PATTERNS
OF
COMMONING

Edited by *David Bollier* and *Silke Helfrich*

The Commons Strategies Group
in cooperation with Off the Common Books

Published by
The Commons Strategies Group
Amherst, Massachusetts / Jena, Germany / Chiang Mai, Thailand

in cooperation with
Off the Common Books
71 South Pleasant Street
Amherst, MA 01002 USA

A German-language version of this book, with minor differences, is available from
transcript Verlag of Bielefeld, Germany, under the title *Die Welt der Commons Muster
gemeinsamen Handelns*, edited by Silke Helfrich, David Bollier and Heinrich-Böll-
Stiftung. In addition to the print edition, it is available on the Web at http://band2.
dieweltdercommons.de.

An earlier, companion volume of essays about the commons, *The Wealth of the
Commons: A World Beyond Market and State* (2012), is available from Levellers Press
of Amherst, Massachusetts or online at http://www.wealthofthecommons.org. The
German edition, *Für eine neue Politik jenseits von Markt und Staat* (2012), is available
from transcript Verlag or online at http://band1.dieweltdercommons.de.

Library of Congress Cataloging-in-Publication Data

Patterns of Commoning
Edited by David Bollier and Silke Helfrich

ISBN 978-1-937146-83-2

PATTERNS
OF
COMMONING

Edited by *David Bollier* and *Silke Helfrich*

The Commons Strategies Group
in cooperation with Off the Common Books

Contents

Acknowledgments | xi

Overture
David Bollier and Silke Helfrich | 1

PART I
PATTERNS OF COMMONING

Helmut Leitner | 15
Working with Patterns: An Introduction

Silke Helfrich | 26
Patterns of Commoning:
How We Can Bring About a Language of Commoning

Elinor Ostrom | 47
Eight Design Principles for Successful Commons

German Commons Summer School | 48
Eight Points of Orientation for Commoning

Marianne Gronemeyer | 50
Conviviality

Intermezzo I
Can Commoners Become Self-aware of Their
Collective Potential? | 53

PART II
NOTABLE ACTS OF COMMONING
ACROSS CULTURES & CENTURIES

Long-Lasting Commons

Eric Nanchen and Muriel Borgeat | 61
Bisse de Savièse: A Journey Through Time to the Irrigation System in
Valais, Switzerland

Monica Vasile | 65
The Role of Memory and Identity
in the Obştea Forest Commons of Romania

Zelealem Tefera Ashenafi | 71
The Resilience of an Indigenous Ethiopian Commons

Neighborhood Commons

Soma K P and Richa Audichya | 77
Our Ways of Knowing:
Women Protect Common Forest Rights in Rajasthan

Véronique Rioufol and Sjoerd Wartena | 83
Terre de Liens: Experiencing and Managing Farmland as Commons

Marcela Olivera | 86
Water Beyond the State

Jannis Kühne | 92
Notable Urban Commons Around the World

Biocultural Commons

David Bollier | 103
The Potato Park of Peru

Erika Styger | 108
The System of Rice Intensification
and Its International Community of Practice

David Holmgren | 113
Twelve Design Principles of Permaculture | 113

Arts and Culture Commons

Michael Peter Edson | 117
Fire and Frost: The Virtues of Treating Museums,
Libraries and Archives as Commons

Dario Gentili and Andrea Mura | 122
The Birth of a Theater Commons in Rome:
Fondazione Teatro Valle Bene Comune

Salvatore Iaconesi | 126
Digital Arts as a Commons

Alain Ambrosi and Frédéric Sultan | 132
Remix The Commons: An Evolving Intercultural Space for Commoning

David Bollier | 136
AS220 of Providence, Rhode Island: A Commons of, by and for Artists

Larry Harvey | 140
The Principles of Burning Man

Collaborative Technology Commons

Dorn Cox | 145
Farm Hack: A Commons for Agricultural Innovation

Julio Sanchez Onofre | 151
Arduino and the Open Hardware Revolution

Tristan Copley-Smith | 154
The Growth of Open Design and Production

Interview with Architect Van Bo Le-Mentzel | 159
On Openness, Commons & Unconditional Basic Work

Astrid Lorenzen | 167
Fab Lab St. Pauli in Hamburg

Jacques Paysan | 170
OpenSPIM: A High-Tech Commons for Research and Education

Code and Knowledge Commons

Cameron Neylon | 179
Open Access Pioneer: The Public Library of Science

Mike Linksvayer | 182
Converting Proprietary Software into a Commons:
The LibreOffice Story

Mary Lou Forward | 186
OpenCourseWare and Open Education

Films and Videos About the Commons | 190

Exchange and Credit Commons

*Jukka Peltokoski, Niklas Toivakainen, Tero Toivanen
and Ruby van der Wekken* | 195
Helsinki Timebank: Currency as a Commons

Interview with Will Ruddick | 199
How the Bangla-Pesa Tapped the Value of an Informal Community

James Stodder and Bernard Lietaer | 204
WIR Currency – Reinventing Social Exchange

Tools and Infrastructure for Commoning

Enric Senabre Hidalgo | 209
Goteo: Crowdfunding to Build New Commons

Kate Chapman | 214
Commoning in Times of Disaster:
The Humanitarian OpenStreetMap Team

Ellen Friedman | 218
Mapping Our Shared Wealth: The Cartography of the Commons

David Bollier | 223
Licenses for Commoning:
The GPL, Creative Commons Licenses and CopyFair

David Bollier, Lara Mallien & Santiago Hoerth Moura | 227
New Ventures in Commons-Based Publishing

Spaces for Co-Learning

Hannelore Hollinetz and Martin Hollinetz | 237
Otelo – Open Technology Labs in Austria

Marcos García | 240
Medialab-Prado: A Citizen Lab for Incubating Innovative Commons

Maria Bareli-Gaglia | 243
Voyaging in the Sea of Ikarian Commons and Beyond

Claudia Gómez-Portugal M. | 248
Learning as an Open Road, Learning as a Commons

Omni-Commons

An Interview with members of Cecosesola | 258
"We Are One Big Conversation": Commoning in Venezuela

Ariadna Serra and Ale Fernandez | 265
Cooperativa Integral Catalana (CIC):
On the Way to a Society of the Communal

Intermezzo II
The Internal Dimensions of the External World:
On Commons and Commoning | 271

PART III
THE INNER DYNAMICS OF COMMONING

Étienne Le Roy | 277
How I Have Been Conducting Research
on the Commons for Thirty Years Without Knowing It

Andrea J. Nightingale | 297
Commons and Alternative Rationalities:
Subjectivity, Emotion and the (Non)rational Commons

Anne Salmond | 309
The Fountain Of Fish: Ontological Collisions At Sea

Nigel C. Gibson | 330
The Ethical Struggle to Be Human:
A Shack Dwellers Movement in South Africa

Arturo Escobar | 348
Commons in the Pluriverse

David Sloan Wilson | 361
Generalizing the Commons

Andreas Weber | 369
Reality as Commons: A Poetics of Participation for the Anthropocene

Finale | 393

Index | 395

Acknowledgments

It is fitting that the preparation of this book has itself been a process of com-moning. We, as editors, have supplied the thematic frameworks, editing and production, but the book is quite literally the original work of a network of more than sixty contributors from twenty countries. It has been a gratifying process to see so many divergent strands fall into place, among dozens of others, creating a vibrant tapestry of stories and analyses about contemporary commons. Our first expression of thanks, therefore, goes to the contributors to this anthology who took the time and energy to share their insights and rich accounts of their commons. Something changes within each of us when we can see the broader context of our own individual projects – and witness this inspiring, larger whole together.

Throughout the two years that it took to produce this book, the Heinrich Böll Foundation has been a determined champion of the commons and sup-porter of this book. We owe a significant debt of gratitude to Heike Löschmann, the head of the Department of International Politics at the Böll Foundation, for her steadfast commitment to this ambitious project. Heike worked closely with us in providing astute recommendations, editorial suggestions and help-ful liaison with many friends of the commons. We are also deeply thankful to Barbara Unmüßig, President of the Foundation, for her unwavering support for commons scholarship and activism, and for this book in particular. Years ago, Barbara recognized the immense strategic potential of the commons paradigm for reinventing political cultures around the world.

This book was an exemplary act of commoning in the arrangements for its publication. The publisher for our previous anthology of commons essays, Levellers Press – a worker-owned cooperative based in Amherst, Massachusetts, USA – has been in the vanguard of innovative publishing practices for many years. (See profile on pp. 227 to 330.) With this collection of essays, we decided to take charge of publishing ourselves, as Commons Strategies Group, in coopera-tion with leading commoners around the world and with the self-publishing arm of Levellers Press, Off the Common Books. Thanks to pre-orders of this book by more than thirty commons-friendly organizations and individuals, we were able to finance the production of more than two-thirds of the book's press run: a case of commoners helping each other, themselves and the greater good. This has enabled us to offer the book at a much lower price than similarly produced books; use a Creative Commons license to make the text available for copying and sharing; and retain key decisions about marketing and distribution while enjoying access to conventional distribution channels.

We extend our hearty thanks to the contributors to our "limited crowdfunding" campaign for their faith and confidence in us and this project! And we once again wish to thank Steve Strimer, the publisher of Levellers and Off the Common Books, for his great resourcefulness and good cheer as a partner in commons-based publishing. Faith Seddon did a terrific job in converting our manuscript into beautiful pages.

From the start, this book was conceptualized and edited in two languages, German and English. Naturally this required considerable coordination and extremely careful translations. These were sometimes quite difficult because of specialized and unfamiliar terms associated with the commons, "commoning" and "enclosure." We were fortunate that Sandra Lustig and Brigitte Kratzwald were able to provide meticulous translations for both the German and English editions of this book. Once we had completed the manuscript, editor Bernd Rheinberg at the Böll Foundation provided valuable suggestions for improving the book.

Since *Patterns of Commoning* is the second of a planned trilogy of anthologies about the commons, we hope to begin work soon (after a decent interval for rest!) on the third volume. It will focus on the political and policy challenges of advancing the commons paradigm and the culture of commoning. We hope to discover an even wider circle of commoning when we release that book in 2017.

David Bollier　　　　　　　　　　*Silke Helfrich*
Amherst, Massachusetts, USA　　*Jena, Germany*

Commons Strategies Group
July 15, 2015

OVERTURE

By David Bollier and Silke Helfrich

In Valais in the Swiss Alps, an elaborate system of irrigation canals has existed for half a millennium. In the high-altitude Sacred Valley of the Incas, in Peru, the Quechua people have cultivated the richest diversity of potatoes anywhere on the planet since time immemorial. Since the time of Stephen the Great in the late 1400s, people in the Eastern Carpathians have managed their forests jointly through community-based institutions known as *obştea*, a tradition that has even survived fifty years of state dictatorship in the twentieth century. These examples demonstrate that commons are nothing if not enduring. Yet at the same time, they are highly vulnerable because nation-states claiming absolute territorial sovereignty tend to see commons – with their focus on collective governance, use-value over exchange value, and indifference to political jurisdictions (e.g., bioregions, Internet communities) – as perplexing or threatening. For their part, global corporations commanding vast resources and legal privileges often seek to destroy commons because they are seen as an alternative regime for meeting needs and thus a threat to the hegemony of the market system.

Despite such challenges, human beings show an irrepressible impulse to work together to create, maintain and protect those relationships and things that are dear to them. The impulse is evidence of a deep need and satisfaction as well as of pride and the will to survive. The process of *commoning* – of joint action, of creating things together, of cooperating to meet shared goals – is ubiquitous. It can be seen in modern urban skyscrapers as well as in remote rural villages destroyed by earthquakes in Nepal; in artistic communities and educational and research settings; and in the community forests of India and the many self-organized communities of cyberspace.

Commoning may be a hardy social phenomenon with an ancient pedigree, but in modern industrial societies, it enjoys only modest understanding and respect. We still seem to venerate and fear those people of monetary wealth and power and dismiss people who cooperate to come up with successful solutions that can benefit everyone. The latter remain largely nameless or are even belittled as starry-eyed dreamers because they do things that do not make money. "That won't work in the real world," people often say dismissively, ignoring the diversity of actual commons. Also ignored: the many different caring activities (usually performed by women) that are the basis for the "real economy," the social construct otherwise known as "the market." This fixation with achieving all goals through market exchange is producing a moribund global monoculture of homogenous social relationships – a culture that disdains innovative types of social interaction and collaboration unless they can generate money. The drive to commercialize everything from genes and water to sounds and words, and to create human dependencies on proprietary technologies and their manufacturers, is fracturing our social and ecological landscape – our common spaces. Time itself and consciousness are subordinated to the elaborate systems devised to accumulate capital. The dominant market culture tends to cast individualism as the ultimate fulfillment and to denigrate collective-action solutions, whether in rural communities or peer-to-peer networks, as "impractical" or "utopian" – as if individual and collective interests were somehow mutually exclusive.

In fact, the opposite is the case. A thriving individuality is not only essential to successful commoning, as many stories of commons in this book show, it is a condition for "being commonable," or capable of participating in a commons. Conversely, commoning contributes to strengthening and stabilizing the individual self; it nurtures identity and long-term commitments. In other words, it is not only possible to align strong individuality with strong commons; the two are necessary for each other. They generate and enhance each other. The question is not whether we can align strong individualism with strong commons, but how. And here is where *Patterns of Commoning* seeks to provide insight by examining some remarkable forms of commoning in the most varied places in the world.

It is customary in many social science circles – especially in economics – to equate commons with resources managed jointly. Yet commons are not things, resources or goods; they are an organic fabric of social structures and processes. They may be focused on managing a certain resource – land, water, fisheries, information or urban spaces – and those resources may have a strong influence on how governance structures and economic production occur. But excessive attention to the physical resources or knowledge that a commons relies upon can distract us from its beating heart: the consciousness of thinking, learning, and acting as a *commoner*.

Commoning as a Living Process

The drama of *commoning* is an active, living process – a verb rather than a noun. We consider it to be an aspect of the human condition, an ongoing social process that never repeats in exactly the same way. This is one reason that trying to define the commons using definitions and methodologies from the natural sciences is futile. Commoning involves so much idiosyncratic creativity, improvisation, situational choices, and dynamic evolution that it can only be understood as *aliveness*. It defies simple formulas or analysis. Any theoretical framework for understanding commons must therefore enter into a deep and ongoing engagement with the everyday practices and experiences of commoning. Theory and practice must be in intimate conversation with each other. They might be compared to the fluid complementarity of a musical score and orchestral performance, which exist only in relation to one another and together produce a symphony. Just as it is impossible to learn to play the violin from simply reading music, the commons (or any social phenomena) is fundamentally an *experiential practice* that cannot be understood through theory alone.

If the primary focus of commons is not on resources, goods and things, but on interpersonal and human/nature relationships, then institutions of any kind – business, political, civic, educational – must reliably promote three things: respect for ecological boundaries, stable community and voluntary cooperation. Many economists who consider commons to be a specific class of goods struggle to identify regularities or "laws" that supposedly govern them, with the goal of recommending appropriate institutions or policy mea-sures. Behavioristic schools of thought in other disciplines tend to share this outlook and try to use methods taken from the natural sciences to understand social processes, systematically ignoring the importance of empathy, social relationships and culture. These traditional approaches are utterly unsuitable for understanding the social phenomena of commons, which are at their core "relational social frameworks."

This perspective may abandon the universal regularities that conventional science aspires to identify, but it opens up a rich, empirical field of vision for de-vising innovative solutions to old problems. Instead of seeing "the environment" as something separate and distinct from humanity, the commons can help us realize that we are *part* of nature and that because of this, we destroy ourselves if we destroy nature. Instead of focusing on resources as *stocks* of things that a price mechanism transfers among people, we can focus on complex *flows* of resources that are accessed and used according to the rules made by commoners themselves. Instead of looking to impersonal market transactions as the only way to meet needs, we can see that commoning is a practical alternative that can emancipate people from the pathologies of market culture and its logic.

There is no convincing reason to assume that the commons can work only within small networks or face-to-face communities, and not at societal or transnational levels. We have already seen the rapid scalability of network-based institutions across the globe (free and open source programming communities and Wikipedia, among countless others), and institutions to support location-specific commoning (of fisheries or permaculture, for example).

This book initially deals with another important strand in the commons narrative: the personal and social dynamics of concrete practices, values, rituals, traditions and experiences, all of which generate meaning and identity for people. A commons can survive only if it can nourish and protect this deeper level of commoning, because it is what makes a commons enduring, flexible and resilient. This is why policymakers and "experts" cannot simply design and build commons, let alone institutionalize them in a cookie-cutter way. Commoners must do this work themselves (although not necessarily alone and without support). The outcomes will reflect their particular history, geography and culture.

In this volume, we will not be able to explore the theoretical significance of diverse forces that shape commons, whether they be intentional communities or digitally based peer networks, but we do wish to show how important the inner social dimensions of commoning are. These include a sense of shared purpose, congruent talents and interests, common experiences in a given locality, simple affection, and simple necessity. The range of commons described suggests that there are few parts of life or production that could not be structured to work as a commons.

In a book that we published in 2012, *The Wealth of the Commons: A World Beyond Market and State*, we offered a panorama of perspectives on commons around the world, the enclosures that threaten many of them, and the productive forces that they can unleash. In this book, the second of a planned trilogy, we wish to probe more deeply the internal dynamics of commons, in contrast to standard economics. In so doing, we reject the standard economic repertoire of analytical constructs and categories based on an idealized fiction of *homo economicus*. We human beings are more than "rational" economic agents and maximizers of individual utility. It is not widely appreciated that the archetype of *homo economicus,* mostly thought of as a *male,* and significantly, as an isolated individual, is still considered an ideal, even though it has nothing to say about our common humanity or our essential sociality. In addition, *homo economicus* is a human being without a history or personal development; it has obliterated the idea that we *become* what we are. It fails to recognize our need to belong to a larger society and its traditions, language, laws and so forth.

This book is based on precisely the idea that human beings do not develop and mature as isolated individuals, but only as creatures *in relationship* to others. "I am because we are," as the Nguni Bantu expression "Ubuntu" puts it. It is pointless to construct an idealized abstraction as a counter-image to *homo economicus* because the actual realities are so myriad. Hence our desire here to explore the realities of commoning as a complex human experience, a phenomenon that is carried out by real people situated in unique places and living unique histories.

What unites the many commoners you will encounter in this book is their desire to have the freedom (and the societal conditions) to meet their needs in creative, fair, self-devised ways, without being dependent on markets or the state. This desire reflects their instinctual need and desire to work with others – an idea that is seen as secondary in modern, market-oriented cultures where people are so often seen as utterly autonomous and "self-made" individuals. This mythology ignores the actual dependence of individuals on money and therefore on the market. The commons paradigm helps us recover some elemental human truths – that we learn to be individuals through relationships and that autonomy itself is *nested within* a web of relationships. Autonomy can only be learned and lived through relationships, and commons provide an appropriate framework for this to happen.

Of course, individual endowments and personalities do not disappear in webs of relationships, but it is important to note that they do originate in social and cultural contexts, in real physical spaces, and the time/world concepts that frame our social existence. Our personal skills, outlooks, language and identities emerge and develop only through participation in larger collectives. Happiness research has elicited the insight that when people imagine a good life, they do not imagine themselves as calculating individuals constantly seeking to maximize their own utility at the expense of others. They see happiness as a social state of grace.

It should be no surprise, then, that our sense of social ethics arises from our engagement with larger networks of relationships. Our morality does not fall from the sky, nor can it simply be announced and promoted. Ethical values emerge *through* our interactions. When children begin to grow beyond egocentrism and understand the perspectives of others, they begin to develop ideas of right and wrong. Similarly, scientists regard sharing food and lending aid to a neighbor as contributing to evolutionary success. Experiencing such humanity ultimately contributes to developing a morality that honors socially constructive attitudes and behaviors. It is not a stretch to conjecture that, through a commons, we can find the means to reinvigorate a vibrant, functional social ethics – something that the nation-state and market culture have been singularly unable to achieve.

Patterns of Commoning is an attempt to show that these dynamics are not some historical curiosity from medieval times, but a robust contemporary reality. More than a sampler of eclectic, interesting instances of commons – which, incidentally, stand on their own and can be read and reflected on as separate essays – this book seeks to depict *patterns* of commoning. Our approach is inspired in part by the work of the architect, urbanist and philosopher Christopher Alexander, whose 1977 book *A Pattern Language* sought to identify the attributes of buildings and architectural spaces that have an "aliveness" to them – a theme he developed further in his 2005 book *The Nature of Order*. Alexander was searching for a quality that was elusive and still without a name, but which he attempted to describe using words such as "vitality" and "wholeness" and "eternal" to point to the essence he had in mind. He developed pattern languages as a tool to understand and solve complex problems, and as a heuristic for expressing not simply the principles of design, but the artful relationships among the individual elements of the whole that mysteriously generate a sense of aliveness.[1]

This rigorous yet open-ended focus on relationships inspired us to apply the pattern approach to the commons. The commons, too, is about complex, living systems and how they emerge and grow. Just as a footpath may emerge over time because it serves the interests of thousands of walkers, so a commons may emerge, and persist, because its specific "social morphology" is pleasing and effective for participating commoners. In a commons, a biophysical resource – a forest, a body of water, an energy source, emotional energy, labor, knowledge – becomes co-mingled with social practice and diverse forms of institutionalization, producing a single, integrated system that must be considered as a whole. Patterns help us to identify similarities among diverse commons without homogenizing or oversimplifying them. Patterns of commoning help us avoid analytic frameworks that are generally too rigid, reductionist, totalizing or alienated from the messy dynamics of life. Of course, we are taking only a first step in this book to delineate patterns of commoning. We hope that this rudimentary effort will initiate the development of a richer pattern language of commoning and the commons.

---

1 | For more on patterns and pattern languages, see the essay by Helmut Leitner on pp. 15-25 .

The Score for this Book

We have tried to structure this book as a kind of musical composition. This overture is the prelude, after which we introduce in Part I the main topic – commoning. We link commoning to the term conviviality, which social critic Ivan Illich popularized as a concept to describe versatile, user-friendly tools and institutions that people can adapt to serve multiple needs and interests. *Patterns of Commoning* is organized as three thematic movements, each of which is connected by an "intermezzo," before concluding with a finale. Our hope is that, like any serious piece of music, we can convey the power and eloquence of certain striking motifs as they recur in different variations and contexts.

Part I will help orient the reader by explaining at greater length the idea of patterns of commoning. Key motifs here include the struggle of people to devise reasonable, effective rules and institutions to stabilize and protect their commoning; to reconcile the tensions between individual and collective interests; and to develop cultures that honor fairness, responsibility and accountability.

Commoning is at bottom a process by which we enter into a participatory culture and can sketch an idea of how we want to live together as a society. We will also see throughout the book the ways in which shared emotional commitments and a sense of identity are essential to commoning – and how commons, over time, subtly change the inner lives and behavior of commoners.

An inescapable theme for any commons is the daunting challenge of protecting it against enclosure and destructive interference, whether the threats come from markets, the state or free riders.[2] We deliberately decided in this book not to focus on enclosures, in part because we dealt with that extensively in our previous anthology, *The Wealth of the Commons*. The focus in this volume is more on constructive acts of reclaiming endangered commons and creating new ones as well as the ceaseless struggle actively to protect them.

In Part II, we present brief profiles of more than fifty different commons. Our goal here is to show the incredible range of commoning across time, geography, resource domains and cultural tradition. We intentionally departed from the usual classifications of commons such as natural resource and knowledge commons, or material and immaterial commons. There were several reasons for this approach. The most important one is simply that *every* commons requires both a material and an immaterial basis, and every commons, no matter its core focus, is always based on producing and sharing knowledge. Material resources *and* knowledge are the bases for *all* commons, and so the familiar habit of dividing them up based on these criteria strikes us as specious.

---

2 | In commons in which knowledge is produced and maintained, the problem is not generally free riders, but vandals and disrupters who prevent the community from managing its code, text, photos or data in orderly ways.

Instead, we have divided the profiles in Part II into loose groupings of similar commons: long-lasting commons, neighborhood commons, biocultural commons, arts and culture commons, collaborative technology commons, code and knowledge commons, exchange and credit commons, tools and infrastructure for commoning, spaces for co-learning and omni-commons. Of course, this classification is not intended as a new taxonomy; it is simply our attempt to bring together generally related commons.

If there is a strong emphasis on open source projects and digital platforms among the profiles of Part II, it is because this realm is surely one of the most robust vectors of commoning in contemporary life. The open source paradigm is a fiercely effective and popular form of commoning – on the Internet, in Fab Labs, hackerspaces and elsewhere – precisely because these spaces welcome innovative minds concerned with positive social change. Because open platforms and infrastructures are so hospitable to self-organized commoning, conventional institutions of governance and commerce are eager to capture and control them, as we see in the growth of the commercially oriented "sharing economy," attacks on net neutrality, and corporate and governmental surveillance and data collection.

In the commons profiled in Part II, it becomes apparent that commoning transcends the misleading mental dichotomies that modern cultures have invented. It lets us re-integrate that which seemed to have been divided into "public" and "private," "objective" and "subjective," or "tangible" and "intangible." This has far-reaching consequences because our categories of thought limit the spectrum of imagined possibilities for action. If we think only in terms of "public" and "private," we will see only public (governmental) or private actors and, if state coffers are empty, we will see few options beyond "public/ private partnerships." We will literally have no language to imagine "public/ commons partnerships," for example.

In Part III, we ask how commoning can become deeply rooted in our world and to what levels it can penetrate. Seven notable contributors probe these questions by exploring "the inner dynamics of commoning"– the title of this concluding section. These interpretive essays depict the foundations of commoning in different cultural and historical contexts – for example, the inland fisheries of Scotland, the current struggles in the shanty neighborhoods of South Africa, the sea-faring Maori people of modern New Zealand, and land-use issues in West Africa and France.

It becomes clear from these analyses how commoning helps us develop a worldview that integrates who we are with what we do – and that has the power to shape our world. In this sense, the essays of Part III resemble bright spotlights that carefully explore a recently discovered cave: We see many strange and glorious things illuminated in this deep cavern of human experience known as commoning, but we have barely begun to probe its deeper reaches. As yet, we do not really know what we are capable of achieving collectively. Immersed as some of us are within our digitized and thoroughly monetized lifeworlds, the potential expansion of the many and diverse forms of commoning is still in its infancy. The same is true of efforts to re-imagine commons-based governance, law and production.

By considering the ontological dimensions of commoning – that is, the basic experiences of being, seeing and knowing as a commoner – the essays of Part III point to the necessity of rethinking the very categories and notions that we use to describe the world. We learn how "pluriversal" ways of knowing, acting and being lie at the heart of the commons paradigm – and how these new perspectives and categories of thought can help us build a new world. Instead of simply imagining "a democracy fit for the market" – a stunted, cynical exercise that dominates contemporary politics – the commons can help us re-imagine democratic self-determination and freedom in sweeping new ways, helping us expand the scope of what is thinkable and therefore doable. Much further research – and new experimental projects – will need to be done to explore these possibilities, of course.

The Role of Subjectivity and Intersubjectivity

Academic scholars of the commons will notice that the way we approach and frame the commons differs from the metatheoretical research framework known as Institutional Analysis and Development (IAD). This framework was developed by the pioneering commons scholar and Nobel Prize Laureate Elinor Ostrom, working with others, as a tool to assess numerous variables in far more than one thousand commons institutions across disciplinary boundaries. Making sense of variables in commons is a vexing challenge for research design because it is often unclear which internal dynamics are significant and defining for successful social processes, and which are incidental and contextual.

Our focus is not intended to challenge or displace the IAD approach, but rather, to enrich and extend it. That is, we wish to set aside what we find less compelling, (for example, the modeling of social change inherent to it) and to introduce and explore the animating role of subjectivity and intersubjectivity as central elements of commoning. We believe that commons must be "seen from the inside" – through the experiences, feelings, histories and cultures of every participant. This helps explain why it is not really possible to "design" a commons from the outside and import a specific set of "best practices" or "golden rules" to manage a particular commons. A commons must arise from the personal engagement of commoners themselves. It is unavoidably the product of unique personalities, geographic locations, cultural contexts, moments in time and political circumstances of that particular commons. Yet finding a workable *common* language to generalize about commons remains an important challenge. It can help commoners draw connections between their experiences and the aspirations of others, and help all to see the wider ramifications and potential for societal transformation.

To be sure, there will be many legal, financial and organizational forms that are useful to advance the principles of commons at larger scales. But it is important to distinguish these legal and administrative forms from the social practices of commoning itself. They should not be confused as the essence of a commons or as necessarily producing commons. History shows us that legal and organizational forms can be captured and co-opted, and made to serve very different purposes. For example, many co-operatives today have become so driven by managerialism, market competition and profit orientation, that they are oblivious to their members and co-operative principles. Capital-driven logics now dominate so many microfinancing projects that the sovereignty and eman- cipation that once came through commoning have been lost. Similar dynamics have afflicted other administrative forms such as credit unions, indigenous councils and nonprofit organizations, not to mention state-managed institutions that are ostensibly intended to serve the public interest. The clear lesson is that legal and administrative structures, no matter how well-designed, cannot serve as reliable substitutes for commoning and its social norms and practices. The future will surely see new attempts at "common-washing" by projects parading the *forms* of commons without living the realities of commoning.

There is nonetheless an important role for law and public policy to play in making commons administrative structures more trustworthy, well-managed and accountable. Indeed, the state must help promote the social construction of commons by fostering hospitable conditions for commoners to do what they do. Even bureaucrats and politicians working within traditional conceptions and structures of the state and law can support the development of commons to solve problems that neither the market nor state can solve. In the end, it is only when leaders "think like a commoner" that the state can actually become more commons-friendly; yet to do this, it must liberate itself from the logic of the market and bureaucratic "rationality." Hence the mind-bending conundrum of living within an archaic normative system of existing governance, production, law and culture – the market/state – while simultaneously trying to transcend it by creating a new, more cooperative order. This is a topic we intend to explore in our next anthology about the commons.

The Commons as a Different Worldview

Commoning is a radical concept because it insists upon the active, knowing participation of people in shaping their own lives and meeting their own needs. A commons is not just about allocating a common-pool resource, something that a computer algorithm could arguably achieve. A commons requires active, ongoing participation with others in implementing and maintaining a shared purpose. Just as market culture makes and shapes specific ways of being, so does commoning. Thinking in categories of commons and generating action from that thinking (and vice versa) helps to develop personal capacities and competencies that are essential to a happy, flourishing, creative life. A person's intentionality and affective, emotional labor matters. All this cannot simply be designed into an organization or a procedure through legal or administrative means.

In other words, commoning is a form and process that *flows through us*, similar to "calculative thinking" (K.H. Brodbeck). Through countless acts of commoning, we develop essential capacities and competencies that self-replicate and spread throughout an entire collective. The resulting culture becomes a kind of emotional and cognitive "air that we breathe" – a way of perceiving and experiencing the world that flows through us and is taken for granted. Until such time as the culture of the commons becomes a richer collective experience, the language of the commons is a valuable tool for helping us to (re)discover this different way of being, knowing and doing. It helps us become self-aware of commoning as a learned practice that is simultaneously as old and as modern as making music.

The fact that commons are timeless raises profound questions about many premises of modern civilization. It is worth quoting Étienne Le Roy in his essay "How I Have Been Conducting Research on the Commons for Thirty Years Without Knowing It." He writes that once you begin to take the commons seriously, "the whole edifice on which modern Western civilization is based, previously believed to be well-founded, collapses onto itself: the state, the law, the market, the nation, work, contracts, debts, giving, the juristic person, private property, as well as institutions such as kinship, marital law and the law of succession, is suddenly called into question."

For example, the commons calls into question the idea that discrete individuals and objects are the self-evident, privileged categories of analysis. We need a procedure that systematically takes "more than one" into account. Methodological individualism is unable to sustain this, as is the already criticized thinking in either/or patterns or the whole symbolic apparatus of mainstream economic thinking, which derives from the Newtonian worldview and its linear paths of causality and supposed regularities. Significantly, "the economy" is seen as an objective machine that somehow stands above us and apart from our combined actions and consciousness – as if human beings did not exist.

Set against the powerful global dominion of the market and nation-state, which are conceived of as abstract entities (and which are by no means as old as is commonly assumed), it is tempting to see any single commons as an insignificant mote. Yet acts of commoning, by connecting us with the deeper circuits of living systems and with other commoners, have their own inexorable power, especially when those circuits begin to interconnect and expand, as they are doing now.

It is our hope that *Patterns of Commoning* will hasten this process of rediscovering commons and developing a deeper understanding of them. They are a precious platform from which to defy the stalemate and despair of our time with living, creative and durable alternatives.

PART I

PATTERNS OF COMMONING

"To be truly radical is to make hope possible rather than despair convincing."

Raymond Williams, British historian

Working with Patterns: An Introduction

By Helmut Leitner

On August 6, 2000, I happened upon an unadorned website with valuable knowledge and interesting discussions. Every page had an edit button that gave me access as a contributor and coauthor with the same rights as everyone else. That was new and exhilarating, like receiving an unexpected present. I didn't know that this was the first wiki prototype, a more advanced version of which was to achieve worldwide recognition as Wikipedia a few years later. And I had no idea that in 2001 I would be one of the first German speakers to register and contribute. I found out that this prototype *Wiki Wiki Web* had been invented so that people could jointly collect and elaborate software patterns and that as the *Portland Pattern Repository*, it was playing a part in revolutionizing thinking about software development. At the time, I had no way of knowing that I would be involved in organizing the first Wiki conference WIKISYM, that I would later write a book on pattern theory, and that this and many other events would permanently change and influence my thinking – especially about community and society.

The present chapter cannot tell that story, but elaborates important aspects to help people interested in the commons (the participants in the commons movement) to become acquainted with the concept of *patterns*. Using patterns enables people to communicate common ideas about complex relationships more easily and to seamlessly combine theoretical research with its practical application.

In 1977, architect and unconventional thinker Christopher Alexander published the book *A Pattern Language* that became a nonfiction bestseller in the English-speaking world (Alexander et al. 1977). The book describes important architectural structures. Although the second volume *The Timeless Way of Building* forms a whole with the first one, it had a much smaller audience (Alexander 1979). It describes universal design processes. These two books together deal with top-quality design at scales large and small, with the goal of creating living cities, living regions and life-supporting architecture.

The ambition is that all people should feel full of life and be able to live well in freedom. This requires their involvement in the design process and in making decisions about architecture. When developing his theory, Alexander studied architectural history in its entirety, and he demonstrated that this kind of practice was possible in his own projects. His work rejects mainstream architecture, which usually follows the rules of the capitalist construction industry, and step by step, he provides the building blocks and connecting pieces of an alternative program.

Transferring these ideas from architectural structures to other structures in their own cultural and societal environments suggested itself to many readers. This resulted in reform-minded approaches for design and decisionmaking in all kinds of areas: democracy, the education system, organizational design, the health system and personal development. Wherever something is designed or shaped, it seems plausible to apply Alexander's ways of thinking. In almost every area of society, people have the feeling that a change toward more community-based rationality and participation is needed. In the summer of 2015, as this book went to press, the international conference "PURsuit of Pattern Languages for SOcietal Change" (PURPLSOC) convened scientists of *all* disciplines for the first time to reflect on patterns for societal change (PURPLSOC 2014).

A professor at the renowned University of California at Berkeley, Alexander spent decades conducting research, working as an architect, and writing a dozen books. In particular his final four-volume magnum opus *The Nature of Order* (Alexander 2002) should be mentioned here; it integrates the research of biological systems and finds far-reaching parallels between natural and cultural structures and processes.[1]

At this point in the chapter, which is a translation from the German, the translator and the author would both like to inform readers about an English language problem. Alexander's research made him understand complex systems – such as cities and works of art and culture – as living systems, as growing and unfolding like biological organisms and biospheres. Both kinds of systems, biological living systems and non-biological complex systems, as well as combinations of those two, follow the same principles.

Having no English word for the quality of such living systems in a general sense, Alexander wrote about a "quality without a name," which gave his texts a somewhat mystical touch. Other authors abbreviated this to the acronym QWAN. This quality is central because a designer should

---

1 | Editor's note: The author of this chapter has published an accessible introduction to Alexander's work: Helmut Leitner, *Pattern Theory: Introduction and Perspectives on the Tracks of Christopher Alexander*, Graz, Austria, 2015.

optimize for it. Alexander tried to define this quality in twenty pages of *The Timeless Way of Building*, using words like *alive, whole, comfortable, free, exact, egoless, eternal, not simply beauty, not only fitness for purpose,* and *slightly bitter*. In later books, he used the word *wholeness* instead.

Other authors talk about systems being lively, vivid or life-supporting, or refer to their vitality or liveliness. These replacements never work fully: readers have to build a concept in their minds without having a single corresponding word. This is difficult for most people, at least in the beginning. Oddly enough, this problem doesn't exist in German because it has the adjective *lebendig* in a non-biological sense that fits Alexander's concepts exactly. In German, people talk about *"einen lebendigen Unterricht"* (a lively/vivid teaching) or *"die Lebendigkeit einer Geschichte"* (the wholeness/vitality/power of a story). Therefore, the theory of complex living systems, in the tradition of Christopher Alexander, is much easier to understand, teach, and write about in German. In the following text, such circumscribing words are italicized to support readers in grasping that they point to a common general concept.

But back to the story. In *A Pattern Language*, Alexander describes fundamental architectural knowledge modules and wisdoms. The book's 1,171 pages are jam-packed with 253 problem-solving, reusable concepts that he calls *patterns*. Presented on roughly three to six pages each, these *patterns* are sometimes called *design patterns*, especially in the field of software development, and they describe expert knowledge in a form comprehensible to laypeople and students. The descriptions of the patterns follow the same format. Each can be read and understood on its own and can be used like a building block for learning about and designing very different projects and processes. We can select those patterns that are important to us at a particular moment, just as we take individual tools from a toolbox. Alexander enables each of us to take our own path of learning through this body of knowledge, similar to the way we use a cookbook or an encyclopedia. Just as the words in an encyclopedia attain their expressive power only in the fabric of their rule-based relationships and thus become language, so do individual patterns become a *pattern language*, a device for expressing design ideas, only in the fabric of the other patterns and their functional relationships (Figure 1).

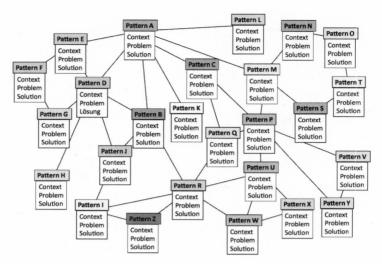

Figure 1: A pattern language as a network.

In practice, most projects are inevitably "works in progress," so it is easiest to speak of "patterns of X (e.g., X=commoning)" to identify a collection of patterns of continuously improving quality. Over time, the completeness of patterns and the quality of their descriptions will improve until a pattern collection really deserves the label "pattern language." Then, it amounts to a toolbox equipped with everything required. However, the terms *"pattern collection/collection of patterns"* and *"pattern language"* are often used uncritically and practically synonymously.

From Pattern Description to Pattern Language

The descriptions of the individual patterns in a pattern collection follow a certain outline that thus becomes a standard for descriptions to be applied by everyone working on that particular pattern collection. Such outlines are often taken on by other groups of researchers, but are sometimes changed when the original group applies them; a new standard can emerge in this way.

Alexander selected one format for architecture, Kent Beck a different one for software programming, Rob Hopkins a third for transition processes, etc. (Figure 2). Someone who develops a pattern language must outline certain aspects for the description and then stick to the outline selected. If necessary, it is always possible to expand and change it. What is important is that each piece of information has its precise place and that the different aspects are not mixed when deriving statements. This makes it easier for individuals and groups to collaborate, both in a particular field of application and across disciplines and topics.

Christopher Alexander (Architecture)	Rob Hopkins (Transition)	Peter Baumgartner (Education)
pattern name	pattern name	pattern name
internal ranking	picture	picture
picture	challenge	context
context	solution	problem
problem		forces
forces		solution
solution		stumbling blocks
resulting context		pros & cons
		examples
		user roles
		tools
		related patterns
		references

Figure 2: Example outlines for pattern descriptions.

Pattern collections are a foundation for dialogue between everyone involved. Our world can be understood as if it were interwoven by conscious and unconscious patterns, whereby each pattern is linked to other patterns. Changes in our world appear in new patterns emerging or existing ones changing. All design patterns taken together as a whole form humanity's cultural heritage, which can only belong to all of us together. Pattern descriptions are a form of sharing this heritage with others and making it accessible to all people in their own lives and surroundings. Pattern descriptions are tools for involvement in decisionmaking as well as participation in continually making the world a better place in a common, creative, cooperative and consensual process. However, we have yet to begin doing so rationally and at a larger scale.

Christopher Alexander became very well-known to his readers and followers. He demonstrated both theoretically and practically how people can jointly design parts of the world in a *life-supporting* way, rejecting profit as the goal of optimization, which is why he is considered a moral authority in the field of architecture. Yet only a few individual architects have been able to liberate themselves from the capitalist rules of the construction industry. The construction industry as a whole remains captive to the strictures of capitalist economic logic and thus on a collision course with the reality of a world that cannot be exploited limitlessly. It exacerbates the problems of our day: environmental devastation, overexploitation of resources, and climate change, to mention just a few. In other words, the desired architectural revolution has not yet taken place, but the approach – to arrive at *life-supporting* structures by means of participatory design – has in the meantime proven fruitful in many other areas beyond architecture.

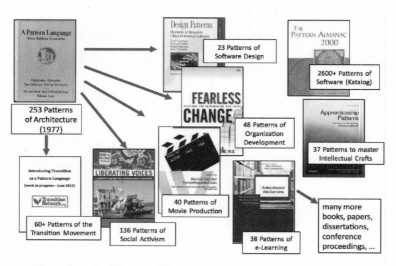

Figure 3: The variety of publications following the influential book A Pattern Language.

From Pattern Research to the Design Process

Hundreds of books about patterns have been published in various disciplines (figure 3). More and more theses and dissertations as well as scientific articles are being published as well. Working with patterns in software development is being taught at some universities and has become mainstream. One indicator of the significance of thinking in patterns is *Wikipedia*, which would not exist without Christopher Alexander and his theory of patterns, as sketched out in the introduction above.

The path to patterns consists in starting with practical experience and using it as the basis for elaborating useful experiential knowledge in a joint process, and reflecting on it, refining it, and deepening it with reference to theory. Once the patterns exist as a collection of texts and data, also called a *repository*, they can be worked through and prepared for practical work in different ways (Figure 4).

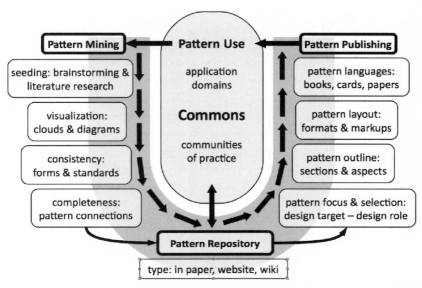

Figure 4: U-shape workflow model for researching and publishing patterns, pattern collections and pattern languages.

The end result is not necessarily a book. Lighter-weight forms may also be appropriate for making pattern knowledge more widely known and helping it take effect: brochures, websites or stacks of seminar cards. The latter are popular for workshops in particular because they can be used flexibly to help people talk about experiences, ideas and concepts, and put what they've learned into practice. Figure 5 shows a group of students at Keio University in Tokyo elaborating *"patterns of presentation"* during class (Iba 2012).

Figure 5: A group of students developing patterns. Photo courtesy of Takashi Iba.

Patterns are just *one* side of Alexander's approach, albeit the one that is perceived and discussed most intensively. In addition, Alexander provided a circular model (Alexander 1979) of an ideal-typical creative process which can be imagined as forming the basis of every instance of design (see Figure 6).

It is comprised of six sectors. In sector 1, the system is perceived holistically; in sector 2, a point for approaching the next developmental step is sought out; in sector 3, a pattern from the relevant pattern language is selected, which in sector 4 is adapted to the concrete problem situation at hand; in sector 5, the newly developed system situation is tested for success or failure; and finally, in sector 6, the transformation – the result – is either accepted or undone. Then, the creative cycle begins again.

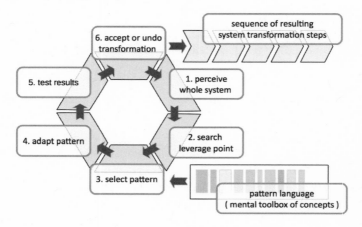

Figure 6: An ideal-typical model of the creative cycle.

Alexander's Ethics – An Ethics of Design

This creative circle, as an ideal-typical model, must be powered by ethical principles to work and bear fruit for everyone (Figure 7). Otherwise it is just a value-free and value-less mechanism that can be misused like any other tool.

A first requirement: Successful design requires holistic perception of the system at hand and its potentials. This can succeed only if one gets involved in the specific features of the situation on the ground as well as the people affected and their needs; and what is more: the people affected should best be involved in the design process as well. Thus, Alexander was an early representative of participatory building and design. However, he did not advocate it as a moralist; his reason for doing so was an empirical insight on the part of designers: optimal design is possible only by means of participation. Our states, democracies, communities, schools, universities, organizations, etc., are sustainable only to the extent to which they make this idea a reality – by opening up to people, their commitment and their creativity. This theoretically founded openness is the reason why open source, open knowledge, and open everything are successful. One reason for the success of the open project Wikipedia was the intentional application of Alexander's principles of stepwise improvement and openness for participation. The closed project that had preceded Wikipedia, Nupedia, with its concept based on articles written by experts, had previously been a hopeless failure.

Second, as mentioned above, patterns are our common cultural heritage. Each and every person draws upon this age-old source, whether or not he/she is aware of it. Whether patterns are used explicitly or implicitly is irrelevant. By imparting competence in the use of patterns, the explicit descriptions of patterns and pattern languages simply enable people to enhance their self-organization and creativity.

Third, the evaluation of a system-changing transformation in step 5 is oriented toward the *vitality* of the system. *Vitality* is the value upon which the search for system improvements, the selection and adaptation of patterns, and the final decisions about all transformations, is founded. Understood properly, this concept of *vitality* includes concepts such as sustainability, support of life and resilience, and rounds them out.

Fourth, this design theory results in priority for humans and for life in its totality over efficiency and profit maximization. This permits the formulation of a *creative imperative*: "Always design and act in a way that people and life have priority over individual interests and profit." In short: "Design for people, not for profit."

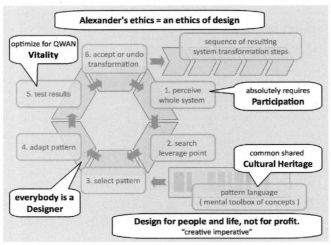

Figure 7: Ethical aspects of the creative cycle.

Alexander systematically opened up the creative realm to all people; he urged for everyone affected to be informed and emancipated so that they can participate in designing the world. The message: "Everyone is a designer."

Paradigmatic Overview

I will stop here and do a visual summary of what has been shown so far. Pattern research can be far more than formulating patterns for solving problems and the corresponding pattern languages. The following pyramid (Figure 8) illustrates the fields of application.

Each level builds upon the level below, but does not necessarily require progressing to the next-higher level. For example, software developers are currently happy with level 2, while in pedagogy, for example, the ethical topics of level 4 are of particular interest. Each field of application has its own characteristics in addition to the common features.

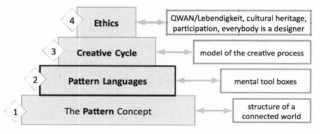

Figure 8: A four-level pyramid model of pattern research.

Patterns and the Commons Movement

In the future, the commons movement will be faced with a development that must be connected to further mobilization and dissemination of the knowledge that is *alive* within the movement and its actors. The situation seems complex, especially because of the diversity of historical and current manifestations of commons projects in all cultures. It is a challenge to identify fundamental concepts – ideal-typical models for all commons projects – in all this diversity. As if that were not already complicated enough, there is the additional task of conceiving of important problems of contemporary life – e.g., climate protection – as commons projects and arriving at solutions by this route.

The situation is complicated, yes, but the necessary concepts and methods are available. Work is in progress to connect the theory of patterns and the practice of the commons. Another two important parts of Alexanders's theory help us to understand in even more detail the properties of living structures and the principles of living processes. In the following essay, Silke Helfrich will apply the principles from this introduction to patterns and show their relevance for the commons movement.

> *"What is the most powerful force in the world?*
> *A big pattern-change idea."*
>
> – *Bill Drayton, founder of Ashoka*

References

Alexander, Christopher, Ishikawa, S., Silverstein, M. 1977. *A Pattern Language: Towns, Buildings, Construction.* New York: Oxford University Press.

Alexander, Christopher. 1979. *The Timeless Way of Building,* New York: Oxford University Press.

————. 2002. *The Nature of Order: An Essay on the Art of Building and the Nature of the Universe,* 4 Volumes. Berkeley, California: The Center for Environmental Structure.

Iba, Takashi. 2012. "Pattern Language 3.0: Writing Pattern Languages for Human Actions." http://de.slideshare.net/takashiiba/plop2012.

Leitner, Helmut. 2007. *Mustertheorie – Einführung und Perspektiven auf den Spuren von Christopher Alexander,* Graz, Austria: Nausner & Nausner Verlag.

Leitner, H. 2015. *Pattern Theory: Introduction and Perspectives on the Tracks of Christopher Alexander.* Graz, Austria: Helmut Leitner. Printed by CreateSpace.

PURPLSOC. 2014. Conference PURPLSOC, July 3-5, 2015, Krems, Austria, http://purplsoc.org.

Schuler, Douglas. 2008. *Liberating Voices: A Pattern Language for Communication Revolution.* Cambridge, Massachusetts, and London: MIT Press.

Helmut Leitner *(Austria) is a natural scientist and graduate in chemistry from the Technical University in Graz, Austria. He works as an independent software developer, systems analyst and consultant. In 2000, as a pioneering user of wiki systems, he started to research online communities, the precursors of social media, using approaches based on patterns. His recent work focuses on the dissemination of the pattern approach and on supporting the growth of the pattern research community.*

Patterns of Commoning:
How We Can Bring About a Language of Commoning

By Silke Helfrich[1]

The neighborhood I live in still sleeps and works according to the rhythm of companies that earned their reputations in the nineteenth century. It's very late at night. A chat window pops up on my computer: Helmut Leitner is still awake, too. He had spent three months working through our volume *The Wealth of the Commons: A World Beyond Market and State* (2012) to "arrange and piece together eighty articles on the commons like a puzzle," according to the chat log. Months later, in January 2014, I meet Helmut Leitner for the first time at a conference in Vienna. The abstract of his talk – "Patterns of Enlivenment" – catches my attention: "Pattern languages and a bit of theory [enable] holistic thinking in the service of enlivenment, transparency, participation, and sustainability." Even more enticing, Leitner claims that a "set of instructions for dealing with cooperative forms of economic activity and life" could be fleshed out, drawing upon the insights in our volume on the commons and other sources.

At first I am skeptical about the description of pattern languages as "sets of instructions," since I believe that Christopher Alexander's approach offers far more to commons theory than merely being a concrete manual for collaboration in social spheres of a manageable size. After all, Alexander calls for designs that foster enlivenment: living cities, living communities, a living democracy; and ultimately he also calls for a science of enlivenment that disengages natural sciences and some social sciences from the metaphor of the machine. Alexander works toward a paradigm shift – from thinking about individual components that are separated from one another, toward thinking about the richness of relationships among loosely connected components. His pattern language discourse does not focus on what separates things, but on

1 | I am very grateful to Franz Nahrada for his encouragement, his foresight, and his depth; and much obliged to Jacques Paysan, Florian Rommel, and especially Helmut Leitner for their support, their solidarity and their numerous, exceedingly helpful editing suggestions.

what connects them, i.e., he helps us learn to see living organisms embedded in a rich field of connections.

Patterns Make Us into Commoners

Patterns are usually revealed through processes that highlight the role of purpose, genesis, subjectivity and meaning, which reductionist approaches far too often neglect. Just as water is doubtless more than the combination of two hydrogen atoms and an oxygen atom, so are commons more than the combination of resources, communities and rules. The insight on which this book is founded, that commons do not simply *exist*, but are created – "There is no commons without commoning," as Peter Linebaugh says – sheds light on why a deeper understanding of commons requires an approach that is capable of taking purpose, genesis, subjectivity and meaning into account. What is more: *through* the process of taking such an approach and pondering patterns of commoning, we change our understanding of ourselves in specific ways. Or to modify Linebaugh: There is no *commoner* without commoning. Becoming aware of the patterns of commoning gives us more clarity in thinking about commons and our identities of living within them.

All this explains why the pattern approach sketched out by Helmut Leitner in the previous essay is suitable for getting to the bottom of the idea of the commons while at the same time making it easier to communicate how commons can succeed. A pattern approach...

- is context-related (cultural, political-economic, social, and ecological contexts);
- is based in concrete livelihoods;
- supports self-reflection;
- generates experiences of resonance;
- recognizes one's own experience as a pathway to insights; and
- has no predetermined outcome.

A patterns approach permits people to orient themselves to complex and dynamic systems, and can be applied to (smaller) community processes as well as (larger) societal ones. Patterns of the former are more specific, of the latter more general.

In June 2014, half a year after encountering Helmut Leitner in Vienna, I am sitting comfortably beside a raspberry bush in the lovingly tended garden of the Culture Nature Farm in Bechstedt, Germany. It was the third Commons Summer School, which included a workshop on "Patterns of Commoning." We had already placed the concept of commoning at the center of our deliberations, so that the participants were already aware of the fact that commons *are made*.

But this insight did not answer the question: How? After all, at times it seems more difficult to "do commons" than to "imagine commons." Yet the more (often and intensively) we ponder this question of *how to common*, the more often our thinking departs from conventional schools of thought, including, ultimately, institutional economics, and enters uncharted territory.

General and Specific Patterns

The relationship between "general/higher-level" and "specific/lower-level" patterns can take on at least two forms:

   1) Spatial/inclusive

For example: A commons project includes "self-determined rules" as an indispensable component. "Commons project" would be the general/higher-level pattern. "Self-directed rules of a commons project" would be the specific/lower-level pattern.

   2) Abstracting/general

For example: The *dual control principle (second pair of eyes)* is to be found in various specific action situations – in bookkeeping, aviation (pilot/co-pilot) or politics (President/Vice President) – and it is less general than a *backup principle*, which is to be found in nature (our two eyes, ears, and kidneys, for instance) or in technology (backups of files).

Commons Theory on a Multilayered Foundation

Political scientist Elinor Ostrom's design principles for commons institutions (see p. 47) have become widely known ever since she was awarded the Nobel Prize in Economics in 2009. Ostrom was largely concerned with "diverse *institutional arrangements* for governing common-pool resources (CPRs) and public goods at multiple scales" (Ostrom 2010:641, emphasis added). Her method was based on the standard frameworks and concepts of institutional economics, but – and this is her special accomplishment – she focused on the fact that the arrangements sought are not to be found only in a dichotomous choice between the market and the state. This well-supported insight is a point of no return, both in political and scientific terms. As an empathetic, dyed-in-the-wool academic, Ostrom sought to understand the "broader institutional regularities among the systems that were sustained over a long period of time and were absent in the failed systems" (Ostrom 2010:652). She, as well as other schools of thought on the commons on which she had a formative influence, used the Institutional Analysis and Development (IAD) modeling (see Figure 1).

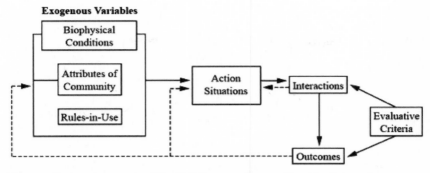

Figure 1: Basic components of the IAD framework, as outlined by Ostrom.[2]

It serves to analyze situations in which people are confronted with various demands, norms, and rules, some of which are contradictory (Conway 2012). Such contradictions are part of everyday life. Everyone is familiar with them – for example, the criterion of individual "mobility" in order to be available "for the labor market," which requires that you have a car to be available for where and when you're needed. This privileged criterion, however, affects one's usage of public transportation and even its being provided in the first place: the more people who use their own cars in a certain area the less sense it makes to sustain public transport services.

At a more abstract level, IAD modeling is complemented by the Social-Ecological Systems Framework, which is based on numerous variables that constitute a whole social-ecological system and is therefore included in the analysis of a commons. Taken together, IAD and SES form a kind of double analytic system that consists of groups of building blocks (or "variables", see illustration) – such as biophysical conditions, characteristics of the community and rules – that affect the concrete "action situations." Although this approach is quite detailed and differentiated, it ultimately clings to the notion that changing the number and quality of these analytic building blocks affects the desired result more or less directly, as if one were causal to the other.

Of course, some things do cause other things. Nonetheless, the dynamics of a commons cannot be captured by an input/output calculus; there is more going on than causality. Likewise, the "ingredients" that constitute the system matter. An outstanding meal cannot be prepared using inferior ingredients, and conceiving education as a market activity oriented toward the requirements of "the economy" that is driven by grades and test scores cannot bring about a well-rounded, socially concerned human being. So, too, commons do not result simply by combining certain rules and building blocks; they can hardly emerge,

---

2 | The modeling shows that the "Ostrom School" is not self-critical about its ontological categories of thought, and accordingly has a somewhat schematic understanding of social *processes.*

for example, from rules that are inimical to commons or from groups of hard-core loners. The sum of building blocks does not constitute the whole because integrated systems have their own, larger logic. Both are important ways to understand commons, but one must recognize that the conceptual framing of the commons that I as an observer propose – i.e., the "how do I imagine commons?" – in effect predetermines what will be analyzed and perceived in the first place. In effect, one's analytic categories *constitute* one's understanding of the commons. If education is conceived of as a commodity whose primary function is to serve the labor market, for example, it will hardly seek to "trans-form as much of the world as possible ... into oneself," as Humboldt describes the proper scope of education. Or people who think of eating only in terms of providing calories will not necessarily set out to find fresh foods.

In short: The way in which we imagine and model a system has a direct bearing on how we conceive its creation, structure and character.

So commoning does not simply succeed when all the factors and conditions have been optimized and all institutions comply with the stipulated design principles. Ostrom herself emphasized that ultimately there is no reliable chain of cause and effect. Yet we can address this "gap" in causality by complement-ing Ostrom's Law with a holistic approach that is capable of incorporating the characteristic of social processes that have their own meaning and purpose.

This is where I locate the potential of pattern theory for commons theory. While suitable institutions can provide frameworks for cooperative institutions, patterns of commoning contribute to developing concrete skills *within* these institutions, providing sharper definition to the as-yet undertheorized concept of commoning. It is important to address the internal, intersubjective dimen-sions of commons because abstract terms detached from concrete practice are not well-suited to communicating dynamic social phenomenon that have many of their own idiosyncrasies. This problem can be countered by patterns of commoning. Patterns have the potential to capture the principles and inner dynamics of self-organization, helping to make them more easily reproducible and able to bring about a more profound social-ecological transformation. Patterns theory does not insist upon strict causal relationships; instead it helps identify the subjective, contingent complexities of any commons. Here, patterns can be seen as structures within which things crystallize so that commoning can develop in as many different spheres and on as many levels as possible.

The basic point: Ostrom's approach should be enriched in the medium term by two complementary tools: a pattern language of commoning, which this article attempts to outline, and a pattern language of a "commons-based society," which has yet to be developed.

Patterns Make Commoning More Effective

Helmut Leitner's effort to assemble descriptions of commons projects like pieces of a puzzle and to comb through them, seeking out patterns, is worthwhile because it makes commoning more effective. That is why we are sitting in the garden in Bechstedt and jointly developing patterns on the issue of "borders and exclusion in commons;" Who's inside? Who's outside? And why?

That is why I host another workshop a few months later in Montreal, Canada, where three dozen people from projects, networks, universities and public agencies debate the art of commoning[3] in general and develop patterns for conflict resolution in particular. The event prompts me to reflect on a very classic problem of collective processes – "sharing of costs" – from the perspective of patterns. This perspective lays bare the connections between processes that appear all over the world in specific forms that vary based on time, location, environmental and social conditions, as well as people's sensitivities. All these processes harbor patterns, the hypothesis goes, and laying them open not only helps us to understand the processes of commoning, but also facilitates their integration into everyday life and institutions. Not in the sense of a how-to manual or a "set of instructions" for commoning, but definitely in the sense of a catalyzing action and reflection. The more commoning seems normal to us, the more easily and effectively the various commons – the "peninsulas against the current," in Friederike Habermann's words – can be networked with each other, and the more intensively they will support societal transformations.

So, how can such patterns be developed?

Valueless Patterns

The creative cycle of pattern generation, as outlined in Figure 6 in Helmut Leitner's chapter, amounts to a reflexive practice for problem-solving. This creative cycle is initially independent of ethical or moral meaning, but it gradually becomes endowed with values as people generate, exchange, test and change them in everyday interaction with each other.[4] It is this *performative creation of meanings* that generates values in a community. One could call this creative process the essence of commoning. In other words: We act, and through our actions, we generate the criteria and standards through which we can ascribe value(s). Values are understood here as an expression of creative energy and imaginative potential for action; they are neither objectively nor categorically

---

3 | Conference, "The Art of Commoning," November 6-8, 2014, Montreal. More at http://www.aohmontreal.org/en/l%E2%80%99art-de-l%E2%80%99en-commun.

4 | Values are understood here as that "through which actions gain significance for the person acting" (Graeber 2012:13). The idea is based on the assumption that "not things, but actions are valued" (ibid:94).

determined by anything in particular; they are developed anew each time that commoning occurs, again and again.

Accordingly, values do not exist *before* commoning as some kind of predetermined blueprint. There is no god, no state and no purportedly objectifying process that can *set* the values of a commons in advance. And yet, from a commoning perspective, values become an essential element of successful commons that patterns of commoning must take account of. In the process of developing patterns, one must therefore ask over and over whether a value so elementary to the commons as "freedom based on relatedness"[5] is strengthened or made vulnerable.

To enter into commoning is to search for patterns that help to shape our way of living together as voluntary experiences, free from external coercion and constraints. Free cooperation as a basic principle is not only for small size communities; all of society can ultimately only be maintained if in principle cooperation can also be taken away or given up. In simpler words: People must also have the option to leave a group, or to "exit." There can be no justification for forcing cooperation.

In commoning, as in all social processes, successful solutions can be replicated only to a limited degree. Needless to say, there are no silver bullets. So patterns remain a means of showcasing commoning in such a way that the salient, constant features become visible without having to banish certain other features from reality or ignore contextual elements. It goes without saying as well, that many of these patterns are right in front of us, they are just not well articulated in language or made culturally legible. As Franz Nahrada, an expert on pattern languages, has put it: "It simply isn't the case that pattern languages are something fundamentally new; they are implemented so naturally in our lives that we probably wouldn't even have found out what is actually essential if they weren't threatened so strongly by many, many negative societal developments. So we have to act with a special awareness to reconstitute these 'natural' behaviors."[6] This reconstitution comports with Elinor Ostrom's understanding of her work as identifying *the conditions* for cooperation to flourish. Her question was not whether people want to cooperate, but rather how to help them do so.

---

5 | This is a freedom related to the necessities of life, the freedom of others, and the basic understanding of the individual as a social being who is connected to others. This is different from a concept of freedom that focuses on the freedom of the individual to do anything he or she wants with an indifference to social and ecological boundaries.

6 | Franz Nahrada, personal correspondence, April 2014.

Developing Patterns

Fostering cooperation, helping to make commons: that is what patterns can achieve. Combined in a pattern language, they orient us as we search for the structural elements for creating solutions for commons-related problems that work in particular contexts. Patterns let us assess the productive potential of different prospective solutions and compare them with each other (Transition Network 2010). The process of developing them should be understood not as abstract knowledge about the success of commons, but rather as practical, accessible knowledge about how to solve very concrete questions of concern to the networks or peer-to-peer communities on electronic networks. Patterns stimulate focused reflection. The knowledge created in this way directly influences the actions of commoners and shapes the contexts of their future activities. Patterns of commoning can promote the basic openness of a process, help guarantee that everyone involved is actually part of the discussion and decision making, and raise the question again and again: How does this process support everyday needs and the enlivenment of life?

One of the most important features of every pattern language is to not see it as a *model*, but as a *platform* that enables us to take the first steps in adapting specific patterns to our own particular circumstances. A pattern language is necessarily incomplete knowledge, but still it represents the best knowledge that we have and it can be further developed jointly as needed. People familiar with developing patterns know that the process helps elicit insights that "we already know" deep inside but which have not yet been made visible and explicit. The patterns shed light on the conceptual foundation of commoning and give them a clear formulation that makes it more comprehensible to outsiders and thus more easily replicated.

In the best case, a pattern is to be formulated in a language appropriate to the respective subject matter – in our case, commoning, it must be a language that is itself open and that remains enlivened. This way, a pattern language of commoning co-creates a common language of commoning – one that not only lets commoners see the hidden social logic and practices that hold them together, but also helps communicate key commoning themes that shed light on the similarities between (for example) community seed banks and free software, both of which seek to protect their shared resource against enclosures. Again: Patterns are above all a pattern *language*: a means of forging community and socialization par excellence.

During the development of each pattern (language), the question first arises: How to start? How to "set foot" in a system with so many details and contextual complications and begin to systematically analyze it? Some ways of accessing it are summed up here:

How to start? Methods of developing patterns[7]

- Brainstorming
- Text analysis of descriptions of commons projects and commoning processes
- Derive from categories and key concepts of the field to be examined (specialist literature)
- Elicit patterns through internal discussions by commoners
- Examine meta- or general patterns to deduce specific patterns (see box above)
- Look to patterns from other pattern languages for inspiration
- Test alternatives to already existing patterns
- Extrapolate from scientific discourse about particular patterns
- And others yet-to-be-discovered.

In other words: many paths lead to the creation and identification of patterns: By looking more deeply at projects, we can draw on tried and tested practical examples and the knowledge about problems specific to the commons. Processes of communication, cooperation, mediation, and conflict resolution in other areas of society may provide useful material for developing patterns. We can also study the repertoire of methods of social innovators and movements – permaculture, transition, nonviolent communication, systemic consensus-building, "Scrum" agile project management[8] and many others – to identify patterns that have already been developed. (See box on pp. 35-36.)

---

7 | I came to recognize these methods of developing patterns from talking with Takashi Iba at the University of Tyrol, and from reflections at the Third Commons Summer School, in 2015, and at the Art of Commoning in Montreal, on November 15, 2014.

8 | See: https://en.wikipedia.org/wiki/Scrum_(software_development).

Patterns inspired by other pattern languages: Iteration and Iterator

Iteration

From the pattern language: "Groups work: patterns enlivening human encounters."

Description: If at first you don't succeed, try again a second or even a third time. The outcome of the first round of an activity or conversation will inform the next round and will deepen, broaden, and generate new understanding and new possibilities. To achieve a stronger effect, repeat a process several times or come back to it later.

Example: At the beginning of a group meeting lasting several days, you will presumably feel alone among strangers. Halfway through the meeting, some faces will be familiar, and you may have forged some relationships. By the end, you will probably feel more integrated into the group. Every day is a new iteration, whereby you always start over from the beginning, but at a higher level each time (from Group Works Deck)[9]

Iterator

Description: Software developers use iterator patterns in programs to access elements of a set, or put more simply: a list. Iterator patterns operate according to the basic principle: "if there is another element on the list, then provide it." Iterators are usually generated by a code function called "iterator()".

Example: Iterator pattern in the programming language Java: Every Iterator pattern makes functions called next(), hasNext() as well as an optional function called remove() available. An iterator pattern outputs a special value that marks the beginning. That is why, after initialization, the function next() has to be run first, which marks the first element of the list to be searched. The function hasNext() is used to find out when the program has arrived at the last element. The following example shows a simple case of using iterator patterns in Java:

```
Iterator iter = list.iterator();
//Iterator<MyType> iter = list.iterator(); in J2SE 5.0
while (iter.hasNext()){
  System.out.println(iter.next());
}
```

---

9 | http://groupworksdeck.org/patterns/Iteration

> *To illustrate:* This is like reading a text following these instructions: "If a word follows, then read it and show it on the monitor. If no word follows, you have reached the end of the text and completed the task." In each step of accessing the text, called an iteration, exactly one word of the text is available for processing. The entire text can be processed in many iterations. An algorithm described like this is so abstract that it can be used in many situations, for example, iteratively working your way down a street, looking at the sewerage connection of each and every house, or working your way down the questions on an exam. (Source: Iterator, https://de.wikipedia.org/wiki/Iterator)

The first patterns of commoning that I would like to present here were developed to address typical problem areas of commons. Normally, sufficient inspiration for developing patterns during a workshop (as we did) can be gained by using people's own descriptions, practical experiences, and knowledge as a jumping-off point. At the beginning, the context and the problem(s) in a concrete action situation are defined as precisely as possible. Then, everyone jointly focuses on one problem or one aspect of it. In a sense, it's just circling around the identified problem in a conversation collectively. The basic idea of this approach is to first open the floodgates and present all the solutions that the people involved can contribute from their experience and their imagination. This prepares the ground for things to emerge that were previously unimaginable.

At first, it is important not to pursue a single idea for solving the problem, but instead to keep asking the questions: "What else is there?" "And what else?" "Which other solutions are imaginable?" In this way, the elaboration of patterns takes place step by step, and also iteratively in each and every phase of the exploration. During such a conversation, the abundance of our ways of managing a situation and shaping our social realities and devising solutions to common problems becomes more visible, while the limits of each possible solution are sketched out too. In short: The procedure remains anchored in immediate, practical issues.

Patterns of Commoning

> *Celebrate and celebrate often. Celebrate the small things and*
> *celebrate the large things. Celebrate failure (and success!)*
> From the Transition Network's collection of patterns (2010)

In the course of connecting various perspectives, there often comes a moment when a group develops a confidence and conviction about a pattern – that describes a common reality shared by all. Co-intelligence scholar Tom Atlee would call this moment "collective magic." One workshop participant, while thinking about agricultural commons, formulated this idea in these words: "I had a new thought every time someone spoke. Now I feel I'm not thinking only about rules and structures, but about the people. People sulk sometimes. Structures don't." Indeed: and this has to be taken into account. People have emotions, in each and every commons there is an emotional memory. Pattern theory relies on this insight: patterns permit people to access not only the rational approaches to a topic, but also the emotional ones. In this way, they activate the experience of collective resonance, which is often experienced as magical.

While Ostrom's design principles delimit the normative horizon of institutional design, patterns can make accessible what happens *within* these "institutions" and at their borders. They help elicit answers to questions such as: How do people make sure that nobody feels taken advantage of? How do people deal with power and dominance within a commons? How can discrimination on the basis of gender, ethnic group, ability, descent etc. be addressed? How can the commons succeed in everyone contributing what they can? And how are commons protected from enclosure or reprivatization – in the midst of capitalism?

Beginning with an answer to the last question, I will introduce four examples of patterns of commoning. The structure that I will use to describe them resembles those Helmut Leitner introduced in his essay.[10] Recall that it consisted of a series of items that move from context → problem → solution → result → specific pattern name → related patterns.

Case 1: The Logic of the Commons vs. the Logic of the Market

The Context

Real estate markets treat buildings and land like any other commodity, which frequently results in speculative investments that drive land prices and rents up, making housing unaffordable for many people. To address this problem, a network of residential projects across Germany, the Mietshäuser Syndikat, devised a decentralized organizational structure in an ambitious attempt to "claim apartment/residential buildings as commons" (Rost 2012:285).

The Problem

Just as the situations of individual people living in residential projects change in unpredictable ways, so do societal conditions. Project finances can fail or the transition to a new generation may bring unforeseeable challenges. A building purchased jointly decades ago can become more valuable on the open market,

---

10 | See Figure 2 in Helmut Leitner's contribution on p. 19.

making it seem attractive to sell it. In all these cases, the building, which had been deliberately removed from the sphere of the market, could now be returned to it. To preclude such a possibility, a building association could lay down in its bylaws, that residential property is to be *permanently* removed from the market. Yet the people involved in the association could still change their bylaws with a qualified majority. So the governance provisions don't seem to be secure enough to protect the property as a commons in the long term

The Solution

Most but not all of the residential projects organized in the network of the Mietshäuser Syndikat are set up as cooperatives: therein, an assembly of all tenants ("association of residents") decides democratically, within the framework of its bylaws, how to make the best use of its respective building, how to manage it, oversee construction projects and secure financing. In other words, the respective association or cooperative of residents settles all matters that are linked to managing the collective property as such; however, it does not decide by itself, how to resolve questions relevant to ownership, such as sale of the property. This is made sure through a simple legal construction: The title of ownership for a particular collective property is not in the name of the property's association of residents only, but it's with a classical limited company. This limited company has just two partners, the association of residents and the Mietshäuser-Syndikat itself, each of which has different interests. In the event that a decision to sell needs to be made, there are only two votes – one from the association and one from the Mietshäuser-Syndikat. The property can be sold only if both bodies agree, which essentially gives each a veto over a proposed sale. This simple concept relies on both a classic separation of powers and the principle of consensus.

The Resulting Situation

This legal scheme raises the institutional barriers to re-privatizing and selling housing that was conceived of, created, and financed as a permanent commons. At the same time, this solution does not entirely rule out sale of the property, which may prove reasonable in individual cases. In the event that it has to solve problems relevant to the bylaws, the association or cooperative of residents receives support from the Mietshäuser-Syndikat.

The Patterns
- Protect commons from the logic of the market
- Use a trusted entity for strategic co-decisions.

Case 2: The Relationship of Give and Take

The Context

Among the members of a German community-supported agriculture (CSA) project, there is a broad consensus that giving and receiving should be decoupled from one another to help achieve structural change in the economy, society and their own organization.[11] As a community within an EU "model region," this CSA is eligible for support for experiments in alternative forms of economic activity, a general situation that provides favorable conditions for launching new ideas and projects.

Some farms in the region have been working with this CSA. They practice organic farming, but have come up against limiting factors time and again, especially if they produce dairy products and meat in addition to vegetables and fruit. The problem arises between the CSA and one of the organic farms (which is not the common supplier of this CSA). Both value each other highly, and they both are even planning for the organic farm to become a partner in the CSA project.

The Problem

One standing challenge of community-supported agriculture is to make do with what is produced while spending only the amount of money raised from the CSA members at the beginning of the growing season. These two factors – what a supplier can produce and what the community can contribute – places limits on how much produce the CSA can supply year-round, a limitation that members generally accept. The concrete problem in our case is that the CSA, in 2014, needed more potatoes to provide to its members. So a CSA representative asked a nearby organic farmer and friend (not the usual CSA supplier) to donate the potatoes she could not sell to other customers to the CSA. The farmer, who herself is involved in many community-minded activities, says no – and the resulting argument took on a sharp tone: "That is a matter of principle. I'd rather feed the potatoes to the animals or put them on the compost heap. ... If a potato doesn't cost anything on the market, does that mean that a CSA organization can take it for free?" The CSA member replied: "To me, it is a

---

11 | "Decoupling acts of giving and receiving" and thus no longer applying the principle of exchanging goods or services of equivalent value, is a general pattern of societal transformation. The "bidding round" is one of its specifications, in other words, a specific pattern. It is used in CSA projects and other groups to make this decoupling a practical reality. In this way, everyone receives what they need and everyone gives what they can. When the bidding round begins, the community's total financing needs for the coming year are presented, i.e., all costs arising in the context of producing the range of goods (e.g., seeds, wages, use of machinery). Then every member writes down the amount of money s/he is willing to contribute to the budget. The bids are collected and added up. If the sum fulfills the needs of the budget, then the bidding round is over. If that is not the case, then a second round begins.

matter of course that if you have something you don't need, then you give it away." And: "In the end, a "NO" means that you would rather let something rot away someplace, than give it to the CSA."

The Solution

No solution is found to this conflict at the moment. But, when the people involved think about and discuss it later, it becomes clear that the dispute isn't really about the potatoes, nor about giving away or selling, nor is it a personal conflict. The organic farmer concludes: "It's about sensitivities, about recognition. And it's about the fact that I can make these decisions myself. Otherwise, something's wrong."

The Resulting Situation

The CSA has to buy potatoes elsewhere or meet its need in some other way. The farmer considers that to be a necessary learning curve for the CSA. Furthermore, when both sides have a conversation about this situation, it becomes clear that each has very different basic assumptions that were not properly understood by the other side. Both sides are interested in finding better solutions in the future. The key to do so successfully lies in the following patterns, among others.

The Patterns

- Voluntariness is key.

→ "It's about the fact that I can make these decisions myself. Otherwise, something's wrong."

- Recognize explicitly the other's contribution.

Related patterns

- Disclose basic assumptions
- Decouple the acts of giving and receiving
- Value people vs. added-value
- Create a sense of fairness for all

Case 3: Making Decisions Jointly

The Context

About thirty adults and thirty children live and work as a community in a rural setting. Most of the land is wooded, there are a few meadows and fields. As a rule, decisions are made by consensus, i.e., it isn't necessary for everyone to vote "yes" every time, and people can support a decision passively, yet in principle they can exercise a veto. People like and respect each other. There are conflicts, as everywhere, but overall, they have a strong interest in inclusion and a lot of shared experiences as a community.

The Problem

The group has decided to go with a *strict* consensus, concerning whether to allow livestock farming in the community. That means: if somebody votes "no", this person actually exercises a veto. Therefore, the very framing of the question (allow livestock farming or not) implies that people who wish to raise animals will be excluded even if only one person votes against the proposal.

At a certain moment, one woman congenial to the group has applied to become a member. The group in principle supports her application, but she wants to keep some dairy cows to support herself. Some members cannot back this decision even though they would like to welcome this individual as a new member. Not keeping animals is very important to them.

The Solution

One positive factor in finding a productive solution is the group's many years of experience with consensus decisionmaking. That framework provides for four options:

- Yes
- Abstain
- Agree, with reservations
- No

The group decides to introduce another option:

- Agree, with strong reservations

The Resulting Situation

Thanks to the introduction of the new option, three people who had maintained their vetoes for three years feel that their views are sufficiently taken into account. They feel they are now in a position to lift their vetoes and agree to admit a new member even though this member raises cows.

The Pattern

- Expand options for decisionmaking

Related Patterns

- Disclose basic assumptions

Case 4: Conflict Resolution Within a Commons Project

The Context

In a large building with many large rooms suitable for groups, rental payments are to be secured for several years by about thirty people (and potentially more users of the building in the future) on a voluntary basis. Members do not all know each other well, and the ways in which they use the rental property differ widely. Compared to market prices, the rent is low. Even so, the financial situation of most users is precarious. This makes it difficult to plan finances and maintenance. Everybody seems to assume that "somehow there will be enough money."

The Problem

In order to make sure that the rent is paid on time every month, the group makes a joint decision about a *recommended* amount per person and month. This is then communicated a number of times by mailing list. But in principle, the contribution is voluntary and not mandatory. Each one is supposed to contribute according to what s/he is able to contribute. After a few months, the group is in the red. The problem is not solved by sending alarming e-mails to members informing them about the actual payments by individuals (without mentioning names). The precise reasons for deficit remain in the dark.

The Solution

In a conversation using a talking stick, everyone involved takes advantage of the opportunity to describe how he or she personally deals with the issue. This brings individual motives to light. In addition, some basic assumptions that had never been mentioned explicitly are formulated for the first time ("But that's just a small amount per person.")

The Resulting Situation

The group continues to refrain from requiring individuals from paying specific sums. Yet the deficit disappears. Talking about each and every individual's feeling of fairness and at which point they "stop giving gladly" has raised people's awareness on the complexity of the situation. People apologize to each other when they understand individuals' other ways of dealing with the rent question.

One reason that many people mention for not increasing their contributions is their "individual feelings of fairness" → "It would no longer be what I'd gladly give."

The Pattern

- Making the invisible visible

Related Patterns

- Transparent financial situation
- Disclose basic assumptions
- Create a sense of fairness to all
- Talking stick

Many more examples could be described and tested against real-world experiences. In this way, one pattern after another emerges; they can relate to one another like words in sentences,[12] connecting to one another, and finally growing to form a pattern language that is always open and adaptable to new conditions, just like the language we use. When we reflect on these patterns or develop them jointly, different levels of abstraction become visible. Some patterns can be used in collective processes of a manageable size; others describe a different societal logic, for example, "protect commons from the logic of the market" or "decouple acts of giving and receiving." and "make the invisible visible."

Of course, developing patterns won't suffice; commons-friendly structures must also be developed to create the conditions and support the long-term persistence and proliferation of commoning. Such structural changes (through public policy, law, organizational forms, etc.) require political commitment for commons and commoning. Yet often the opposite occurs, intentionally or not – but always effectively.

Anti-patterns

In fact, many public policies or structural economic conditions today can be described as anti-patterns. Anti-patterns are "patterns" that are not adapted to the diverse individual needs in enlivened systems. Nobody would assume that a single model of shoes would fit everyone or that a single model of a house replicated millions of times would fulfill everyone's dreams of their own home. It is also clear that not all students learn in the same way, or at the same time of day – and yet teaching is often organized in this way. The following excursus shows just how ubiquitous anti-patterns are.

Minimum Wage or Commoning?

A mandatory minimum wage – 8.50 gross euros per hour – was introduced in Germany on January 1, 2015. According to many, the law represents an attempt by the political community to set limits on the business community. This way of thinking follows the pattern "state versus market". Actually, the minimum wage intervention by lawmakers seems plausible for situations (like the one we currently live in) with clearly defined roles: entrepreneurs and owners on one side, wage earners on the other. All too often, the latter can't make ends meet because of their low wages. All too often, one side dictates conditions. This results in a never-ending conflict between interests with periodic interventions by the social welfare state as a way to smooth out contradictions that in essence stem from a segmented world where all too often others make decisions for us. In this world, producers are not only forced to compete with each other; an active life is separated into "work" and "life." All too often, "working to earn

---

12 | The "related patterns" following the examples demonstrate this.

money" crowds out any other possible motivations for work, including the idea of "working to live."

In such a context, the minimum wage – which is supposed to create a minimum level of equality in formal terms – can never create a feeling of social justice.

Why is that? The minimum wage law applies to people who are very unequal in personal circumstances in a formally equal way. It applies to temporary employment agencies in the construction and cleaning industries as well as to railway workers, to asparagus and strawberry farms using a lot of seasonal labor as well as small farms and craftspeople's businesses without internal hierarchies. During a discussion with organic farmers and people working in the sector, I hear that the minimum wage, which makes sense to them "in principle", cannot be sustained in practice, especially on family farms where agriculture is a way of life, not "a job" and where people must work as much as necessary in a given day (during harvest time, for example). But the new law is very strict and detailed, farmers tend to come up with "creative bookkeeping" to comply with it, but nobody feels good about these petty subterfuges.

The situation is complex: Someone asks during the discussion, "And what if farmers went on strike, but not for minimum wage, but for a 'skilled craftsman's wage'?" Another one suggests a "minimum wage per day"? Would that be a pattern, with no upper limit on the number of hours worked per day? Isn't this the same as just switching from an hourly to a daily rate? The actual living and working situations of the people who participate in our discussion vary immensely. The way they are affected by the minimum wage law varies as well. Yet everyone agrees on one thing: Such an approach has no room for a simple idea such as "working is enjoyable." Reflecting on his own situation, one middle-aged man who has spent decades working toward different concepts of work and life reports how he observed himself starting to think about whether a farm worker "was productive enough for his hourly wage" – a thought he had never had before. The man lost sight of the idea of work as something integral to one's life and even enjoyable. In such a context, having a chat on the farm loses its innocence and becomes potentially an issue to be sanctioned. The new setup changes everything; it highlights in a somehow tragic way that "clocking hours doesn't really go with agriculture." Similar dynamics apply to many other occupations – scientist and artist, artisan and mountain guide, geriatric nurse and physician. The list is endless. Counting and care don't go together.

So, farmers and other sectors are experiencing how the formal equality created by a law that makes sense "in principle" generates new injustices. For example, a man who has taken early retirement may work a few hours per week on a farm on a 450 euros per month basis (in a special program according to which no taxes or contributions to the social welfare system are deducted), and in fact receive now 8.50 euros per hour gross under the new minimum wage law. Whereas, trained farmers or gardeners work 50 hours or more per week on the same farm until all the work that needs to be done is actually done and would never make 8.50 per hour. "You can't 'adapt creatively' so many hours in the payroll accounting."

"Can there be creativity in actual pay instead?" someone finally asks. The first answer comes from a communal farm in the Black Forest that has experiments with a different concept: no wages are paid, and yet everyone can live according to their abilities and needs. The basic idea of this farm is incompatible with the minimum wage approach. Instead, this farm cultivates the attitude: "Everyone makes their best effort, then we'll have everything we need." Formal equality is not an issue on that farm. For example, if there were two apprentices only one of whom had financial support from his parents, then "we would all decide together how to handle the situation." As a result, it is "possible that every person gets a different amount, and still everyone agrees." If two people have different needs and get the same amount, then one person has what s/he needs, and the other doesn't. That would not be fair. The group succeeds with this different way of solving the problem. And their way is based on patterns of commoning, which should be made explicit so that these patterns can inform the decisions of others.

Conclusion and Outlook

There are many reasons that we need to develop a pattern language of commoning. Pattern languages are capable of finding the treasures within our implicit knowledge, which too often go ignored or unexpressed. Specific patterns of commoning will help us to get beyond counting and measuring everything and instead encourage us to focus on deeper, more "enlivened" relationships. Patterns provide useful tools for conflict-resolution and help make insights discovered elsewhere visible as possible ways out of our problems without mandating rigid solutions; they respect our freedom and need to make decisions and shape our livelihoods for ourselves. The process of developing patterns of commoning can be a wholly natural and even playful process available to anyone. It is a way of learning a common vocabulary while disseminating a meme, as if in passing: commons. As a way to cultivate a greater self-awareness of the realities of commoning, pattern languages can significantly accelerate the cultural transformation now underway, helping embryonic forms of commoning become new social norms and expanding the practices of commoning so that a commons-based society can emerge.

References

Conway, Ryan T. 2012. "Ideas for Change: Making Meaning Out of Economic and Institutional Diversity," in David Bollier and Silke Helfrich, editors. *The Wealth of the Commons: A World Beyond Market and State.* Amherst, MA: Levellers Press, pp. 361-368.

Graeber, David. 2001. *Toward an Anthropological Theory of Value: The False Coin of Our Own Dreams.* New York: Palgrave.

Group Works: A Pattern Language for Bringing Life to Meetings and Other Gatherings, http://groupworksdeck.org/patterns/Iteration.

Nahrada, Franz. 2014. Discussion on Open-Source-Biologie at keimform.de, http://keimform.de/2014/open-source-biologie.

Ostrom, Elinor. 2010. Beyond Markets and States: Polycentric Governance of Complex Economic Systems, in: *The American Economic Review*, 100(3):641-672 (June 2010).

Rost, St. 2012. Mietshäuser Syndikat, in Silke Helfrich and Heinrich-Böll-Stiftung, editors: *Commons – Für eine neue Politik jenseits von Markt und Staat*, transcript, pp. 285-287.

Transition Network. 2010. Introducing Transition as a Pattern http://transition-culture.org/wp-content/uploads/Seeing-Transition-as-a-Pattern-Language-conference-booklet-latest-version-1.1.pdf.

Silke Helfrich *(Germany) is an author and independent activist of the commons who blogs at www.commonsblog.de. Bollier and Helfrich cofounded the Commons Strategies Group in 2010 with Michel Bauwens of the Foundation for Peer to Peer Alternatives.*

Eight Design Principles for Successful Commons

One of the great achievement of the late Professor Elinor Ostrom was the identification of eight key design principles for successful commons, which were set forth in her book, Governing the Commons: The Evolution of Institutions for Collective Action (1990). *There have been elaborations and suggested modifications to these rules, but they remain a landmark set of reference guidelines for understanding why commons succeed or fail.*

1. **Clearly defined boundaries**: Individuals or households who have rights to withdraw resource units from the CPR must be clearly defined, as must the boundaries of the CPR itself.

2. **Congruence between appropriation and provision rules and local conditions**: Appropriation rules restricting time, place, technology, and/or quantity of resource units are related to local conditions and to provision rules requiring labor, material, and/or money.

3. **Collective-choice arrangements**: Most individuals affected by the operational rules can participate in modifying the operational rules.

4. **Monitoring**: Monitors, who actively audit CPR conditions and appropriator behavior, are accountable to the appropriators or are the appropriators.

5. **Graduated sanctions**: Appropriators who violate operational rules are likely to be assessed graduated sanctions (depending on the seriousness and context of the offense) by other appropriators, by officials accountable to these appropriators, or both.

6. **Conflict-resolution mechanisms**: Appropriators and their officials have rapid access to low-cost local arenas to resolve conflicts among appropriators or between appropriators and officials.

7. **Minimal recognition of rights to organize**: The rights of appropriators to devise their own institutions are not challenged by external governmental authorities.

For CRPs that are parts of larger systems:

8. **Nested enterprises**: Appropriation, provision, monitoring, enforcement, conflict resolution, and governance activities are organized in multiple layers of nested enterprises.

Eight Points of Orientation for Commoning

The wording of Ostrom's design principles is aimed at social scientists who study the management of common-pool resources from a neutral, non-participatory, scientific perspective. As a result, the principles are not as accessible to the general public, nor do they reflect the personal experiences and first-person voice of commoners.

The first German Sommerschool on the Commons, which took place in Bechstedt, Thuringia in June 2012, decided to remedy this problem. Participants took part in intense debates over what a new set of principles for commoning – based on the Ostrom principles – might look like if they reflected the personal perspective of commoners themselves. The result is a statement, "Eight Points of Orientation for Commoning," which can be seen as a re-interpretation – remix? – of Ostrom's design principles.

* * *

The eight design principles formulated by Elinor Ostrom and others distill the lessons of a huge number of case studies from around the world. They are written from a scientific perspective and continue to be of great significance for the commons movement. We approach the commons from the perspective of active commoners, meaning the people who create and maintain working commons. We are more concerned with creating spaces for community and cooperation than with institutions. As for the resources themselves, we are more interested in how to preserve and use them, than in making distinctions between material and non-material, traditional or new commons. We therefore refer to all types of commons here.

For us Ostrom's design principles provide a template for the following points of orientation. We hope that commoners may find them useful in reflecting on their own practice.

Commons do not exist in a perfect world, but rather in one that is hostile to commons. Therefore it is important that commoners be aware of the treasure they hold in their hands, to preserve it and help it flourish.

1. As a commoner I clearly understand which resources I need to care for and with whom I share this responsibility. Commons resources are those that we create together, that we maintain as gifts of nature or whose use has been guaranteed to everyone.

2. We use the commons resources that we create, care for and maintain. We use the means (time, space, technology, and quantity of a resource) that are available in a given context. As commoner, I am satisfied that there is a fair relationship between my contributions and the benefits I receive.

3. We enter into or modify our own rules and commitments, and every commoner can participate in this process. Our commitments serve to create, maintain, and preserve the commons to satisfy our needs.

4. We monitor the respect of these commitments ourselves and sometimes we mandate others whom we trust to help reach this goal. We continually reassess whether our commitments still serve their purpose.

5. We work out appropriate rules for dealing with violations of our commitments. We determine whether and what kinds of sanctions shall be used, depending on the context and severity of a violation.

6. Every commoner can make use of a space and means for conflict resolution. We seek to resolve conflicts among us in an easily accessible and straightforward way.

7. We regulate our own affairs, and external authorities respect that.

8. We realize that every commons is part of a larger whole. Therefore, different institutions working at different scales are needed to coordinate stewardship and to cooperate with each other.

A German translation of the Eight Points of Orientation for Commoning is available here: http://web03.webcoach.at/w16/commons/index.php/Acht_Punkte. A French translation is available here: http://www.savoirscom1.info/2012/11/ huit-points-de-reference-pour-la-mise-en-commun-des-biens-2.

Conviviality

By Marianne Gronemeyer

> *"I have no expectations from technology, but I believe in the beauty,*
> *in the creativity, in the surprising inventiveness of people,*
> *and I continue to hope in them."*
> Ivan Illich (Cayley 1992:111)

This creativity and inventiveness are not, as we often believe, products of extraordinary individual minds. Instead, they originate from a culturally shaped cooperation that they also serve. And this collaboration could be described more aptly as "conviviality."

"Conviviality" is *still* a foreign word, one that triggers the question, "Well, what does it mean?" At the same time, it risks becoming an all-purpose word that can be fitted into globalized "Uniquac" (Illich) without further ado, a word that *technocrats* invented to justify their misdeeds, and that *alternative-minded people* happily imitate – and which both groups confuse with proper language. It is tempting to protect this beautiful world by not using it – yet that would obviously be futile.

"Con-vivial" has two parts. The prefix "con," derived from the Latin *cum*, means "together with," and "vivial" is easy to recognize as coming from the Latin verb "vivere" = "to live."

Conviva is a fellow diner; *convivium* is a party of invited guests, a feast, a circle gathered around a table; *convivere* means "living together, dining together," and in English, the adjective means "sociable, joyful," certainly also in the sense of "slightly tipsy." The kind of gathering called conviviality apparently requires a table around which people can gather, a pitcher of wine to be emptied and bread to be broken together in order to have a good conversation. Of course, the table can also be an empty circle around which people are seated on the floor. Ivan Illich mentions another utensil: a burning candle. After all: "In other words, our conversation should always go on with the certainty that there is someone else who will knock at the door, and the candle stands for him or her. It is a constant reminder that the community is never closed." (Illich 2005:105-151) But is "conviviality" in this sense inviting? Or does it rather tend to be a threshold that people can trip over?

The difficulties that this word poses, besides its meaning, lie less in that fact that even people proficient in using foreign vocabulary are not familiar with it, but more in the fact that in our habits of speaking and hearing, we have become entirely deaf to the good sound of the little word cum, just as we have become unreceptive to its meaning because of the circumstances and the practices of our lives. Com/Cum is a very widespread prefix that appears in German as "kom" or "kon." Yet most of the composite words formed with it have turned its former meaning on its head. The preposition cum, which used to denote cooperation on equal footing – as though it sought to capture the meaning of "commoning" in just three letters – is increasingly serving to describe a sharp, relentless conflict in the struggle for advantages, power, or influence. "Com-petition" no longer describes common striving, but the effort to outdo one another; competitors vie for scarce resources. "Con-sensus" is no longer a spirit generated jointly, but prescribed equality. "Con-sumption" no longer means using something jointly and thoroughly; instead, people consume things to become the object of other people's envy. "Con-formity" does not mean taking on a form through a common effort, in other words, educating oneself together and through one another, but rather being put in shape to be utilized arbitrarily.

I selected these four distortions of the meaning of words with care. They represent the destructive force of the great monopolies that have set out to rule the world as an alliance: The economy holds the world monopoly on distribution and fuels *competition* for scarce resources; science has claimed the world monopoly on explanation and demands *consensus* about its authority to interpret; technology asserts the monopoly on designing the world and is grooming the world for *consumability*. And bureaucracy claims the world monopoly on regulation and does not rest until everything is brought into line in procedural *conformity*. "Thou shalt agree with me and trust my evidence," says natural science. "Thou shalt desire to prevail over your neighbor," says economy. "Thou shalt have machines work in your place, have them serve you and care for you," says technology. "Above all, thou shalt not disturb things," says bureaucracy.

But: "Places devoid of power can always be found. The institutional clutches on life exist partly in appearance only," wrote Peter Brückner about the possibility of finding such a place, even under the conditions of the Nazi period (Brückner, 1982:16). It would take nerve to ignore the omnipotence of the system. What mattered would be to perceive its enormous power without recognizing it. But where might such places devoid of power be found?

Perhaps they are no longer to be *found* today, but first need to be *established*. A place devoid of power is a place for deserters. The deserter is the "no-longer-participant" par excellence; he disobeys orders, he deprives the authorities of his collaboration by going absent on the quiet, but above all, without leave. "Places devoid of power" emerge by people filling them through their presence, people *practicing* conviviality.

The word "convivial" is still able to resist being disfigured by consumerism and being incorporated into jargon. "Convivial" – as is "commoning" – is still a stumbling block in our path, helping us to remain vigilant in the face of smokescreens muddling both our senses and the meanings of words by devastating the most valuable good from which fruitful cooperation can emerge: our language. And there cannot be enough stumbling blocks in an increasingly bulldozed world in which all thresholds, borders, and obstacles have been made to disappear so that everything runs like clockwork, while at the same time, walls, fences, and insurmountable barricades are erected to keep everything and everyone foreign off our backs.

Conviviality needs a *language* that is both objectionable and triggers ideas, a language without which there is no understanding but only "consensus" achieved by manipulation, *research* that speaks a personal language full of experience; *practice* that does not compete, but cooperates and shares; and *technology* that helps to make the best out of the power and the imagination that everyone has (Ivan Illich). "Conviviality" aims to be:

- nonviolent, but not tame;
- appealing to the senses, but not inimical to thought;
- power-less, but not without strength;
- regulated, but not bureaucratic;
- modest, but not lacking in aspirations;
- cognizant/in the present, but not trendy;
- self-determined, but not overly self-assured;
- determined by others, but not patronized;
- unpretentious, but not simple;
- in love with success, but not with victory;
- oriented toward complementarity of differences, not toward marginalization of the other.

Commons are either convivial or only a variant of globalized (and institutionalized) sameness.

References

Brückner, P. 1982. Das Abseits als sicherer Ort, Berlin. [no English translation published, according to Library of Congress and British Library catalogs]
Cayley, D., Editor. 1992. *Ivan Illich in Conversation*, Ontario.
Illich, I. 2005. *In the Rivers North of the Future*. Toronto: House of Anansi Press.

INTERMEZZO I

Can Commoners Become Self-aware of Their Collective Potential?

"At the end of the day, we are what we do to change who we are."
–Eduardo Galeano

As the idea of patterns of commoning suggests, commons are not objects, but actions. In Part II, we would like to illustrate the many forms that commoning takes by examining more than fifty noteworthy commons throughout the world.

The actions that breathe life into commons require at least three insights of everyone involved. First, a recognition that commons do not belong to one person alone. They belong to a community of shared interest that spans past, present and future generations. In this sense, the conventional idea of "ownership" is a category error – an inappropriate frame of reference for understanding commons.

This leads to a second insight, the idea that a commons is all about the relationships among everyone involved. Those relationships cannot be linear, hierarchical or merely bureaucratic because in a commons the terms of human relationship require authentic social connection and care. They must be based on a basic equality of responsibility, entitlement and mutual respect while also recognizing the diversity and uniqueness of the community. This is not just a matter of moral or ethical preferences; it is a necessity for the operation of a stable, robust commons.

Third, a commons needs to affirmatively develop the systems – social, legal, technological – to protect the integrity of its commoning from entropy and hostile outside forces, especially corporate enclosure. This is a perennial struggle of any commons. However, self-protective measures have become extraordinarily important in a time when global capitalism is relentlessly exploiting "free" and unpriced resources as feedstock for its voracious market machine.

These are just a few of the preconditions from which a logic of the commons can emerge – a logic that stands in notable contrast to the logic of the market and its emphasis on absolute individual rights, impersonal exchange, short-term profit and constant economic growth. And yet commons, drawing upon different human capacities and working through different institutional forms, actually produce a great deal of value. We can see this in the forest commons of India and Romania, the Potato Park of Peru, the Helsinki Timebank and Cooperativa Integral Catalana. As these examples also show, commons do not only produce what we need, they shape who we become: our values, practices, relationships, commitments and very identity.

However, there is no such thing as a "pure" commons – for the simple reason that commons cannot be understood as abstract idealizations. They can only be understood in their actual, embedded social circumstances. It is no wonder that any search for a single definition of "the commons" will come up empty-handed! One must understand a commons in its particularity.

This is inescapable because the identity of a commons does not reside solely (or even primarily!) in the resource that is shared. Its character is defined by how we experience it subjectively and emotionally – and that will vary by the people, culture, geography and other conditions and circumstances. A commons resembles a morphological form that shapes both physical matter and social organization and culture. New things will emerge in this world as they are generated anew time and again. Slowly, commoners develop a self-awareness of their acts of commoning, stabilizing them through rules, rituals, traditions, language and ethics. Through the practice and experience of commoning, some very different forms of knowing arise or are preserved. They slowly take root and eventually change our patterns of thinking and our frames of reference. In this fashion, a commons can transport us into a different way of being.

That, truly, is why commons have such emancipatory potential. They can help incubate new ways of seeing, being and knowing. Such emergent sensibilities can help us escape ossified categories of dominant paradigms of thought, politics and economics. They can also help us nourish new foundations for thinking that can free us from the misleading dichotomies of contemporary life – subjective and objective, individual and collective, private and public, rational and irrational.

Despite the diversity of commons that we survey in Part II, one thing stands out: they all slip the mental shackles that contemporary capitalism seeks to impose. The dominant categories of private property, capital, money, profit and wage labor do not play a central role in any of them. These commons are animated by a different logic, a different repertoire of human motivations and emotions than the logic of maximizing individual gain at the expense of nature or other human beings. We are aware of the fact that the old, familiar categories of understanding will continue to be applied to these notable commons (they even emerge in some self-descriptions of commons), if only because we still live in societies forged by archaic categories and must act in a commons-unfriendly political and economic environment. But if you look closely, it is clear that each of the commons profiled in Part II ushers us into a transitional zone of possibilities; they point to a new framework of analysis and set of experiences. However, it will take time, research and dialogue for the contours of such a framework to become more evident and widely understood.

In working with the authors on their essays, we found it fascinating that so many of them thought that things we were interested in were not worth mentioning. To them, certain realities of their commons were self-evident; they simply took them for granted. For example: how decisions are made, how conflicts are dealt with or how the project relates to the state. On many occasions, we learned about these important features of daily commoning only through a process of discussing the authors' drafts with them. It was not always possible to finish discussing our questions, let alone find adequate answers and present them in the space available. Still, we believe these essays provide a rich foundation for further inquiry and for commoners to "live the questions" as a fruitful way to find answers.

Some of the remarkable commons we present here do not even consciously consider themselves as such. Indigenous Ethiopians have been managing the Menz-Guassa grasslands for centuries – well before social scientists or activists applied the term to their relationship to the earth. Contributors to the Public Library of Science journals do not necessarily self-identify as commoners; nor do the participants of the Burning Man festival.

For this reason, one might agree with the authors of the recent Corner House Report: "The term 'commons' tends to be a term of political art and not of self-description." (Lohmann/Hildyard, 2014:16) Tech-savvy initiatives in particular tend to focus on their experimental or technological components, or on their openness. See, for example, the profiles of the Public Library of Science journals, Arduino, Open Design, OpenCourseWare and Fab Lab St. Pauli. They do not necessarily recognize that their very processes of commoning point to a very different type of economic activity and way of living. That is one of the points of the profiles of commons in Part II: to help showcase some similarities of radically different commons and to foster a greater self-awareness of these social patterns.

Even though a common may be a small player in a cultural backwater (the idea of open mapping to help with humanitarian crises, for example), we can begin to see in Part II how virtually any commons begins to connect to a larger pattern. We see collaborative ways of creating pools of knowledge; the networking of like-minded commons with each other; the drive to take into one's own hands the infrastructure needed to meet daily needs; and precautionary tactics to prevent enclosure of shared wealth and commoning. All commons also have a potent but latent political significance that should not be understated. Whether and how they will manifest remain an open question.

Yet commons flourish without regard to the political viewpoints or worldviews of participating commoners. That not only makes commons strong, it makes them far more than a political or ideological phenomenon. They are pockets of a highly distributed cultural future that is struggling to crystallize a new worldview and sensibility. Commons may appear to be islands, yet if we connect the dots among the dozens of commons profiled here, making invisible patterns more visible, we cannot help but agree with Norbert Rost's insight, "Islands grow to form continents if we connect them intelligently."[1]

—*Silke Helfrich and David Bollier*

Reference

Lohmann, Larry and Hildyard, Nicholas. 2014. "Energy, Work and Finance," Corner House Report, March 31, 2014, available at http://www.thecornerhouse.org.uk/resource/energy-work-and-finance

---

1 | http://www.spiekerooger-klimagespraeche.de/node/171

PART II

NOTABLE ACTS OF COMMONING
ACROSS CULTURES & CENTURIES

"When offered a choice between A and B, remember there's a whole alphabet out there ..."

Stephen Collis, poet

LONG-LASTING COMMONS

"Most commons have never gone by that name. For most of history there was no need for such a generic term. The differences between the practices referred to – estover, minga, ejidos, *locally-maintained irrigation systems, communal fields and pastures, traditions of gleaning or gathering or turf-cutting or setting aside "pin money" or seeds, sharing software development, or even just maintaining considerate silence after dark – were more important."*

Corner House Report (London), 2014

Bisse de Savièse: A Journey Through Time to the Irrigation System in Valais, Switzerland

By Eric Nanchen and Muriel Borgeat

In Valais, Switzerland, a network of "artificial canals" was rediscovered in the 1980s. They were "drilled and built into mountainsides, enabling the irrigation so important to land cultivation by transporting water across several kilometers," as Auguste Vautier recounts (1942:19). Above and beyond their original purpose, the canals have become important for tourism today, contributing to the establishment of popular hiking trails, among other things. The irrigation canals are of interest in connection with the commons because of their long history of collective management.

Irrigation canals were mentioned in the Swiss Alpine canton Valais for the first time in thirteenth century documents that referred to structures that had likely been built 200 years before. Yet it was not until the fifteenth century that the Golden Age of the *bisses* dawned. Historically speaking, the development of the network of canals can be explained by events that left deep scars across Europe: the plague of 1349 and the epidemics that followed. The population of Valais was hit hard by these epidemics and was decimated by at least 30 to 50 percent. The decline of population density in the Alps in turn meant that land that had previously been used for growing grain was freed up for other purposes. At the same time, the demand for beef increased sharply in the cities of northern Italy. These two factors prompted the farmers of Valais to increase their herds of cattle and to convert their land into hayfields. They had to build the famed canals to transport water from the mountains to their pastureland. So the owners of the hayfields and pastures joined forces, and "collective operations [began] which often involved the entire village community," as one researcher of the canals, Muriel Borgeat, has said.

In the nineteenth century, population pressure and the expansion of vineyards sparked a new phase of irrigation canal construction. In 1924, there were 300 irrigation canals totaling approximately 2,000 kilometers (Schnyder

1924:218). The last survey in the canton of Valais, in 1992 (unpublished), found 190 extant irrigation canals spanning a distance of at least 731 kilometers.

One of these canals is part of the Savièse irrigation system. It was built in several stages. More than a century after it was put into operation in 1430, it was expanded through an impressive wall of rock in order to increase its holding capacity. Hundreds of years later, in 1935, a tunnel through the Prabé Mountain was finally completed, making it easier to maintain the system and to pipe the water across the high plateau. The sections of the *bisse* built at dizzying heights were then abandoned. Only in 2005 did some enthusiasts of the Association for the Protection of Torrent-Neuf[1] decide to reconstruct this emblematic part of the *bisse* with the support of the municipality of Savièse. This section bears witness to the high-wire acts undertaken by earlier generations in order to secure irrigation.

The traditional form of common management of the *bisse* has endured. Since the Middle Ages the feudal lords granted the rural communities water-use rights, either to the entire community or to a group of people who joined together in a community of users, a *consortage*. Such a *consortage* has always had a special statute that determines the rules for use of the system, details of construction (what, by whom, how), maintenance, financial management, and monitoring of the canal system. In the spring, the canals had to be cleaned, and sections damaged in the winter had to be repaired so they would again hold water. Women attended to sealing the wooden channels, collecting twigs and branches and stuffing holes. Today, municipal employees take care of this job, occasionally supported by passionate volunteers.

Members of the *consortage* were granted certain rights to use water proportional to the area of land they cultivated, and for a precisely defined period of time. Each family's coat of arms and its allotment of water rights were carved into a wooden stick. The rights were distributed at regular intervals. "Water thieves" – people who violated the rules of distribution or disregarded the relevant time periods – were punished. "Water theft was considered a serious offense, and the community treated the thief with contempt" (Annales Valsannes 1995:348).

Managing the gates controlling the flow of water was a responsibility of great power because water supply was so fundamental to the farmers. Setting the gates was usually a task reserved for the canal guards (*gardes des bisses*) who saw to the proper condition of the system and guaranteed passage of the largest amount of water possible. Of course, this form of communal organization also reflected a commitment to shared values such as solidarity. Yet as historian and archivist Denis Reynard told us in an interview in July 2014, "It was first

---

1 | Editors' note: The Bisse de Savièse is also called Bisse du Torrent-Neuf.

and foremost economic reasons that forced the landowners to join forces.
It was a way to keep the system going. It was always a necessity, first for farming cattle, and in the nineteenth century, for growing wine. Joint management was a good solution." When we ask whether this management system will endure over the long term, he gets more concrete: "It works if people have a common economic interest – for example, in farming, cattle raising or growing wine. If that isn't the case, then it has no future."

Up to this day, the *consortage* of Savièse is responsible for irrigating the vines. Since common economic interests no longer connect the farmers as strongly as in the past, maintenance of

The *bisse* irrigation canals in the Swiss canton of Valais have been managed as commons since the eleventh century.

the canals has become problematic. One possibility would be for the municipality to take over management of the system. The establishment of the Association for the Protection of Torrent-Neuf sparked new interest in the *bisse* as a piece of cultural heritage. "That made restoration possible, but it isn't a *consortage*," explained Reynard.

The *Bisse de Savièse* is majestic. It has been repaired, and it is located in the midst of a protected Alpine landscape. Thanks to the association, management today still functions similarly to the original system. Yet use of the system has changed. As a tourist attraction, cultural heritage and irrigation infrastructure – all at the same time – the *bisse* tells the story of the development of a Valais commons over the course of centuries.

References

Akten der Internationalen Kolloquien zu den Bewässerungskanälen, Sion, September 15-18, 1994, sowie 2. bis September 5, 2010, *Annales valaisannes*, 1995 and 2010-2011.

Reynard, Emmanuel. 2002. *Histoires d'eau: bisses et irrigation en Valais au XVe siècle*, Lausanner Hefte zur Geschichte des Mittelalters (Cahiers lausannois d'histoire médiévale) 30, Lausanne.

ders. 2008. Les bisses du Valais, un exemple de gestion durable de l'eau?, Lémaniques, 69, Genf, S. 1-6.

Schnyder, Theo. 1924. "Das Wallis und seine Bewässerungsanlagen," in Schweizer Landwirtschaftliche Monatshefte, S. 214-218.

Vautier, Auguste. 1942. *Au pays des bisses*, 2. Auflage, Lausanne.

Eric Nanchen *(Switzerland) is a geographer and director of the Foundation for the Sustainable Development of Mountain Regions (www.fddm.ch). He focuses on development policy, in particular the effects of global and climatic changes on the Alpine world.*

Muriel Borgeat *(Switzerland) is an historian and project director at the Foundation for the Sustainable Development of Mountain Regions. Her research concerns the history of Valais and Rhône.*

The Role of Memory and Identity in the Obştea Forest Commons of Romania

By Monica Vasile

In the Vrancea Mountains of Romania, the Eastern Carpathians, people in dozens of villages have used community-based institutions known as *obştea* to manage forest commons since the sixteenth century.[1] The original sense of the word, coming from Slavonic, is "togetherness," and it underlines the participatory essence of the institution. The traditions of *obştea* are so deeply rooted among Vrâncean villagers that the forest is not regarded simply as a resource; it is a powerful source of collective identity, social practice and pride that has near-mythological resonances. The effectiveness of *obştea* as a customary institution, however, has been profoundly affected by the rise of extractive technologies, the fifty-year reign of communism (1948-1989), and by the surge of modern markets. Through it all, people have cherished their affective relationship with their forests and the *obştea* form of forest management. The institution of *obştea* was not founded at a precise moment or as a contractual organization. Legend tells us that in the sixteenth century Stephen the Great endowed the founders of seven villages for their military merits with communal ownership of the Vrancea Mountains.

Villages of the region jointly possessed the mountains for generations (only interrupted by state ownership during the communist regime), a unique

---

1 | Forest commons can be found all over the Carpathian Mountains in diverse organizational forms. At present, an approximate number of 911 registered forest associations, commons (*obşte* and *composesorat*), in Romania own 14 percent of the total forested surface of the country, the rest being state-owned or individually owned. They account for very different resource bases, some associations owning large plots of high-quality old forest, others small young forests. Also, the rights distribution system is different from place to place, most commons being based on inequality and genealogies, while very few of them are based on equal rights and residence, such as the ones described in this chapter. Income shares from the forest yield can also be distributed in various ways. Some associations invest in communal utilities (such as public buildings reparations, village infrastructure), while others simply distribute cash dividends to the members. For more detail on contemporary issues see Vasile 2006, 2007, 2008, and Vasile and Mantescu 2009. For a historical perspective see Stahl 1958 (in Romanian) and 1980 (in English).

circumstance in Romania and a rarity in Europe. Initially, the whole region owned the entire mountain area (Stahl 1958) in *devalmaşie*. The first division of the land among villages occurred in 1755, followed by another five divisions until the last one in 1840. The divisions were made to meet the pasturing needs of each village and to resolve a political conflict.[2] By the end of the nineteenth century, villagers' access to their forests became more and more restricted as exploitation technologies improved and wood became a valuable commodity associated with money, and social status. During this period, several powerful foreign forestry companies, especially from Austria and Italy, struck deals with local elites for leasing and exploiting large areas of forest. In several villages, with the money yield, the old elites worked for the best of the community, building schools, village halls and communal baths. In others, the locals' collective memory remembers elites who deceived people to sell their use rights, often for a pack of cigarettes. The foreign companies ended their activity in Vrancea by the beginning of the First World War, after committing massive deforestation.

The Romanian state introduced its first forestry statute, The Forestry Code, in 1910, giving *obştea* formal legal recognition. The law required villagers to obtain vouchers from a local committee (without payment) to harvest lumber, as well as certificates to transport it. These regulations were mostly seen as unnecessary formalities and were not strictly followed at the time. Instead, customary norms continued to serve as effective regulation.

The *obştea* might have slowly transformed from a socially embedded institution into a modern organizational form except that, in 1948, the Communist Party came to power and the state seized all communal forest property. In the 1950s there were a number of serious fights in Vrancea between villagers belonging to the Anticommunist Resistance Movement, and communist authorities. Several people were killed, and some were imprisoned. These events, along with an outmigration of educated people from rural areas, led to a loss of capable local elites. Many *obştea* traditions were lost or receded.

Locals' experiences during the communist period varied a great deal from village to village, and even within the same village. Some people worked as wage earners within state structures. Others stole wood from their former common property with the tacit acceptance of local authorities. A black market for wood arose alongside the legitimate market, facilitated by bribes paid to party officials. I found in my study of forest usage during the communist period that "having" and "owning" were not very important. More important was access and use, which were facilitated in many ways, both legal and illegal, usually involving state officials and corrupt practices.

---

2 | The historian H.H. Stahl (1958) notes that, besides the pasturing necessities, each village needed to make a monetary contribution when a powerful boyar claimed the territory, a dispute resolved at the "great trial of Vrancea."

Immediately after the fall of communism, restitution politics gave way to new property relations (Hann 1998) and regulation and governance entailed a lot of legal fuzziness (Verdery 1999).

Collective property rights were re-established only in 2000. Meanwhile, local businesses involved with timber extraction flourished. These new businesses did not contribute to local economic development; they offered mostly black market, and low-wage jobs, but they played an influential role in the evolution of *obştea* institutions because many of them, in flagrant conflicts-of-interest, also served as decisionmakers.

Nowadays, twenty nine *obştea* institutions continue to function in Vrancea, managing around 65,000 hectares of forest. Each village owns between 1,500 and 14,000 hectares for a population that may range from 800 to 5,000. The restoration process stipulated that the *obştea* institutions should follow the model of the old organizational structures and that each *obştea* has the right to modify their statutory norms, according to local situations, with the agreement of the village assembly.

Men and women have equal property rights, although men participate more in assemblies and do more of the forestry work. The guiding principles of managing forestland in the Vrancea Mountains were (and still are) *indivisibility, inalienability* and *equal sharing*. A fundamental characteristic is the equal participation of every individual. But the individual does not hold any measurable right or own a precise plot; the only entitlement is the "right to be a member." Membership includes the right to vote in the village assembly and to receive an annual quota of wood, which changes according to assembly-based decisions about individual shares. An executive committee, ruled by a president, together with the village assembly, manages each common forest. Villagers elect the committee and the president by a secret democratic vote. The committee handles all administrative operations, including organizing the village assemblies, auctions for selling timber, and distributing annual shares of wood to commoners. The participatory framework is excellent in principle, but in practice there are problems with poor attendance at assemblies, fears about the integrity of vote-counting, conflicts of interest, and a limited pool of capable councilors.

Today, an average of 20 percent of *obştea*-managed wood goes toward household consumption and the rest (usually in the form of monetary profit) towards improvement of local infrastructure. Locals receive as their share a quantity of one to three cubic meters of firewood per year, per family, and the same quantity of timber, with the right to sell it locally, and not beyond the borders of the *obştea*. The estimated value of the wood in 2006 for a household of two adults was about 80 euros per year, or about 5 percent of the average annual household income of 1,500 euros in the villages studied.

The legend of the commons' origins stands as a source of legitimacy for present-day property arrangements. This "once upon a time story" is widely remembered and frequently repeated, with the forest perceived as a "legacy from Stephen the Great." It amounts to a kind of emotional capital that villagers in the Vrancea Mountains draw upon to reassert their collective local identity and history. The symbolic and affective dimension of property, as managed by *obştea*, is thus reinforced. Most locals cannot conceive the idea of dividing up their forests because it would violate "the old way." Some people see the rights to use the mountains as a compensation for the *vrânceni* (as people there are called) for not having access to the prosperous, arable land of the plains. Collective property is seen as a simple historical fact – a given. Even though the quality and quantity of the allotted forest land varies from one village to the next, the initial act appears as indubitable: "*This is the way Stephen gave it to us!*"

Not surprisingly, feelings, perceptions and meaning matter a great deal in the participation of members and in the management of *obştea* – and these emotions are dynamic and evolving over time and different circumstances. The relationship between these locals and their forest is more complicated than the familiar "peasant attachment" to the land because what they own essentially involves a diffuse material resource and a shared experience: a use-right in the commons. Yet, from the survey I conducted in 2005-2006[3], 42.2 percent say that feel "a lot" like proprietors of the commons. Another 32.7 percent consider themselves proprietors "to some extent" and 24.1 percent "not at all." Memories, lived and repeated to others, enhance people's emotional attachment to the commons. Older locals seem to have a fonder regard for their communal forests than the younger generation, and are more supportive of the current organizational practices.

I found in my extensive fieldwork with ten communities in the region[4] that people spoke of the forest as property in contradictory terms. The meaning of property is locally expressed in two different registers – property as an affective symbol of inheritance and identity, and property as a material, functional resource for use. They use a rhetoric of community pride in owning and managing historic lands using established practices and traditions, as well as a rhetoric of deprivation, as local or national elites illicitly seize most of the forests' benefits. Feelings of deprivation and injustice arise when *obştea* is perceived through the lens of its ruling structure, as a group of "corrupt

---

3 | The survey is based on a representative random sample of 304 persons in four villages of Vrancea region.

4 | The author undertook extensive fieldwork during 2004-2006 and subsequently paid shorter visits to previously studied areas in 2007, 2008 and 2012.

opportunists." Eighty-nine percent of respondents in my survey perceive that *obştea*, understood as its managing committee, does nothing or too little for the communities.

In the post-communist era, there has been a resurgence of pride and memory of the pre-communist-era *obştea*. Yet, there are also struggles to deal with corrupt practices, conflicts over the fair distribution of wood and profits, and poor local leadership. Part of the problem is that the legal framework of commons is not clear or detailed on many matters. Another problem is that there are no local mechanisms to resolve conflicts in low-cost ways. Both customary and state laws appear to be ineffective when corruption is too pervasive or when conflicts escalate. Ambiguous circumstances can easily result in an "adhocracy" that allows self-interested opportunists to exploit the collective good.

Yet despite these challenges, I have found in my studies of Vrâncean villages that there is a remarkably strong support for *obştea* as an institution of collective identity and purpose. Managing the forest is not all about calculations, performance, material value and revenues. It is also about affective relationships and symbolic meaning as reflected in collective memory, tradition and identity. These affective dimensions keep people interested in and involved in the processes related to their forest property even if the external forces of the state, market and local officials may work in other directions.

References

Hann, Chris. 1998. "Introduction: The Embeddedness of Property." In C.M. Hann, editor, *Property Relations: Renewing the Anthropological Tradition.* Cambridge: Cambridge University Press.

Stahl, H. Henri. 1958. Contributii la studiul satelor devalmase romanesti [Contributions in Studying Romanian Joint Property Villages]. Bucuresti. Editura Academiei

———. 1980. *Traditional Romanian Village Communities.* Cambridge: Cambridge University Prss.

Vasile, Monica. 2006. "*Obştea* today in the Vrancea Mountains, Romania. Self Governing Institutions of Forest Commons." *Sociologie Romaneasca* [Romanian Sociology]. 4(3):111-130.

———. 2007. "Sense of Property, Deprivation and Memory in the Case of *Obştea* Vrânceana." *Sociologie Romaneasca* [Romanian Sociology]. 5(2):114-129.

———. 2008. "Nature Conservation, Conflict and Discourses around Forest Management: Communities and Protected Areas from Meridional Carpathians." *Sociologie Romaneasca* [Romanian Sociology]. 6(3-4):87-100.

Vasile, Monica and Liviu Mantescu. 2009. "Property reforms in rural Romania and community-based forests." *Sociologie Romaneasca* [Romanian Sociology]. 7(2):95-113

Verdery, Katherine. 1999. "Fuzzy property: rights, power, and identity in Transylvania's decollectivization." pp. 53-81. In M. Burawoy and K. Verdery, editors. *Uncertain Transitions: Ethnographies of Change in the Postsocialist World.* Rowman & Littlefield Publishers.

Monica Vasile *(Romania) is currently visiting fellow at the Integrative Research Institute on Transformations of Human-Environment Systems (IRI THESys) at Humboldt University in Berlin, where she researches issues of environmental and economic anthropology. She was previously a research fellow at the Max Planck Institute for Social Anthropology in Halle (Saale).*

The Resilience of an Indigenous Ethiopian Commons

By Zelealem Tefera Ashenafi

Ethiopia is home to one of the oldest, most effective conservation management systems in sub-Saharan Africa, the Menz-Guassa Community Conservation Area, an 11,100-hectare region that is home to a rich endowment of grasslands, plants and rare animals such as the Ethiopian wolf, gelada and Abyssinian hare. The history of the indigenous land tenure system known as Atsme Irist[1] reveals a great deal about how people in Menz have been able to regularly use, but also preserve, valuable grazing lands and ecosystem services for more than 400 years.

The varied structures of indigenous land tenure systems in Ethiopia evolved through a complex set of processes, but one of the most notable examples is Atsme Irist. In the Ethiopian district of Menz, which includes the Guassa area, the Atsme Irist system for centuries gave the Menz people a right to claim a share of land held in common with other rightful landholders based on an historical ancestor. According to local sources, the Menz pioneer fathers, Asbo and Gera, started the indigenous management of the Guassa area in the seventeenth century. Gera had noticed an expanse of open land in the eastern part of Menz, Guassa, and demarcated it as his pastureland. Later, Asbo and Gera subdivided the land in two parcels based on the outcome of a horse race; a boundary was drawn at the place where the first horse dropped from fatigue.

The two pioneer fathers set aside the Guassa area for the primary purpose of livestock grazing and use of the guassa (*Festuca*) grass. Those who could establish kinship with Asbo or Gera through either parent were entitled to claim a share of the land from elders controlling the allocation.

---

1 | For more on Atsme Irist in Menz, see Z.T. Ashenafi, "Common Property Resource Management of an Afro-Alpine Habitat Supporting a Population of the Critically Endangered Ethiopian Wolf (Canis Simensis)," PhD thesis, University of Kent, Canterbury, UK.

The Qero Indigenous Management System

To promote the rational use of their common property resources in the Guassa area, members of the land holding group there adopted the Qero system. This indigenous institution worked by inviting members of two areas, Asbo and Gera (named after the pioneer fathers), to choose a headman (known as "Abba Qera" or "Afero") to protect and regulate the use of each area. The Abba Qeras were mostly elected unanimously in the presence of all users of the common property resource. The terms of office of Abba Qera could last from a few years to a lifetime, depending on the performance of the office holder.

Guassa user communities were further subdivided into parishes – six for Asbo and eight for Gera – with one headman esquire for each parish who was answerable to their respective Abba Qera. This division of land under parishes gave the land consecrated status because parishes are under the protective patronage of the long-established Orthodox Christian Church in Ethiopia.

Under the Qero system, the Guassa area could be closed off from any type of community use for as long as three to five consecutive years. The length of closure largely depended upon the growth of the *Festuca* grass and the need felt by the community. For example, a successful crop harvest might result in a longer closure of the land while a drought might persuade the Abba Qera to reduce the length of a closure.

When the Abba Qera of both Asbo and Gera agreed that the Guassa grass was ready for harvest, they would announce to the rightful owners of the Guassa user community the date of the opening, usually at church ceremonies, market places, burial ceremonies or other public gatherings. The Guassa area was generally opened at the height of the dry season of that particular year, usually in February. Once the grass cutting was over, the livestock took their turn to graze. When the wet season approached, the community prepared to leave. The date of closing was culturally predetermined as July 12 (Hamle Abo), the annual date of the "Apostle's Fasting Breaking Day," the second biggest fasting season next to Lent for the Ethiopian Coptic Orthodox Church.

The Qero system imposed a number of rules and bylaws to protect the Guassa area, which were carried out by the entire community working together under the leadership of the two Abba Qeras. The Abba Qeras frequently chose dates to patrol their respective areas, with mandatory participation by every able household head. Failure to participate could result in severe punishment, including, in extreme cases, the burning down of the person's house.

Women in those times retained ownership rights through their kinship ties to Asbo or Gera and thus the right of their children to inherit land access. However, women were restricted to work around the homestead. If they tried to go out with men to the Guassa area it was regarded as preposterous. Therefore, in those days the Qero system was a male-dominated venture of common property resource management.

Rules prohibiting use of the Guassa area during the closed season could be quite severe. If someone was found cutting or grazing livestock in the Guassa area during the closed season, he or she could be forced to pay 100 sacks of cabbage seeds, a wet lion skin, a one-testicled servant, or other item that is simply not available in Menz or anywhere else! Such penalties were meant to deter people from violating the Guassa bylaws, but could sometimes result in a person being stripped of his Astme Irst right of owning land and be forced to leave Menz permanently. As time went by, the penalties under the Qero system were changed to less severe ones as modern law and rights of individuals became societal norms during the rule of King Haile Selassie. For example, when someone was found cutting grass in the Guassa area, the most frequent punishment for violating a bylaw involved a serious beating. If someone thatched his house using *Festuca* grass that was cut during the closed season, his house was burned down. If livestock were found grazing, the livestock was slaughtered and the skin would be given to the parish church to make a drum. These types of severe punishment under the Qero system signified how important the common property resource was to the livelihood of the community, its individuals and their communal holdings.

Resilience of the Qero System in the Face of Change

Following the 1974 Socialist Revolution in Ethiopia, the then-governing regime proclaimed the Agrarian Reform in 1975. All land that was in private owner-ship or communal tenure was transformed into the state or public land tenure system. This in turn brought the Qero system in Menz to a formal end. The transformation of land ownership from communal tenure into the state or public land tenure system abolished the regularity of the Qero system. Suddenly the reliability of resource management that all rightful owners collectively depended upon was no longer fully functional.

State ownership not only instituted different property rights for land usage, it ushered in less sustainable and socially inequitable land use practices because the stewards of the land under the Qero system were replaced by nine farmers' associations adjacent to the Guassa area. As one informant from a farmers' association said, "Those people whom we used to exclude from the Guassa management became owners of the Guassa overnight and everybody started to scrabble for the resource."[2] The new state-based management resulted in a

2 | Cited in Zelealem Tefera Ashenafi and N. Leader-Williams, "The Resilient Nature of Common Property Resource Management Systems: A Case Study from the Guassa Area of Menz, Ethiopia," available at http://dlc.dlib.indiana.edu/dlc/bitstream/handle/10535/1953/AshenafiZelealamCPR.pdf?sequence=1

more bureaucratic, corrupt and less effective management of the Guassa – in practice, an open access regime.

However, commons tend to have a great capacity to adapt to sudden surprises and shocks – the essence of resilience. That has been the case with the Qero system. After the Qero system was abolished by the state, Menz peasant associations decided to form another indigenous management system, which it called the Guassa Conservation Council Committee, with a new management system and online bylaws, which have adapted to the present sociopolitical order of the country. The new system consists of nine peasant associations (Kebeles) that elect five representatives, each of whom are descendants of Gera and Asbo. The five members of the committee include the chairman of the Kebele, an elder (women or man), a religious leader, a representative of the women and a representative of the youth. For the first time women are included in the management of the Guassa area under the new system. The system governs usage of the Guassa by about 9,000 households.

The Committee oversees a system of twenty "community scouts," and works with local police to prosecute people who use the Guassa in unauthorized ways. It also upholds the Idir system, a widely respected indigenous social institution that helps members in difficult times. The Qero system punishments are now less severe (100 birr, or about a US$5 fine for cutting grass), but serious offenses such as ploughing grasslands are brought before district courts.

Thanks to a 2012 policy change by the Ethiopian government, the capacity of the Guassa communities to conserve its vital grasslands' biodiversity was strengthened and recognized by law. The United Nations Development Programme has honored the Guassa community with its prestigious Equator Prize in 2004, and the community conservation practices have been a model for the Frankfurt Zoological Society and other community-based conservation initiatives within Ethiopia.[3] In 2013 the Guassa community was awarded the first Mountain Protection Award by the International Mountain Protection Commission (UIAA).[4]

Zelealem Tefera Ashenafi *(Ethiopia) works as country representative of the Frankfurt Zoological Society in Ethiopia overseeing ecological monitoring, community-based conservation, community-based tourism and rural development activities. He received his PhD from the Durrell Institute of Conservation and Ecology (DICE), University of Kent, UK, and was a project leader with the Ethiopian Wolf Conservation Programme of University of Oxford.*

---

3 | United Nations Development Programme, 2012. *Guassa-Menz Community Conservation Area, Ethiopia*. Equator Initiative Case Study Series. New York, NY.

4 | http://mountainprotection.theuiaa.org/awards/2013#.UyxdZUudTOc

NEIGHBORHOOD COMMONS

*"The word without action is empty, action without the word is blind,
and action and the word outside the spirit of the community is death."*

Proverb of indigenous people of southwestern Colombia

Our Ways of Knowing:
Women Protect Common Forest Rights in Rajasthan

By Soma K P and Richa Audichya[1]

Nichlagarh, an adivasi village in the forest region of Southern Rajasthan, is caught between the bureaucratic regime of the Forestry Department (FD) of India and progressive legislation that claims to restore the traditional rights of commoners. While the state has its own ideas about how villagers should manage their forest commons and their lives, the women of this adivasi community have stepped forward as the knowledge keepers, managers of the forests and champions of democratic representation to protect the right to common.

Like most villages in the Abu Road region of Rajasthan, India, Nichlagarh is a predominantly adivasi village. Consisting of about 650 households in five hamlets, the village is spread over an undulating hilly, forested terrain, with streams, water check dams (*nadis*) and patches of mixed deciduous forests. Most women work hard on their fields or foraging from the forest to meet the needs of their households, while men work on their small tracts of agricultural land or work outside the village or on others' fields. The women regard the forests as their domain and their culture, and their lives are intricately woven into the weft and warp of their forest commons. It was the adivasi women who drew attention to the region in 2010 when they took the initiative to organize a *Dharna*, or nonviolent mass sit-in strike, and blocked traffic on the highway. They were demanding recognition of their rights to the forest.

Sharmi Bai, 45, is the dynamic president of the *panchayat*, or village council, whose leadership in mobilizing the community has twice earned her victory in the local election by large margins. Before the 1960s, the villages enjoyed free access to the forest and its grazing lands, but those lands have

1 | This case study is based on the research conducted in collaboration with Jan Chetna Sansthan of Abu Road, Rajasthan, an organization dedicated to adivasi women's rights. Support provided by Manju, Pushpa, Kailash, Laxman and Dinesh in the compilation of this case study is gratefully acknowledged. This case study is part of a larger study based on a grant received from Action Aid, which is also gratefully acknowledged.

become increasingly restricted since the Forest Department took control; and in 1981 with the advent of the Forest Conservation Act, its control by the Forest Department was complete. Today women lament the loss of their autonomy and the decline in the health of the forests. "If they [the Forest Department] had given us [women and adivasi people] community rights earlier, the forest would not have disappeared," said women of the hamlet located closest to the forest commons, who witness its devastation every day.

For the adivasi, the forest has been the center of their existence since ancient times. It gives them everything – wood, timber, food, rope, shelter, clothing. Its large leaves from deciduous trees such as the saal and the palaash are used to make umbrellas and even footwear. The forest gives bark that provides medicine, gum and oil. It seems as if everything that people need could be either found or grown just by scattering a few seeds. In the higher reaches of the hills, musli and other foods once grew. People recalled that they would harvest a little for their needs and sometimes a little extra for exchange. "The trees and shrubs and grasses and herbs – they nurtured us," said Sharmi Bai. "We tended to the forest and regulated its use among ourselves, not by principles of management but by processes of sharing."

"We cut the wood from the trees for our multiple uses," said Bai, "but we did it mindfully to ensure that there was adequate and more forest wealth was restored. We know how to harvest crops, even museli and kaneri (a valuable small gourd vegetable plant), without harming the shoots or destroying the nodes that would spring into new shoots. We would take care to pick the stocks of plants to ensure that there was enough left to replenish for our next cycle, so we nurtured the forest collectively, not by dividing it among ourselves but by tending to it collectively. Anyone seen to be destructive or greedy would be reprimanded and we would help each other to sustain and collect for our needs."

Despite their significant roles in managing forest commons, women were not allowed to participate in the traditional spaces where customary rights were determined. Given the patriarchal social structure of these tribes, women are not viewed as rights holders. Yet communities have recognized their roles and rely on them to advocate for rights and meet survival needs.

The Forest Rights Act of 2006 (FRA) ushered in a major set of changes to create legal entitlements to traditional rights for forest dweller communities. The enactment sought to correct the "historical injustices" wrought upon the traditional forest dwellers. But the FD viewed the forest as its fiefdom and sought to govern it using modern principles of forest management, which focused on only a few species and failed to recognize traditional methods of sustaining forests and traditional forest livelihoods.

The FD in its colonial legacy viewed forest dwellers and dependent communities as encroachers. It sought to curtail their rights or evict them from their forests through varied legislative and executive means, often causing serious risk to life and livelihoods. More recently, the FD had on the one hand come down heavily on communities to penalize them for encroachments and "illegal felling," while itself allowing timber felling and extraction. It also allowed the allotment of forest lands to industries after only cursory community consultations, causing great distress and displacement of tribal communities in several regions.

The Forest Rights Act challenged the FD's control over the forests by expressly restoring traditional rights of forest dwellers to govern their forests through both individual claims and community rights. However, the FD, flouting the clear intent of the Act to give tribal communities autonomy in governing their forests, continues to resist this law by allowing recognition to only a small portion of the claims filed and challenging claims for community forests under the provisions of the FRA.

The Forest Rights Act and the PESA Act (Panchayats Extension to Scheduled Areas)[2] make provisions for communities to claim traditional rights for defining the extent and governance of the commons, validating their traditional systems and practices; these two laws seek to restore the autonomy of tribal communities to determine how their forests should be governed, and restrict the powers of the FD, which has resisted the implementation of these enactments. The recognition of women as key and legitimate actors in the democratic, decentralized forest governance of traditional tribal forums, has strengthened their roles. It has also strengthened the commoning process, enhanced livelihoods, and strengthened the region's food security and environmental sustainability for future generations.

Dhani Bai of Mataphalli came to the village four decades ago, at a time when everyone was entitled to a stake in the natural resources within the village. Every new bride was aware of the rules, and knew the boundaries of her village. But under the Forest Department regime, said Dhani Bai, "the forest is now off-limits to us and we have to look elsewhere for grasses, herbs and other needs because the boundaries have now been constructed by the Forest Department to prevent us from gaining access to our resources. But we are the ones who tended to the needs of the forest in the first instance!"

Especially between 1980 and 2005, villagers routinely found large amounts of wood being pilfered from the forest, even after reporting such theft. "The powerful contractor lobbies try to get our young boys to steal the wood for their

---

2 | Under the PESA Act 1996, *panchayats* are mandated to "take care of the customs, religious practices and traditional management practices of community resources." http://www.moef.nic.in/sites/default/files/jfm/jfm/html/strength.htm.

profit," said Dhani Bai, "but we know what the consequences of such actions will be. They will cause the land to dry and our water to recede." Gradually, Forest Department management caused changes in how forest resources are managed and how communities relate to each other and to the environment. In the village hamlet of Verafalli, home to sixty-five families, there is little land available for any scattered sowing, and neighboring forests are out of bounds. Forest Department guards and rangers confiscate any tools and penalize anyone found to be grazing their animals in the forests.

In response to the *kabja* or capture of their traditional forests, women describe the different practices that have evolved to manage forests even within their own village vicinity. One section of Verafalli has continued to manage the forest as a commons, resisting the trend to fence off sections to individual households. Adapting practices from the past, the village has instead negotiated norms for the use and management of about five acres of forest. Women here have resisted attempts to divert these tracts to other uses and attempts by the Forest Department to incorporate this area to their control. While the state has yet to recognize Verafalli's claim to the lands under the Forest Rights Act, the community under the women's leadership has managed to ensure free access for cattle grazing and produce-collection for those who have been traditional users, or about seventy households.

"The more that the state delays or neglects the implementation of the Forest Rights Act, especially the claims for community rights," Sharmi Bai lamented, "the more likely it is that communities will move towards apportioning forest rights to individual families' households." Thus in Matafalli, another hamlet of the same village closer to the river, forest lands have been apportioned as separate parcels for each of the hamlet's sixty-five families. This has resulted in endless wrangling and theft. "Even my own patch where I have planted fruit trees is not free from assault," Sharmi Bai noted, showing us the area where the commons has now been fenced by individual households.

Of course, these arrangements have changed the social relationships be-tween families as each protects its own patch, denying others access to even paths on their land. This does not bode well for the cohesion of the community and its common interests. Nor does it bode well for the health of the forests, said Sharmi Bai: "If we start thinking about the forests as property then our common, cohesive social processes will get eroded. We will only look to the forest as trees and wood like the contractors and the FD [Forest Department] do, and soon it will all become agricultural land." This would not be the case if FRA were to be implemented in its true spirit, in her view. " Water used to be plentiful in this region, but now it is becoming scarce. There are multiple hand pumps in the village, but with the destruction of the forests the other crisis is also not far behind. We must restore our rights and protect our forests. It is our way of life."

For the adivasi, the forest has been the center of existence since ancient times.

Dhani and other women remember the severe famine in the 1960s when they survived on fruits, herbs and greens from the forests even though they were closed to the community. With no other options, most migrated to a nearby town to earn a wage. The wages allowed the community to survive, but it also allowed an influx of products from the market and traders eager to buy the local produce. As families grew and forests became depleted, each household now seeks to have at least one child in government service and others in jobs to provide for household needs. Hopes of the FRA being implemented effectively notwithstanding, their changed relationships with the forest have reduced their self-provisioning, on the one hand, and their dependency on wages have made them more dependent on markets. The traditional *melas* (local fairs) at the Khetia Bapasi – a local deity whose place of worship in the forest brought community men together to decide on community management affairs – are now reduced to a ritual. The jurisdiction of such gatherings is limited to discussions about the village and community lands because the Forest Department is now the dominant authority for managing forests and their use.

While basic entitlements to the forests remain unaddressed, notwithstanding the mandate of the Forest Rights Act, the new District Commissioner who oversees the Abu Road region has proposed new schemes to strengthen livelihoods in the region, and to promote water harvesting and watershed management. Forest commoners are understandably skeptical. They have seen the ineffective, politically motivated behaviors of the state – and appreciate and struggle to retain the effective and sustainable processes of their own commoning. The women of the forest commons have seen how their own knowledge, social collaboration, community ethic and leadership are likely to be a better means for protection of the forest commons over time than narrow scientific expertise and politically motivated policies that cater to the economic moguls. The women see strength in the provisions of the FRA, which recognizes a process of decentralized self-governance based on respect for their traditional rights: a process that will help them restore depleted commons and maintain those that exist through their traditional practices.

Soma KP *(India) is a researcher, policy analyst and support person to community based institution-building initiatives, with more than three decades of experience in the area of gender, development and natural resource based livelihoods.*

Richa Audichya *(India) is director of Jan Chetna Sansthan, an NGO that works with a women-centered approach to adivasi people's rights and leadership development – the focus of her work for more than twenty years.*

Terre de Liens:
Experiencing and Managing Farmland as Commons

By Véronique Rioufol and Sjoerd Wartena

A feeling of joy and achievement runs through the group of ten people gathered in Robert's kitchen. After three years of planning, they have come to celebrate: Ingrid and Fabien will soon be able to settle down and develop their farming business. The farm is theirs!

In this small, pastoral village of the French Pre-Alps, establishing young farmers is an act of will. Everywhere, small mountain farms are closing down; work is hard and the business not deemed profitable enough. When aging farmers retire, they do not find a successor. The best land is sometimes sold off to one of the few more or less industrialized farms that remain. Overall, villages are progressively abandoned or become havens of secondary residences.

In Saint Dizier, a small village of thirty-five inhabitants, local people have decided differently. Municipality members, local residents and farmers have decided to preserve agriculture as a component of local economic activity and lifestyle. They also view farmers as young, permanent residents for the village. So they keep an eye on land put for sale, and have contacted farmers and landowners to learn their plans for the future. The municipal council has sought public subsidies to acquire farmland and rent it to young farmers, but with no success.

In 2006, villagers started to work with Terre de Liens, a recently established civil society organization focused on securing land access for agroecological farmers. Everywhere in France, high land prices and intense competition for farmland and buildings have become a major obstacle for young farmers. Obstacles are even higher for those doing organic agriculture, direct sales or other "alternative" forms of agriculture, which usually are not deemed profitable enough by banks or worthy of public policy support.

So when a farm goes for sale in Saint Dizier, everyone is ready. In just a few months, the small group approaches the owners and all relevant institutions with a stake in the transaction. Above all, they start raising money among local residents, family and friends. And it works. Through word-of-mouth, public events and fairs, they soon manage to raise 50,000 euros locally. Then, Terre de Liens, through its national network of supporters, raises another 100,000 euros. People choose to invest in the project because they want to promote organic agriculture, to preserve mountain farming, to protect the environment, or to give young farmers a chance. Soon, Ingrid and Fabian start to graze a herd of 160 ewe and to produce cheese; they also develop a microbrewery, work on an agrotourism project and lease part of the land to a fruit grower.

The group continues to meet regularly. They discuss the terms of the lease and the protection of the environmental assets of the farm; they plan for the repair work needed on farm buildings; they support Ingrid and Fabian in developing direct sales; and they facilitate exchange of equipment and services between local farmers. When another farm goes for sale, they repeat the operation and, after two more years of mobilization, they are met with success. In just over five years, this small village of thirty-five inhabitants has gained three new farm businesses. Four new families with children have settled permanently.

Throughout France, Terre de Liens fosters similar dynamics for preserving agricultural land and supporting a new generation of farmers. Participants are driven by the conviction that agriculture is everybody's business. They recognize that the way land is used and distributed is key to improving the quality of local food production, not to mention ecological forms of farming and livelier rural areas.

The fundamental premise of Terre de Liens is that the value of farmland lies in its contribution to food production, lasting ecosystems and human life. So when people invest in the group's farmland, they choose not to make a profit. Technically, they are shareholders of a private company, but practically, they know that the land will not be sold back as long as Terre de Liens continues to exist.

In any case, they will receive no financial dividends. At best, they may have an inflation-based re-evaluation of the value of their shares at some point, and may qualify for income tax rebate, on a limited scale. The benefits that investors seek are nonfinancial ones: direct connection to a farm, good local food, fertile soils and biodiversity, preservation of a local

Terre de Liens in numbers

> 12,000 citizens mobilized
> 120 farms acquired
> 2400 hectares in organic, peasant farming
> 200 future farmers supported every year
> 1 ethical company, 1 foundation, 19 regional and 1 national association
> 35 million euros in ethical investment and 5 million euros in donations
> Share = 103 euros
> Tens of partnerships with local authorities

activity and a sense of belonging. They also enjoy partaking in new forms of experimentation and social bonding around food and agriculture.

Terre de Liens is still a recent movement facing many challenges: improving the monitoring and management of farms and buildings, reaching beyond its first circle of supporters, consolidating its financial resources, etc. To date, it has saved 120 farms, recruited 12,000 supporters and forged tens of partnerships with local authorities. These achievements, while modest in the larger context of French agriculture, are a strong sign that, if given a chance, large numbers of citizens want to promote more intelligent land planning, agroecological forms of farming and more robust rural areas.

Terre de Liens is advancing this agenda by liberating land from the commodity system.[1] For the moment, it is done via "capitalist" instruments such as private property and finance. But the organization and its supporters believe that developing a "solidarity-based economy" can nourish the idea of treating farmland as a commons, with eventual support by law.

Today, there is an urge to grow and connect the Terre de Liens initiative with similar alternatives elsewhere in Europe and in the world. The decline of smallholder farming is a fact of contemporary life. So are the disastrous consequences of conventional farming for the environment and public health, and the desertification of rural areas. There is resistance, however, especially among a new, emerging generation of farmers who are eager to integrate farming with its social surrounding, and to produce food for local and regional markets. In this sense, Terre de Liens is part of a much broader transition aimed at restoring living, community-connected ways of farming and rural life.

Véronique Rioufol *(France) is Terre de Liens' European Relations Coordinator. She has a background in international relations and political studies and has worked in human rights organizations. She joined Terre de Liens in 2010 because she views it as a successful experiment for social change. She has contributed to setting up the European Network on Access to Land, of which Terre de Liens is a member.*

Sjoerd Wartena (France) worked at the Amsterdam University library and moved to France in 1973 to become a goat farmer. He was active in the organic agriculture movement and in 2003 cofounded the Terre de Liens association and was president for its first ten years. He considers this organization the logical consequence of his adaption to the traditional way of farming he discovered in France, which he believes to be a healthy and "modern" alternative to destructive large-scale farming.

---

1 | Véronique Rioufol and Sjoerd Wartena, "Terre de Liens: Removing Land from the Commodity Market, and Enabling Organic and Peasant Farmers to Settle in Good Conditions," 2011, available at http://www.terredeliens.org.

Water Beyond the State

By Marcela Olivera

Autonomy and horizontality are distinct characteristics of traditional forms of organization in Bolivia. They support an everyday, practical, tangible understanding of what "public" means as well as how to shape a participatory democracy that can exist even without the state and the government. The water committees in the south of Cochabamba, Bolivia's fourth-largest city, epitomize such autonomous and horizontal structures. In spite of many adversities, their network is still very active, and it has become more visible to the public following the so-called "water war" of 2000, when massive demonstrations stopped the attempts to privatize Cochabamba's public water supply.

Many people associate this water war with a notion of real democracy. But a war – any war – means violence, a waste of energy and resources, deaths, and strife; in contrast, democracy (as we know it in the West) is supposed to avoid all this. The water conflict was not only a struggle to defend resources; it was part of a larger, historical struggle of Bolivian women and men to secure the right to make decisions about their own affairs through autonomous and horizontal procedures. The conflicts of the water war, then, were an expression of the urgent and repeatedly postponed desire for real democracy.

In September, Cochabamba's Municipal Drinking Water Supply and Wastewater Management System (*Servicio Municipal de Agua Potable y Alcantarillado de Cochabamba*, SEMAPA) was sold to the corporation Aguas del Tunari, whose largest shareholder was the US construction and project management company Bechtel. The sale must be understood in the context of the long-term structural adjustment programs that the World Bank and the International Monetary Fund have imposed on Latin America – including Bolivia – since the mid-1980s. These programs have facilitated the sale of common assets to private investors and corporations.

Following the privatization of Cochabamba's water system, the people living in the Cochabamba Valley saw excessive price increases; the cooperatives and the water committees actually managed the water, but they did not have state concessions to do so. That meant that Aguas del Tunari was able to sue them on the grounds of illegal competition and even take over the committees' administrative structure. These dismal realities were the reason why the "Coordination for the Defense of Water and Life" (*Coordinadora de Defensa del Agua y la Vida*), popularly known as the "Water Coordination" (*Coordinadora del Agua*), was established. After several months of negotiations with the government and confrontations with the army, the *Coordinadora* succeeded in driving out Aguas del Tunari.

Many things came to light only as a result of this water war in 2000 – for instance, the countless forms of organization, including the Cochabamba water committees, that are not supported by structures of Western democracy. Since the clashes at the beginning of the millennium, these committees have played a very important role in the work of the Water Coordination, together with the other population groups actively involved in the struggles.

Although the Cochabamba water committees are based mostly in the southern part of the city, they do exist throughout the urban periphery. Half the city's population – more than 200,000 people – lives in the southern part of the city, which is divided into six districts. In this area alone, there are between 100 and 120 water committees; according to Stefano Archidiacono of the nongovernmental organization CeVI, there are 400 more across the entire city. In other words, this is a remarkable phenomenon of social participation: thousands of people organizing themselves to manage their water supply.

While two structures in Bolivia rarely function in precisely the same way, it is still clear that the water committees share the same basic commitment to water as a living being, as something divine, as the basis for mutuality and complementarity. Water is considered a being that belongs to everyone and no one. It is the expression of the greatest possible flexibility and adaptability; it helps nature to constantly create and transform life. Without it, social reproduction would be impossible. Accordingly, this understanding as well as the customs and traditions of the communities are mirrored in the ways in which the water committee meetings are conducted; they serve as a vehicle for forming urban communities similar to those in rural areas.

In the past, the water was distributed in different ways in Cochabamba. Even though in the city itself, the urban water utility was the main supplier, almost two-thirds of Cochabamba's urban districts or neighborhoods drew water directly from rivers, wells or rainwater collection systems. In some neighborhoods, the residents pooled money to establish their own water supply systems and to secure their operation and maintenance. Other communities fall back on cisterns or even private supply systems in large containers as a kind of water truck. The emergence and the success of these commons provide people with the opportunity to decide for themselves how the water is obtained – whether and where cisterns are built, a well is drilled, or (partial) connections to the municipal water supply are desired.

The origins of the autonomous practices used by the water committees today can be traced back to the Inca empire. They are hardy social norms that outlived the colonial period. For this reason, the committees are often understood as a kind of modernized communitarian practice. In an article, "The State and Autonomy in Bolivia: An Anarchist Interpretation," published by Bolpress, Carlos Crespo explains this understanding of autonomy: "It is not an ideal that is to be achieved, but rather a daily practice of the ethnic groups, communities or user groups" (Crespo 2001). These horizontal processes have always been the social and political practice when dealing with the state and the powers governing at any particular time: since the days of the Incas, all through the colonial period, during the republic, as well as today in the plurinational state of Bolivia. That is also the message of a manifesto published by factory workers during the Cochabamba water war: "Neither public nor private. Managed by the people themselves!"

The water committees represent a vision of autonomy and independence from the state; this is also linked to the fact that they are established in the so-called poverty belts at the city's edges. Farmers who have settled there and have brought their Andean tradition (known as *ayni*) of working in turns and in solidarity to their new urban communities, encounter miners who live there. They have brought their organizing experience to the local communities in these neighborhoods forgotten by the state.

The water committees are also a product of self-empowerment and effective processes of autonomy. They are based on practices recognized neither by the state nor by the international community – and that need no recognition in order to exist. The members of each community distribute among themselves the roles and tasks that have to be shared to supply each neighborhood with water. The committees network with one another, and they exchange information about their strategies for action in order to learn from each other. They do not organize in opposition to the public utilities, but *for* their competence to decide for themselves how and to what extent they want to be connected to the public supply systems. They are a genuine expression of the autonomous shaping of a political community.

How does that work in practice? During a meeting in 2008, a neighborhood in the south of Cochabamba decided to find out the best way to bring water to their area. They collected their knowledge and their insights and then discussed whether it would be better to urge the local municipal company to lay pipes for their neighborhood or to build a huge cistern themselves and to negotiate a fixed-price contract with a private water tank company so that it would be full at all times.

The water committees always approach and solve the most important social questions at the level of the community (*comunidad*), which is why they have a different perception of social movements than the state, which tends to present them as merely making demands on the state. People organize in the committees in order to take their own matters into their own hands, not to ask the government for favors. They organize in other areas besides water, too. Even if water concerns were the catalyst for establishing the water committees, they also deal with many other issues, such as individual members' well-being, community security, parties, soccer and more. One committee member explained it in these words: "When someone dies, we sit down and think about how we can make a donation to the family, or at the end of the year, we present each committee member with a basket of everyday consumer goods. During our meetings, we also talk about private matters" (Zeballos 2013). The water committees are so independent in their actions that in some places, they are called "zones liberated from the state." The people do not organize in order to make demands on the state or to negotiate their rights, but in order to determine and shape the conditions of their own lives themselves.

The current situation in Bolivia is complex, and the numerous water committees are reaching both technical and financial limits. Their negotiations with the state on questions of their autonomy are often full of obstacles. The technical problems concern everyone in their processes of organization and consolidation, which is why there are very deliberate reflections on such issues, including discussions of the community's own limits. An example of this is Gastón Zeballos, a leader of the committee of San Miguel Km 4, participating in the first international meeting of water management organizations from Uruguay, Colombia, and Bolivia (URCOLBOL) in Montevideo in October 2013. During this meeting, the Bolivian participants were more interested in technical questions such as chlorination, drinking water purification and wastewater treatment than in any other topic. As Gastón Zeballos explains, "We are interested in the technical aspects mostly because we have the social aspects under control. In our committees, we have active participation and equal rights, social control and rotation. What we're lacking is the other part."

By that, Zeballos means money, especially when indispensable projects are on the agenda that are absolutely beyond the committees' own means, such as investing in sewer systems in the areas for which the individual committees are responsible. Such projects require support and investments by the state, a form of support that must manifest itself in the will to respect the autonomy of the water committees and their specific view of what the community in question needs. That implies actually making the investments in water supply and water management available and affordable for all, rather than benefiting a specific constituency, especially during the political campaign season.

When Evo Morales became president in 2006, it was hoped that his government would strengthen and broaden the social movements' autonomy and their processes of self-organization. The opposite was the case. The state expanded its sphere of influence, including in water management, increasingly intervening in matters that were previously beyond its reach, resulting in a highly centralized political and technical administration. The most recent water management laws give the state the power to intervene in the communitarian systems – which it previously did not recognize – and to make decisions about them.˙

In the *Convention on the Right to Water*,[1] which the Bolivian government put forward at the United Nations, and the Declaration on the Rights of Mother Earth, the Morales government gave nature the status of a bearer of rights, simultaneously creating a "rights" framework that transfers the responsibility and power over water management from the people affected to the state. Although these efforts were widely applauded internationally, and Evo Morales is considered a pioneer concerning environmental reforms, it is precisely this strategy that weakened the forces of self-government. The traditional forms of management are rendered null and void, and anyone needing access to water can only turn to the state or appeal to laws and courts.

The water committees are faced not only with technical and economic challenges, but must also deal with the attempts by the state to co-opt them. Yet their success to date shows that Bolivians organizing on an equal footing with one another have retained their ability to manage their common resources autonomously. They have also established their own counterpowers and a concept of democracy seeking to maintain existing structures.

References
Crespo, C. 2001. Estado y autonomía en Bolivia, una interpretación anarquista, bolpress.com, http://www.bolpress.com/art.php?Cod=2011041902
Zeballos, G. Interview with the author, August 2013.

This essay is based on an article that originally appeared on the North American Congress on Latin America website, Fall 2014.

---

1 | Editors' note: On July 28, 2010, the General Assembly of the United Nations passed Resolution 64/292, recognizing the human right to water.

Marcela Olivera *(Bolivia) is a water commons organizer in Bolivia and Latin America. After graduating from the Catholic University in Cochabamba, Bolivia, she worked for four years in Cochabamba as the key international liaison for the Coalition for the Defense of Water and Life, the organization that fought and defeated water privatization in Bolivia. Since 2004 Marcela has been developing and consolidating an inter-American citizens' network on water justice named Red VIDA.*

Notable Urban Commons Around the World

By Jannis Kühne

A wide variety of urban commons around the world are challenging the idea that people's needs can only be met via city governments, urban planners and lawyers. Expertise matters, of course, but a growing number of urban commons is showing that it is not only possible but highly attractive to create commons through which citizens can actively participate in the design of their city spaces and the programs and policies that govern them. The norm in most cities is a system of rigid bureaucratic control and market-driven "service-delivery." People are treated as impersonal units of need. In dozens of cities around the world, urban commons are showing the distinct limitations of this approach. It is entirely possible to meet people's basic needs – for food, housing, social services and community connection – by giving them a more active, creative role and responsibility in maintaining their cities. Below are several noteworthy examples.

Bologna, Italy – City of the Commons

What would it be like if city governments, instead of relying chiefly on bureau-cratic rules and programs, actually invited citizens to take their own initiatives to improve city life? That's what the city of Bologna, Italy, is doing, and it amounts to a landmark reconceptualization of how government might work in cooperation with citizens. Ordinary people acting as commoners are invited to enter into a "co-design process" with the city to manage public spaces, urban green zones, abandoned buildings and other urban issues.

The Bologna project is the brainchild of Professor Christian Iaione of LUISS, university in Rome, in cooperation with student and faculty collabora-tors at LabGov, the Laboratory for the Governance of Commons. LabGov is an "inhouse clinic" and think tank that is concerned with collaborative governance, public collaborations for the commons, subsidiarity (governance at the lowest appropriate level), the sharing economy and collaborative consumption. The tagline for LabGov says it all: "Society runs, economy follows. Let's (re)design institutions and law together."

For years Iaione has been contemplating the idea of the "city as commons" in a number of law review articles and other essays. In 2014, the City of Bologna formally adopted legislation drafted by LabGov interns. The thirty-page Bologna Regulation for the Care and Regeneration of Urban Commons outlines a legal framework by which the city can enter into partnerships with citizens for a variety of purposes, including social services, digital innovation, urban creativity and collaborative services.[1] Taken together, these collaborations comprise a new vision of the "sharing city" or commons-oriented city. To date, some ninety projects have been approved under the Bologna Regulation. Dozens of other Italian cities are emulating the Bologna initiative. The Bologna Regulation takes seriously the idea that citizens have energy, imagination and responsibility that they can apply to all sorts of municipal challenges. So why not empower such citizen action rather than stifling it under a morass of bureaucratic edicts and political battles? The conceptualization of "city as commons" represents a serious shift in thinking. Law and bureaucratic programs are not seen as the ultimate or only solution, and certainly not as solutions that are independent of the urban culture. Thinking about the city as commons requires a deeper sense of mutual engagement and obligation than "service delivery," outsourcing and other market paradigms allow.

Instead of relying on the familiar public/private partnerships that often siphon public resources into private pockets, a city can instead pursue "public/commons partnerships" that bring people together into close, convivial and flexible collaborations. The working default is "finding a solution" rather than beggar-thy-neighbor adversarialism or fierce political warfare.

To Iaione, the Bologna Regulation offers a structure for "local authorities, citizens and the community at large to manage public and private spaces and assets together. As such, it's a sort of handbook for civic and public collaboration, and also a new vision for government." He believes that "we need a cultural shift in terms of how we think about government, moving away from the Leviathan State or Welfare State toward collaborative or polycentric governance."

SSM Sozialistische Selbsthilfe Mühlheim
(Socialist Self-Help Mühlheim), Germany

Sozialistische Selbsthilfe Mühlheim (SSM) is a self-organized residential and work project with a tradition and a vision. SSM evolved in the wake of a squat in an old Schnapps distillery in the Mühlheim district of Cologne. After negotiating with the city of Cologne for four years, SSM signed a rental contract

---

1 | http://www.comune.bologna.it/media/files/bolognaregulation.pdf

for the distillery buildings. It took the legal form of a *Verein*, an association controlled by its members.

This arrangement has given SSM some assets that it can use to generate revenues to sustain itself as a nonprofit. It rents out one part of its hall for events, for example. And since one of SSM's activities is liquidating households, another part of the building is used for furniture storage. The project also runs a secondhand store. The group has always taken pride in not becoming politically or financially dependent; it began without any supporting funding and is financially self-sufficient today.

Since its founding in 1979 about twenty people have been living on the SSM site. Their common space enables them to live independent lives without social isolation, and their community ethic is prized by members as a way to counter the capitalist, consumerist sensibilities of the surrounding city. SSM members seek not only to take control of their own lives, but to advance more humane, ecologically responsible urban policies. For example, SSM took a strong activist role in opposing the demolition of the *Barmer Viertel* neighborhood of Cologne – one of SSM's many public-spirited initiatives that have earned it respect and admiration among city officials as well as the general population.

In light of such activism, the abbreviation SSM could reasonably stand for "self-help and solidarity come to life in Mühlheim." The community has been providing communal housing since 1979 and creating jobs that conventional markets do not find lucrative enough to create. SSM members confidently use the term "socialist self-help" to describe their projects. SSM is a commons because it relies on self-organized governance and public-spirited action, combined with the self-reliance, sense of responsibility and ecological commitments of its members. It is a living social system that is independent and durable, and therefore able to enter into constructive engagements with both the market and state. Confirming its wide respect, SSM won the "Soziale Stadt 2012" prize ("Social City 2012") from a business organization, the Association of German Housing and Real Estate Companies.

Garden City Letchworth, Great Britain

For most city-dwellers, one of the great challenges they face is the high cost of living and housing expenses due to investor speculation. In the early twentieth century, Ebenezer Howard tackled this problem by proposing the idea of a "garden city" that would blend the benefits of both country and city living and be financed through collective ownership of land. The central idea of Letchworth is to keep land ownership in the hands of the community while allowing housing and other buildings to be sold or leased to individuals.

Garden City Letchworth[2] was started more than a century ago by ethical investors, Quakers and philanthropists and other socially concerned individuals. In 1903, founders Raymond Unwin and Barry Parker purchased 2,057 hectares of land near London at a reasonable price and then made it available to the members of the community for building. In this way, people came to own the roofs over their heads but co-owned the land on which their houses had been built. Despite low wages for many people, the community-oriented form of ownership made it possible to avoid high rents.

The collective ownership of the land also generated revenues through housing rentals and business leases. This in turn made it possible for the community to finance schools and hospitals. Everyone, not just investors, could benefit. Howard described his ideas in detail in his 1898 book *Tomorrow: A Peaceful Path to Real Reform*. For decades the economic value generated by Letchworth's infrastructures – water, sewerage, gas, electricity, roads, schools, hospitals – were mutualized to benefit all of its inhabitants. This helped the city to become relatively self-sufficient. Inspired by the Letchworth example, other garden cities followed, such as the Welwyn Garden City in the 1920s.

Following World War II, the appeal of the garden city model declined. People still enjoyed living in leafy surroundings, but a more individualistic ethic replaced the idea of community in general and community ownership of land in particular. In 1995, the Garden City Corporation in Letchworth became the Garden City Letchworth Heritage Foundation, a not-for-profit organization that finances itself. The plots of the residences created in the beginning are still in the hands of the Community Land Trust (CLT). Today more than 33,000 people live in Letchworth, on land that belongs to the CLT.

In Europe and the US, there is a renewed interest in the idea of community land trusts as a way to decommodify land and mutualize the benefits of land ownership. In such discussions, Garden City Letchworth remains an inspiration and archetype. "There is indeed a wind of change now building for rethinking and updating the garden city model," says British land trust expert and community researcher Pat Conaty.

City Repair Project, Portland, Oregon, USA

In 1996, the people who lived in Sellwood neighborhood of Portland, Oregon, decided to reclaim a street intersection, Ninth Avenue and Sherrett Street, to create "Share-It Square." They filled it with a tea stand, a children's playhouse and a community library. This was the beginning of an ongoing volunteer

---

2 | An excellent contemporary account of Letchworth Garden City can be found in a report by Pat Conaty and Martin Large, editors, "Commons Sense: Co-operative Place Making and the Capturing of Land Value for 21st Century Garden Cities" (Co-operatives UK, 2013), available at http://www.uk.coop/commonssense.

project, the City Repair Project, a self-organized urban commons designed to foster a sense of community participation and make the urbanscape more inviting and sociable.

Every May, the City Repair Project hosts a ten-day series of workshops called "Village Building Convergence" in places around Portland. The events have created dozens of projects that enliven the city through "natural buildings" and permaculture designs. Thousands of volunteers have built benches and information kiosks using "natural materials" such as sand, straw and "cob" (unburned clay masonry). The kiosks are a place for sharing neighborhood information, such as requests or offers of services (babysitting, housecleaning, massage, gardening). They are also places where people can share their homegrown vegetables.

At first, city officials resisted the idea of a neighborhood claiming a public space for itself by painting the pavement and creating small structures. But then they realized that the convivial neighborhood life at at Share-It Square was a great way for people to become more involved with city life. In 2000, the City of Portland passed an ordinance authorizing "intersection repair" throughout the city. With the help of City Repair volunteers, a neighborhood that obtains the consent of 80 percent of its residents within two blocks of an intersection, can design paintings and creative public spaces for the centers of the intersection.

Much of the inspiration for the City Repair Project has come from Mark Lakeman, the self-styled "placemaking coordinator" of the initiative. The group's stated mission is to facilitate "artistic and ecologically oriented placemaking through projects that honor the interconnection of human communities and the natural world. We are an organized group action that educates and inspires communities and individuals to creatively transform the places where they live."

In practice, this means everything from "intersection repairs" to public installations, block parties and conferences, and educational events and festivals. The commoning catalyzed by City Repair allows people to make decisions about their own immediate neighborhoods and to actively shape the future of the community. Sometimes that amounts to finding out the name of the neighbor who's been living across the street for the past twenty years.

Vila Autódromo, Rio de Janeiro, Brazil

For more than thirty years, the Vila Autódromo favela community in Rio de Janeiro has been fighting the city government's plans to evict everyone and build a new upper-middle class neighborhood. At first, the resistance came from fishers and other people with low incomes who had built their huts on the banks of Jacarepaguá Lagoon. Then, as real estate values rose in this area adjacent to the upscale neighborhood of Barra da Tijuca, developers wanted to build luxury apartments, highways or sports facilities in the Vila Autódromo.

The city government has offered a shifting set of reasons for eliminating the neighborhood – the needs of the Olympic Games in 2016, growing traffic, the environment. But the real reasons seem to be about money. As one commentator put it, "The general assumption is that skyrocketing land values have put pressure on city officials to make the space available to developers, the same interests that fund local politicians and newspapers. Yet the Brazilian constitution stipulates that those who occupy unused urban land for more than five years without contestation by land owners should be granted legal claim. And Vila Autódromo has been there since 1967."[3]

Residents in Vila Autódromo are accustomed to doing things for themselves. Decades ago, they built their own houses, installing all of the electrical connections, water pipes, septic systems and telephone lines, with no government assistance. So it was not so difficult for them to form their own residential association. Their resistance helped them win formal land use rights from the government in 1994. But residents could never be sure that the government would not forcibly remove them. Many have already succumbed to the government's strategy of paying residents large sums of money to move, leaving many parts of the neighborhood in a state of abandoned disrepair.

To propose a different vision for their neighborhood, the residents' association came up with its own local development plan, a Plano Popular, in 2012, with the support of students and professors at state universities and the Rio de Janeiro university ETTERN.[4] The grassroots proposal called for better infrastructure, restoration measures for the banks of the lagoon, and better-quality urban design for the community. In December 2013, the plan beat out 170 other applicants and received the Urban Age Award, presented annually by the London School of Economics and Deutsche Bank to creative urban initiatives.

Yet still the Vila remains under threat by a hostile city government and developers. In early 2014, construction of new housing, where the government plans to resettle the Autódromo residents, began just a kilometer away. Some residents accepted attractive cash compensation offers from the city officials, which had the effect of dividing residents and sapping energy from the protest. By January 2015, construction had begun for new buildings adjacent to the houses of residents still fighting the projects. Whether the residents will prevail in their resistance is uncertain, but they have already made one thing clear:

3　| Aron Flasher, "Rioonwatch" [Rio Olympics Neighborhood Watch website], February 12, 2012, at http://www.rioonwatch.org/?p=2988

4　| http://www.ettern.ippur.ufrj.br

it is best to pursue urban design with the active, collective participation of a neighborhood's residents, in ways that meet their real interests and needs, than to sell off such "development" rights to the highest bidder.

Resident-Managed Housing, Astrachan, Russia

Following the dissolution of the Soviet Union, practically all of the state-owned housing stock in Russia was privatized in the early 1990s. While roughly 80 percent of the apartments are privately owned, managing the jointly owned stock – from the roof to the outdoor facilities – has generally remained either a responsibility of the state or has been handed over to private real estate companies. Maintenance and upkeep declined so greatly that approximately 40 percent of the apartments in Russia must now be completely refurbished. In some places the answer to the problem is being solved through self-governance by residents. This possibility arose in 2005 when the government passed a law enabling the residents to manage apartment buildings themselves or through housing cooperatives.

One early set of cooperators were residents of apartments in Astrachan, a city of 500,000 people in southern Russia. Residents of Eleventh Red Army Street in Astrachan decided to manage their apartments themselves through a council of residents known as *Soyuz Zhiteley*.[5] The residents' council levies a monthly charge of 8.7 rubles (roughly 17 euro cents) for every square meter of an apartment, which is then earmarked for repairs and maintenance.

Roughly one-fifth of Astrachan's apartments, a total of 1,900 apartment buildings, are now managed by their residents. Similar initiatives exist in Moscow, St. Petersburg, Sochi and many smaller provincial cities. Management by the residents is a good alternative to the often corrupt private real estate management companies. It also helps to counter the expropriation of adjacent green spaces between the prefab apartment buildings, which developers consider suitable land for high-priced high-rises.

Not surprisingly, President Vladimir Putin's government is opposed to resident-managed repairs and maintenance in apartment buildings. He would like to overturn the 2005 law that authorized the arrangements and housing cooperatives. If successful, residents would become individually liable for repairs and maintenance again, leading to a decline in building upkeep. The residents' associations would also be more vulnerable to fraud and embezzlement of their contributions for repair and maintenance.

The figures show what this kind of discrimination against residents' management means in concrete terms: in 2007, the government promised

---

5 | *Soyuz* means "council." In Astrachan, 200 organizations of residents of individual buildings are organized under the umbrella of this Russia-wide organization.

380 billion rubles to refurbish apartment buildings. However, these monies have been granted only to buildings managed by private real estate companies or cooperatives, and not a single ruble to housing managed by the residents.

Jannis Kühne *(Germany) studies urbanism at Bauhaus University in Weimar where he does research on urban commons. He has done internships in Bamako, Mali (DRCTU) and Rio de Janeiro, Brazil (NAPP) as well as a semester of study at the Federal University of Rio de Janeiro, where he worked on the issue of favela upgrading and* remoção branca *(the displacement of residents in pacified favela).*

BIOCULTURAL COMMONS

"Only in the last moment in history has the delusion arisen that people can flourish apart from the rest of the living world."

E.O. Wilson

The Potato Park of Peru

By David Bollier

Drive an hour northeast from Cusco, Peru, and you will encounter some beautiful high mountain lakes, historic Inca ruins, and the richest diversity of potatoes on the planet. Approximately 2,300 of the 4,000 known potato varieties in the world are grown here, making it one of the most biodiverse regions on the planet. The 7,000 Quechua people who live on this high-altitude Sacred Valley of the Incas have, with their ancestors, cultivated and improved Andean potatoes for seven millennia. That impressive record stems from a holistic way of life that blends deep spiritual traditions and cultural values with cultivation techniques, barter and exchange practices and ecological stewardship.

Potatoes are, of course, a central element of Quechua culture. When a reporter from *Gourmet* magazine visited the region, she was amazed to discover that "each potato, it seemed, had its own special or ceremonial use: There were potatoes to eat at baptisms; potatoes, like the bride potato, for weddings; and others for funerals. Potatoes like the red *moro boli* were high in antioxidants, while potatoes such as the *ttalaco* – a long, banana-shaped tuber – must be either soaked and steamed or made into a potato alcohol."

Some potatoes must be grown on steep slopes above 13,000 feet. Some can be grown nearly anywhere. It is not uncommon for a single farmer's field to produce hundreds of different varieties, many of them quite rare.

The six Quechua communities see themselves as living in reciprocal relationship with the land, each other and the spirit world. The approach has been called *ayllu* – a political and socioeconomic system in which "individuals with the same interests and objectives [are] linked through shared norms and principles with respect to humans, animals, rocks, spirits, mountains, lakes, rivers, pastures, food crops, wildlife, etc.," write Alejandro Argumedo and Bernard Yun Loong Wong (Argumedo & Loong Wong 2010; Argumedo 2008. These monographs are the source for many facts in this essay). People strive for a balance between the *ayllu* of the *Runas* (humans and their domesticated crops and animals), the *Sallaka* (wild plants and creatures) and the Auki *Ayllu* (sacred beings, including mountain protector spirits).

In this cosmovision, the Earth is seen as giving potatoes, other crops, animals and the living landscape to the people – gifts that must be reciprocated through the giving of *pagos*, or offerings, in return. The spiritual engagement with *pachamama*, or Mother Earth, is not incidental, but a key factor in the Quechua's deep respect for the earth's limits, generativity and agrobiodiversity. "The main objective of the *ayllu*," Argumedo and Loong Wong explain, "is attainment of well-being, which in Quechua societies is defined as *Sumak kawsay*." The term refers to living a harmonious and healthy relationship with *pachamama*.

The point of agriculture in Quechua societies is not to raise maximum crop yields for market sale and profit. It is to faithfully implement the principles associated with the *ayllu*, which lies at the core of the Quechua's stable, regenerative agroecological practices that have evolved within the Andean landscape – a region that has a variety of different "vertical" microclimates at different altitudes, often at short distances from each other. Thus the altiplano region may grow potatoes and quinoa, notes Argumedo, while fields in lower valleys may grow maize, and higher pastures may be used to raise llamas (Argumedo & Loong Wong 2010).

In recent decades, multinational biotech and agricultural corporations have increasingly sought to appropriate the fruits of such distinctive ecosystems and convert them into market commodities. They often buy up or evict traditional communities, dismantle traditional agriculture and claim patents in seeds, genes and other organisms. Regions with rich biodiversity such as Peru are a prime hunting ground for such corporate predators, whose acts of biopiracy seek to privatize genetic and physical resources that have been managed as commons for generations.

To prevent such market enclosures of shared wealth, the indigenous peoples of the Cusco Valley joined with the nonprofit group ANDES[1] in the 1990s to develop an ingenious legal innovation, the Indigenous Biocultural Heritage Area (IBCHA). The idea, launched in 2000, was to create a *sui generis*[2] legal regime to preserve and promote native potato varieties and protect the fragile ecosystem by recognizing the role of indigenous "biocultural heritage" practices (Argumedo 2008:49-57).

The communities established a protected agroecological region called the "Potato Park" – "Parque de la Papa" – to protect more than 12,000 hectares

---

1 | ANDES in Spanish is an acronym for the Quechua-Aymara Association for Sustainable Communities. The Peruvian nonprofit is dedicated to defending indigenous rights to genetic resources, genetic knowledge and landscapes.

2 | "Of its own kind or class" – a unique legal instrument for a special circumstance.

considered essential to the agrobiodiversity of the Pisaq region and conserve traditional culture, knowledge and livelihoods. The Potato Park is a community-led and rights-based approach to conservation that points toward a very different model of "development" than conventional market-based ones.[3] The villages of the Potato Park all share authority in running it, with each one electing a chairperson to coordinate the work of the association. Special attention is paid to integrating traditional spiritual values and practices into the everyday operations and policies of the Potato Park.

Under the IBCHA system, communities that belong to the Potato Park have agreed to selectively share their "living library" of potato genetic knowledge with scientists. In a special agreement with the International Potato Center (CIP) – a nonprofit food security organization that works with the global research partnership CGIAR – the Potato Park has shared more than 200 of its 900 native potato varieties with scientists, and is facilitating experiments to cultivate new (non-GMO) potato varieties that can resist climate change. They also have a special interest in "repatriating" potato varieties that were lost when modern, commercial farming methods were introduced. The Potato Park refuses to allow the patenting of any genetic knowledge, however, believing that private property rights are incompatible with the sacred and collective status of the potatoes. The agreement is widely seen as a model that other agroecological cultures could emulate. It both recognizes the sanctity of community control over the potatoes while allowing modern scientific study and certain forms of communal business activities.

Thus, besides preserving Quechua cultures and assisting scientific inquiry, the Potato Park is hosting socially and ecologically sensitive forms of development such as agroecotourism, "nutraceuticals," (dietary and nutritional products) and pharmaceuticals. The Potato Park has a processing center for natural medicines and soaps, a network of local pharmacies and a video communications center. It has a formal registry of the Park's biological diversity and uses "geographical indicators" (legal rights for place-based products) and trademarks to protect its stewardship authority over local genetic diversity (Argumedo and Pimbert 2005:11).

Women play a key role in many of the economic activities of the Association of Communities of the Potato Park (the formal name of the project). There is, for example, the Sipaswarmi Medicinal Plants Women's Collective, which sells natural medicine and soaps, and the Tijillay T'ika Women's Audio-Visual Collective, a women's co-operative that makes videos in the native language about local resources.

---

3 | See essay by Arturo Escobar, "Commons Beyond Development: A Pluriversal Perspective," on pp. 348-360.

Although the Potato Park does not have state recognition within either Peruvian national law or the International Union for the Conservation of Nature (IUCN), that does not mean the association is without legal protection. The IBCHA agreement is legally compatible with existing systems of national and international law, and is seen as an inspiration for similar projects along the Ruta Cóndor agrobiodiversity corridor in the Andes. Meanwhile, many Potato Park agreements and actions are legally enforceable in conventional ways, such as the scientific study agreement with CIP and the Potato Park database that can be used to thwart patent applications for indigenous medicinal plants and knowledge.

In any case, some of the most consequential forms of law are not formal and state-based, but customary and vernacular. It is in local villages that agro-ecological and biocultural practices are actually managed and enforced, in ways that official, state-based law could never do. The IBCHA agreement is really an attempt to bridge this divide – to use formal law to recognize distinctive, context-specific customary law so that intergenerational cultural knowledge and practices can be recognized as legally valid and practically effective.

In the end, the Quechua culture of commoning remains the stabilizing force. In the village of Chawaytire, there is an all-organic restaurant Papamanka run by a women's association, which acts as a custodian of indigenous traditions and recipes. Proud of its heritage, the restaurant shares its indigenous folkways without pandering to the tourist trade. When the *Gourmet* reporter asked a waiter to cut into one of the potatoes to see the color inside, she declined, explaining that cutting a potato without eating it is an insult to *pachamama*.

Such reverence, which may appear irrational to the modern mind, is a key reason why the Quechua have been able to maintain the integrity of their biocultural traditions and fragile ecosystem. The success of the Potato Park suggests that the "rationality" that needs greater questioning is the one that believes a bioculturally diverse ecosystem can be plundered for its cash value without quickly destroying it.

References

Argumedo, Alejandro. 2008. "The Potato Park, Peru: Conserving Agrobiodiversity in an Andean Indigenous Biocultural Heritage Area," in Amend, T., Brown, J., Kothari A., Phillips, A., Stolton, S. editors. *Protected Landscapes and Agrobiodiversity Values.* Vol. 1 in the series, "Protected Landscapes and Seascapes." IUCN & GTZ. Heidelberg, Germany: Kaspareg Verlag.

Argumedo, Alejandro and Bernard Yun Loong Wong. 2010. "The Ayllu System of the Potato Park, Cusco, Peru." Satoyama Initiative, United Nations University Institute of Advanced Studies, March 5, 2010, available at http://satoyama-initiative.org/en/the-ayllu-system-of-the-potato-park.

Argumedo, Alejandro and M. Pimbert. 2008. *Protecting Indigenous Knowledge Against Biopiracy in the Andes.* London. IIED.

David Bollier *(US) is an author, activist, blogger and scholar of the commons. He is cofounder of the Commons Strategies Group and the author of* Think Like a Commoner *and co-editor of* The Wealth of the Commons, *among other books.*

The System of Rice Intensification and Its International Community of Practice

By Erika Styger

When the rainy season came early to the highlands of Madagascar in 1983, the rice seedlings in the nursery were still too young for transplanting, and French Jesuit priest Henri de Laulanié had to make a decision: either to wait another two to four weeks to transplant (which would obviously result in a lower yield due to delayed planting) or to go ahead and transplant the seedlings as they were. He decided to transplant the tiny fifteen-day-old seedlings – a practice then unheard of. The yield from this plot outperformed, by far, all others in the area. Surprised by the results, Father de Laulanié and the young farmers he worked with were inspired to continue experimenting based on additional field observations.

Over the next five years, farmers tested transplanting seedlings at twelve, ten, nine and eight days. They also planted only one seedling per hill; increased the spacing between hills; and even allowed soils to dry intermittently. This differed greatly from the conventional practice of planting thirty- to sixty-day-old seedlings at three to six seedlings per hill with close spacing, and with continuous flooding of soil throughout the season.

Results were encouraging. The plants became obviously healthier and stronger. The number of tillers per plant increased from 20 – 25 to 60 – 80, and yields increased proportionally. Yields increased from 1 metric ton per hectare (t/ha) to 2 – 5 t/ha, with a few plots reaching as much as 6 – 7 t/ha. Although results were consistent, Laulanié writes that by 1988 neither agricultural research institutes nor government extension services took the results seriously and were not even curious enough to visit the fields.

This did not stop the farmers from continuing to experiment with the new cultivation practices that they called the System for Rice Intensification, or SRI. In 1990, Laulanié and several of his close Malagasy friends established a local nongovernmental organization, *Association Tefy Saina*, to promote SRI and rural development in Madagascar.[1]

In 1994, the Cornell International Institute for Food, Agriculture and Development (CIIFAD), based at Cornell University in New York, began working on agricultural improvement in the peripheral rainforest zone around Madagascar's Ranomafana National Park. Introduced to SRI by *Tefy Saina* and surprised by the reported results, the Cornell team undertook its own tests. After obtaining consistently high yields for three years, they started to share the knowledge about this new methodology with rice researchers outside Madagascar.

Over the next twelve years, from 1998 to 2010, a small team at Cornell University shared information on SRI with newcomers and collected accounts of field experiences and reports from people testing SRI in their own countries. Knowledge was openly shared through lectures, seminars, personal visits, chance encounters while traveling, emails, publications and the small website that was set up at Cornell to collect and organize the incoming information. This website – sririce.org – has become today the world's largest repository of information on SRI.

By providing a platform to share new ideas and results from the field, and to respond to questions, the Cornell University team found that an informal working network had developed on an international scale – a novel kind of commons. This was neither planned nor funded, as it had started out as a small unofficial side-project.

Similarly, in each country, unique initiatives and communities of practice developed independently. Thousands of individual farmers, curious about SRI, often in close collaboration with researchers and technical staff, tried SRI for themselves, recognized the benefits and shared information about it within their own networks. Witnessing the advantages, others joined in and developed their own national SRI networks that took steps to further spread and innovate SRI methods. Each network is somewhat unique, and has developed its own organizational structure and way of functioning.[2]

In time, given the ever-increasing demand for information about SRI, the Cornell team found the means to formally establish the "SRI International Network and Resources Center" (SRI-Rice) in 2010. Its original mission was to make available and advance knowledge about SRI and provide international networking support. But SRI-Rice soon expanded its role to directly consult on project planning, provide technical advice and develop guidelines and materials for training, data monitoring and reporting.

---

1 | Laulanié, H 1993. Le Système de Riziculture Intensive Malgache. *Tropicultura*, 11(3):1-19.

2 | See http://sri.cals.cornell.edu/listservs/index.html for a detailed listing.

Since 1998, when Cornell started sharing information about SRI, many practitioners and researchers in Asia, Africa and Latin America have evaluated the SRI methodology. These wide-ranging efforts have confirmed that the SRI methodology is applicable under conditions in ecological zones ranging from humid to arid, and from lowlands to uplands. Today, improved crop productivity as a result of applying SRI principles has been confirmed in more than fifty countries.[3]

What Makes SRI So Different?

We have learned that successful introduction of SRI to a country depends mostly on: 1) *leadership*: motivated individuals bringing the SRI methodology to farmers and promoting positive results; 2) *depth of technical knowledge* and adaptation of the practices to a given environment, and 3) *available funding*, which has been mostly found from local, in-country resources.

There are other reasons for SRI's surprising success:

The SRI methodology is easy to understand and easy to implement – although practices must be adjusted to local environments. As SRI is a knowledge-based methodology, once farmers become familiar with the SRI principles and most common practices, they can easily test SRI and adapt the system to their own environments. Practices are not prescribed; SRI is not a fixed package, and does not offer a "silver bullet" solution. Nevertheless, as farmers adjust their practices, the challenge becomes to capture what works well and share it with others. For this purpose, SRI-Rice has started to develop a simple and accessible Internet-based "citizen-science" platform where farmers and technicians can directly share their results and ideas with the rest of the world.

The impact is visible and clear. Applying SRI methodology increases yields by 20-50 percent and often more, while using less seed, less water and fewer or no chemical inputs. Farmers gain a direct benefit in only one season, and can do it with their available resources simply by changing their agricultural practices.

SRI's surprising effectiveness provokes interest. Plants develop faster, are more vigorous and become more productive. Farmers, researchers, technicians are surprised the first time they witness the development of an SRI field! SRI arouses their curiosity and raises new questions about best agricultural practices. Soils, water, plants, soil biota and nutrients can be managed more productively. Farmers do not need to look for new seed varieties, fertilizers and other chemicals to improve productivity. They become motivated to think and experiment beyond previously perceived boundaries.

---

3 | http://sri.cals.cornell.edu/countries/index.html

An example is the "System of Crop Intensification" (SCI), which has evolved when SRI farmers and field technicians adapted the SRI principles to other crops, such as wheat, finger millet, sugarcane, mustard, legumes and vegetables. This has benefited several hundred thousand farmers, especially in India.

SRI is open-source. It does not belong to anyone, but is shared as a commons. Nobody "owns" either SRI theory or practice. This can be unsettling to some, be they researchers or program developers, who like to think in terms of well-defined and predetermined theories and methodologies. At SRI-Rice, we work to make knowledge freely accessible to the public, as it should reach as many smallholder farmers as possible. The drawback is that the value of open-source knowledge is often not appreciated. Because it is freely available, it is sometimes perceived as being without value. However, this open availability has been instrumental to SRI's success in many of the countries where SRI has been adopted.

SRI has had and still has doubters and skeptics. In the early 2000s, when SRI began to be tested for the first time in various countries, a short-lived but heated debate sprang up. Some rice scientists doubted that such substantial benefits could be obtained by changing agronomic practices alone. Who could believe that this simple methodology synthesized by an unknown Jesuit priest and refined by a global network of ordinary farmers would outperform the recommendations from the global research community?

Although SRI-Rice plays an important role for the SRI community of practice, the impact of its networking and advisory support over the past seventeen years is difficult to quantify. Outputs and outcomes are often indirect and nonlinear. Sometimes efforts show no results, and sometimes support is responsible for the success of a large program. The current estimate is that about ten million farmers benefit from the SRI methodology, although this might be underestimated, as it is difficult to know how the knowledge about SRI has spread.

The international community of practice is growing, but remains informal. Anyone interested in SRI can join the community. There is no membership and no selection criteria, but also no formal support. This has two implications. On the positive side: the community and the network, composed of several hundred genuinely dedicated and self-selected individuals, maintains itself; they remain part of the community even if there is little direct support. The downside is that many of the community members do not know of each other, thus large potentials for collaboration and creating synergies among partners are not tapped.

In response to that, SRI-Rice facilitates the formation of regional networks, so that technical exchange and learning can more easily happen across country borders, often based on similar ecological zones. We were instrumental in developing the "Improving and Scaling up SRI in West Africa" project, funded by the World Bank, where SRI partners from thirteen countries collaborate closely on SRI and where SRI-Rice provides technical support (sriwestafrica. org).

Nevertheless, it might be time to think about how to better structure or formalize the international network, creating opportunities for encounters and collaboration while keeping the spirit of the commons at its heart.

The Way Forward

There is a great potential to build on what has already been accomplished. There is a high demand for knowledge from smallholder farmers in Africa, Asia and Latin America, and the international community of practice is available to work with them. More than ever, we know how to best adapt the SRI methodology to various climates and cropping systems. Farmer-driven agricultural innovation, stimulated by the SRI methodology, can become a model to further improve other crops and components of smallholder farming systems.

Erika Styger, *PhD (United States), is Director of Programs, SRI-Rice, Cornell University, Ithaca New York (eds8@cornell.edu), which she set up and has headed since 2010. Prior to joining Cornell, Styger worked for more than twenty years on agricultural research and development programs in Africa, including three years introducing and developing use of SRI with farmers in Mali.*

Twelve Design Principles of Permaculture

Permaculture is a type of sustainable agriculture and ecological design and engineering that self-consciously attempts to work in constructive alignment with natural dynamics. At once a philosophy and set of social practices, techniques and ethical norms, permaculture seeks to ensure that all life systems can remain healthy and flourish. This goal can only be met if human beings regard nature as a holistic system that includes human society, which in turn must reintegrate surplus production and waste back into natural ecosystems.

Permaculture design, practices and ethics can be considered a form of commons-based agriculture, engineering and production. The essence of permaculture has been summarized by David Holmgren in his book, Permaculture: Principles and Pathways Beyond Sustainability, *in the following twelve principles.*

1. **Observe and interact.** By taking time to engage with nature we can design solutions that suit our particular situation.

2. **Catch and store energy.** By developing systems that collect resources at peak abundance, we can use them in times of need.

3. **Obtain a yield.** Ensure that you are getting truly useful rewards as part of the work that you are doing.

4. **Apply self-regulation and accept feedback.** We need to discourage inappropriate activity to ensure that systems can continue to function well.

5. **Use and value renewable resources and services.** Make the best use of nature's abundance to reduce our consumptive behavior and dependence on non-renewable resources.

6. **Produce no waste.** By valuing and making use of all the resources that are available to us, nothing goes to waste.

7. **Design from patterns to details.** By stepping back, we can observe patterns in nature and society. These can form the backbone of our designs, with the details filled in as we go.

8. **Integrate rather than segregate.** By putting the right things in the right place, relationships develop between those things and they work together to support each other.

9. **Use small and slow solutions.** Small and slow systems are easier to maintain than big ones, making better use of local resources and producing more sustainable outcomes.

10. **Use and value diversity.** Diversity reduces vulnerability to a variety of threats and takes advantage of the unique nature of the environment in which it resides.

11. **Use edges and value the marginal.** The interface between things is where the most interesting events take place. These are often the most valuable, diverse and productive elements in the system.

12. **Creatively use and respond to change.** We can have a positive impact on inevitable change by carefully observing, and then intervening at the right time.

ARTS AND CULTURE COMMONS

"Revolutionary moments do not spread by contamination but by resonance....An insurrection is not like a plague or forest fire – a linear process which spreads from place after an initial spark. It takes the shape of a music, whose focal points, though dispersed in time and space, succeed in imposing the rhythms of their own vibrations."

The anonymous Invisible Committee, France

Fire and Frost: The Virtues of Treating Museums, Libraries and Archives as Commons

By *Michael Peter Edson*

It was usually a note in the newspaper, a few pages back. Or, if the blaze was big enough and a camera crew arrived quickly, a feature on the evening news. It seems like house fires were more common when I was young, and the story was often the same: "As they escaped their burning home," the newscaster would say, "they paused to save a single prized possession..." And it was always something sentimental – not jewelry or cash but a family photograph, a child's drawing, a letter, a lock of hair. Ephemera by any measure, and yet as dear as life itself. Museums are simple places. Libraries and archives too. Collect, preserve, elucidate. Repeat forever. We don't think about them until the smoke rises, but by then it's usually too late.

When Hitler ordered the destruction of Warsaw in 1944, the army tried to set the national library – the Biblioteka Narodawa – on fire, but the flames smoldered.[1] It turns out that the collected memory of a civilization is surprisingly dense and hard to burn, so a special engineering team was brought in to cut chimneys in the roof and holes in the walls so the fire could get more air. Problem solved. Museums, libraries and archives are simple places, but once the flames take hold they burn like hell.

Or sometimes they freeze: the icy cold of ignorance and neglect can be as deadly as the hot end of a torch. The last and only specimen of the fruit bat *Pteropus allenorum* sat preserved in a jar on a museum shelf for 153 years before it was finally studied and identified as a new species – but by then it was extinct.[2] The Bachman's warbler, "famous for its unusually thrilling song," was hurtled

---

1 | Knuth, Rebecca, *Burning Books and Leveling Libraries*, Praeger, 2006; and as told to the author by the library director, October 2011.

2 | *Discover Magazine*, "'New' species gather dust on museum shelves for 21 years before being described," November 19, 2012, http://blogs.discovermagazine.com/notrocket-science/2012/11/19/new-species-gather-dust-on-museum-shelves-for-21-years-before-being-described/#.U8upGoBdUxo. (Many thanks to Dr. Elycia Wallis of Museum Victoria for sharing this story.)

into extinction in 1939 when bird watchers found and proudly shot the last two of them.[3] A quarter of Americans don't believe in climate change;[4] almost half don't believe in evolution;[5] a third don't know their next-door neighbors,[6] and while the rest of the world clamors for greater access to knowledge and literacy the UK has closed hundreds of community libraries. "Libraries that stayed open during the Blitz will be closed by budgets," wrote Caitlin Moran, "A trillion small doors closing."[7] Lost opportunity kills like smoke and flame, but it's harder to see.

Fire and frost – ignorance of science, neglect of our physical environment, and failure to cultivate human potential – we can't afford them anymore: there is too much at stake.

Civilization requires wise and engaged citizens, and for hundreds if not thousands of years we have built and sustained museums, libraries and archives in our communities to advance this goal for our own survival – to stimulate knowledge creation and creativity; foster learning and independent thinking; support civic engagement and dialogue; encourage emotional intelligence and well-being; and to deepen our knowledge of the past and clarify our plans for the future. We need museums, libraries and archives to accomplish these tasks on a massive scale – we can't possibly have too much success in them – but taken as a whole, our institutions, operating in their traditional ways, are a remarkably blunt instrument for spreading the enlightenment. For every person who walks through museum doors there are billions who can't or won't; for every item cataloged and available to library and archive patrons, millions are absent or withheld; collections that have been in the public domain for centuries are enclosed by paywalls and unnecessary restrictions; and the expertise and passion of the public lies dormant and invisible.[8] Why?

The issue, it turns out, is not a conflict of values but of habits: old ideas about scope and scale – who has a voice, who does the work, and who gets to benefit – die hard. Like most organizations, museums, libraries and archives

---

3 | Bryson, Bill, *A Short History of Nearly Everything*, Broadway Books, 2003, p. 476.

4 | Yale Project on Climate Change Communication, "Americans' Global Warming Beliefs and Attitudes in April 2013," at http://environment.yale.edu/climate-communication/article/Climate-Beliefs-April-2013#sthash.SfADnW8K.dpuf.

5 | Gallup: "In U.S., 46 Percent Hold Creationist View of Human Origins," June 1, 2012, at http://www.gallup.com/poll/155003/Hold-Creationist-View-Human-Origins.aspx.

6 | Pew Research Internet Project, "Neighbors Online," June 9, 2010, at http://www.pewinternet.org/2010/06/09/neighbors-online.

7 | Caitlin Moran, "Libraries, Cathedrals of Our Souls", November 11, 2012, at http://www.huffingtonpost.com/caitlin-moran/libraries-cathedrals-of-o_b_2103362.html?ncid=edlinkusaolp00000003&utm_hp_ref=fb&src=sp&comm_ref=false.

8 | Sanderhoff, Merete, "Common Challenges, Common Solutions," slide 26, September 20, 2012, http://www.slideshare.net/MereteSanderhoff/common-challenges-common-solutions-okfest-20092012.

forged their dreams in the twentieth century when success was equated with impressive buildings full of experts, big collections and visitors through the doors. That was reality, there was no Internet yet, and one could hardly imagine any other type of measures of excellence. And the concept of a commons seems perverse and strange in that context: in the world of the bricks-and-mortar, what self-respecting museum would share its privilege and authority with the crowd, and who but barbarians would accept it? What responsible institution would relinquish control of its data and invite billions of people to collaborate, or free collections from copyright and abandon hope of squeezing profits from licensing and fees?

But even back in 1853, people like Joseph Henry, the first chief administrator of the Smithsonian Institution (now the world's largest museum and research complex, based in Washington, DC), saw that museums, libraries and archives could accomplish great deeds in society – not by only looking inward at their own experts and collections, but by looking outward, to the imagination and energy of citizens. "The worth and importance of the Institution is not to be estimated by what it accumulates within the walls of its building," wrote Henry, in the Smithsonian's first annual report, "but by what it sends forth to the world."[9]

It is a beautiful sentiment: we just lacked the means to fully realize it until now. Free, unrestricted digital access is the key, and the creativity and action of citizens – commoning, as it is called throughout this book – is what turns it in the lock.

The New York Public Library recently put 20,000 high-resolution public domain maps online. "What's this all mean?" asks Matt Knutzen of the library's map division, "It means you can have the maps, all of them if you want, for free, in high resolution. We've scanned them to enable their use in the broadest possible ways by the largest number of people."[10]

Amsterdam's Rijksmuseum owns some of the most priceless masterpieces in Western art, but rather than hoard them, they give them to the world. The Rijksmuseum has over 150,000 high-resolution public domain reproductions of works of art on its website, and the museum encourages and celebrates re-use of these resources through its innovative Rijksstudio project and API.[11] "We're a public institution," said Taco Dibbits, the Rijksmuseum's director of collections, "and so the art and objects we have are, in a way, everyone's property."[12]

9 | *Annual Report of the Board of Regents of the Smithsonian Institution for the Year 1852*, Washington, DC: US Government Printing Office, 1853, via http://siarchives.si.edu/history/exhibits/henry/joseph-henrys-life#c1.

10 | Knutzen, Matt, "Open access maps at NYPL", March 28, 2014 http://www.nypl.org/blog/2014/03/28/open-access-maps.

11 | https://www.rijksmuseum.nl/en and http://www.rijksmuseum.nl/en/rijksstudio.

12 | "Masterworks for One and All," *New York Times*, May 29, 2014, available at http://www.nytimes.com/2013/05/29/arts/design/museums-mull-public-use-of-online-art-images.html.

Eighty-eight institutions from sixteen countries have contributed 1.3 million images to The Flickr Commons, an ongoing project to increase access to, and interaction with, public photography collections around the world. All images in the Flickr Commons are presented with "no known copyright restrictions" and are free to use for any purpose, by anyone.[13]

Europeana, a European Commission initiative to increase access to cultural resources,[14] provides a single point of access to over 3.9 million public domain and CCØ public domain books, artworks, and other museum, library, and archive items from almost 400 collecting institutions.[15] "Entrusted with the preservation of our shared knowledge and culture, not-for-profit memory organizations should take upon themselves a special role in the effective labeling and preserving of Public Domain works," reads Europeana's *Public Domain Charter*. "As part of this role they need to ensure that works in the Public Domain are accessible to all of society, by making them available as widely as possible."

And the Wikimedia Commons, "a database of 22,022,531 freely usable media files to which anyone can contribute," is perhaps the best, most used, and most productive cultural commons in the world, despite the fact – or *perhaps because of the fact* – that it is run not by institutions, bound by tradition, but by volunteers, inspired and empowered to take action and create value through their own efforts.[16] The Wikimedia Commons provides images and other media resources for Wikipedia's 35 million articles, and while a growing number of those resources are contributed by museums, libraries and archives, many more are contributed by individual citizens – commoners and activists – who scour the Web for relevant images and reference materials, scan pages from books, organize and execute collaborative projects, and even upload photographs from their own visits to museum and cultural sites to help improve the quality and breadth of Wikipedia articles.

Because of its foundation of free and open resources and its network of volunteers, the Wikimedia Commons operates at a magnificent, global scale – transcending professional, institutional, and national boundaries to serve over 500 million Wikipedia readers a month in 280 languages. Even the world's

---

13 | https://www.flickr.com/commons. Thanks to James Morley and his Flickr Commons statistics tool (http://www.whatsthatpicture.com/flickr/commons-stats.php) for the image counts.

14 | http://europeana.eu, and FAQ, http://pro.europeana.eu/europeana-faq. Thanks to James Morley and Christoph Braun for help with record counts. Europeana Public Domain Charter, http://pro.europeana.eu/c/document_library/get_file?uuid=d542819d-d169-4240-9247-f96749113eaa&groupId=10602, 2010.

15 | CCØ ("CC Zero") is a legal deed for dedicating a work to the public domain, which existing copyright law makes no provision for doing.

16 | http://commons.wikimedia.org/wiki/Main_Page. 32 million articles is as of June, 2014, http://stats.wikimedia.org/EN/TablesWikipediaZZ.htm. Wikipedia use statistics are from the Wikimedia Foundation 2013-2014 annual report: http://wikimediafoundation.org/wiki/Annual_Report.

greatest museums, libraries and archives cannot hope to match that reach and impact – especially if they cling to the methods and measures of the past.

The work of the world's cultural institutions is a matter of great consequence now, as wise and engaged citizens are our best hope to quench the flames of fear and hatred and thaw the bitter cold of ignorance and neglect. And with the fire and frost upon us we have only a few moments to take action: What should we ask our museum, library, and archive institutions to do? How should they act to scale and amplify their impact in society? The commons offers the way forward.

Michael Peter Edson *(USA) is a strategist and thought leader at the forefront of digital transformation in the cultural sector. Michael is a Presidential Distinguished Fellow at the Council for Libraries and Information Resources (USA), he serves on the OpenGLAM advisory board for Open Knowledge, and he works at the Smithsonian Institution in Washington, D.C. The opinions in this essay are his own.*

The Birth of a Theater Commons in Rome: Fondazione Teatro Valle Bene Comune

By Dario Gentili and Andrea Mura

Founded in 1727, Teatro Valle in Rome has been a playhouse for illustrious artists like Mozart, Rossini and Pirandello. The oldest theater in the city, it has achieved international recognition in recent years as the symbol of a pioneering struggle over the idea of the commons (*beni comuni*). The origins of this battle can be traced to a 2011 voter referendum in Italy that proposed a sweeping privatization of public water supplies and their conversion into market commodities. Defeated by more than 90 percent of voters, the "water referendum" elevated the commons to the center of the national debate, problematizing the legal category of "public goods."

A day after the referendum, a number of arts workers and ordinary citizens occupied the venerable building with the idea of protecting it from the risk of an impending privatization. The occupation immediately drew attention to the inadequate funding and mistreatment of the theater by the Italian Theatre Authority (ETI), a public administrative entity closed in 2010. Because the law regarded the theater as a "public good," the city council was authorized to invite private investors to tender competitive bids in a regulated process to acquire the theater. Thus the privatization of Teatro Valle was not only lawful but, given the city's budget woes, eminently attractive.

Given this legal logic, occupiers realized that the most effective remedy against this juridical thinking and further threats of privatization would be to treat Teatro Valle as a commons. The temporary occupation soon gave rise to the *Teatro Valle Occupato*, a protest that eventually lasted three years. Its long-term objective became not only the preservation of the theater, but also an affirmation of a new "right to the city" and to the commons. Artists, researchers, activists and ordinary citizens brought new energy to the ambitious political and cultural project of extending the idea of the commons to encompass immaterial goods.

The occupation also opposed neoliberal policies of commodification, and pioneered a new experimental approach to reconceptualizing law itself. By no longer fighting *against* the law, but *through* the law, the occupiers launched a battle for legal recognition of Teatro Valle as a commons, assisted by prominent legal theorists and by a working constituent assembly of the commons.[1] Occupiers wished to distinguish their actions from traditional squatting; this would instead be a battle for the recognition of the commons through which existing legal tools would be emancipated from their familiar, more conservative uses.

The occupiers' chief innovation was a formal institution of private law functioning as trust-like legal entity – the "Foundation," or more formally, *Fondazione Teatro Valle Bene Comune* (Teatro Valle Common Good Foundation). Stretching the juridical definition of the theater exposed a crucial tension between *legitimacy* and *legality* in the management of the theater. The Foundation sought to ratify the occupiers' possession, use and active production over and against the contrary formal claims of property ownership. This would open up a new legal approach to managing "public goods" while clearing the path for a law of the commons to emerge in the future and possibly be incorporated into the Constitution. The goal was to call attention to the deficiencies of the traditional divide between private and public goods and to offer an alternative to the naturalization of private property.

Teatro Valle Occupato conscientiously worked to comply with all requirements for the creation of its new legal entity, which, although not formally recognized yet, soon began to act as a de facto institution. This included the crafting of a legal Charter to set forth the scope of its authority, principles and structure.[2]

The "Commune" (*la comune*) or "Assembly of *communards*" – an assembly composed by the active participants of the theater (*communards*) – figures as the "sovereign political organ" of the Foundation (article 12). It gathers twice a month, and remains an open and ever-changing body, reflecting the actual presence of the *communards* at the meetings. The Commune is in charge of all crucial decisions about the theater, ranging from the preservation and development of the Foundation, amendments to the Charter, organization of specific groups, and, crucially, the programming of cultural and political activities. Decisions require unanimous agreement through an inclusive, nonauthoritarian, noncompetitive and shared decisionmaking method. Although it can take a lot of time before full agreement is reached, this deliberative procedure ensures that all minority positions find expression, encouraging collective engagement. All *communards*, whether originally expressing a majority or minority position,

---

1 http://www.opendemocracy.net/can-europe-make-it/maria-rosaria-marella/constituent-assembly-of-commons-cac

2 www.teatrovalleoccupato.it/wp-content/uploads/2013/10/statuto-fondazione-teatro-valle-bene-comune.pdf

must favor the general implementation of final decisions. However, a principle of pragmatism allows a reversion to majority vote in cases where unanimous agreement cannot be reached after two consecutive meetings.

The *communards* and all those supporters who have paid an annual membership fee or have contributed with occasional work (*soci fondatori*) constitute a second main body, the General Assembly (*Assemblea Generale*). This Assembly gathers once every year and decides annual budgeting. Finally, a Directive Board (*Consiglio*) presides over the execution of the activities decided by the Commune, performing a coordinating function. A President of the Board is chosen among its members, becoming the temporary legal representative of the Foundation. The criteria for the composition of the Board and the selection of the President, with candidates nominated also among the non-*communards* in the General Assembly, evidences the inclusive character of the Foundation.

In its Charter, the Foundation is committed to the "full realization of culture as the common good" (article 5), seeking to link the widely cherished history of Teatro Valle with the fundamental principles of co-working, inclusivity, direct and participatory democracy, constituent and collective action, and common creation. As reconfigured with this new type of governance, Teatro Valle hosted a variety of outstanding events with international artists, activists and intellectuals between 2011 and 2014, prompting the European Cultural Foundation to confer on the Theater its esteemed Princess Margriet Award in 2014.

However, as is often the case in Italy, despite international support, domestic resistance to Teatro Valle Occupato was massive. News media and public figures campaigned for the eviction of occupiers and for repressive measures against them. They accused occupiers of "unfair competition" against other cultural institutions in the city and the "misappropriation" of a public good "taken from citizens" (read private investors).

The political climate shifted in February 2014 when the Prefect of Rome (the general representative of the State at the local level) rejected Teatro Valle's claim to be recognized as a Foundation, arguing that it did not have legal *"ownership" of the "place"* (the material theater), which the law sees as a public good managed by the city council. In short, the Prefect saw possession as an insufficient title to the Valle premises – the very principle of use that the assembly of occupants meant to affirm.

In the face of an eviction ultimatum by the municipality in July 2014, a permanent general assembly open to all citizens began to gather in the theater with the aim of discussing present and future strategies of the Foundation. This effort succeeded in securing a public negotiation with the city council and the Teatro di Roma, an entity running public theaters in the capital, which would be entrusted by the Mayor with the management of the Valle at the end of the occupation.

After two weeks of open debate, the occupiers resolved to abandon the Valle voluntarily on August 10, 2014, accepting the Mayor's formal claim that a project of refurbishment and structural improvements needed to begin immediately. This transition from occupation to renovation was accepted on condition that the theater would remain public for 100 years, and that the city council and the Foundation would jointly draft a "Convention" regulating the future of the theater.

Although a dramatic choice, the Foundation acknowledged that its initial objectives – stopping privatization of the theater and experimenting with a new form of democratic governance – had been accomplished. Moreover, the agreement entailed the beginning of a "new phase" that would now fully recognize the Foundation as a *space* (for commoning) rather than *a place* (for managing a public facility), allowing the experience of the occupation to continue and transcend the physical building of Teatro Valle. In the framework of the future Convention, this will likely lead to a formal recognition of the Foundation; to an official appraisal of its cultural and political achievements over the last three years; and to a formal commitment to valorize this experience with a co-management between the Foundation and the Teatro di Roma. This outcome would preclude any future bids to privatize the Valle.

Going forward, public institutions will need to entertain new and diverse hybrid forms of governance, while the Foundation will have to prove that its governance is far more open, transparent and inclusive than the type of management traditionally associated with the public/private nexus. The challenge will be to show that a governance drawing on the commons will function not just as the simple rejection of private or public property, but as a real, experimental and socially robust alternative.

Dario Gentili *(Italy), a philosopher, carries out his research at Italian and European universities and institutions. His publications include:* Topografie politiche. Spazio urbano, cittadinanza, confini in Walter Benjamin e Jacques Derrida *[Political Topographies. Urban Space, Citizenship, Borders in Walter Benjamin and Jacques Derrida], Quodlibet, Macerata 2009;* Italian Theory. Dall'operaismo alla biopolitica *[Italian Theory. From Operaism to Biopolitics], Il Mulino, Bologna 2012.*

Andrea Mura *(Italy) is Research Fellow in Political Philosophy at the Open University's Faculty of Social Sciences. He has published widely in the fields of continental philosophy and psychoanalysis, and is the author of a major monograph in comparative political thought,* The Symbolic Scenarios of Islamism *(Ashgate 2015).*

Digital Arts as a Commons

By Salvatore Iaconesi

Since their beginnings, digital arts have provided great impetus to the commons, driven in part by their irreverent resistance to the ideas of copyright and of intellectual property. Arts criticize existing codes of politics and culture – through surrealism, irony and other means – creating new imaginary orders. On the one hand they sense emerging consensual realities and communicate them in their own peculiar ways; on the other hand they always tend to push a bit further beyond what is perceived as possible or real, by enacting simulacra and narratives.

Both of these modalities of the digital arts are linguistic in nature. They challenge language, and create new idioms – words, sentences, phrases, meanings – in ways that are meant to be interpreted and performed.

So it is not entirely incorrect to say that artists' main occupation is to create performative platforms for people's expression, and to give people new opportunities to re-create the elements of their world by interpreting the artwork (which is, after all, a symbolic representation of the essence of its times, from the artist's point of view). Art instigates a shared performative dialogue about how we shall perceive our shared reality.

In this sense, artists are indispensable enablers for the creation of our political and cultural commons. Whether their artworks are freely shared (as happens with many digital artists, for example) or not, they continuously contribute shared fragments of collective imaginaries that ultimately constitute our cognitive and psychic commons.

The digital arts pursue this mission through two key, coexisting modalities – the creation of frameworks and platforms for expression, and the re-appropriation and transformation of existing culture. The ubiquitous availability and accessibility of digital media enable artists to produce radical communication performances with relatively low effort, rivaling the expensive, highly produced performances of corporations and governments. This simple fact explains why digital arts are able to create so many insurgent new liberated spaces that can be appropriated, accessed, shared and used as commons.

Let's examine a few.

The **Human Ecosystems** project enacts a participatory and inclusive process revolving around public data and information.[1] Data about the behaviors of people in given neighborhoods – transit patterns, hotspots of creativity, commerce, crime, and so forth – are aggregated from various social networks in cities and then compiled to reveal hidden "relational ecosystems" in that city. The idea is to transform real-time digital data streams into source material for visualizing hidden patterns of human interaction. City agencies can use the data to engage communities in participatory decisionmaking and policy-shaping processes. Academics and urban planners are studying the data-based "human ecosystems" to gain new insights into urban design and cultural anthropology. Artists are developing new types of artistic interpretations and public performances about city life. Citizens, designers, researchers, entrepreneurs and public administrators participating in Human Ecosytems workshops are learning how to use this data for diverse purposes, such as the design of innovative city services and peer-to-peer business models.

One outgrowth of the Human Ecosystems project is the concept of **Ubiquitous Commons**. Millions of citizens are generating vast quantities of digital information via their mobile phones, web visits, public databases and more every day. There are rich new opportunites to create new types of public spaces that could function as commons. The Human Ecosystems project wants to ensure that that happens. But this requires that public datasets using social networking platforms be made freely available and accessible so that the information can be used as a data commons.

With appropriate access, artists can use the data to create visualizations of how emotions, topics and modalities of expression flow across time and geography in the city, or generate sounds which render a city's emotional expression. Researchers can use the data to make new ethnographic or sociological insights. Citizens and public administrations can use the data to understand how to engage communities and cultures in the city, forming human networks to participate in shared decisionmaking processes. Designers can use the data to invent anything from toys[2] to innovative services, adding value to the knowledge and expression produced ubiquitously across the city. The interests and relations discovered on social networks can be used to initiate productive dialogues about what citizens really want from urban spaces and city government, and reveal how they actually behave.

---

1 | http://human-ecosystems.com/home

2 | For example, the Emotional Compass: http://human-ecosystems.com/home/
an-emotional-compass-new-ideas-for-wayfinding-in-cities

Many processes of commoning find their origin in political activism. The radical transformation of the ways in which people have learned to communicate through the Internet have brought on major changes in the very definitions of what is (and could be) a "movement" in the digital age. The Arab Spring, the 99 Percent, Occupy[3] and Anonymous[4] – often in conjunction with the digital arts – are causing a metamorphosis in how we think about personal identity, public space, authorship and aesthetics.

Increasingly, ad hoc movements based on digital collaboration are becoming powerful creative forces in their own right, shaping how people relate to each other and express themselves to the wider society, and self-organize to challenge the state. In Italy, for example, there is a rich history of collaborations between arts and political movements in the digital era. Some of the most notable ones have invented fictitious, shared public identities as a commons-based vehicle for artistic and political commentary. An early example was **Luther Blissett** (later renamed Wu-Ming), a collective identity used by hundreds of cultural activists starting in 1994 for participatory writing processes and for post-dadaist political actions.[5] "Blissett" has been the "author" of countless situationist pranks, performances and even a historical novel that sold hundreds of thousands of copies in more than ten languages.

A more recent example is **RomaEuropa FakeFactory**, a participatory fake cultural institution that was created in response to the stodgy, traditionalist cultural policies of Rome's city administration in 2008. The REFF argues, "Defining what is real is an act of power. Being able to reinvent reality is an act of freedom." Its commitment to fake, remixed, recontextualized and plagiarized art projects has made it an international movement, eventually recognized officially by governments and organizations.[6]

Serpica Naro[7] and **San Precario**[8] are two movements that protested against the politics of austerity and its role in eliminating jobs and worsening precarity. Serpica Naro is a fictitious activist fashion designer created by the San Precario and Chainworkers collectives. She is intent on subverting the fashion system's proprietary luxury brands and marketing, and building instead "open brands" that invite mass participation and creativity. San Precario is a faux saint – the Patron Saint of Precarious Workers and Lives – who was invented in 2004 to protest the growing use of "flexible" working arrangements without social security or other benefits. There is even a specific prayer that can be made to

---

3 | http://en.wikipedia.org/wiki/Occupy_movement

4 | http://en.wikipedia.org/wiki/Anonymous_(group)

5 | http://en.wikipedia.org/wiki/Luther_Blissett_(nom_de_plume)

6 | http://romaeuropa.org

7 | http://www.serpicanaro.org

8 | http://www.precaria.org

San Precario, which asks for paid maternity leave, protection for chain store workers and holidays for call center operators.

A final collective artistic endeavor that has mobilized dissent toward the politics of austerity, especially as it affects public education, is **Anna Adamolo,**[9] a fake ministry of education and the Minister herself, Anna Adamolo. The persona has been used as a way for the Italian people to collectively express their protests against the government. One email issued by Anna Adamolo, for example, declared, "Today, we symbolically build on the Net a new Ministry, the Ministry that we all would want to have in Italy, where the voices of the temporary workers, of the students, of the teachers, of all the citizens, are finally heard."

All three projects are focused on using fictitious public identities as ways to create shared spaces for responsibility and purpose. All are based on creating a mythological persona that can be used to organize a commons: a collaborative vehicle through which to protest and express alternative proposals and solutions. In effect, these characters are a series of *meta-brands* – carefully constructed cultural memes that can be accessed and used by everyone.

Again, the patterns for creating digital arts commons are minimal and direct: establish a platform for expression (in these cases, meta-brands, collective identities, fake cultural institutions that act in open-source ways) and a participatory performative dimension (a movement, its mythopoiesis, its practices, meetings, events). For example, the Serpica Naro movement has turned into a toolkit for open source fashion in the digital age, and has developed a rich archive of knowledge and models. San Precario has produced a series of collaboratively collected kits, how-tos, tutorials and surreal protest models against precarity and austerity. Anna Adamolo now hosts an archive of art performances, lessons, open courseware on multiple subjects as a form of artistic practice. It has even proposed new models for formal and informal education systems.

Digital arts often manifest themselves in surprising ways in physical territories, leading to the creation of commons. In Sicily, Italy, **the Museo dell'Informatica Funzionante** – the Museum of Working Informatics in Palazzolo Acreide – has created a vast collection of old computer systems that people can use both physically and remotely via the Internet. They can enjoy using the amusingly obsolete computers, learn basics of electronic and computer science, and share a piece of our history.[10] The museum is a place where people can conserve, repair and preserve our heritage in digital formats and hardware, but also use the documentation, software, electrical schemes, books,

---

9 | http://annaadamolo.noblogs.org

10 | http://museo.freaknet.org/en

manuals and media of various kinds. This place is, in fact, the only known place in which older software artifacts can function in their native environment, allowing anyone to study and understand the transformation of user interfaces, communication and collaboration functionalities, visual cultures and more.

The point of many art projects is to create new commons through the creation of archives, communication patterns and knowledge sharing. In **"Sauti ya wakulima,"**[11] (The Voice of the Farmers), artist Eugenio Tisselli used a few smartphones, some old, cheap mobile phones and other low technology devices to invite farmers from the Chambezi region of Tanzania to document their agricultural practices. The community, working with the artist, then used smartphones and mobile applications to publish images and voice recordings on the Internet, creating a shared digital space that allows easy, curated access to the community's knowledge and memories. The project has enabled the farmers to communicate with extension officers and scientific researchers in remote locations, and to develop more advanced small-scale agricultural techniques for their harsh environmental conditions. All while making, through art, a powerful act of communication and awareness.

As the previous examples demonstrate, many of the most successful patterns for the creation of commons in the digital arts deal with the creation of archives: open collections of artworks, knowledge, data, content and more. This issue is fundamental to digital cultures that care about preserving the past and avoiding a digital dark age – "a possible future situation where it will be difficult or impossible to read historical electronic documents and multimedia, because they have been in an obsolete and obscure file format."[12] By creating archival materials only in open, documented, accessible and usable formats, they greatly enhance a society's ability to preserve digital art, culture and knowledge production for future generations.

Perhaps the most forward-thinking example is the **Internet Archive**, a non-profit founded by tech entrepreneur Brewster Kahle to provide free public access to vast stores of digitized materials. The Internet Archive includes websites, text, audio, moving images, software and 4.4 million public-domain books.[13] Located in San Francisco and operating through donations and collaborations with the Library of Congress and the Smithsonian, the Internet Archive also provides specialized services for adaptive reading and information access for the blind and other persons with disabilities.

Are digital archives really commons, or just open platforms? A commons, after all, requires an active social engagement and a "space" for collaboration

---

11 | http://sautiyawakulima.net

12 | http://en.wikipedia.org/wiki/Digital_dark_age

13 | https://archive.org

and mutuality built around a set of shared values and visions. And yet open platforms are also important vehicles for aggregating and sharing the most prized elements of a culture.

One digital project which does succeed in creating a space for participation around a shared set of values is **HowlRound**,[14] a self-styled theater commons dedicated to the proposition that theater is for everyone. Instead of begging for crumbs from the formal, hierarchical, market-driven universe – while compromising their artistic vision in the process – HowlRound wanted to reinvent nonprofit theater as a commons. Its starting point is that "artists should have more say in how the American theater is run" – which, in the eyes of HowlRound commoners, is theater that is authentic, innovative, community-connected and accessible to all. Its website, video streaming, online journal, conferences and web archives are now a hub for all sorts of American community and nonprofit theater people.

This, in the end, could be the best way to describe how digital arts have built successful patterns of commoning: through artists' sensibilities they have enacted transgressive actions which have created liberated spaces in the culture, most of the time in open defiance of intellectual property-based economies, in order to enable inclusive participation and free access and use of artworks, knowledge, information and data. The forms of commons enacted in the digital arts varies – from subversive situationist performances through institutional collaborations and everything in-between – but each reflects the active presence of shared values and ethical approaches, enabled by a shift in the perception of the possible. This creates a perception of the possibility of a "new normalcy field," which is among the most important elements that the arts can make – a continuous redefinition of what the world is, and of what it means to live in a society.

Salvatore Iaconesi *(Italy) is a robotic engineer, philosopher, artist and hacker. He teaches Digital Design and Near Future Design at La Sapienza University in Rome and at ISIA School of Design in Florence. He is the founder of Art is Open Source, an international network of researchers, artists and designers dedicated to working across arts and sciences to gain better understandings, and to expose them to the transformations of human beings and their societies with the advent of ubiquitous technologies. Iaconesi is a TED Fellow, Eisenhower Fellow and Yale World Fellow. He is also an independent expert for the European Commission in the areas of ICT [information and communications technologies], design, open data and P2P models for education and production.*

---

14 | http://howlround.com/about

Remix The Commons:
An Evolving Intercultural Space for Commoning

By *Alain Ambrosi and Frédéric Sultan*

"How would you define commons in one sentence?" "Remix The Commons"[1] saw the light of day in 2010 when we shouldered a video camera and started asking many people from different social and educational backgrounds, cultures, and with various ranges of experiences this "little" question. And we received quite spontaneous answers, as if everyone had a profound insight about the concept. Of course, the responses are as diverse as the people we interviewed, and although always incomplete, each answer contributes a building block that dovetails with other building blocks to form a definition of commons.

A well-known Canadian environmental expert told us at a commons conference in Berlin in 2010, "Commons are an attitude." A year later, a Senegalese participant of the World Social Forum in Dakar stated, "Commons are what we all share," and yet another said, "They are something I feel committed to."

In May of the same year, one of 15,000 demonstrators on Plaça de Catalunya in Barcelona used the image "a soccer team (that plays well!)." At a 2012 Earth Day rally in Montreal, Canada, one participant responded, "Commons are what belongs to everybody," and the next one added, "commons are what belong to nobody." During the Rio+20 Conference in Brazil, an Ecuadorian government minister talked with us about commons and *buen vivir*.[2]

At a commons festival in Helsinki in 2014, we had to reformulate the question so that we could pose it to a Lithuanian dancer: "How would you dance commons?" Her spontaneous response: "But that's impossible alone!" Then she invited the interviewer to participate in a "moving" commons definition.

---

1 | In the original French "RemixBiensComuns."

2 | On the connection between commons and the Andean concept of *buen vivir*, see "*El buen vivir* and the commons: A conversation between Gustavo Soto Santiesteban and Silke Helfrich" in David Bollier and Silke Helfrich, eds., *The Wealth of the Commons. A World Beyond Market and State* (Levellers Press, 2012), pp. 277-281, available at http://wealthofthecommons.org/essay/el-buen-vivir-and-commons-conversation-between-gustavo-soto-santiesteban-and-silke-helfrich.

By August 2014, our collection had grown to more than 100 brief definitions in thirty-five languages from about forty countries. Naturally, we also
included definitions that are more precise and elaborate and that reflect the
long practical experience of commoners and the research findings of commons
theorists.

All of these substantial and diverse answers to our simple question illustrate
both the universal character of commons and the difficulties arising when one
tries to both delineate such a definition while keeping it open and dynamic.
And they made clear to us that an intercultural perspective is indispensible.

Remix The Commons considers itself a place of intercultural encounters,
sharing, and joint production of video and audio documents, short films, and
media and cultural projects about commons. The initiative is supported by an
international collective of people and organizations convinced that collecting,
exchanging, and remixing stories and images about commons is an active,
sociable way to get to know the concept and make it one's own.

Remix The Commons itself works like a commons. The work is organized
around an open and collaborative platform which is a website that enables
storage, exchange, cataloguing, remixing, and dissemination of multimedia
documents. We also always find places and opportunities that make it easier
to jointly develop concepts for media productions and to design and breathe
life into them. In other words, an intercultural, free and collaborative catalog of
multimedia documents on the commons is available to commons practitioners,
academics, educators and cultural activists. They can use it and enrich it with
contributions of their own.

The history of the project is closely linked to the emergence of the commons in the current societal debate and in the proposals put forward by social
movements since the crisis of 2008. An initial draft was presented at the
International Commons Conference (ICC)[3] in November 2010. It was based
on the video documentary of the interdisciplinary meeting on "Science and
Democracy" that had kicked off the World Social Forum in Belém in Amazonia
in January 2009. The commons had a place at the final session of this World
Social Forum, and the manifesto "Reclaim the Commons"[4] was published in
several languages on this occasion. That same year, the academic community
saw Elinor Ostrom awarded the Nobel Peace Prize for her work on the commons, and the documentary "RIP: A Remix Manifesto,"[5] which pays tribute

---

3 | http://www.boell.de/en/node/277225. See also http://p2pfoundation. net/
International_Commons_Conference_-_2010.

4 | http: //bienscommuns.org

5 | A documentary by Brett Gaylor on critical reflection of copyright in the era of digital
technologies. The film accompanies the mashup artist Girl Talk, shows interviews with, among
others, the then Brazilian Minister of Culture and world-famous artist Gilberto Gil as well as

to humanity's creativity as the outcome of collaborative creation in space and time, circulated in the independent cultural scene.

Remix The Commons is maintaining its close connections with the international meetings of social movements, and this colors the development and realization of our concrete projects. We participated in the discussions and documentation of the commons at the World Social Forums in Dakar in 2011 and in Tunis in 2013, at the Summit of the Peoples at Rio+20 in Rio de Janeiro, and at the Afropixel Festival in Senegal in 2012. We were part of international meetings on social and solidarity-based economic activity as well as open festivals à la Villes en Biens Communs 2013 in the French-speaking countries and Pixelache in Finland in May 2014. We are now concentrating on events that bring out the art of commoning[6] and contribute to the development of an international network of commons schools.

Our roughly 300 videos have been viewed more than 15,000 times and are constantly reproduced, disseminated and used for many purposes. The videos consist of interviews, case studies, reports about concrete projects and activities, reflections upon them, and theoretical and political statements on commons. The videos also consist of a large collection of individual commons definitions in the respondents' native languages, as mentioned at the beginning of this piece. That collection is currently being mapped on an online map that locates each speaker and his or her statement on a world map, which is very helpful for workshops and educational events about discovering the diversity of commons. Such workshops – for example, "commons breakfasts" or "commons summer schools" – illustrate how collaborative knowledge production works in open networks.

As the commons have grown in visibility on the international stage of culture and politics, Remix The Commons is constantly adapting to the rapid shifts in sociopolitical contexts. This is evidence of the agenda-setting power of a movement that is still very heterogeneous, but is increasingly influencing socioeconomic and political agendas. Amidst this veritable cultural revolution, Remix The Commons is committed to using the Internet to shape new cultural interest in commoning and to develop new methods of communicating these trends.

This requires that we meet numerous challenges, for example, countering "commons-washing," which seeks to trivialize the innovative and revolutionary character of commons. We must also confront incessant enclosures of information and natural resources, and devise joint strategies, collaborations and means

---

US law professor Lawrence Lessig, one of the founders of Creative Commons. Available at: https://www.nfb.ca/film/rip_a_remix_manifesto.

6 | See http://www.aohmontreal.org/en

of communication for commoners in the cultural arts and trades, education, and communication in order to share knowledge. In George Pór's words, "We have to raise our culture of communication to the level of commoning" – and make it as intercultural, user-friendly, participatory and inviting as possible.

Alain Ambrosi *(Canada) is a designer and producer of intercultural projects, independent researcher, author, videographer and producer of the Remix The Commons Project. His long involvement in improbable international collaborations has led him to aspire to the status of utopian's apprentice.*

Frédéric Sultan *(France) is a French commons activist. He co-facilitates the Francophone Network for the Commons, launched in 2012, and helps people create or claim commons in their communities through cultural and educational actions.*

AS220 of Providence, Rhode Island:
A Commons of, by and for Artists

By David Bollier

Nearly everyone knows AS220 as one of the most happening places in Providence, Rhode Island. The "AS" stands for "Artists' Space"; 220 was the initial address of the distressed building that it originally occupied in 1985. AS220 is now an incredibly vital cultural commons that offers everything: rehearsal spaces, poetry slams, live music and dance performances. Figure drawing, affordable artist studios, a Fab Lab and a print shop. Public access to specialized art equipment, cheap apartments for struggling artists, and more.

While AS220 has all sorts of interactions with businesses, government and philanthropy, it is really an unheralded model of a commons for producing and enjoying the arts. It is financially self-sustaining, independently managed and organically connected as a co-producer with various artistic communities.

AS220's success as an arts commons stems from its fierce vision of what authentic art should be – and its resourcefulness in acquiring three large buildings in a once-troubled section of Providence's downtown. The buildings, consisting of more than 100,000 square feet, enables AS200 to generate its own revenue through storefront leases while providing huge amounts of affordable downtown building space to host artistic enterprises. After more than three decades, AS200, with a budget of more than $3 million and 60 employees, is a self-confident, financially secure overdog for the underdog – artists.

AS220's ownership of downtown real estate may be the financial secret of its longevity, but it could not have survived without its deep commitment to the arts as a commons. This originated in a manifesto written by three artists, Steven Emma, Martha Dempster and Umberto Crenca, in 1982, in which they called on artists to "stop harboring false hopes and come to terms with the present deteriorating situation in the arts." They urged resistance to all attempts by the state, philanthropy, arts agencies and award systems to control or manipulate artists. "Art has been removed from being an integral part of our society and has been relegated to mere processes which have lead to the production of dry, academic, pedantic, superficial, mechanical and mass-produced works of art devoid of all integrity, honesty and meaning...." the artists wrote. They demanded that art be "allowed to flourish unhampered because art is one of the last areas of culture where humanity defines his spiritual nature."

Crenca, better known as "Bert," founded AS220 shortly thereafter and is its artistic director today. He is mostly a painter, but now spends much of his time overseeing the diverse artistic enterprises hosted by AS200 and the real-estate management that sustains this rare empire of vernacular arts and culture. The organization has always been primarily a group effort, however, achieved through the talents of people like Lucie Searle, who manages all of the real estate projects, Managing Director Aaron Peterman, helpful board members, a staff of dozens, and active collaboration with the state and city governments and the business community.

Calling AS200 a nonprofit organization fails to capture its real achievement or inner logic. While it is legally chartered and managed as a nonprofit organization, its deep cultural commitment is to protect the integrity of artistic freedom and creativity. It has refused to become a supplicant desperately trying to please stuffy donors or produce preconceived notions of "what sells" in artistic markets. It realizes that its core mission is not to make money in the marketplace, satisfy foundation program officers, spur urban development or please politicians. Its goal is to help artists to be artists, and to nourish artistic communities as artistic communities.

Walk around the three AS200 buildings and the fruits of this ethic can be seen everywhere. Fascinating and fantastic artworks abound: prints, murals and paintings on the walls, music wafting through the hallways, and posters advertising upcoming exhibitions and performances. AS200 is no genteel, sanitized haven for the fine arts as some society matron might conceive of them. It is a place where both amateur and accomplished photographers, poets, dancers, painters, musicians, hip-hop artists and digital fabricators with 3D printers can be themselves. The AS220 vibe is funky, experimental, transcendent, offbeat and startling.

A conspicuous example is the colorful eighty-foot mural that adorns the side of one of AS220's buildings. It was designed by Shepard Fairey, the street artist famous for the iconic poster used by Barack Obama's 2008 presidential campaign. Fairey contributed the mural for next to nothing because of a favor that Bert had shown him years earlier when Fairey had been an unknown artist.

The commitment to local art is shown by AS220's policy toward rock bands. In the mid-1980s, it was extremely hard for local bands playing original music to get booked at any Providence clubs. Only large, national touring acts or local bands doing cover songs could get gigs. In response, AS220 instituted a "no covers" policy requiring that any song performed in its performance spaces must be in the public domain or licensed under a Creative Commons license. In explaining its policy, AS220 notes, "We believe that corporate control of music hurts our culture as a whole and hinders the free development of artistic expression. The 'blanket licensing' scheme enforced by the major music licensing corporations....helps fund major labels that perpetuate homogenized music, marginalize independent labels, engage in pay-for-play radio and undermine musicians."

The "no covers" policy was later carried over to a special electronic jukebox in its bar and grill that contained only original songs; no cover tunes allowed. This enabled AS200 to avoid paying any fees to performance-licensing bodies such as BMI because the jukebox *doesn't have* any industry-produced music. (The jukebox was retired when the staff person who created the jukebox left AS220, leaving no one else with the skills to maintain or fix it.)

This organization's approach to exhibition spaces is also locally minded and inclusivist. Its mission statement declares, "Exhibitions and performances in the forum will be unjuried, uncensored and open to the general public. Our facilities and services are available to all artists who need a space to exhibit or perform from traditional sources because of financial or other limitations." The main gallery space at AS220 is routinely booked for years in advance. (But there are other gallery spaces as well.)

Several things are striking about AS220 as a cultural commons: its sheer scale, its diversity of arts activities, and its self-confidence. The place is no platform for co-branding or crypto-marketing. It does not treat people as consumers ("exit through the gift shop"), but as human beings. It doesn't pander. These institutional traits stem from AS220's commitment to be an enterprise for and run by artists.

Authentic art is always compelling, which helps explain why AS220 has ended up becoming a highly effective catalyst of economic development in downtown Providence. Its projects directly serve more than 90,000 people every year. Thanks to such traffic and the kinds of people attracted to AS220's music, galleries, performances and classes, the neighborhood has improved over the years. Nearby buildings that were once beset by drug dealers and prostitutes have been renovated. A fancy hotel has moved in. Other new businesses have arisen.

Beyond its artistic integrity and inclusiveness, AS220 has flourished by showing ingenuity in acquiring and renovating buildings. "Its venture into real estate was spurred on by recognizing that it needed to own its own space if it was going to be viable and sustainable," said David Dvorchak, communications director of AS220. After losing its lease in one building and facing rising rents at another (due in part to its own positive effects on the neighborhood), AS220 was determined to be the master of its own destiny. Its programming needs also required more space.

So in 1992 it acquired a 21,000 square foot, three-floor building on Empire Street that was almost totally abandoned, and within one year had complied with all building codes and filled all of its space with artists, including a dance company and theater. According to an AS220 history, "This was accomplished with a very limited budget of $1.2 million, tremendous community support, highly imaginative fundraising and most significantly, tons of sweat equity."

Today the building is home to a community darkroom, twenty studios for artists, a space for youth artists, three gallery spaces, a music performance space with eight to ten events per week. AS220 hosts monthly "Geek Dinners" as a networking event for local tech leaders. It also hosts monthly sewing circles, a monthly comedy series and figure drawing sessions and panel discussions. On the street level, a bar, restaurant and barber shop lease retail space from AS220.

Over the years, the organization acquired two other mixed-use buildings and renovated them to provide space for even more artistic projects. Its real estate holdings are now worth an estimated $25 million.

It is tempting for outsiders to regard the success of AS220 as simply a story of savvy real estate investment and development. But if AS220 were market-driven, its vision would have quickly curdled into commercial, sentimental pap. The organization was fortunate to have leaders that saw its real estate assets as ways to maintain its own independent vision, unbeholden to investors, politicians eager for conventional development or imperious donors.

What a concept: empowering artists by giving them space and autonomy, and building a hosting infrastructure with real equity assets, good leadership and a commitment to commoning. The revenue from its infrastructure helps lower the overhead costs for creating challenging art – and this in turn makes it easier to build a culture of artistic authenticity. The autonomy forces artists to take responsibility for themselves, both economically and artistically. And by helping isolated artists discover their voices and develop robust peer communities, the people of Providence have acquired real alternatives to the vacuous pop entertainment that the culture industries peddle. They have a place where they can become artists themselves.

David Bollier *(US) is an author, activist, blogger and scholar of the commons. He is cofounder of the Commons Strategies Group and the author of* Think Like a Commoner *and co-editor of* The Wealth of the Commons, *among other books.*

The Ten Principles of Burning Man

Burning Man is a self-organized week-long gathering of more than 60,000 an-archists, technologists, artists, urban designers and other creative people that has convened in the desolate Nevada desert since 1995. It is notable for its massive and daring artworks, flamboyant performances and radical self-expression, and for its influence on many "real world" activities during the rest of the year – urban design, humanitarian relief and more – through its Burners Without Borders affiliate. As a "pop-up city" of considerable size, Burning Man participants have had to develop a distinct cultural ethic for successfully managing such a huge instant-city.[1] Founder Larry Harvey came up with "The Ten Principles of Burning Man" in 2004 to serve as guidelines for the community. Burning Man organizers regard them as the key to their success as a self-governing community of radical individualists.

1. **Radical Inclusion.** Anyone may be a part of Burning Man. We welcome and respect the stranger. No prerequisites exist for participation in our community.

2. **Gifting.** Burning Man is devoted to acts of gift giving. The value of a gift is unconditional. Gifting does not contemplate a return or an exchange for something of equal value.

3. **Decommodification.** In order to preserve the spirit of gifting, our community seeks to create social environments that are unmediated by commercial sponsorships, transactions, or advertising. We stand ready to protect our culture from such exploitation. We resist the substitution of consumption for participatory experience.

4. **Radical Self-reliance.** Burning Man encourages the individual to discover, exercise and rely on his or her inner resources.

5. **Radical Self-expression.** Radical self-expression arises from the unique gifts of the individual. No one other than the individual or a collaborating

---

1 | See Peter Hirshberg, "Burning Man: The Pop-Up City of Self-Governing Individualists," in John H. Clippinger and David Bollier, *From Bitcoin to Burning Man and Beyond: The Quest for Identity and Autonomy in a Digital Society* (ID3 & Off the Common Books, 2014, available at https://idcubed.org/chapter-5-burning-man-pop-city-self-governing-individualists.

group can determine its content. It is offered as a gift to others. In this spirit, the giver should respect the rights and liberties of the recipient.

6. **Communal Effort.** Our community values creative cooperation and collaboration. We strive to produce, promote and protect social networks, public spaces, works of art, and methods of communication that support such interaction.

7. **Civic Responsibility.** We value civil society. Community members who organize events should assume responsibility for public welfare and endeavor to communicate civic responsibilities to participants. They must also assume responsibility for conducting events in accordance with local, state and federal laws.

8. **Leaving No Trace.** Our community respects the environment. We are committed to leaving no physical trace of our activities wherever we gather. We clean up after ourselves and endeavor, whenever possible, to leave such places in a better state than when we found them.

9. **Participation.** Our community is committed to a radically participatory ethic. We believe that transformative change, whether in the individual or in society, can occur only through the medium of deeply personal participation. We achieve being through doing. Everyone is invited to work. Everyone is invited to play. We make the world real through actions that open the heart.

10. **Immediacy.** Immediate experience is, in many ways, the most important touchstone of value in our culture. We seek to overcome barriers that stand between us and a recognition of our inner selves, the reality of those around us, participation in society, and contact with a natural world exceeding human powers. No idea can substitute for this experience.

COLLABORATIVE TECHNOLOGY COMMONS

"The major difference between a thing that might go wrong and a thing that cannot possibly go wrong is that when a thing that cannot possibly go wrong goes wrong it usually turns out to be impossible to get at and repair."

Douglas Adams, *The Hitchhiker's Guide to the Galaxy*

Farm Hack: A Commons for Agricultural Innovation

By Dorn Cox

In 2011, a community of farmers, designers, developers, engineers, architects, roboticists and open source thinkers came together in Boston, Massachusetts, to explore a simple yet radical idea – that great improvements in agriculture could be achieved by reducing barriers to knowledge exchange. They were convinced that transforming agricultural technology into a commons would result in a more adaptive, open and resilient food system, one that would reflect the values not just of the grower but of the larger community as well. The path toward a more distributed and just agricultural and economic system, this gathering of people concluded, would come into being through the collective development of new working prototypes and universal access to a constantly improving repository of best ideas and practices.

Thus began Farm Hack, an ambitious volunteer project that brought together the seemingly disparate cultures of technologists and agrarians. The start of Farm Hack came with an offer from M.I.T. to host a teaching event that could connect engineers with farmers' needs. The National Young Farmers Coalition had just started a blog called "Farm Hack" and launched the first program, followed closely by more events held in partnership with GreenStart and Greenhorns agrarian networks and maker/hacker networks.

The Farm Hack community quickly expanded through online and in-person social networks across the east and west coasts of North America. Within three years, it became a user-driven, collaborative community of ideas and tools with many thousands of active participants. Hundreds of thousands of visitors from every continent were soon contributing tens of thousands of hours to the platform. Farm Hack has become a rapidly growing repository of agricultural knowledge, containing scores of open source designs and documentation for farming technologies and practices. In effect, Farm Hack is an emergent, networked culture of collaborative problem-solving.

Hacking has been defined as the art of coming up with clever solutions to tricky problems by modifying something in extraordinary ways to make it more useful. Hacking also means rejecting the norms of consumer culture, and imagining ways to modify, improvise, and create new, accessible, custom solutions for particular problems. Not surprisingly, both hacker and maker culture are a natural fit for the sustainable agricultural movement. Both cultures formed in response to ongoing, hegemonic attempts to control users' access to basic technologies and other resources. Both arose from a realization that open access to knowledge is the best strategy to counter dominant industry interests. This has long been an inherent part of agriculture in general, and a critical part of sustainable agriculture in particular. On most farms, identifying a problem, thinking of a solution, testing that solution and assessing its efficacy while thinking of the next iteration is a daily practice.

Within its first year, the Farm Hack website featured documentation for over 100 innovative agricultural tools. They ranged from manufacturing instructions for newly created farm-built hardware such as garlic planters, to the remanufacturing of an "extinct" farm-scale oat huller. The community contributed designs for greenhouse automation and sensor networks and business models for organic egg enterprises.

The power of open source exchange is illustrated by the quick pace and diversity of modifications and improvements made to tools on Farm Hack. One of the first greenhouse monitoring projects was turned into an electric-fence alert system, which quickly evolved into an automation and data logging system, which then spun into businesses selling kits. An organic no-till roller made open source by the Rodale Institute in Pennsylvania was quickly modified in New Hampshire, then Quebec, and then France and Germany; the latest versions being built in New York are based on German and French improvements made six months earlier. In this production model, inventors increasingly may not be able to predict the ultimate use of their tools, as the ultimate use will be collaborative and emergent.

Despite being an all-volunteer organization, operating without a budget until 2014, Farm Hack partnered with dozens of organizations, universities, open source and maker communities in the US and Europe to expand the network. In addition to providing an online forum and repository for the community's knowledge and tools, Farm Hack has hosted in-person and online events to document and improve tools, foster sharing and build skills. In these events, the group carries on the agrarian club tradition of mixing participatory education with lots of good eating, drinking and socializing.

With growth of the community came greater financial burdens of hosting and guiding the conversations and idea exchanges. The community also needed to evolve in its role from organizing and planning, to facilitating, guiding and recruiting new contributors. Initial funding to support these needs came indirectly through the founding partner organization budgets supplemented by contributions from community volunteers. It was three years before the first general grant support was secured. A university extension program wrote a grant on behalf of Farm Hack to document, measure and extend the reach of USDA Sustainable Agriculture Research and Education (SARE) funded projects.

To manage the challenges of growth and expansion in its third year, the Farm Hack network adopted a set of ten principles; participants wanted to maintain the representative open agrarian values of the network as they interacted with established power structures. The collaborative and flexible structure of the organization, and rapidly evolving tools for remote collaboration, became important ways for the organization to evolve while remaining representative and emergent. For example, a collaborative tool currently in development, by the community and for the community, is a best practices template for open source project contracting to help navigate the tension of having paid and volunteer efforts working side by side. The template is exploring the awarding of bounties and other rewards for commercial contracts, special recognition to volunteer efforts, and pooled payments or retainers on a project-by-project basis for participants.

Open Source Software Converges with Agrarianism

Farm Hack has blended a rich set of old and new traditions – the Enlightenment salon ideals of the eighteenth century and those of the open source software movement. Both believe that the natural state of knowledge is to be free. Farm Hack also looks to the Physiocratic worldview of nature-governance articulated by Quesnay, Jefferson, Locke and Franklin, who regarded the productivity of the soil, and the education of the populace to provide for their own livelihood, as necessary for liberty and the health of a culture. From this perspective, agricultural production is the root of sustainable civilization. It is not just an occupation, but a foundation for the shared cultural values of a healthy society.

Well before the Internet, Enlightenment thinkers pioneered the idea of crowdsourcing with their community-created *Encyclopedie: A Systematic Dictionary of Sciences, Arts and Crafts*, first published in 1751 and written with over 2,250 contributors. More than 250 years later, the contemporary open source software community is pioneering the development of networked tools, such as wikis, forums and collaborative documents, all of which facilitate social cooperation and trust. Building on these models of voluntary reciprocity, Farm Hack implicitly challenges the prevailing norms of conventional agricultural economics and research. It challenges not only what types of questions are asked in agricultural research and development, but also who asks the questions, the types of tools that are produced, and how they are financed.

The Farm Hack community believes *that the tools, seeds, and techniques used in agriculture should both reflect and benefit those who intend to use them, not just those intent on selling them*. Through an ongoing amateur inquiry that connects farmers with other farmers, designers, engineers, and thinkers, Farm Hack has embraced, woven together, and expanded upon preindustrial and modern hacker/maker ideals. Its open, social collaboration creates the potential for every farm to become a research farm, and every neighbor to be a manufacturer, drawing upon a global library of skills and designs.

An Alternative Template for Agriculture

By documenting, sharing, and improving farm tools and associated knowledge, Farm Hack is not just framing agriculture as a shared foundational economic activity. It illustrates an alternative template for local manufacturing and provides greater citizen choice, control and local self-determination. The primary limiting factor in agriculture shifts from the (negative) extraction of scarce natural resources to the (positive) expansion of skills and systems understanding of all participants. Farmers are able to learn better ways of harnessing the complex biogeochemical flows of atmospheric carbon, water, and nitrogen into productive and resilient agroecosystems. The emphasis shifts from efficient extraction of resources to skilled regeneration of resources using all available knowledge.[1] The focus becomes improving rather than diminishing the natural resource base.

By contrast, the broken proprietary model for conventional farm research, development, and commerce is deeply committed to various biological "dead ends" such as sterile seeds and breeds, and chemicals that destroy the soil. It relies on closed technologies that often cannot be shared, adapted or reproduced, and that often introduce artificial inefficiencies whose chief purpose is to protect a proprietary business model. To move beyond this perspective is to recognize that there is potentially more innovation happening on farms every day than in all universities and industry

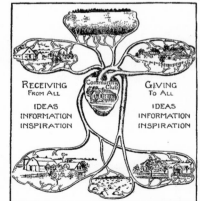

FIG. 281. The community club, rightly organized and conducted, can serve as the heart of the community through and by which a stream of inspiration and encouragement is sent to every member.

Encyclopedia of Practical Farm Knowledge, published by Sears and Roebuck, 1918. Available at archive.org.

1 | See essay by Eryka Styger on the System for Rice Intensification (SRI), on pp. 108-112.

labs combined. Yet, because of a scarcity mindset, very little on-farm innovation is typically shared beyond the farm gate or developed on a wider scale. By challenging this mindset and building trust across geography and promoting nontraditional interdisciplinary community interactions, a culture of knowledge sharing and innovation can emerge. That's essentially what has allowed Farm Hack to grow in such a rapid, robust manner. Its participants realize that farms have less need to compete with each other than with global economic and climatic forces.

Another contribution to the rapid expansion of Farm Hack's community has been its reliance on the network structures and administrative tools pioneered by other open source communities, including Drupal (blogging software), Wikipedia (wiki collaboration), Open Layers (Java script software), and Apache (server software). It has been able to build trust, grow, and adapt while making its own unique contributions back to the commons. Another important tool used by Farm Hack is the Collective Impact Framework, a structured approach that allows organizations to use collaborative tools to form common agendas and adopt shared measurement tools, mutually reinforcing activities and continuous communication among diverse sorts of participants.[2] This Framework has been adopted in order to enable the community to identify and reduce overlapping, duplicative efforts, and to build upon the cumulative achievements of the broader open source community.

Farm Hack's online platform is a prototype for implementing this framework in the context of open source agriculture practices. Just as symbiosis is as powerful an influence as competition in nature, Farm Hack believes that it can help turn the conventional agricultural research and development system on its head. By creating tools and social norms that reward, refine, test and evaluate collaborative production, it is possible to stimulate rapid, reliable community knowledge and innovation.

In 1726, Jonathan Swift famously wrote, "Whoever could make two ears of corn or two blades of grass to grow upon a spot of ground where only one grew before, would deserve better of mankind and do more essential service to his country than the whole race of politicians put together." The quote embodies Farm Hack's partial but expanding achievement: By creating open source repositories of knowledge and technologies, it is bypassing the dominant political and economic power structures behind industrial agriculture. Farm Hack is shifting the balance from those who derive their power through the control of scarce resources and knowledge to those who mix their creative skills with nature in order to create abundance.

---

2 | John Kania and Mark Kramer, Collective Impact, *Stanford Social Innovation Review*, Issue 73 (Winter 2011), available at http://www.ssireview.org/articles/entry/collective_impact.

Dorn Cox *is a farmer in Lee, New Hampshire (US), where he continues to develop and refine open source agricultural research and development systems to improve farm productivity and resilience. He is a founding member of Farm Hack, the New England Farmers' Union, GreenStart, the Great Bay Grain Cooperative, and the Oyster River Biofuel Initiative. He has a B.S. from Cornell University and a PhD from the University of New Hampshire.*

Arduino and the Open Hardware Revolution

By *Julio Sanchez Onofre*

The revolution in collaboration that started with free and open source software in the 1990s has moved on to an even larger frontier, open source computer hardware. At the forefront of this revolution is Arduino, a global commons of designers and producers of microprocessing boards that can be freely copied, shared and produced. Because the boards are low-cost yet highly versatile, Arduino technology lies at the heart of such cutting-edge projects as the Kikai, an Argentinian 3D printer that created an arm prosthesis at a cost of less than $50, unmanned aerial vehicles (drones) and a nanosatellite platform (for satellites that weigh less than 10 kilograms) known as ArduSat.

Arduino was the brainchild of Italian Massimo Banzi and his colleagues David Cuartielles, Tom Igoe, Gianluca Martino and David Mellis. Originally an educational project for students, the Arduino collaborators in 2005 expanded the venture as a way to make cheap but sophisticated computer boards more available to the open source community. It is also seen as a way to bring artists, engineers and creatives together to find new ways of using technologies for the greater good.

Since its founding, Arduino has become part of the larger worldwide movement of open innovation, technology and creativity. The reference designs for Arduino hardware are licensed under a Creative Commons Attribution-ShareAlike license, and the source code for its software is licensed under the GNU General Public License (GPL). While Arduino technologies can be freely copied by anyone, Arduino has created its own line of self-produced "Arduino At Heart" branded products. The official product sales support the Arduino enterprise while still allowing competitors to make "clones" at cheaper prices.

Arduino is officially a business whose chief asset is its trademark, the name Arduino and its logo. Anyone can use the Arduino designs for free, but if they wish to sell them under the Arduino name, they must pay to use the trademark. Besides licensing the Arduino trademark, the firm produces its own line of Arduino-branded devices. Paradoxically, the ability of others to freely use Arduino designs does not undermine sales of the Arduino-branded products because this openness has merely enlarged the market for Arduino technology while boosting trust in the Arduino brand compared to cheap knock-offs. Massimo Banzi's design firm also makes money creating customized Arduino-based products.

Besides computer boards, Arduino offers its own self-designed kits, materials for wearable technologies and 3D printers, tools, books, manuals and workshops. There is now a vast global community of Arduino users, with many regional networks and groups devoted to special types of microprocessing boards.

Arduino enthusiasts and companies see the open hardware platform as an important infrastructure for building a new economy based on collaboration and collective knowledge. While Arduino systems can perform familiar tasks such as remote control of a car or the doors of a house, they also have great potential as the core of cheap but powerful smartphones; systems to collect, purify and distribute water in marginal areas; and systems that can generate clean, renewable energies.

But achieving the full potential of Arduino-based open platforms will require more focused public education about its capabilities. In this regard, Arduino – and other open technologies – still have a long way to go. While many governments have created digital agendas to boost their economic and social development through information technologies, few public schools have recognized the great promise of open source principles by teaching students about open source coding or open hardware development.

Even in countries like Spain that require young people to take programming courses in school, the government and schools have ignored the open source revolution, preferring to make agreements with big companies such as Microsoft, Oracle and SAP to teach students about (and buy) their proprietary software. The same blindness affects government procurement of information technology, where governments tend to buy technology from the big firms instead of encouraging or requiring open source technologies that could improve their domestic research and development.

There are some bright signs, however. There is now a global robotics competition for students called RoboCup, which hosts a number of competitions using Arduino kits in the creation and programming of machines. Some big companies like Intel and MediaTek with their own proprietary microprocessors have decided to design products that can communicate with Arduino platforms, thus expanding their usefulness and appeal.

The unmet challenge is for governments to put Arduino and other open source technology at the core of their development agenda and educational programs. The benefits would be especially significant for smaller, emerging economies which otherwise depend on expensive foreign technologies with restrictive intellectual property terms.

Arduino is that rare commons that has successfully combined stable social collaboration with market sales. As an open technology, it has significantly advanced innovation in computer hardware while enhancing economic opportunities for millions of people.

Julio Sanchez Onofre *(Mexico) is a tech journalist for the newspaper* El Economista *in Mexico City.*

The Growth of Open Design and Production

By Tristan Copley-Smith

It's difficult not to appreciate the unfolding potential of the open source movement. The concept is beautifully simple: "When we share together, we are
stronger." It taps into a broad range of human sensibilities, from the practical,
to the creative, abstract and even spiritual. This is a relatively young and apoliti-
cal movement, whose nature and intention are to collaborate. As a result, it
attracts a diverse mix of developers, tinkerers and users eager to experiment
with new ways to meet familiar challenges, from software to hardware, from
data collection to government, from environmental activism to agriculture.

But open source projects tend to exist in somewhat of a paradox. They
are propelled by extremely skilled and well-educated people, but the financial
compensation for projects is often low or nonexistent. Even though they are
sometimes used by communities of many thousands or millions of people,
the output of projects is often expected to be free of charge. While open source
methods are responsible for many profound innovations in our lives, most
societies have yet to understand or appreciate the meaning of "open source."

If open source projects do not always make money, what propels them to
continue growing? How does an open source project get started, and how does
it evolve? What are some things to embrace and avoid when working on open
source projects? The following noteworthy initiatives offer some instructive
answers.

Open Source Ecology

The ambitious goal of this small organization is to develop fifty open source
industrial machines that can be used to build a civilization from scratch. This
includes everything from bread ovens to ploughs and 3D printers. In each case,
the idea is to make useful tools out of cheap, accessible parts and share how
to do so on the Internet.

OSE is the brainchild of Marcin Jakubowski, whose original mission to start
a sustainable farm was hindered by the fact that proprietary agricultural tools

are expensive and difficult to repair. To help his farm and his wallet, Marcin began building his own tools like a tractor and a press to make compressed earth bricks useful for building. He documented his work rigorously on a blog and YouTube channel, catching the attention of other tinkerers who began contributing time and resources to support Marcin's efforts.

Marcin's goals evolved quickly from developing a farm, to inventing an ecosystem of modular open source tools called the Global Village Construction Set. The project aims to supply anyone with designs and tutorials to build their own machines, thus enabling people to become more autonomous as farmers and less dependent on industrial producers. Adopting radical open principles, Marcin began documenting his work on a public wiki, including theories, detailed plans, and even financial information. A successful crowdfunding campaign and a supporter subscription system helped fund early development, but for the first few years, the project was often financially precarious.

After building a productive following of hundreds, several successful prototypes, and a community living space onsite, OSE's proof of concept seemed to be emerging. The project received several lucrative grants to continue development, and an invitation to speak at the celebrated TED conference.

Although OSE was attracting a lot of attention, its infrastructure, both in terms of governance and the physical space at his farm in Maysville, Missouri, was not able to deal with the flow of people wanting to collaborate. Marcin's brainchild needed other brains to grow, but living conditions were poor and he lacked basic skills in community management. After several fallouts with OSE collaborators, he became seen as unappreciative of the community and the organization evolved into a one-man show where credit for the work of many seemed to be going only to Marcin. This was obviously harmful to the collaborative environment, and led to an unhealthy, disempowering dynamic within the community. OSE needed structural stability, but with the team constantly changing, the project began to suffer. However, the vision and goals were compelling enough that money and people continued to pour in.

Currently OSE seems to be stabilizing, but the lofty ambition of developing fifty Global Village Construction Set machines still seems far off. This is the story of a project that evolved organically, but perhaps too fast and without stable governance. With a focus on machines and not on people, the vision has suffered, but there remains great potential for its future, should these issues be resolved.

Perhaps OSE's most profound achievement is the influence it has had, which reaches far beyond the thirty acres of farmland in Missouri. In pioneering open agriculture and engineering with such ambition, new shoots are rising to adopt and spread these methods, as seen in robust collaborative projects such as Farm Hack (see pp. 145 - 150).

WikiHouse & Open Desk

As recent graduates in 2011, architects Alastair Parvin and Nicholas Ierodiaconou found themselves hired by an innovative London design practice called Zero Zero Architecture. Both shared a passion for open design and were given the opportunity to experiment with their ideas.

While exploring CNC [computer numerical control] fabrication, the two architects and their team used automated printer-like technology to design files that could be fabricated from plywood, which in turn allowed them to develop a construction system made of large, flat wooden pieces. These pieces could be assembled quickly and with unskilled labor to make the structural shell of a home.

After publishing the Wikihouse construction system as open source files available to anyone, the project encouraged others to adapt its creations for different environments. They released a manifesto outlining the core principles of the organization, and invited people to sign up in their own individual chapters. This allowed a collaborative network to form without compromising anybody's autonomy. The community, twenty chapters strong in 2015, is able to connect with the project without requiring management from Wikihouse and its small team. Wikihouse is now registering as a nonprofit foundation, using grants and pre-made kits to fund development.

Open Desk is an online platform developed by Alastair and Nicolas for selling furniture that is designed and produced through open source principles. Although structured as a for-profit company, Open Desk is a collaborative community of designers, makers and buyers. Designers propose furniture designs that can be made using the same plywood fabrication technique used by Wikihouse. The proposed designs are voted upon by the community, and if demand is high, they are added to the official product line. Users have the choice to either download the files and make the product themselves (for a small fee) or buy a prefabricated product though the site. Orders are assigned to a fabrication facility local to the client, and revenues are split three ways between the designer, the manufacturer and Open Desk.

The system is not entirely open source because use of the designs must be purchased (albeit only for a small amount) and they come with licenses that prohibit commercial reproduction of the products (although noncommercial, personal copying is allowed). This has been done in an effort to protect and incentivize Open Desk's designer community.

Open Desk and Wikihouse were intentionally founded on open principles in an effort to foster communities of designers and users. By changing the traditional model of design and manufacturing, they are allowing for global collaboration linked to local production, slowly inverting the standard "producer to consumer" production model to something more participatory, innovative and accessible.

Public Lab

Public Lab is an organization that creates cheap, open source hardware and software tools to help citizens document and investigate environmental problems together. It began in 2005 when a group of loosely affiliated activists set off to Louisiana in the wake of the BP oil spill. There, they began documenting coastal oil pollution using low-tech kite mapping techniques. Over the past few years, the organization has grown into an international community whose members are working to understand their natural environments with greater scientific precision, and to hold to account those responsible for damaging them.

Public Lab describes itself as a community supported by a nonprofit organization. Through their store, they sell low-cost open source monitoring kits, which are legally considered donations. This allows them to secure foundation grants while also earning revenues from sales of their monitoring products. As an open source hardware developer, Public Lab provides guides on how anyone can make their tools at home for free.

Public Lab's real value is not in the tools, but what is done with them. The balloon mapping kit, for example, allows users to create exceptionally high-resolution aerial photographs (to map oil pollution or coastal erosion) for exceptionally low costs. The images can then be uploaded to Public Lab's website where users can stitch them together using open source software, and where the maps can be analyzed by the community. The resulting images (if good enough) are even scraped by Google and added to their mapping services. (This is an example of how open-platform corporations often appropriate things from the commons for their own profit-making purposes, and why many digital commoners are now turning to Commons-Based Reciprocity Licenses – see pp. 225-226.)

Public Lab is a fine example of how a dedicated community with useful open-source tools can populate a digital commons with valuable data. The website is heavily editable in the manner of a large public wiki/notebook hybrid so that everyone's work is documented. The community is motivated by a curiosity or concern, and the Public Lab website gives people access to the tools and information they need to help investigate. The resulting discoveries can be documented, shared and used to lobby for political change.

Jeff Warren, one of Public Lab's cofounders, calls this "speaking the language of power." Rather than petitioning for change through traditional means of protest, which may or may not be respected by authorities, the hard scientific data produced by the Public Labs community gives it powerful factual justifications to launch official investigations.

Public Lab is a project which evolved organically from a group of activists who realized they were developing an important new form of community activism based on the power of open data, open hardware and open source software to influence government policymaking and enforcement.

Conclusion

What motivates these projects to contribute to our commons? I think the answers vary a great deal. Open Source Ecology is driven by a desire for autonomy in farming. Wikihouse wants to lower barriers to custom design. Open Desk is expanding creative designs and localized production. Public Lab is pioneering new forms of effective, scientific activism.

What connects these diverse efforts is an acknowledgment of the increased power of our work when it is combined, and not limited by proprietary restrictions. There is another salient force here: a recognition that business as usual often serves to separate us from what is really important and cannot create the scale or speed of change needed to address the multitude of challenges we face in the modern world.

Tristan Copley-Smith *(US) is a documentary filmmaker and communications expert aiming to empower positive disruptions in technology and society. He has worked with organizations like Wikileaks and Open Source Ecology to build supportive followings and communities, and is cofounder of the Open Source Beehives citizen science project.*

On Openness, Commons & Unconditional Basic Work

An Interview with Architect Van Bo Le-Mentzel

Van Bo Le-Mentzel has invented all kinds of useful things, among others, do-it-yourself blueprints for furniture and tiny houses. He has become known for social DIY projects such as "Hartz IV[1] Möbel," the Unreal Estate House,[2] and the One-Square-Meter House.[3] He is now transferring the concept of these projects – unconditional freedom to use something for one's own purposes – to his own life and that of his family with a campaign called #dScholarship that he started in 2014. "There's a genius in every one of us. Wake it up!" Following an interview about #dScholarship, with which the architect, always in a good mood, would like to have "the crowd" finance a whole year of his work, a journalist said, "In a way, the campaign is looking for patrons in a world in which counts and feudal lords no longer exist and people are not under the patronage of others. The Protestant, democratic version of indulgent permanent financial support. Or in Van Bo's words: a first step toward an unconditional basic income."[4]

And the exciting thing is: this basic income does not depend on the state or the anonymity of contributors, but on the recipient's relationship to them. A commons-based basic income, as it were – one that decouples the goods and services rendered from those received in return. One that grants freedom and

---

1 | The Hartz concept is a set of recommendations submitted by a commission on reforms to the German labor market in 2002. Named after the head of the commission, Peter Hartz, then Volkswagen's personnel director, they went on to become part of the German government's Agenda 2010 series of reforms, known as Hartz I - Hartz IV. The latter was implemented on January 1, 2005, and brought together the former program of unemployment benefits for long-term unemployed (Arbeitslosenhilfe) and welfare benefits (Sozialhilfe), leaving them both at approximately the lower level of the former Sozialhilfe. A single person may get up to €391 per month, plus financial assistance with housing and health care, if the claimant meets eligibility requirements that take into account savings, life insurance, and the income of spouse or partner. The heavily criticized Hartz IV system includes a strict regime of control and sanctions, which has made the term "Hartz IV" a synonym for the working and non-working poor and is used as a prefix in multiple contexts.

2 | The Unreal Estate House is a statement against gentrification – a wooden living unit installed on parking lots – where you can live without paying rent.

3 | The One-Square-Meter House measures one meter times one meter and can be flipped on one side to turn the house into a sleeping cabin.

4 | http://motherboard.vice.com/de/read/crowdfunding-fuer-ein-demokratisches-stipendium

enables Van Bo Le-Mentzel to do "basic work." What makes a young man with an infant in a baby sling place half his life in the hands of a community, after coming up with Open Design, a fair-trade shoe project (Kharma Chacks), and after many other stages of his work? Is that courageous or crazy?

Helfrich: Van Bo – a designer of designer furniture or "things that serve their purpose"?

Le-Mentzel: Designer furniture.

Helfrich: Sounds ambitious...and expensive. But you are an architect, and you have designed "Hartz IV Möbel." Could you tell me more?

Le-Mentzel: They're instructions for building furniture that is usually very expensive. I looked to the Bauhaus for inspiration, guided by the idea: every human being should be able to afford a "Bauhaus chair."

Helfrich: How did you develop this idea?

Le-Mentzel: I often wonder what kind of furniture – or other things – would be created if one weren't always asking the question about how they can be sold. I think that many goods would be different. They would be less harmful to the environment and to the workers producing them. And they wouldn't make so many false promises to consumers. Good goods, as it were. (laughs)

Helfrich: Like "Hartz IV Möbel."

Le-Mentzel: Exactly.

Helfrich: What is the role of the open design idea here? You point out that people are explicitly encouraged to imitate Hartz IV Möbel and the Karma Chakhs as well as the do-it-yourself house projects. Other creative professionals have a different perspective.

Le-Mentzel: I believe in open source and support the open design idea, but I have invented other terms for it – terms that presuppose openness without using the word.

Helfrich: For example?

Van Bo Le-Mentzel on his Kreuzberg 36 Chair.

Le-Mentzel: Beta business. What I mean is quickly establishing something new using open source tools, or starting a business together with the crowd, without any aspirations for success: blogs, free platforms like strikingly[5] or etherpads,[6] or the campaign platform avaaz[7] can help here.

Helfrich: That doesn't necessarily mean that it benefits everybody.

Le-Mentzel: That's right, but it presupposes openness, and that changes everything. It simply doesn't make sense any more to have fixed structures, a logo, a business plan, corporate goals, patents, or mechanisms for monitoring success if you're constantly in the beta phase. I'm not interested in being an alpha male in a beta business, either, because it's about moving the idea forward, not about anyone's sensitivities.

Helfrich: Is that merely theory or also practice?

Le-Mentzel: Betahaus – probably Germany's best-known coworking space in Berlin – is very practical. The same is true of bookcrossing[8] or Wikipedia, but also of Hartz IV Möbel. That's more than just theory. The interesting thing, though, is: no competitors, no squabbling, no strict hierarchy, and – very importantly – no bureaucracy or administration. It's completely open-ended. People who work like this have an entirely different attitude about things....

Helfrich:...and they have to do without being able to plan. That means insecurity, but also more space for coincidence.

Le-Mentzel: That's another term I like to use: random design. Intentionally designing for coincidence, with the subtext that failure is desired, too. It isn't about getting from A to B in the most direct way possible. Business plans are A-to-B systems, schools and universities are A-to-B systems. It isn't even about B any more, but about C. About whatever emerges and that can't be planned. Vespucci and Columbus finding the ocean route to America were A-to-C processes. The same is true of many inventions, for example, 3M's sticky notes or Google Maps. They came into being more or less by chance during people's free time. Industry doesn't like random, because random can't be scaled up and can't grow. For instance, you can't invent sticky notes twice. In particular, you can't assign someone the task of inventing them. In a sense, it invents itself. That's exactly why I love randomness!

---

5 | A website that makes it possible for anyone to design a sophisticated website of their own. https://www.strikingly.com

6 | Editors' note: An Etherpad enables people to work together on texts directly on the Internet, with or without registration. Several people can write simultaneously; everyone sees everything in real time. Changes can be saved, and in this way, the writing process can be made transparent.

7 | https://secure.avaaz.org/en

8 | A book tagging and sharing website, at http://www.bookcrossing.com

Helfrich: Who owns Hartz IV Möbel and the Unreal Estate House? Or more generally: who owns what comes out of the open design process?

Le-Mentzel: In any case, it isn't mine. I'm not convinced of the idea of "intellectual property." Knowledge must be free: ideas, compositions, texts, tattoos, designs, colors, words, sculptures, jokes, blueprints, YouTube videos. Incidentally, my favorites are the TEDTalks by Sir Ken Robinson and Hans Rosling and videos that teach you how to build rocket stoves. When knowledge is free, the best for all emerges. Parallel to that, we have to create systems in which inventors, movers and shakers, musicians, and other knowledge creators – and not just superstars like Damien Hirst – can live in dignity.

Helfrich: Many creative professionals and designers use precisely the same argument – namely, being able to live a life of dignity – to defend the idea of intellectual property and copyright (which is based on it). They are supposed to protect creators from imitation.

Le-Mentzel: Yes, that's an important point, at least in the current system that is oriented entirely toward competition and exploitation of ideas and knowledge. But who says that it has to be like that forever? What I fundamentally call into question is this: Let's take Damien Hirst as an example, one of the most successful (and richest) contemporary artists. He makes millions by transforming a real shark into a work of art. I doubt he would have had the same effect with a duck or a Golden Retriever. I think that neither journalists nor poets nor composers could write or produce without being inspired by what they see out in the world, and without the support of others.

What do they pay those who inspire them? Or the sources that nourish them and on which their work is based? Do journalists pay the people they interview? Do photographers pay the objects they shoot – landscapes, skylines, buildings or people – by which they earn money? The bridges of Venice have inspired so many poets and composers. These bridges really need (financial) support. I don't know any creative artists who would donate a part of their profits to repairing bridges.

In addition, the problem with the current systems [of intellectual property] is that they are all performance-oriented. They benefit some – usually well-known artists – but not others.

Helfrich: You're raising the question of fairness.

Le-Mentzel: Yes, of course. The two of us are now conducting an interview for your book.

Helfrich: For *our* book. After all, a lot of people are involved in it.

Le-Mentzel: Which is almost always the case. Now one could ask: Who is actually working for whom? Who owns what is said here? Who has to bill whom? Do I bill you? Or do you bill me? Of course, one can try to deal with this in a contract. That would make the lawyers happy. But one can also try to promote the idea, in this case, the book's success. And when it's about that, I'm not concerned with the question about who owns this interview. It will be published under a Creative Commons license, which guarantees that others can use our ideas and develop them further. I think that's a good idea, and that's why I'm happy to make a contribution. Who knows what our readers will make out of it.

Erich Fromm [the German social psychologist and philosopher] even wrote that some mindful readers actually understand a book better than the author himself. From that perspective, preserving vested rights is extremely backward. Incidentally, I took that as encouragement to republish his classic book *To Have or To Be* with references to current affairs.

Helfrich: You also published *Ayşe Langstrumpf*, a Berlin-Kreuzberg version of Pippi Longstocking [in German: Pippi Langstrumpf], right in time for the seventieth birthday of the world's most famous brat. In your version, Bloom and Thunder-Karlsson are gay, and the monkey Mr. Nilsson is called Mr. Nguyen. So that's what emerges if you're not interested in selling something – *Ayşe Langstrumpf* is not for sale. You simply publish instructions on the Internet how everyone can print their own version of Pippi, based on the original text.

Le-Mentzel: That's exactly how I would publish the book by Erich Fromm. A summary of his life's work. I'll leave out copyrighted parts of the text and add links to the missing passages on the Internet. The book is completed only through interaction with the readers. To me, that has something symbolic. Economic activity begins with people working together. And that's why it's easy to outwit systems that are based solely on money and the notion of individual property. You only have to remove their foundation, and then they're not worth anything at all.

Helfrich: Simple? That's certainly arguable!

Le-Mentzel: You just have to take the price tag off of capitalism – copyright is one of its catalysts – and then trademark protection, copyright and commercial principles are irrelevant. Neither the Hartz IV Möbel nor the Karma Chakhs have price tags. You can't buy them. If you want to have them, you have to make them yourself or manufacture them in a community. Another word for this is "prosumption." Vitra, IKEA, Converse, or publishers' classic strategies are powerless in countering prosumption.

Helfrich: And now you want to get rid of your own price tag?

The One-Square-Meter-House. Photo © by Daniela Gellner.

Le-Mentzel: Yes. That's why I started my own #dScholarship campaign to secure my livelihood for a year. The basic idea is to decouple services from pay. Then I'm not forced to work for money, but can do meaningful things instead. I call that karma work.

I used to work freelance and charged 250 euros per day for illustrations. I have an exclusive contract with a design agency, and it charges its clients four to five times that amount. Everything in the world, not just goods, but also raw materials, people, time, even stellar constellations have been given a price tag. That drives us crazy. Of course, I have already thought about how it can be that other colleagues get twice as much or more for a service that I perform at least as well. The CEOs of Volkswagen and the Techniker Krankenkasse[9] earn a lot more money than Chancellor Angela Merkel. Do these people achieve and work so much more?

Helfrich: Your pitch was for people you don't know to practically give you 375 euros per week, or 1,500 euros per month. Why?

Le-Mentzel: Because that's roughly what I need to live. To be honest, that's the amount, roughly speaking, that my wife and I agreed on. Right now, my steady job pays a lot more than 1,500 euros. I promised her that I would do the #dScholarship project only if amounts to at least 1,500 euros a month.

---

9 | Translator's note: A German health insurance fund.

She already got a fright when I told her that I'd like to give up the privileges of having a steady job with permanent contract. Next year, I won't be billing anyone. I will simply work, without money and without thinking about profit. I call it unconditional basic work.[10]

Helfrich: If everyone simply does what they feel like doing, who will do the dirty work?

Le-Mentzel: Hm, good question. Who's doing the dirty work today? People who need money to survive are paid a small amount, and then they'll do anything: cleaning toilets, digging for ore in mines, picking cotton, doing sex work. Women in India have recently begun working as surrogate mothers for Western career women. To me, that isn't an alternative because these people aren't doing these things voluntarily.

I'm curious to see whether I'll perform unpleasant work next year voluntarily. It's all a question of attitude. When we packed shoes for Karma Chakhs, I declared this tedious work an event: a packaging party with music and a buffet. In Seoul, people voluntarily cleaned the streets when the soccer World Cup public viewing events were over. It was a huge happening. Cultural work is fun. Forced labor isn't. So we should think carefully about how unpleasant work can be made into something cultural. And for the rest, we should develop machines. Open source ones, of course.

Helfrich: And what do the people who support you get in return?

Le-Mentzel: That's the crazy and revolutionary thing. My givers give me the money unconditionally. They get nothing in return. They're all giver types. They know what their benefit is. They know the universal secret of giver networking.

Helfrich: Okay...I'm all ears.

Le-Mentzel: Whoever gives unconditionally will also receive in return. And twice or three times the amount. Givers benefit from giving. It sounds paradoxical, but it's true. My Startnext profile lists precisely how much money I have already given to other crowdfunding campaigns: precisely 6,000 euros. Now I'll get 18,000 euros back. That's exactly three times what I've given. You don't necessarily get it back from the people you helped yourself. That's why it's a universal secret.

Helfrich: What would you do if someone tried to co-opt you?

Le-Mentzel: A foundation offered me 1,000 euros, a businesswoman even offered me 12,000 euros. It's clear that those were calculated proposals. At

---

10 | Translator's note: Van Bo Le-Mentzel coined this term with reference to the unconditional basic income, a proposed alternative to welfare payments.

first, I was delighted, but then I turned them down. The businesswoman can give at most one-quarter of the entire #dScholarship, or 4,500 euros, just like everyone else. And I don't accept money from businesses, only from private individuals. After all, it's about "waking up the genius in me" and not about making me dependent on just a few givers. The genius comes out when there's no pressure. There's a genius in every one of us. In most people, however, the last time it's sighted is when they start first grade. That's why I'm also trying to transfer this #dScholarship to others.

Helfrich: You say of yourself, "I'm a giver." And that the #dScholarship is also supposed to help you contact other givers. Does that mean that we can succeed in putting this other form of economic activity into practice if we all become givers?

Le-Mentzel: I think that we are born as givers. That is because life itself, conception, birth, education works only if someone (parents and many others) give unconditionally. That leaves its mark on us. And we are all team players by nature. Birth is always a team effort. It's only school, grades, competition, pressure, sitting still, obedience, curricula that transform us into beings thinking in terms of economics.

Helfrich: You love controversy...

Le-Mentzel: At least I provoke it. There are two camps. Some people say I'm an egoistic oddball. The others think I'm a selfless, courageous pioneer. Somehow, there isn't anything in between.

Helfrich: So, what are you?

Le-Mentzel: A human being.

Fab Lab St. Pauli in Hamburg

By Astrid Lorenzen

The Fab Lab Fabulous St. Pauli, founded in 2011 by an interdisciplinary, tech-savvy group, is located right in the middle of one of Hamburg's liveliest neighborhoods. It's one of roughly thirty Fab Labs in German-speaking countries. An open workshop, it offers anyone interested access to the usual wood- and metalworking tools (milling machine, punching machine, drill) as well as computer-controlled devices such as 3D printers and a laser cutter. Anyone can produce everyday objects such as small toys or jewelry, prototypes or spare parts, independent of public or private service providers, for the Fab Lab is organized as a registered association and is financed exclusively by membership dues.

Turning a profit is not its goal, as stated in the international Fab Lab Charter drafted in 2007 by Fab Lab founder Neil Gershenfeld. Another important point mentioned in the Charter is open access to the tools. We make that possible every Thursday on Open Lab Day.

The visitors and users of the Lab include school and university students who want to make models for educational projects, engineers and natural scientists who want to find out more about the technologies, and tinkerers who make new things or fix old ones. The Lab also offers neighborhood youths the opportunity to find out about technical jobs. And there are a lot of creative people in the area who use the Fab Lab to build prototypes or models. They experiment with printing materials, print sample copies, or develop a finger for a robot, for example.

The same conditions, developed by the association, apply for everyone: Whoever puts their hands on something takes on the responsibility for it. That works well in general. People only pay for the materials they use. The time other people take to support them is free of charge. However, the Lab does not offer people the opportunity to use its space and machines for ongoing commercial purposes. New knowledge gained in the Lab is supposed to be transferred back to the community.

Fabulous St. Pauli considers itself a networking node, a place where people and neighborhood initiatives active in societally relevant areas such as energy (KEBAP energy bunker), waste, traffic, or urban gardening, can jointly use the technologies they need in order to develop individual and locally adapted solutions for very different problems. For example, a freight bicycle was developed in collaboration with the urban gardening project *Gartendeck*.

Fabulous St. Pauli intentionally grapples with the role of production in the city of today, thereby taking part in the discussion about a new form of development of the city in the Hamburg network *Recht auf Stadt* ("right to the city"). Yet collaboration goes beyond Hamburg and Germany: the global Fab Lab network also provides ongoing exchange of ideas and software as well as visitors from Fab Labs around the world.

The Fab Lab thrives on exchange and on its members' willingness to share their time and their knowledge about using and repairing the machines, in addition to paying their monthly fee. We started out with seven members and have about thirty today, up to eight of whom are most active. Specifically repairing machines is important, because some of our machines were donated by industry and require regular maintenance. Most machines, however, are provided by the members themselves. Individuals' motives differ: some are most interested in talking shop and trying things out, others in carrying out their own projects. Still others believe in offering access to new production processes to as many people as possible.

Right now, it would be difficult to run the Lab without the opportunity to rent space cheaply in a self-governed center. That is why municipal policy is very important if self-organized spaces for experimentation are to succeed. With the resources and the knowledge of the active members, who have backgrounds in computer science, electrical engineering, design, journalism, and numerous other areas, and with an affordable, centrally located venue, a Fab Lab like the one in St. Pauli has the potential to take production into its own hands – at a high technological level. Here, at Fabulous, people can try out and implement individual, innovative products and alternative concepts, independent of market conditions. If supported by public funding, then this potential can develop, as the example of Fabrica, a do-it-yourself project to make cellphones, showed in the autumn of 2014.

The Fabrica Project

The Fab Lab hosted the project "Fabrica—Technology meets art meets DIY culture" from August 13 to September 7, 2014. 3D printing and laser cutting are fun, without question. But this is about more than maker-hype gimmicks. Fabulous St. Pauli also wants to be able to make complex devices that everybody uses – for example, cellphones, the consumer product *par excellence*. They are short-lived, status-laden, produced under questionable circumstances, and locked in black boxes so that consumers have to rely on whatever the manufacturers put inside.

We set up a temporary, decentralized high-tech cellphone factory with a view of the city's harbor. We wanted participants to be able to produce 5 percent of St. Pauli's cellphone demand themselves. The circuit boards were assembled and soldered following the template of an open source phone, the Arduino-based DIY phone developed by David Mellis (M.I.T.). A high-end laser cutter and various 3D printers were available for producing individually designed casings. We wanted to find out what people wanted in terms of future, decentralized production of their high-tech products, and also how nonexperts could participate in producing simple cellphones at a professional level. Finally, we wanted to experiment with the freedom to use components from fair production in our cellphones, gradually increasing their share in each device. What we had in mind was "Fair IT." A lot of people were interested in understanding the products they carry around every day, and even designing and assembling them.

Astrid Lorenzen *(Germany) has been an independent industrial designer for sustainable product design since graduating from the Muthesius University in Kiel. She has been active in the FabLab St. Pauli since 2012. In addition, she is involved in the Sustainable Design Center and in the Working Group Fair IT.*

OpenSPIM: A High-Tech Commons for Research and Education

By Jacques Paysan

Scientific and medical research critically depends on being able to observe very small structures that are invisible to the naked eye. Neuroscientists seeking to find cures for injury-induced paralysis, for example, may want to be able to observe the axons of regenerating neurons on coated nanowires. This kind of experiment often requires extremely high-powered and sophisticated microscopy. While demand for high-end, innovative microscopes is significant, there is only a handful of companies in the world that manufacture such instruments. One reason for this is certainly that the production of high-quality optical equipment in larger scales requires levels of precision and sophistication that are difficult to reproduce. It seems that the smaller the object being observed, the bigger the problems become. The effect of any aberration in the optical system is enlarged along with the desired information. A disturbance of only one thousandth of a millimeter can lead to visible abnormalities. Thus, even with detailed technical knowledge, the manufacturing of high-precision microscopes remains an enormous challenge.

It is therefore a remarkable development that this high-tech domain has recently been invaded by a project, OpenSPIM, in which researchers and engineers are cooperating on all levels under a regime of commons principles. The projects show the power and effectiveness of networked cooperation at the highest levels of scientific research and precision manufacturing.

SPIM is an acronym for "Selective Plane Illumination Microscopy," which is also known by a more intuitive name, light-sheet microscopy. SPIM differs from other microscopic technologies in how it illuminates observed objects. In conventional instruments, the sample is usually illuminated along the optical axis,[1] either through a lens *underneath* the object or through the microscope objective in the viewing direction. In light-sheet microscopy, however, the il-

---

[1] | The optical axis represents a straight line from object to image through the centers of symmetry of all lenses of a microscope.

lumination light traverses the object like a thin sheet from one side to the other, perpendicular to the optical axis and not from below or above. This unusual configuration gave rise to the technology's name – selective plane illumination.

This illumination technique was first developed in the beginning of the twentieth century by Richard Zsigmondy and Henry Siedentopf in their so-called Ultramicroscope. When Zsigmondy was awarded the Nobel Prize for Chemistry in 1925, Professor Söderbaum described this instrument quite nicely in his presentation speech:

> The idea originated from Zsigmondy and was developed in detail by him in cooperation with Siedentopf, an able optician with the firm of Zeiss. The principle of this instrument is briefly that the intensely illuminated object, the solution to be examined, is observed by means of a microscope from the side, i.e., vertically to the axis of the incident light beam. In this way it is possible to differentiate between particles of such small size that they could not be observed under an ordinary microscope, just as the dust particles suspended in the air in our rooms, which are invisible under ordinary conditions, sometimes become visible when the sun's rays shine through the window in a definite direction in relation to the observer.[2]

For understanding the significance of the SPIM principle, it might be helpful to recall some basics of light microscopy. In transmitted light microscopy, nontransparent structures become visible because they absorb light and therefore appear darker. In contrast, reflected light microscopy makes objects visible through a reflection or scattering of light, which makes them brighter. Fluorescence microscopy can be regarded as a special case of reflection microscopy, where the illumination light is used to cause observable fluorescence of specific structures in the specimen under investigation. Fluorescence microscopy has grown dramatically in recent decades, especially with the invention of a variety of new biogenic dyes (e.g., Green Fluorescent Protein (GFP) and its spectral variants), letting researchers now observe processes in living cells, in whole organs, or even in intact living organisms.

The problem with this very powerful approach is the high photon density that is required to cause fluorescence in the sample. During an observation, the sample is exposed to such intense excitation light that dye molecules soon bleach away and the observed samples are damaged or even die. This damage gets particularly severe because the excitation light beam has to travel along the optical axis through the entire specimen; in three-dimensional objects, this destructive flood of photons needs to be repeated for each level of observation.

By using an elegant trick, however, SPIM revolutionizes fluorescence microscopy exactly at this point: The microscope is able to illuminate precisely

---

2 | http://www.nobelprize.org/nobel_prizes/chemistry/laureates/1925/press.html

and exclusively the plane of the object that one wishes to observe. Other parts of the object remain untouched by the intense ray of excitation light, and the points above or below the plane of focus are not even elevated to a glow.

Thus SPIM can actually produce an "optical sectioning" enlargement of thick three-dimensional samples "on the fly." This is something that traditional "confocal microscopy" can accomplish only through an elaborate point scanning procedure. SPIM avoids this process by illuminating the entire plane of focus, which can now be imaged in milliseconds using high-speed digital cameras. This process also makes it possible to gently observe intact living samples for hours or even days and from multiple perspectives, without destroying the sample. Consequently, SPIM is typically used to observe insect larvae, zebra-fish embryos, the growth of tumors, organoids, and regenerating nerve fibers. Because of its versatility, SPIM has quickly attracted a growing community of enthusiastic followers among researchers interested in noninvasive microscopy on living organisms.

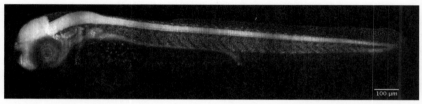

Figure 1: An OpenSPIM image of a 48-hour-old, living zebrafish embryo, in which certain structures like the nervous system and cell nuclei are labeled with the Green Fluorescent Protein (GFP). Photo by openSPIM, under a Creative Commons BY-SA 3.0 license, via http://openspim.org/Welcome_to_the_openSPIM_Wiki.

Globally, an estimated 100 SPIM systems had been "homebuilt" by this community before ZEISS introduced the first commercial light-sheet micro-scope in October 2012. Two years later, members of the SPIM community and curious researchers from all over the world converged on Barcelona to attend the First International Lightsheet Fluorescence Microscopy conference, where they eagerly exchanged experiences and ideas for applying and improving SPIM.

Among the speakers at this conference were Ernst Stelzer and Jan Huisken, who are regarded as key inventors of modern SPIM. The reanimation of the old oblique illumination principle known as SPIM in modern research drew upon academic research in which Huisken was significantly involved as a graduate student in Ernst Stelzer's lab, at the renowned European Molecular Biology Laboratory (EMBL) in Heidelberg, Germany. As a postdoctoral researcher at the University of California, San Francisco, Huisken later continued to adapt SPIM to biological applications before returning to Germany to start his own research group at the Max Planck Institute for Molecular Cell Biology and

Genetics in Dresden (Germany), where he obviously inspired a creative nucleus for further SPIM-related ideas.

It was there where the next breakthrough occurred: "OpenSPIM started, once upon time, at the institute's canteen where they dreamed up SPIM in a suitcase," as his colleague Pavel Tomancak tweeted. "It actually exists!" Supported by the international Human Frontiers Scientific Program, the idea was first developed through a wiki,[3] which, consistent with the basic ideas of the commons, was published under a Copyleft (CC BY-SA 3.0) license.[4] In this wiki, the interested researcher can find a precise list of necessary parts, assembly instructions and video tutorials describing how to build a ready-to-use OpenSPIM instrument in less than one hour, in fourteen discrete steps. From the beginning, the OpenSPIM project committed itself to the principles of open hardware and open software (Pitrone et al. 2013).

Figure 2: OpenSPIM in a suitcase. The camera is seen in the bottom left, the sample chamber in the upper left corner. The box in the center is the laser light-source from which the blue laser is reflected by several mirrors into the sample chamber. Photo by OpenSPIM, under Creative Commons BY-SA license, 3.0, via http://openspim.org/ Gallery.

To fully appreciate the achievements of this project, one needs to understand the complex and challenging data-analysis requirements of SPIM microscopy. Depending on its configuration, a SPIM microscope can generate more than 100 megabytes of data per second, potentially during the course of an entire week, all of which must be handled, stored, analyzed and rendered. Simply storing such vast quantities of data, where individual datasets can comprise

3 | www.openspim.org

4 | Editors' note: See the essay on alternative licensing in this book on pp. 223-226.

up to several terabytes, is prohibitively costly for normal computing systems. The system often requires specific software that can work on cloud computing platforms, i.e., high-performance computing on distributed computer networks. Performing such computation at acceptable speeds on individual machines is highly problematic.

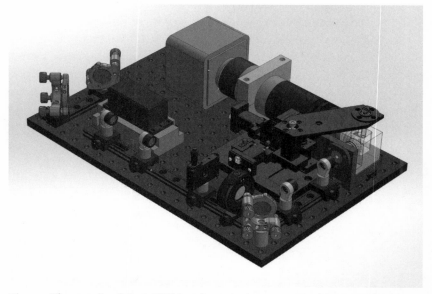

Figure 3: The completed OpenSPIM as shown in the open assembly instruction. Photo by OpenSPIM, under a Creative Commons BY-SA license 3.0, via http://openspim.org/ Step_by_step_assembly.

Fortunately, the open structure of OpenSPIM provides a solid groundwork for mastering these challenges. For example, OpenSPIM uses only open source Arduino electronic components, and the operation of the system is controlled by the free software µManager. Data analysis and rendering are managed by specialized plugins to the software package Fiji/ImageJ, which is an extensive open source software project for the analysis and processing of scientific image data. Much of the work for those plugins has come from a team led by Pavel Tomancak, a congenial Czech who works at the Max Planck Institute in Dresden. This group is not only renowned as a driving force of the OpenSPIM project, but is highly respected for its missionary zeal in hosting workshops, conferences and academic collaborations to share its knowledge within the growing OpenSPIM community.

Since OpenSPIM started two years ago, the design plans for seven OpenSPIM instruments worldwide have been posted on the wiki.[5] The number of unpublished systems is unknown, but more systems are certainly under construction. In any case, global interest in OpenSPIM is remarkable. Curious students and researchers use every possible opportunity to get familiar with the system. Experts say that OpenSPIM does not reach the standards of commercially available or sophisticated home-built systems, but due to its significantly lower costs it is widely accessible to a much broader user community. This makes applications possible, for example, for universities in countries that have very limited research budgets and that could not afford other SPIM systems. Because OpenSPIM is open to all and not proprietary, its usefulness in educational contexts is unparalleled. Anyone who buys a light-sheet microscope can use it, but anyone who assembles an OpenSPIM will also understand it! Beyond that, OpenSPIM also makes research more transparent. Experimental results can be understood and reproduced more easily by peers and thus be verified, which contributes to the integrity and authentication of research results.

Whether OpenSPIM will continue to expand or simply remain an exciting niche project remains to be seen. This will substantially depend on whether or not the SPIM community – including the DIY builders and commercial providers – recognize the value of their ongoing commoning and perceive themselves as active commoners. Will they let their project modifications and improvements continue to flow back to the community and contribute to its flourishing?

If the OpenSPIM platform is seen simply as a launch pad for the proprietary "secret projects" of either businesses or solitary nerds, it is quite possible the project will collapse. The community of OpenSPIM enthusiasts might at some point become exhausted by their voluntary efforts, and find it easier to retreat to their own private, proprietary interests. But there are reasons for optimism: In January 2015, the highly respected journal *Nature Methods*, which is affiliated with the prominent interdisciplinary scientific journal *Nature*, selected light-sheet microscopy as "Method of the Year 2014."[6] This will provide strong tailwinds for the OpenSPIM endeavor!

Jacques Paysan *(Germany) holds a PhD in Neurobiology, and is a commons fan and SPIM Expert. He lives in the Jagst-Valley in Baden-Württemberg.*

---

5 | OpenSPIM should not be confused with customized SPIM systems. Some of the latter are specialized and highly sophisticated systems constructed for specific applications. The costs of such systems can reach hundreds of thousands of euros. In contrast, the costs of an OpenSPIM, depending on its configuration, are typically in the range of tens of thousand euros.

6 | http://www.nature.com/nmeth/journal/v12/n1/full/nmeth.3251.html

CODE AND KNOWLEDGE COMMONS

"Just realized that 'open source' and 'encrypted' are the 'fair trade' and 'organic' of the software world."

Nadim Kobeissi tweet

Open Access Pioneer: The Public Library of Science

By Cameron Neylon

In the 1990s, Nobel Laureate Harold Varmus, a genetic researcher, and California scientists Patrick Brown and Michael Eisen were increasingly frustrated by the many constraints on sharing scientific research. Even though academic researchers were the ones performing difficult, costly scientific research and peer reviews of it – much of it financed by taxpayers – commercial journal publishers have usually demanded the copyrights for published results. This has enabled them to charge subscription fees that are often unaffordable to libraries and to impose legal restrictions on people's ability to access, copy and share research articles. Subscription costs have been rising at above inflation rates for over a decade and American universities now spend more than $10 billion a year on subscriptions to academic journals. Even the most wealthy institutions like Harvard University are saying this is unsustainable.[1]

In an attempt to address this problem, Varmus and his colleagues launched an online petition calling for scientists everywhere to pledge that they would no longer submit papers to journals that didn't make the full text of their papers available to all, unconditionally, either immediately or after a reasonable delay of some months. They also urged scientists to no longer subscribe to or write reviews for such journals.[2]

The response was swift and astonishing: More than 34,000 scientists from 180 nations signed the open letter. However, it soon became clear that signatories could not practically adhere to goals of the letter because there were simply too few publications that would actually provide or allow open access to their articles.

To address this gap, Varmus and other scientists inaugurated a new publishing venture known as the Public Library of Science (www.plos.org). The project's purpose was to help scientists and scholars regain control over their own research by providing "open access" publishing vehicles that would make

---

1 | http://isites.harvard.edu/icb/icb.do?keyword=k77982&tabgroupid=icb.tabgroup143448

2 | http://www.plos.org/about/plos/history

articles freely available to everyone in perpetuity. The original authors retain copyright and license the articles to the world under a Creative Commons Attribution license to enable free re-use, sharing and distribution. (See essay on the Creative Commons licenses on pp. 223–225.) This project built off the earlier development of Biomed Central, a publishing venture with similar aims led by London-based entrepreneur Vitek Tracz, and by other innovative publisher efforts of the late 1990s.

Since its founding in 2003, PLOS has grown from a community protest into the world's largest publisher of free to read, immediately accessible and openly licensed scholarly content. The first PLOS journal, *PLOS Biology*, published its first articles in late 2003, rapidly establishing a reputation for high quality articles. Over the next few years, the project launched *PLOS Medicine* and four community journals focused on research in computational biology, genetics, pathogens and neglected tropical diseases, respectively.

As these six journals grew, the founders began to step up to their original, more ambitious goal of catalyzing a transformation in scholarly communication. The next big step toward this goal was the founding of *PLOS ONE* (www. plosone.org), a new scientific journal in 2006 to cover the whole of science and pioneer a new approach for a scientific journal. For the first time there would be no artificial limits placed on the number of articles published. Submissions would be considered only on the basis of scientific validity and technical quality, not on perceived impact. Traditionally researchers have sought the prestige of publishing in the most selective journals, to the extent that the prestige of the container has become more important than the quality of the articles. This can lead to perverse incentives for both authors and editors to write and select the most sensational claims rather than provide measured evidence. *PLOS ONE* publishes every submitted paper that meets the criterion of being properly done science – a publishing strategy that made *PLOS ONE* the world's largest journal in 2010. All major publishers soon imitated the *PLOS ONE* "megajournal" model by publishing journals of broad scope that do not artificially limit the number of articles published.

Because of its larger readership and the diversity of submitted papers, *PLOS ONE* has also become a pioneer in rigorous pre-peer review validation. It conducts some of the most rigorous checks of all journals for statistical validity, ethical review and reporting guidelines.

PLOS was financed initially by charitable grants and income from philanthropic sources such as the Gordon and Betty Moore Foundation and the Bill and Melinda Gates Foundation (which are associated with the founders of the Intel Corporation and Microsoft, respectively). But it broke even for the first time in 2010 and the not-for-profit has posted a surplus in each year since.

PLOS has committed itself to a transparent approach to financial information, and so pioneered the publishing of detailed income and expense figures alongside the disclosures required by the government for nonprofits. In 2012, PLOS publishing ventures were collectively reaping over US$38 million, with a surplus of US$7 million.

Once its financial sustainability was established, the organization began to focus on new innovations in scholarly communications. One notable project has been Article Level Metrics, a toolset that provides open data to assess in great detail the impact and usage of individual papers.[3] Before this innovation, research articles were traditionally judged more by the reputation of the journal in which they appeared rather than by their own individual merits.

This initiative has had a further impact – the San Francisco Declaration on Research Assessment (DORA), which has been signed by more than 10,000 researchers and 400 organizations.[4] The 2012 statement calls on funders, institutions and other publishers to judge research articles on their own merits rather than conflating the "impact factor" of a journal (the average number of citations for an article) with the quality of a particular scientist's contribution. These ideas are changing how research is assessed and slowly but surely affecting how hiring, promotion and firing decisions are made.

More recently, PLOS has focused on ensuring that research data directly underlying published papers is made freely accessible, except where ethical of other considerations make that inappropriate. PLOS has also developed new tools for structured evaluation of published articles after publication, helping to encourage continuing evaluation of the accuracy of research.

By reimagining scientific publishing as a type of commons, PLOS has been at the vanguard of the massive shift in scholarly publishing. Access to research is increasingly more open, and not restricted or delayed – and scientific inquiry itself has become more rigorous. Equally important, PLOS has been able to provide vital advocacy and pacesetting innovation to the field, which now includes thousands of open access journals and over half a million freely licensed research articles.

Cameron Neylon *(USA) is former Advocacy Director at PLOS, a role he moved to from a career as a researcher. He has an interest in how to make the Internet more effective as a tool for science and writes and speaks regularly on scholarly communication, the design of Web-based tools for research, and the need for policy and cultural change within and around the research community.*

3 | http://article-level-metrics.plos.org
4 | https://en.wikipedia.org/wiki/San_Francisco_Declaration_on_Research_Assessment

Converting Proprietary Software into a Commons: The LibreOffice Story

By Mike Linksvayer

Since the early 1990s Microsoft has held a lucrative near-monopoly in "office suite" software for word processing, spreadsheets, slide presentations and databases. In 2013 alone, Microsoft's business division made US$16 billion profit on sales revenues of US$24 billion – an astounding upward transfer of wealth from software users to Microsoft made possible by copyright law, Microsoft secrecy about its programs, and the power of "network effects" created by widespread usage of its programs.

Microsoft used every trick in the book to lock users into a dependency on its software. One technique, for example, deliberately underdocumented the technical specifications for software, which made it impossible for non-Microsoft programs to interoperate perfectly with Microsoft Office. Because such performance is unacceptable to many industries and users, Microsoft in effect made its software noncompatible with other systems as a way to protect its market dominance and reap enormous profits.

The irony is that software developers were technically capable of using the Internet to collaborate online to produce office suite software. But this was not widely recognized until developers came together in the 1990s, working outside of large, proprietary software companies, to create Linux and the Apache Web server software. The success of these and other open source projects began to put pressure on many proprietary vendors as consumers and developers realized that they had alternatives. Even many large companies such as IBM and Intel started to see business opportunities in contributing to the development of open source software. The code might be free to everyone, but they could make money by providing technical support and service, as well as custom adaptations of the code.

Securing freedom for end-users of software has been elusive, however. Programmers regularly predicted that the next year would become "the year of the Linux desktop," in which open source office apps would become popular, but these visions never materialized.

One bright spot, however, was OpenOffice.org, a corporate-controlled word processing program that a corps of dedicated software developers improbably converted into an authentic software commons. The story begins when Sun Microsystems, a company that once was a pioneer of proto-open systems, began to feel competitive pressure from open systems like Linux. With grandiose aims of displacing Microsoft, Sun acquired a German company in 2000 and released an open source version of StarOffice called OpenOffice.org (OOo).

As a corporate-managed open source suite of office software, OOo was not really a commons. Still, OOo was a full-featured office suite that was generally interoperable (with lots of rough edges) with Microsoft's suite and thus the rest of the world. OOo provided a big incentive for users of nonfree Microsoft and Apple systems to install OOo, save money and learn about open source.[1]

But it was unclear from the start how Sun would work with outside developers and whether OOo could break Microsoft's near-monopoly. Despite Sun's relatively progressive corporate ethic, it gave itself absolute control over project governance for OOo because it wanted to produce a "shrinkwrap" product. This proved to be a big disincentive to non-Sun developers to participate in improving OOo. In response, non-Sun developers in 2002 began providing their own versions of OOo, which they included in popular distributions of Linux in preference to Sun's version. It was as if the commoners would not be thwarted in their drive to create a software commons!

Another force driving this effort forward has been Open Document Format (ODF), a major standards effort to produce an open and fully documented set of formats for office applications. The goal has been to ensure that applications from different vendors and communities could interoperate, thereby eliminating a major source of vendor lock-in. OOo was among the first applications to support ODF in 2005.

Microsoft began its own major effort to sabotage the standards process with a competing format, OOXML. It designed its software with proprietary extensions to OOXML, effectively retaining control over its formats as a tool to prevent users from turning to competing vendors.

While Microsoft succeeded in monkey-wrenching the process (see its current profits), ODF has made both technical and policy progress that will enhance its prospects, such as an authentic interoperability among different programs and legal mandates by various public bodies that only ODF-compliant software may be purchased.

---

1 | A technical "genealogy" of OOo can be found here: https://commons.wikimedia.org/wiki/
File:StarOffice_major_derivatives.svg

Despite Microsoft's resistance to open formats, OOo went on to become the main alternative to Microsoft, in part through the sheer attrition of proprietary vendors. But Sun, which continued to tightly control OOo development, was by the late 2000s a troubled company with its main server business in tatters due to competition from Linux. The prospects for OOo became even more perilous when the software giant Oracle acquired Sun for its server and Java technology. The writing was on the wall: OOo would not contribute to Oracle's profits, and would likely be abandoned.

This dismal prospect galvanized the OOo community to take steps to convert OOo from a declining corporate sideline into a robust software commons. They "forked" the project (started a different development pathway for the code) by creating LibreOffice. Nearly all developers outside Oracle and Sun joined the fork, and nearly all communities with Linux distributions made plans to ship LibreOffice (instead of OOo) to users. A German nonprofit, The Document Foundation, was set up to give the project permanent community-oriented governance. Although these events happened very quickly, they were possible only because the groundwork had been laid by nearly a decade of commoning and community that had developed around non-Sun OOo builds and ODF advocacy.

It was no surprise that Oracle then terminated OOo development. But rather than cooperating with the new LibreOffice, Oracle donated the OOo code to the Apache Software Foundation, a trusted nonprofit steward of open source projects. This resulted in unnecessary acrimony between supporters of LibreOffice and the new splinter project, Apache OpenOffice. However, as two open source projects working on largely the same code, there are strong incentives for the two to collaborate – so LibreOffice happily uses code from Apache Open Office.

LibreOffice has clearly won the hearts and minds of the free and open source community by making it as easy as possible for anyone to contribute – and impossible for any one entity to seize control the project's governance. As a result, LibreOffice's features, user interface and interoperability with Microsoft's quasi-proprietary formats have improved greatly since the fork. This has put it in a better competitive position relative to Microsoft Office than any of its predecessors enjoyed. Its popularity has also been fueled by large-scale adoptions such as the City of Munich, Germany, and other municipalities.

While these developments might normally accelerate LibreOffice's assault on Microsoft's near-monopoly, the shift in computing from desktop applications to the cloud and mobile devices is undercutting such gains. Google Docs, for example, has become an essential organizing tool by providing an online office suite that enables real-time collaboration on documents; it runs on Google's servers and is accessed by individual web browsers. Google Docs does not generate the same sort of near-monopoly profits as Microsoft's suite of office software, but it does entail a much more direct loss of user control: Google can change the software at any time, and access all files edited and stored online. Microsoft has also produced its own online version of Office, with the same properties as Google Docs – leaving commoners to once again play catch-up with proprietary vendors. LibreOffice Online has existed in prototype form since 2011, but only recently gained a dedicated development team. In 2016 LibreOffice Online should provide a robust alternative to reliance on corporate-controlled proprietary services for collaboration and organizing.

The pattern of a corporate steward of an open source project going bad, followed by a community revolt, plays out over and over. The database program once owned by Sun, MySQL, is the next best-known example. This commons-based, post-Oracle fork of code is known as MariaDB. The example of LibreOffice and ODF standards, however, point to the great potential of open governance, open development processes, and collaborative financing and marketing – and, indeed, the promise of public policy advocacy to provide legal support for commons-generated software. With motivations ranging from local skill development to national security, governments around the world are requiring the evaluation of open source options in software procurement (Italy), banning Windows 8 on government computers (China), and mandating support for open formats (UK).

Mike Linksvayer *(USA) serves on the boards of Software Freedom Conservancy, OpenHatch, and AcaWiki, and is a member of the Open Definition Advisory Council and the steering committee for Snowdrift.coop. From 2003 to 2012 he served as Chief Technology Officer and Vice President of Creative Commons.*

OpenCourseWare and Open Education

By Mary Lou Forward

While the world has become increasingly digital, most formal educational systems have not taken full advantage of what the new technologies can provide. The Open Education movement seeks to address this disconnect by providing easier, cheaper and faster access to all sorts of standard learning resources – books, articles, databases, videos and other curricular materials. By using open networks and open content, Open Education also lets students and teachers separated by great distances interact with each other, opening up new types of learning opportunities.

Open Education is based on three basic ideas – that education is critical for personal and societal growth; that education is, at its essence, about sharing and building on knowledge; and that digitization and the Internet have created unprecedented opportunities to improve education worldwide by enabling sharing at a global scale. At the core of Open Education is a commitment to establish a vast pool of openly shared educational resources that are accessible and adaptable to everyone. The movement also shows a deep collaborative spirit to develop educational approaches that are responsive to every learner's needs.

The Evolution of Open Education

The Big Bang of Open Education occurred when the Massachusetts Institute of Technology (M.I.T.) announced in 2001 that it would open its entire curriculum for the world. M.I.T.'s President at the time, Charles Vest, saw the potential of such sharing and asked a faculty committee to examine how M.I.T. might use the Internet to advance knowledge and educate students more effectively. The committee recommended that the university digitally publish its entire curriculum, including undergraduate and graduate courses, on the Internet.[1] M.I.T. called its initiative OpenCourseWare (OCW).

---

[1] | For more information on the evolution of OCW at M.I.T., see Cecilia d'Oliveira, Steve Carson, Kate James and Jeff Lazarus, "M.I.T. OpenCourseWare: Unlocking Knowledge, Empowering Minds," *Science*, 329(5991):525-526 (July 30, 2010). http://www.sciencemag.org/content/329/5991/525.full

The faculty concluded that, rather than start a market-based online educa-tion program, a better way to advance knowledge and support education would be to make its teaching materials accessible to anyone who wanted to see them. At the time, Creative Commons was establishing its free, standardized public licenses to allow copyright holders to authorize the sharing, re-use and modification of a copyrighted work.[2] The M.I.T. OpenCourseWare initiative decided to use the Creative Commons licenses as a way to allow users worldwide to make their own translations and share everything from physics lectures to mathematical problem-sets.

In short order, other universities, recognizing the power of open sharing to transform educational practice, began their own open courses. Soon an increasingly diverse body of openly shared educational materials, collectively called Open Educational Resources (OER), were being created by people around the world. Groups have formed to translate OER into other languages, build online repositories, and promote international cooperation.

The Opensource Opencourseware Prototype System[3] has organized more than 2,000 volunteers to translate over 3,500 open courses into Chinese. The OER Commons[4] and the Connexions project – now Open Stax College[5] – at Rice University formed two of the earliest OER repositories. To support the growing movement, the OCW Consortium[6] was formed in 2005 (changing its name to the Open Education Consortium in 2014). It has grown into a world-wide community of hundreds of higher education institutions and associated organizations committed to advancing open education.

More recently, governments around the world have begun promoting open education. Under a 2010 grant program, the US Department of Labor has provided US$2 billion in funding over four years to help institutions create or improve educational programs for training workers in high demand areas. All educational materials created under this grant program must be openly licensed,[7] making it the first major government initiative anywhere to fund OER development and use. Other governments are moving forward as well. At UNESCO in 2012, the Paris OER Declaration was formally adopted.[8] In 2013,

2 | For a good overview of the history of Creative Commons, see http://www.wired.co.uk/news/archive/2011-12/13/history-of-creative-commons. See also David Bollier, *Viral Spiral: How the Commoners Created a Digital Republic of Their Own* (New Press, 2008).

3 | In English: http://myoops.org/en. In Chinese: http://www.myoops.org/twocw

4 | http://www.oercommons.org

5 | http://cnx.org

6 | www.oerconsortium.org

7 | http://www.doleta.gov/taaccct

8 | http://www.unesco.org/new/en/communication-and-information/access-to-knowledge/open-educational-resources/what-is-the-paris-oer-declaration

the European Commission announced its Opening Up Europe program, which includes a major effort to boost use of OER.[9]

Users and Projects

When M.I.T. first announced its OpenCourseWare program, it was assumed that the chief users would be other faculty members in search of useful teaching materials. It became quickly apparent, however, that the majority of users of OER are individual learners engaged in both formal and informal learning. Based on site user surveys, it is estimated that more than 400 million people worldwide are accessing high quality educational materials every year. They use OER for a variety of reasons – to help them perform better at work; to enhance coursework studying; to help them on a specific project; etc. – producing benefits that go well beyond what was initially envisioned.[10]

With each passing year Open Education projects have proliferated and diversified. Indonesia has developed an open education strategy as a way to address its uneven educational provisioning due, in part, to the country's geography. The government aims to use OER to share educational materials, train faculty, customize resources for local circumstances, provide distance education and share expertise.[11] The Virtual University of Pakistan[12] is using OER as a way to make education available to everyone, develop hybrid education models at universities, and provide additional resources for students.

In the US, many community college students drop out of school because they cannot afford the high textbook prices. In response, Maricopa Community Colleges, the largest community college district in the country, started the Maricopa Millions project. The initiative aims to save students over US$5 million in five years by using OER instead of traditional, purchased textbooks. With the support of the Center for Teaching and Learning, faculty select appropriate OER materials for their courses and students do not need to buy expensive learning materials. In the course catalog, these courses are designated as "no cost," alerting students to the savings and raising awareness of OER as an attractive alternative.[13]

---

9 | See http://europa.eu/rapid/press-release_MEMO-13-813_en.htm and http://www.openeducationeuropa.eu.

10 | For examples of user profile surveys, see http://www.oeconsortium.org/projects/surveyresults, http://www.oeconsortium.org/wp-content/uploads/2013/11/OCW-User-Feedback-Report_Final_May-2013.pdf, and http://ocw.mit.edu/about/site-statistics.

11 | See http://issuu.com/ocwconsortium/docs/oerinindonesia for an overview of this strategy and the challenges it seeks to address.

12 | http://ocw.vu.edu.pk

13 | See https://www2.maricopa.edu/welcome-to-the-maricopa-millions-oer-project and http://www.slideshare.net/OCWConsortium/the-evidence-towards-impact-the-maricopa-millions-oer-project

More and more governments are starting to embrace open education as a pathway to more effective and accessible education.[14] The British Colombia Open Textbook Project,[15] financed by the ministry of education and managed by BC Campus, is developing dozens of openly licensed textbooks in the highest-enrolled academic subject areas. All textbooks use a Creative Commons license and are available free of charge in ebook formats and at cost for print-on-demand editions. The Open Learning Initiative is a social benefit organization using OER to bring basic education to rural and impoverished areas around the world, from Nepal to Rwanda.[16] Other projects, such as the Flexible Learning for Open Education, are focusing on ensuring that materials are accessible to people with disabilities and to support learners with different learning preferences.[17]

Future Directions

Realizing the full benefits of OER in the future will depend on people's aware-ness of its valuable benefits, and on developing new initiatives at all level. To help make the OER possibilities more visible, Open Education Week[18] is an annual effort in March to raise awareness about the movement and its impact on teaching and learning worldwide. A lot has been accomplished over the past fourteen years, but the growing momentum around OER suggests an even bigger, more robust movement in coming years.

Mary Lou Forward *(USA) is Executive Director of the Open Education Consortium, a worldwide community of hundreds of higher education institutions and associated organizations that supports the development of open, online and digital educational projects and policies.*

---

14 | For example, see Open Scotland http://openscot.net, Opening Up Slovenia http:// www.k4all.org/openingupslovenia, and the US commitment to open education as part of its Open Governance Partnership activities: http://www.whitehouse.gov/blog/2014/09/26/ promoting-open-education-help-teachers-and-students-around-world

15 | http://bccampus.ca/open-textbook-project

16 | http://www.ole.org

17 | http://floeproject.org

18 | http://www.openeducationweek.org

FILMS AND VIDEOS ABOUT THE COMMONS

There are hundreds of worthy films and videos dealing with issues related to the commons in one way or another – forestry, finance, water, copyright, and more. However, the number of them that deal directly with the commons as commons are fairly few. Below, some of the more noteworthy productions of the past five years. All films and videos are in English unless otherwise noted.

The Commons

A documentary film about communities all over the world reasserting sustainable, responsible futures using ancient commons principles. The film visits cooperatives, ecovillages, commons lawyers, Occupy activists, Internet commoners, indigenous peoples, community banks and others around the world to explore how commons work for them.
USA, 2015. Produced and directed by Kevin Hansen.
http://commonsfilm.com

The Promise of the Commons

A beautifully produced film that focuses on natural resource commons in the global South, with special attention to land grabbing and land rights in India, Nepal, and Mexico.
India/China, 2013. Length, 50 minutes. Produced by Environmental Education Media Project, with the India-based Foundation for Ecological Security. Written by environmental educator John D. Liu and directed by Patrick Augenstein.
50-minute version: https://www.youtube.com/watch?v=3uN2b1syMsA
20-minute version: https://www.youtube.com/
    watch?t=59&v=AFnNy0WkWbE
16-minute version: https://www.youtube.com/watch?v=EJe19J0B8x8

Peter Linebaugh: Who Owns the Commons? on The Laura Flanders Show

An interview with historian and author Peter Linebaugh on the 800th anniversary of the Magna Carta and the significance of that legal document and the struggle behind it today.

USA, 2015. Length, 18 minutes. Produced by GRITtv.

https://www.youtube.com/watch?v=nSF3m_Uav6Y

The Commons

A left-libertarian-anarchist perspective on the commons that explains the logic of capitalism and the potential of the commons to meet needs beyond the state and market. The video features a variety of slides and a voiceover narration.

USA, 2013. Produced by Anarchist Collective. Length, 36 minutes.

https://www.youtube.com/watch?v=P0BXCiKOsKY

Script for video narration: https://theleftlibertarian.wordpress.com/2013/09/11/the-commons-beyond-the-state-capitalism-and-the-market

This Land is Our Land: The Fight to Reclaim the Commons

Author and activist David Bollier provides a survey of notable enclosures of the commons, especially in the American context, and the growing international movement to reclaim the commons.

USA 2010. Length, 46 minutes. Directed by Jeremy Earp & Sut Jhally. Written by David Bollier & Jeremy Earp.

http://www.mediaed.org/cgi-bin/commerce.cgi?preadd=action&key=146

SHORT VIDEOS

Better Not More: Principles and Practices Towards the Next Economy

This video provides an overview of activist movements to decommodify nature, re-imagine the character of work, liberate knowledge and democratize wealth.

USA. Length, 5 minutes. Produced by Kontent Film and EDGE Funders Alliance.

https://vimeo.com/124550319

Mutiny! Why We Love Pirates and How They Can Save Us

Kester Brewin, a mathematics teacher in South East London, explains what our love of pirates tells us about renewing the commons. The talk draws upon his 2012 book, *Mutiny!*
UK, 2013. Length, 13 minutes. Produced by TEDx Exeter (UK).
https://www.youtube.com/watch?v=escnWFDUYhI

A Commons Conversation

Participants in a workshop hosted by the Institute for Advanced Sustainability Studies (IASS) and the German Institute for Human Rights provide a thoughtful introduction to subsistence and traditional commons, especially in Africa, with a focus on secure land tenure and food security.
Germany, 2014. Length, 5 minutes. Produced by the Institute for Advanced Sustainability Studies and German Institute for Human Rights.
https://vimeo.com/109114444

Remix The Commons

The website for this collaborative multimedia project (see profile on pp. 132-135) features dozens of short video interviews with commoners from around the world, focusing on key ideas and practices.
France/Canada, 2010 - 2015. In English and French.
http://www.remixthecommons.org/en

Commons in Action

A series of short animated videos about a variety of different types of commons.
USA, 2014. Each is less than three minutes. Produced by the International Association for the Study of the Commons. Animations by Viumasters.

  1. Knowledge Commons
  2. A Japanese story
  3. Grupo de Estudios Ambientales' story
  4. Foundation for Ecological Security story
  5. Grupo Autonómo para la Investigación Ambiental's story
  6. Open Spaces Society story

All videos are available at http://www.iasc-commons.org/impact-stories.

EXCHANGE AND CREDIT COMMONS

"Whatever has a price can be replaced by something else as its equivalent; on the other hand, whatever is above all price, and therefore admits of no equivalent, has a dignity."

Immanuel Kant

Helsinki Timebank: Currency as a Commons

By Jukka Peltokoski, Niklas Toivakainen, Tero Toivanen and Ruby van der Wekken

In October 2009, while expecting another futile climate summit in nearby Copenhagen, a small group of friends in the Kumpula neighborhood of Helsinki got together to discuss practical alternatives. Surely there was something that could be done by people themselves! The result of that first meeting of neighbors was a "credit exchange" called the "Kumpula exchange rink," in which the first seventeen participants agreed to exchange goods and services with each other. Some of the exchanges included such services as providing language translations, swimming lessons and gardening.

A year later, the Kumpula exchange rink, renamed the Helsinki Timebank, began to attract more citizens who wanted to participate in this satisfying alternative economy known as timebanking. The main principle of timebanking is that everyone's time, work and needs are of equal worth. One hour of babysitting is equal to one hour of helping an elderly neighbor or providing accounting services. It is fair to say that this essential principle of timebanking stands in stark contrast to the premises of the current money system and capitalist markets, which value everyone's time and effort in highly unequal ways. Timebanking provides an alternative by helping people meet important personal and household needs in more socially satisfying, equal ways.

By 2014 some 3,000 members had registered with the Helsinki Timebank, and more than one-third had participated in at least one exchange. To date, some 19,000 total hours have been exchanged through the Helsinki Timebank, which includes internal work to maintain and develop the timebank. Worldwide there are thousands of timebanks that enable individuals and diverse types of organizations to exchange services, and sometimes goods, according to timebanking's principles. The Timebank is a part of the Community Exchange System (www.ces.org.za), which lets people exchange goods and services without money or markets. (The network hosts timebanks and local currencies, facilitating "intertrading" among them.)

Timebanks are often seen as irrelevant to the "real economy" because they are not dealing with "economic issues" or markets. They tend to be described as self-help tools, as solvers of certain social problems, as charities, and as a new form of volunteering. They are seen as platforms for people to develop skills and exchange nonprofessional services while strengthening their sense of community connection. Yet in meeting real needs without money while building what economists call "social capital," timebanks deserve to be taken every bit as seriously as markets.

Developing Currency into a Commons

Since its founding, Helsinki Timebank has striven to be a platform of deliberation. It is managed by a core group, open to all members, which discusses how to develop the timebank and meet ongoing challenges. All larger and substantial decisions are made in consultation with all Timebank members, or by voting. For instance, the decision to convert the local exchange rink into Helsinki Timebank in 2010 and to name its local currency "Tovi" (Finnish for "a moment") was made through a membership vote.

When a large cosmetic firm with its own exchange rink wanted to join Helsinki Timebank, it provoked spirited discussion about what kinds of services and relations should be supported and how to define the Timebank's boundaries. Inspired by the example of the Solidarity Economy movement, members in May 2013 drafted the Helsinki Timebank's ABC, a statement of its values and working principles. The ABC defines the Timebank as a platform for "reciprocity, We-spirit, ecological sustainability, economic justice, and local and participatory culture," among other principles that guide participants in deciding what types of organizations may join Helsinki Timebank.

When a local food cooperative wanted to join Helsinki Timebank, it was a perfect fit – and an ingenious way to blend the local market with the credit currency. The cooperative makes locally produced food available to people with time-credits – and in return it gains access to the community and resources for which time-credits can be exchanged.

Another example of commoning can be found in the "Time Heals Network," which grew out of Helsinki Timebank.[1] This peer-to-peer network offers emotional support to people when their lives take a turn for the worse; the services are credited to the providers in time-credits. Peer supporters themselves may have acquired their expertise through formal education, employment or life experiences. The system is based on reciprocity – sometimes one helps someone else, sometimes one receives help. The network also uses the timebank to help people meet concrete needs like housekeeping and childcare.

---

1 | http://www.aikaparantaa.net/english.html

The time currency in itself, the Tovi, is not a commodity, but a token in a "credit commons" that allows people to exchange services, earning and spending credits. The process of defining the principles and rules of the credit currency is itself a process of *commoning,* a term used by historian Peter Linebaugh in discussing medieval English commons. In this sense, Helsinki Timebank's time credits function as a pedagogical tool that helps people learn about cooperation and organization. Strangers are able to meet each other and develop new ways of relating to each other. Thanks to a timebank, the valuable human skills that people have – even among people outside of the labor market, such as the elderly and disabled – can be made visible and put to good use. Timebanks help people reproduce ordinary life without the mediation of markets. A timebank as such is a platform for commoning.[2]

One major act of commoning at Helsinki Timebank was the development of an internal taxation mechanism. When the provider of a service receives time-credits, a percentage of the time-credits earned are automatically transferred to the account of an ethical economic actor of choice in the Helsinki Timebank; this could be a food cooperative, another local CSA, or the Time Heals Network, for example. The time-tax function lets Timebank members strengthen actors and organizations that exemplify the values listed in the ABC. It also supports work that is important to timebank members, and strengthens and develops the community. In a larger context the time-tax and time-credit can be seen as ways that Helsinki Timebank supports solidarity economy-building and the commons in Finland.

Facing the Challenge of State Policy

At the end of 2013, Finland tax authorities came out with new taxation guidelines that required taxing skilled work services received through timebanks according to their market value (in euros). Helsinki Timebank contested this decision, arguing that it destroys the essential principle of equality at the heart of timebanking. It called for an exemption from euro taxation so that the actual potential of timebanking in Finland – including also the benefits of the (internal) time-tax – could be assessed. The dialogue was opened between Helsinki Timebank and the City of Helsinki in 2014 and is still continuing.

---

2 | According to historian Peter Linebaugh commoning seems to have four historical practical dimensions. First, commons were embedded in a particular ecology or human attitude of a certain community. Commoners, or members of premodern laboring class, did not build their lives according to the will of a sovereign or law, but by asking and exploring practical questions on how to organize commons to guarantee subsistence for each member of the community. Second, commoning was deeply embedded in the labor process. Third, commoning was and formed a collective. Fourth, commoning was organized from the grassroots, and it was independent from the state or central authority. See Linebaugh, Peter. *The Magna Carta Manifesto.* Berkeley: University of California Press, 2008, pp. 44-45, 72.

The struggle that Helsinki Timebank now faces is to maintain its autonomy as a deliberative commons guided by strong ethical values while securing formal legal recognition and respect in Finnish society. One initiative seeks to find ways for the City of Helsinki to recognize the Timebank's internal time-tax and incorporate it into the local economy. If successful, the time-tax could be used to support many different forms of coproduction (between timebankers and the city). It could also be used to start up all kinds of autonomous creative projects as commons, creating services or goods that are deemed important by both the city and timebank members. Importantly, this could open up new forms of power transfer and sharing within the city – a commonification of the public sector![3]

An interesting future question is whether timebanking could be used as a tool for ethical entrepreneurs to share common resources and gain relative autonomy from markets. This would help the new economy strengthen commons and reduce dependence on highly capitalized markets and competition. Unfortunately, in Finland, this road is now blocked by rigid taxation guidelines that prevent the exchange of professional services via timebanks. It would appear that the guidelines are intended to prevent timebanking from growing and challenging the dominance of both market and state, and the capitalistic order itself.

Jukka Peltokoski *(Finland) is a political researcher and pedagogue, an activist in the precarity movement, a commoner in Commons.* **Niklas Toivakainen** *(Finland) is an active member of Helsinki Timebank, and a member of Commons.fi and the Finnish Solidarity economy collective.* **Tero Toivanen** *(Finland) is a doctoral student in World Politics at the University of Helsinki.* **Ruby van der Wekken** *(Finland) is an active member of Helsinki Timebank, and a member of Commons.fi and the Finnish Solidarity Economy collective.*

---

3 | This resonates with what Michel Bauwens of the P2P foundation) refers to as the "Partner State," which would guarantee the basics of livelihood for all while increasingly providing infrastructure for citizens to act on their own initiatives. Such enabling and supporting of citizen action would constitute not a privatization or marketization, but a commonification of the public realm.

How the Bangla-Pesa Tapped the Value of an Informal Community

Interview with Will Ruddick

People usually don't realize that money is an invention that works only because a community stands behind it, willing to use it in exchanges for goods and services. Most currencies are creatures of national governments that manage and back them. But what if a poorer community created its own currency to foster social exchange? That's what happened in the informal settlement, or slum, known as Bangladesh in the town of Mombasa on the Kenyan coast.

With the help of Will Ruddick, a community development specialist in Kenya since 2009, dozens of small business owners in Bangladesh agreed to accept a new currency, the Bangla-Pesa, in exchange for fresh produce, bicycle repairs, tutoring, taxi rides and other goods and services. The new commons-based currency has stimulated a big boost in the local economy while helping families that earn little in the formal economy (and thus have few Kenyan shillings) to earn another currency, Bangla-Pesa, which lets them meet their basic needs. Since its launch, over three million shillings of trade have been transacted using the currency. Its success has recently inspired the launch of a similar currency, Gatina-Pesa, for the neighborhood of Gatina, in Nairobi, Kenya's capital city.

We interviewed Ruddick, the founder of the Bangla-Pesa to learn more about his remarkable experiment in community-based money.

Will, what are the origins of the Bangla-Pesa?

The concept of the Bangla-Pesa is not new. It was first introduced in Kisumu Ndogo, Shauri Yako and Mnazi Mmoja slums in Kongowea. A number of us brought the idea to Bangladesh in March 2013 as a way to strengthen and stabilize the economy of the neighborhood. Bangla-Pesa is an accounting mechanism of reciprocal exchange or mutual-credit system. Members can accept only as much Bangla-Pesa as they can use in one day for local needs, like food and water. No one is allowed to have more than 400 Bangla-Pesa at any one time. In developing these programs, we incorporated a system of guarantors to the currency and a community fund to make the system more secure and sustainable.

How did you get people interested in using Bangla-Pesa?

The majority of people here live in poverty and are unable to meet their basic needs. Therefore, our goal was to use the currency to encourage economic activity, which in turn would help people who don't earn much conventional money to be able to buy food and other necessities. People were only too happy to participate in such an experiment.

We saw the currency as a tool to let members of the network trade among themselves. The Bangla-Pesa is a business-to-business voucher system that only registered members can participate in. In this sense, the Bangla-Pesa is a complementary currency to official money. Technically it is a credit clearing system for multilateral reciprocal exchange. People outside the trading network like the Bangla-Pesa because it is used to support community activities like clean-ups; they also know that it can be used to buy goods and services at more than 100 shops.

What sort of system did you organize to launch Bangla-Pesa?

We organized more than 200 microenterprises into a community-based organization called the Bangladesh Business Network. Everyone formally registered as a member and agreed to accept the Bangla-Pesa in exchange for whatever they could offer – food products, services, transportation. Each business must agree to back 400 Bangla-Pesa with their goods and services. Each business must also have a group of four members that endorse their membership. Bangla-Pesa serve as vouchers or promissory notes for members' goods and services.

What was the initial response to the new currency?

People in the neighborhood quickly saw the value of using it. It helped them meet their needs even though they don't have much "real money." But state authorities became quite agitated. They feared that the Bangla-Pesa might try to displace or challenge Kenya's national currency, the shilling. Six of us who had started the currency were arrested by the Changamwe police and put in jail. The police were apparently worried because there are secessionist groups like the Mombasa Republican Council within the area. The government saw the Bangla-Pesa as a threat to it and the national currency.

The six of us were charged with possession of illegal currency papers in late May 2013. All of the businesses in the Bangladesh Business Network were told to stop using the currency. We found it all perplexing. Why should a simple mechanism that helps people self-organize themselves to make ends meet pose a threat to the country's Central Bank?

So how did you persuade the government that the Bangla-Pesa is not a threat?

We pointed out that the Bangla-Pesa cannot be traded for shilling. They aren't convertible into each other. We also emphasized that Bangla-Pesa are a trading voucher more than a currency in the strict sense, since its value is pegged to the Kenyan shilling. I think we also convinced the prosecutor that our goal was and is to uplift the living standards of the poorest. Three months after our arrest, in August 2013, the public prosecutor found we had broken no laws and dropped the charges.

What happened next?

The arrests stopped the economic stimulus that Bangla-Pesa had provoked because suddenly no one could use them. But then we re-launched the currency in November 2013 with the backing of the entire community, including local leaders and government officals. Since then, trading in Bangla-Pesa has resumed in a big way.

How does the Bangla-Pesa help people?

Take the case of Maciana Anyango, who is sixty-four. She is a widow and the sole breadwinner and takes care of her disabled seventeen-year-old daughter and a son who trained as a driver but has not secured a job yet. She says, "I used to be without food because we wouldn't have enough Kenyan shillings. Now I can eat even when I don't have the real money because I still have the Bangla-Pesa to use."

Or consider a bicycle operator who has the capacity for twenty customers a day, but in general only has ten. Now he can give rides to those businesses in exchange for goods and services they have in excess, such as a woman who has extra tomatoes to sell. This helps the community weather poor economic periods. There are hundreds of millions of people around the world like this. They have goods and services to offer. So why can't they create their own means of exchange, backed by what they have and can do?

Is the Bangla-Pesa mostly about business – or are there other reasons that people join?

People join because it's good for the community. Fredrick Ochieng is an electronics repairman with a family of seven; such larger, extended families are not unusual in African societies. Ochieng says that he wanted to join to help provide for his family and for things for his children, like merry-go-rounds, and to help the community with things like the trash clean-up. And in fact, since starting to use Bangla-Pesa, it has helped him get to know people in the community as he got to know members of the network and they incidentially became new customers, when they have a problem with their phones.

What makes the currency itself different from the national currency, the Kenyan shilling?

Bangla-Pesa's value is the same as the Kenyan shilling, but is not exchangeable for it. Bangla-Pesa is a voucher that circulates only among the community. And that means that the value generated within the community stays within the community, and does not flow to people outside of the neighborhood. As a result, the Bangla-Pesa, unlike other currencies, does not generate more poverty. Furthermore, unlike the Kenyan shilling, whose value fluctuates with inflation, the vouchers expire after one year. Bangla-Pesa can be renewed with a sticker upon payment in Bangla-Pesa to the community fund. This creates an annual renewal cycle for community service work.

How does the Bangla-Pesa system constitute a commons?

The Bangla-Pesa is managed by a nonprofit organization called KORU, which stands for "Kenyans Organizing Regional Unity," which I cofounded with Jacky Kowa, a native Kenyan who works on women's rights and health issues. The group's members are elected, and it acts as a validator and steward of the currency. KORU addresses any disagreements that may come up among members.

The Bangla-Pesa is a symbol and instrument for community wealth because it is backed by the common pool of goods and services of the members of the network. The value of the currency is the sum total of the teaching of a teacher, the tomatoes raised by the farmers, the rides given on a motorcycle, and so on. Not more. Not less. So the vouchers represent that community wealth. The vouchers are also a way for people to improve the community. Once accepted into the Network, 200 Bangla-Pesa of the 400 allocated to a business are kept for community service work, such as trash pickup. Members vote on which types of community service work to fund.

Bangla-Pesa have helped created a commons by catalyzing new connections and cooperation among people. Rose Akiny runs a maize mill where she grinds maize to flour, a business that helps her care for her sister's family after her sister passed away. She said, "I found friends who were doing business using Bangla-Pesa, and they backed me and then I backed them. Now I go to their businesses to buy maize, rice and beans, and they come to grind at my mill. I follow other members who have the Bangla-Pesa and learn where to purchase goods. It's is also easy to find people because the members' shops are marked."

How have Bangla-Pesa improved the situations of families and the overall well-being of the Bangladesh community?

The community now trades the equivalent of roughly 100 euros daily using Bangla-Pesa in addition to its usage of Kenyan shillings. A survey on the impact of the program found that about 83 percent of participants saw an increase in their total sales as a result of the vouchers. Bangla-Pesa represent an average increase of 22 percent of total daily sales over a baseline level, compared to no increase in sales using Kenyan shillings. This implies that Bangla Pesa are responsible for that extra 22 percent in economic activity, which might not have materialized without the program.

Women especially benefit from Bangla-Pesa because 75 percent of the small businesses in Bangladesh have women owners. Bangla-Pesa have also made all of its users less dependent on the formal economy and the volatility of markets.

Among many commoners, the dominance of money and market mechanisms in mediating people's relationships is usually seen as very controversial. Obviously there are many ways for people to meet their needs and help each other. How important do you think that a currency, or means of exchange, is for improving people's livelihoods in the settlements that you work with?

It is really important to recognize how people fall into poverty when playing the game of capitalism and the reasons why poverty exists in the first place. Perhaps if we see poverty as manufactured through the control of resources by an elite minority, we can also see how the control of money might itself be a key tool of the elite.

Certainly the people in Bangladesh and Mombasa more generally are "poor" due to lack of education, corruption and lack of jobs. But this is not why poverty exists in the first place. There is a nearly unlimited demand for goods and services, including education, and there is a nearly unlimited supply of people who could provide them. What's missing is a means of exchange between demand and supply. Sadly this needed means of exchange is usually only available as national currency, which is typically controlled by for-profit institutions, banks, whose goal is to benefit by increasing the debt of others.

If communities could instead control their own means of exchange, they could make exchange work for their own purposes. They could lower their dependency on Kenyan shilling by using Bangla-Pesa when possible. Bangla-Pesa creates a buffer for the community that helps it keep life going even during the worst economic periods.

Thank you.

WIR Currency – Reinventing Social Exchange

By James Stodder and Bernard Lietaer

The Swiss WIR ("We" in German) is the longest surviving social or community currency, sometimes called a complementary currency. (This last name reflects an ambition to supplement rather than replace a national currency.) WIR is not a physical currency per se, but a system of credits and debits. Once a buyer and seller negotiate a price in WIR, the seller is credited and the buyer debited that amount. Nowadays, the process can be completed in seconds, on a smartphone. Today's WIR-Bank, originally the *Wirtschaftsring* ("Economic Circle"), was founded in 1934, in the depths of the Great Depression. It was based on the ideas of Silvio Gesell, a German-Argentine merchant and economist who saw how ordinary money circulation had collapsed. Money fearfully clutched rather than freely exchanged only makes a downturn worse.

By reinventing their own currencies based on long-term reciprocity among community members – rather than gold or central bank limits – communities can break this vicious cycle. Hundreds of such currencies sprang up in the Great Depression, as noted by Yale's Irving Fisher, the early monetary economist.[1] Recent research by the authors[2] confirms that WIR circulation does indeed accelerate in a recession; as people hoard their limited holdings of Swiss Francs (SFr), they are more willing to use WIR for market exchanges.

WIR are actually somewhat less valuable than SFr because they are less negotiable: not easily changed for another currency, nor accepted outside the circle of WIR users. But that circle of Swiss circulation is fairly wide. In 2013, WIR counted some 50,000 small and medium enterprises (SMEs) among its clients, enabling 1.43 billion Swiss Francs (SFr) of trade, or US$1.59 bil-

---

1 | Irving Fisher, "100 Percent Money and the Public Debt." *Economic Forum*, Spring 1936, pp. 406-420.

2 | Stodder, "Complementary Credit Networks and Macro-Economic Stability: Switzerland's *Wirtschaftsring.*" *Journal of Economic Behavior and Organization*, 2009. Stodder and Lietaer, "The Macro-Stability of Swiss WIR-Bank Credits: Balance, Velocity and Leverage." Working Paper, Rensselaer Polytechnic Institute, 2014.

lion.[3] About 80 percent of WIR users are SMEs and larger firms; the rest are households.

What is the social basis of the WIR's long-term reciprocity among people? Textbooks on the origin of money usually start with the "double-coincidence of wants" problem: If you and I are both to benefit from barter, it's not enough for you to want what I have – you also need to have what I want. As the division of labor grows, such double-coincidences are harder to find. We need to find long circular chains of single coincidences, wherein A gives Bread to B, who gives Cheese to C, who gives an Apple to A. Money helps solve this problem by serving as an intermediary "good" that everyone wants.

This explanation begins and ends with individual wants. But our species has not survived primarily by such exchange. A century of anthropological and historical research shows that it was gifts – not money or barter – that brought the original human economy into being.[4]

In his *Great Transformation*, Polanyi characterizes the gift economy as "free gifts that are expected to be reciprocated, though not necessarily by the same individuals – a procedure minutely articulated and perfectly safeguarded by elaborate methods of publicity." This is the original solution to the "double coincidence" problem – a network of *multilateral* gifts and reciprocity between individual and group – not just two individuals.

Even the earliest forms of currency were community records, not impersonal stores of value. Lietaer's *Mystery of Money* describes pottery-based currencies centered on ancient temples to Mother Goddesses and medieval shrines to the Virgin Mary. These early monies were a way of remembering personal indebtedness. The Latin root for "monetary" – deriving from the temple of Juno Moneta, the mother goddess who "monitors" all exchange – reflects this fact. The WIR is Juno's descendant, a way of monitoring multilateral (not just bilateral) reciprocity, within a community of named individuals.

Impersonal money as the basis of trade came much later, allowing the economy to stretch far beyond interpersonal community. But this new impersonal money creates its own new problem – How should its quantity be controlled? Too much means inflation and wasted resources; too little causes deflation and unemployment. Precious metals are an arbitrary form of control, and central banks a blunt one. History shows shortages and gluts for gold and silver, and the limitations of central banks are confirmed by current conditions.

---

3 | WIR-Banque, *Rapport de Gestion* 2013, Basel: WIR-Banque.

4 | See, e.g., Marcel Mauss' classic book, *The Gift: Forums and Functions of Exchange in Archaic Societies*; Karl Polanyi's *The Great Transformation*; Frederic Pryor's *The Origins of the Economy*; Bernard Lietaer's *The Mystery of Money*; and James Stodder's "The Evolution of Complexity in Primitive Exchange," in *Journal of Comparative Economics* (1995).

The supply of WIR is not limited by gold or central bank "base money" – it grows by as much or as little as people are willing to trade in it. That willingness is greatest (a) in a recession, (b) in highly cyclical industries like construction and hospitality, and (c) among those shortest on cash. Unlike ordinary money, it flows where it is most needed.

WIR is a community currency, but at even its small-nation scale, it is no longer highly "communitarian." Time Banks (US), LETS (Canada) and Fureai kippu (Japan) are other notable currencies that are closer to their community roots. But like all of these, the WIR recreates an awareness of need-based gift exchange. It may be the form of exchange to which our species is best suited.

James Stodder *(USA) teaches economics and econometrics in the School of Management at Rensselaer Polytechnic Institute and the Management Department at the US Coast Guard Academy. His research is on exchange systems, behavioral economics, inequality and economic anthropology.*

Bernard Lietaer *(Belgium) is the author of* The Future of Money *(translated into eighteen languages), and an expert in the design and implementation of currency systems. He codesigned and implemented the convergence mechanism to the single European currency system (the Euro) and served as president of the Electronic Payment System at the National Bank of Belgium (the Belgian Central Bank).*

TOOLS AND INFRASTRUCTURE FOR COMMONING

"Power does not reside in institutions, not even the state or large corporations. It is located in the networks that structure society."

Manuel Castells

Goteo: Crowdfunding to Build New Commons

By Enric Senabre Hidalgo

If there were to be a formula to describe Goteo, an online platform based in Barcelona with European and Latin American scope, it could be expressed simply:

Hacktivism + crowdfunding + wide social collaboration
= the building of new commons

Each of these activities has always existed separately, of course, but it was the vision of Goteo to integrate them into a single open network that is helping commoners build a new Commons Sector in society. With more than 50,000 users and more than 2 million euros raised since 2012, Goteo has helped launch more than 400 projects that support the commons, open code and free knowledge. The projects span a rich variety of fields – education, the environment, technology, culture, entrepreneurial startups, journalism and more.[1] Among them:

The Smart Citizen kit, an open source environmental monitoring platform and hardware for citizens to open and share their own environmental data;[2]

Quién Manda, a collaborative mapping project that depicts political and economic power relations in Spain;[3]

Open source gasifier, a renewable electricity generator using residual biomass gasification in the Republic of Chad;[4]

Nodo Móvil, a replicable, travelling wifi connection unit for communities, social movements and public spaces;[5]

---

1 | http://www.goteo.org
2 | https://goteo.org/project/smart-citizen-sensores-ciudadanos
3 | https://goteo.org/project/quien-manda
4 | https://goteo.org/project/gasificador-opensource-en-el-chad
5 | https://goteo.org/project/nodo-movil

Spain in Flames, an open data website to allow the visualization of forest fires, their causes and solutions, enhanced with data from investigative reporting;[6]

Foldarapa, a compact, foldable 3D printer made by a community using a P2P distributed production model that helps its users expand production while sharing the profit with others;[7] and

The Social Market, a cooperative project by the Spanish Alternative and Solidarity Network linking more than 230 companies and others committed to solidarity economy values.[8]

Goteo is more than a platform for crowdfunding. It serves as a focal point for distributed collaboration among strangers, each of whom may have something special – physical resources, expertise, infrastructure tools, personal time – to contribute to a particular project. Goteo doesn't just engage individuals; it has become a network of local, independent communities throughout Spain. These range from one in the Spanish region of the Basque country, supported by the Basque government, to others in Andalusia and Barcelona.

The people who belong to the Goteo network tend to play different roles at various times. They may introduce a new project that needs support, contribute funds to help launch a project, or collaborate on it so that it can grow.

Goteo had its origins in the Platoniq collective[9] – a Barcelona-based group that was a pioneer in the production and distribution of copyleft culture.[10] The hackers of Platoniq (including me) were passionate about designing tools for citizen empowerment and social innovation. We mostly used open source, peer-to-peer technologies that can be easily adapted and reproduced.

Some of Platoniq's projects became quite famous. Burn Station (2004) was a mobile, self-service system for searching, listening to and copying music and audio files with no charge – all of it legally under a Creative Commons license.[11] This "taking the Internet to the streets" initiative gained worldwide attention. Another project, The Bank of Common Knowledge, was a series of gatherings in different cities that provided open workshops and manuals.[12] Thanks to hundreds of volunteers, people could learn how to install and use a

6 | https://goteo.org/project/espana-en-llamas

7 | https://goteo.org/project/foldarap-peer-to-peer-edition

8 | https://goteo.org/project/desarrollando-el-mercado-de-economia-solidaria

9 | http://www.youcoop.org

10 | Editors' note: For more on copyleft, see essay on the General Public License and Creative Common licenses on pp. 223-226.

11 | http://www.burnstation.net

12 | http://www.bankofcommons.org

wiki, how to repair domestic technologies, how to set up a free wifi network, how to set up a local consumer group.[13]

In these and other hackathon-like events Platoniq also served a "process medium" or "masters of ceremonies" for technology-based projects. It helped developers and entrepreneurs recruit new collaborators, clarify the problems to be solved, choose the superior body of source code for projects, and develop alliances in moving them forward.

Despite the success of Platoniq's work, it became painfully clear after several years that there was a serious lack of resources to incubate innovative and experimental projects. This need was especially acute for projects based on open source and commons-based principles. Neither public nor private institutions are generally eager to support such projects, and certainly conventional market players see little gain in helping produce innovations that are designed to be copied and shared.

The rise of crowdfunding in 2009 as a new model of digital collaboration began to open up a new field of possibilities, however. It became evident from such early platforms like Kickstarter that distributed funding from hundreds and even thousands of people could be a feasible base of support. The standard crowdfunding process at the time consisted of a specific fundraising goal, a deadline for pledges, an "all or nothing" scheme (sufficient pledges to meet the goal or no funding), and a system of individual rewards or perks for backers.

Some of the participants in Platoniq, especially Susana Noguero and Olivier Schulbaum, decided to investigate the possibilities. They found that backers of open source projects were on average more generous than backers of other projects, and that they also contributed more regularly. Platoniq also explored the subtleties of other distributed systems for raising money online – the microcredits approach used by Kiva and platforms for lending money to entrepreneurs – as well as alliances with local organizations in smaller countries. In the end, we decided that it was time to invent a new platform for funding innovations that contribute to open knowledge and the commons.

Since we couldn't identify any single project or tool designed to support the logic of sharing, collaborating and social impact, we decided to invent one – Goteo. From the start it was a collaborative endeavor. Before programming a single line of code, we entered into a lengthy period of codesign in which we consulted with communities of practice, cultural agitators, open source practitioners, designers, academics and others. We asked the potential users to help visualize the new crowdfunding platform and suggest features that could better meet their own needs and experiences.

---

13 | http://youcoop.org/en/bcc

Goteo was launched at the end of 2011 as the first crowdfunding platform expressly for open and commons-oriented projects. Its design embodied the following values, in order of importance:

Collective return: Aside from individual rewards for backers, the final outputs of any initiative using Goteo must contribute to the commons. For example, projects must use licenses that allow copying, sharing, modification and free use of part or the whole of each created work.

Trustworthy management model: The legal organization that manages Goteo is a nonprofit foundation, Fundación Fuentes Abiertas, which is officially recognized as a public-interest organization. This management model offers tax-deductible benefits for both cofinancers and promoters.

Fostering transparency: Each project must give specific details about where the money collected will go. Coupled with a two-round scheme of fundraising, this requirement means that even very successful campaigns disclose the actual use of money obtained, including extra money beyond the stated goal. Furthermore, Goteo and project promoters both sign a legal agreement that guarantees that the work described in the crowdfunding campaigns – products, services, activities, archives, etc. – are actually produced.

Distributed collaboration: Beyond monetary contributions to projects via Goteo, people are invited to collaborate in the development of projects by offering services, material resources and infrastructure. They can also participate in specific microtasks.

Training: Goteo has advised and trained more than 2,000 people from many domains through dozens of workshops – a commitment that both disseminates our knowledge while building Goteo's social following and economic stability.

Community of local nodes: Goteo is not a centralized hub, but more of a community of communities – a network of local, independent nodes that serve to localize projects and give them context. The first one started in the Spanish region of the Basque country, supported by Basque government, and a second later began in Andalusia. New ones will soon be launched in Barcelona and in Nantes, France.

Public/private match-funding: Goteo is a pioneer in recruiting public/private capital investors to help develop open culture projects through a bottom-up process in a "cloudfunding capital" process: each euro a project receives from a person is matched by another euro from institutions belonging to a social investment fund.

Open source: The core software code of the Goteo website is freely available under a General Public License 3.0 via GitHub, which ensures that it can be used and improved via open source principles.

Goteo's organizational design principles and values mean that its crowd-funding processes are more rule-based than others. It takes more work to ensure that proposed projects comply with basic criteria of openness and commons principles; that projects are actually produced as promised; and that the collective rewards are delivered and made accessible.

But with tens of thousands of users and a 70 percent rate of success for all proposed projects (the majority of crowdfunding platforms rarely reach a 40 percent), we are convinced that Goteo is headed in the right direction. Its success has validated new standards of openness in crowdfunding, and it has attracted some of the most compelling innovators in the field. Although it is difficult to measure, Goteo has also contributed significantly to projects in free culture, open source code and the commons that might otherwise never materialize.

Goteo aspires to somehow "close the circle" with its previous experiences with Platoniq by developing new forms of peer-to-peer creation, crowd incubation and development for projects in the stages before and after crowdfunding. That will have to wait for a while as we concentrate on Goteo's first priority, to finance and consolidate the Commons Sector.

Enric Senabre Hidalgo *(Spain) is a member of the Platoniq collective and cofounder and content coordinator at Goteo.org. He is also vice president of the Observatory for CyberSociety and teaches Software Studies and the History of Digital Culture at the Open University of Catalonia, where he holds a Master's Degree in the Information and Knowledge Society.*

Commoning in Times of Disaster:
The Humanitarian OpenStreetMap Team

By Kate Chapman

Just a few hours after the 7.0 magnitude earthquake hit Haiti in January 2010, a group of collaborators from the OpenStreetMap community began collecting all sorts of topographical data about the country – roads, towns, hospitals, government buildings. Within forty-eight hours high-resolution satellite imagery taken after the earthquake became available, and within a month over 600 people had added information to OpenStreetMap of Haiti.

This online map quickly became the default basemap for a wide variety of responders – search and rescue teams, the United Nations, the World Bank, and humanitarian mapping organizations such as MapAction. It turned out to be the first step in the formation of the Humanitarian OpenStreetMap Team, or HOT, which has gone on to organize dozens of similar humanitarian mapping projects over the past five years.

The project amounts to a "mapping commons" whose freely available geographic data is invaluable to humanitarian responders to natural disasters and crises. The maps are also widely used by communities to help them formulate and pursue their own development goals.

The heart of the HOT project is a large corps of concerned volunteers who are committed to creating online maps freely available to anyone. The maps – all based on the open source collection of maps hosted by OpenStreetMap, the Web map wiki project – are especially valuable in places where base map data are scarce, out of date, or rapidly changing.

HOT relies on OpenStreetMap (OSM), a collaborative global project started by Steve Coast in the UK in 2004 following the success of Wikipedia. Relying on crowdsourced data from more than 1.6 million registered users, OSM maps are compiled entirely by people who survey land with GPS units, digitize aerial imagery, and collect and liberate existing public sources of geographic data. Unlike many other providers whose maps are made by paid professionals and sold as proprietary products, OSM allows anyone to contribute information, correct mistakes and access it anywhere in the world. This allows vast quantities of information to be gathered together on one platform in highly participatory and efficient ways.

The maps themselves are licensed under an Open Data Commons Open Database License (ODbL), which means that the maps are freely available to anyone to "copy, distribute, transmit and adapt" so long as any derivative map information is also available under the same terms.[1] This licensing is very important in disaster situations because it allows responders to have quick, no-cost access to accurate information about a region – something that conventional commercial maps do not ordinarily allow. The freely licensed geographic data also makes it far easier for responders to adapt the raw data to create printed maps and mobile applications.

The Humanitarian OpenStreetMap Team was incorporated as a nonprofit shortly after the spontaneous collaboration of humanitarian mappers in response to the Haiti earthquake in 2010. While HOT has a board of directors and a voting membership that comprise the legal body of the organization, anyone with an OSM user name can contribute to the HOT mission via its "Tasking Manager," a tool that divides up a mapping job into smaller tasks that can be completed rapidly.[2]

HOT is part of a sprawling global commons of geographic mapping volunteers who apply open-source principles and open data sharing to improve the welfare of communities in which they work, especially those at risk of natural disaster or other crises. The project engages participants in two ways: by coordinating volunteers from around the world in using satellite imagery to compile maps, and by providing training and support to OpenStreetMap communities in countries prone to disasters. HOT also globally advocates the importance of free geodata in saving and improving lives in times of political crisis and natural disasters.

In late 2013 Typhoon Haiyan, one of the strongest typhoons on record, hit the Philippines, destroying thousands of homes and displacing thousands of people. The OpenStreetMap Philippines (OSM-ph) community and HOT were not strangers prior to such scenarios; a colleague group of humanitarian mappers, MapAction, had used OpenStreetMap to develop an official response map in 2009 after tropical storm Ondoy.[3] In the case of Typhoon Haiyan, both the OSM-ph community and the HOT community began mapping the

---

1 | The full legal terms of this license can be found at http://opendatacommons.org/licenses/odbl. The cartography of the map tiles, and documentation for them, are licensed under the Creative Commons Attribution-ShareAlike 2.0 license (CC BY-SA).

2 | Background on the origins and governance of HOT can be found at http://wiki.openstreetmap.org/wiki/Humanitarian_OpenStreetMap_Team#Global_Volunteer_Community

3 | http://brainoff.com/weblog/2009/10/08/1495

city of Tacloban together even before the typhoon made landfall. Thirty-three mappers used open satellite imagery to add 10,000 buildings to the map, or about one-quarter of all buildings in Tacloban. This data about the location of health facilities, government buildings, water and electricity sources, and so forth have obvious value to responders who must plan activities in rapid, on-the-fly ways from remote locations. The Red Cross has used the map data, for example, to assist in performing a damage assessment. Over 1,600 volunteers from all over the world contributed some five million map changes in the first month after the typhoon. This data was extremely useful to the Philippines government and international response organizations.

In responding in 2014 to the massive Ebola outbreak, which has infected an estimated 24,000 people and killed 10,000, HOT's volunteer mapping was quite helpful to Doctors Without Borders (Medicins sans Frontieres, MSF), CartONG and the Red Cross. Detailed, accurate maps were vital in helping emergency field workers to navigate Guinea, Liberia, Sierra Leone and Nigeria, and to identify infected people who needed medical care.

Not all of the work of the HOT community is focused on this type of intense disaster response. Often mapping of places that do not have detailed data occurs in preparation for an event. In the case of Lubumbashi in the Democratic Republic of Congo the goal was to create a detailed street map of the city so Doctors Without Borders could better track community health and know when a full-scale response was needed.

This interaction began with a "mapping party" in Berlin at which volunteers got together to extract information from satellite imagery. Once they had mapped much of the city remotely, a member of HOT traveled to Lubumbashi to collaborate with MSF.[4] There, they worked together with the University of Lubumbashi to collect even more detailed street data using a tool called Field Papers, a tool that lets one print a map from OpenStreetMap and then write on it.[5] This provides a way for people to write annotations on paper copies of maps, and then to take a picture of the annotations with a mobile phone. The digital image with notes are then loaded into an OSM editor, and volunteers in remote locations can get together at scheduled mapping events to transcribe the notes and add them to the online OSM.[6]

This is a common pattern of HOT engagement with a community – remote volunteers map communities in need whose settlements and landscape are not well mapped. Ideally, the volunteers are also connected to OSM mappers in those communities, though in some places this is not practical. Another

---

4 | http://hot.openstreetmap.org/updates/2014-04-01_a_week_in_lubumbashi_drc

5 | http://fieldpapers.org

6 | http://hot.openstreetmap.org/updates/2014-05-08_london_hot_congo_mapathon

common HOT approach is to teach communities how to use OSM tools to map themselves, often through field missions such as the one in Lubumbashi.

Much is learned through these collaborations and trips, and that information in turn is used to improve OSM globally. For example, the learning tool LearnOSM[7] was first developed in Indonesia during trainings by HOT. LearnOSM offers clear introductions to key elements the OSM technology with step-by-step instructions in nine languages.

Another example is the special Humanitarian map layer of the OSM map, which contains data of great interest to disaster responders – the location of water and sanitation facilities, road quality, fire hydrants, electricity networks, street lights and social facilities.[8] The map layer can also reveal informal shops clustered together – information that is not usually disclosed by traditional Web cartography that doesn't update the rapidly changing urban environment nor allow Web users to zoom in closely enough.

The HOT experience illustrates the contagious nature of local acts of commoning. What is initially useful to people in one disaster zone often proves valuable to people in another part of the world, and so a cycle of learning and access to tools expands from one community to another, and around the world.

Kate Chapman *(USA), a geographer by training, worked extensively in Indonesia to build an OpenStreetMap community and was Executive Director of the Humanitarian OpenStreetMap Team from its inception in 2010 until 2015.*

---

7 | http://learnosm.org/en

8 | http://hot.openstreetmap.org/updates/2013-09-29_a_new_window_on_openstreetmap_data

Mapping Our Shared Wealth:
The Cartography of the Commons

By Ellen Friedman

If a picture is worth a thousand words, a map is likely worth a thousand pictures. Since 2010, hundreds of commons and "new economy" mapping projects have sprung to life. By depicting thousands of innovative social, environmental and economic initiatives, these maps reveal the complex stories of new systems emerging through the cracks of the old, like dandelions through broken concrete.

The maps serve many purposes at once. They help amass new groups of commoners by giving them shared digital platforms. As the maps become dense with user-contributed information, they show the growth of horizontal, participatory power, especially in reclaiming rights to manage shared resources. These resources include everything from valuable urban spaces and lakes to fruit orchards accessible to anyone, environmental projects and hackerspaces. The many maps depicting commons and people-centered economic projects tell the story of communities rejecting the status quo, reconnecting with the places they inhabit, and creating a renaissance through new relationships.

Below, we describe some of the more notable projects that map commons. (A complete list of maps and weblinks is included on p. 222.)

A significant number of mapping projects focus on urban commons. **Mapping The Commons**(.net), founded in 2010, uses an open-workshop process to ask people to identify important common assets in their cities. Developed by principal investigator Pablo de Soto in conjunction with local research fellows, the Mapping the Commons workshop methodology has been used in Athens, Istanbul, Rio de Janeiro, Belo Horizonte, São Paulo, Quito and Grande Vittoria. Workshop participants describe their relationship to each city's commons and name the unique natural resources, cultural treasures, public spaces, digital commons and social actions that matter to them. Short videos are then produced and overlaid on an online map of the city. De Soto's paper, "Mapping the Urban Commons: A Parametric & Audiovisual Method," received the Elinor Ostrom award in 2013 in the category of "Conceptual Approaches on the Commons."

Italians are forging some of the most innovative projects. **World of Commons** is a map that identifies forms of collective governance that constitute "best practices" for a variety of resources such as housing, public space, pastures, forests, and lands that have been treated as common property since medieval times. The project was created by LabGov, the LABoratory for the GOVernance of Commons in Rome, which itself is a collaboration between Labsus (Laboratory for Subsidiarity) and LUISS Guido Carli Department of Political Science. LabGov is attempting to develop experts on commons governance and new institutional forms. To promote its ideas, LabGov offers a series of educational workshops in partnership with the cities of Rome, Bologna, Taranto, and the province of Mantua. The Bologna Lab has been particularly focused on developing new types of collaborative governance for urban commons. It has mounted a campaign to bring the principle of "horizontal subsidiarity" to Italian cities as a way to give citizens a constitutional right to participate directly in all levels of government.

Another mapping project in Italy is **Mapping the Commons**(.org) – unrelated to the Pablo de Soto venture of the same name. The mapping initiative was part of the initial unMonastery project launched in Matera in early 2014. The unMonastery is a social commune that is trying to help communities suffering from unemployment, empty buildings and a lack of social services.[1] The project engages skilled people and local citizens in a collaborative process to develop innovative solutions. Mapping the region's cultural assets, local traditions, knowledge and stories are used to assist this process.

The Great Lakes Commons Map is unique in its focus on a bioregional ecosystem. The map was launched in May 2012 by Paul Baines, a teacher in Toronto, during a multicity educational tour organized by the Council of Canadians, an activist group that focuses on water as a commons. The Great Lakes Commons is a collaborative effort among many groups – including the Council of Canadians, On The Commons, indigenous peoples, municipalities, and urban and rural citizens – to create effective stewardship and governance of the Great Lakes. The Great Lakes Commons Map invites people to tell their own stories of personal experience and community healing and environmental harm at various locations around the lakes. The map includes lively videos and narratives as well as map layers that identify the locations of First Nations, pipelines and bottled water permits as well as supporters of the Great Lakes Commons Charter. The map is itself a commons in several respects: its stories and data come from people who love the Great Lakes, the map is shareable under a

---

1 | http://unmonastery.org

Creative Commons license, and the map platform is powered by Ushahidi, an open-source crisis mapping platform.

The **P2PValue** project maps a wide variety of digital projects created through Commons-Based Peer Production (CBPP), which is a form of online social collaboration among large numbers of people in producing valuable information and physical products. P2PValue was created by a consortium of six academic partners to support the creation of public policies that benefit the commons.[2] P2PValue has identified over 300 CBPP projects from which it has identified best practices and favorable conditions for horizontal collaborative creations. Because digital commons as artifacts of cyberspace cannot be mapped geographically, P2PValue's projects are listed in a searchable directory. The project is open to public contributions, and all project data and source code are freely available.

Some mapping projects focus on resources and organizational forms in the "new economy" and solidarity economy. **Shareable** and its global **Sharing Cities Network** have hosted dozens of "mapjams" in 2013 and 2014 to bring together urban commoners to compile notable sharing projects. The mapjams produced more than seventy urban maps that identify local coops, commons, public resources, and sharing-oriented platforms and organizations. Shareable cofounder Neal Gorenflo says, "Taking stock of your resources is frequently a precursor to action. Such maps indicate an intention, change the mindset of participants, and are a practical organizing tool."

The focus of **Vivir Bien's** mapping project is the solidarity economy and a variety of noncapitalist, not-for-profit initiatives and organizations. Founded in Vienna in 2010 by the Critical and Solidarity University (KriSU), the Vivir Bien mapping project has a European focus. The project website is Creative Commons licensed and utilizes OpenStreetMap.

The explosion of new mapping projects is itself creating new challenges that are currently being addressed. One of the most remarkable is surely **TransforMap**, which emerged in early 2014 from a collaboration of programmers and various people developing alternatives to the prevailing economic model in Germany and Austria. They concluded that all the maps being created need a common digital space. So they began working on an open taxonomy based on the criteria of human needs, which can be used globally. The global mapping process is guided by the motto: "There are many alternatives. We make them visible." TransforMap is intended to make it just as easy for people

---

2 | The partners include the University of Surrey (UK), Centre National de la Recherche Scientifique (France), P2P Foundation (Belgium/Thailand), Autonomous University of Barcelona (Spain), Universidad Complutense de Madrid (Spain), and Universita deli Studi di Milano (Italy) as well as twenty-seven individual consortium members from Spain, Italy, Netherlands, France, Ireland, United Kingdom, India and Luxembourg.

to locate the closest place for sharing, exchanging, or giving things away in their own neighborhood as it is to find the nearest supermarket. Standardizing the datasets – a mid-term goal – will make it possible to amalgamate data from various existing maps into a single, open and free map, most of which will be made available on OpenStreetMap.

CommonsScope is a project of CommonSpark, a Texas-based nonprofit. CommonsScope features several collections of maps and visualizations about commons and common-pool resources. The website is a portal to several hundred commons-related maps including ones focused on food, community land trusts, social movements, public assets, indigenous cultures and sharing cities. Some of the more notable maps of specialized concerns include **FallingFruit** (a global map identifying 786,000 locations of forageable food), a map of Free Little Libraries (free books available in neighborhoods around the world), a global **Hackerspace** map, a global **Seed Map**, a map of all **Transition** communities, and several **Community Land Trust** directory maps. CommonsScope also features in-depth profiles for existing commons projects. The TransforMap initiative and the P2P Foundation also steward large collections of commons and new economy maps.

Thanks to many enterprising cartographers, a growing universe of commons and new economy maps is helping people see and reclaim all sorts of resources that have been systematically destroyed by colonial and capitalist cultures. The maps are also helping people create new forms of community self-governance and increase awareness of commons stewardship. Taken together, these maps tell the big story of this historic moment – how system-change originating from the grassroots is radically altering civilization from one that exalts private wealth to one where wealth is shared. The maps are far-seeing tools that empower us with the means to accelerate the emergence of a just and thriving world.

Notable Maps and Their Weblinks

CommonsScope	http://www.commonsscope.org
Falling Fruit	http://fallingfruit.org
Free Little Library Map	http://littlefreelibrary.org/ourmap
Great Lakes Commons	http://greatlakescommonsmap.org
Great Lakes Commons Map	http://greatlakescommonsmap.org
Hackerspaces	http://hackerspaces.org/wiki/List_of_Hacker_Spaces
Mapping the Commons(.net)	http://mappingthecommons.net
Mapping the Commons(.org)	http://mappingthecommons.org
National Community Land Trust Network	http://cltnetwork.org/directory
P2P Foundation maps	https://www.diigo.com/user/mbauwens/P2P-Mapping
P2P Value	http://www.p2pvalue.eu
Seed Map	http://map.seedmap.org
Shareable Community Maps	http://www.shareable.net/community-maps
TransforMap	http://transformap.co
Big Transition Map	http://www.transitionnetwork.org/map
Vivir Bien	http://vivirbien.mediavirus.org
World of Commons (LabGov)	http://www.labgov.it/world-of-commons

Ellen Friedman *(USA) is project lead and founder at CommonSpark. Her work as an activist and professional counselor focuses on individual and collective wellness and liberation.*

Licenses for Commoning:
The GPL, Creative Commons Licenses and CopyFair

By David Bollier

It is not widely known that the law regards virtually all artifacts of human creativity as private property from the moment they are created. Scribble a doodle, record a few guitar riffs, and copyright law treats the resulting "works" as a kind of private property over which you may retain legal control for the rest of your lifetime plus seventy years.

This monopoly right is supposedly necessary to incentivize authors to create new works, whether they be software code, recorded music, books or photographs. The assumption is that people won't create without copyright protection and that all creative works must be bought and sold in the marketplace.

But what if a creator wants her work to be freely copied, shared and re-used?

Copyright law makes no express provisions for allowing such nonmarket uses. This fact that became painfully evident when the Internet became a mass medium in the 1990s and people suddenly wanted to share things online for free.

Richard Stallman, a legendary hacker, was one of the first to devise an ingenious solution to the limitations of copyright law. Stallman wanted his fellow software programmers to help improve the code he was writing and to be able to share the results widely. Stallman also wanted to make sure that no one could take software programs private by claiming a copyright in them.

His pioneering solution in 1989 was a "legal hack" known as the General Public License, or GPL, often known as "copyleft." A work licensed under the GPL permits users to run any program, copy it, modify it, and distribute it in any modified form – without obtaining advance permission or making a payment. In practice, the GPL provides legally enforceable protections to works developed by large communities of coders.

The only limitation imposed by the GPL – and it is key – is that any derivative work must also be licensed under the GPL. This means that the terms of the GPL – the rights to copy, share, modify and reuse – automatically apply to any derivative work, and to any derivative of a derivative, and so on. This was a brilliant legal hack because it inverted the automatic privatization of content under copyright law, instead requiring automatic sharing. The more that a program is shared, the larger the commons of programmers and users!

The GPL has proven hugely significant over the past twenty-six years because it ensures that the value created by a given group of commoners will stay within the commons. People can contribute to a software program such as GNU Linux, the famous computer operating system, with full confidence that no one will be allowed to "take it private."

The success of the GPL in the 1990s and early 2000s inspired law professor Lawrence Lessig and a band of fellow law scholars, activists, techies and artists to extend the idea of the GPL to other types of copyrighted content. Once again, the goal was to promote the legal sharing of content. But in this case, the focus was on texts, music, photography, videos, and anything else that can be copyrighted.

In 2002, a new organization, Creative Commons, launched a suite of six standard licenses to facilitate the sharing of such content. Creators were invited to choose what types of copying and sharing they wish to authorize for their works. The "Attribution" license (known by the abbreviation "BY") allows copying so long as the author is given proper credit for the work. The NonCommercial license (NC) authorizes free reuse so long as the new work is used only for noncommercial purposes. The ShareAlike license (SA) authorizes free reuse so long as the new work also uses the same SA license (that is, derivative works must also be freely useable – similar to the terms of the GPL). A NoDerivatives (ND) license authorizes free reuse so long as the new work does not alter the original work. Any of these licenses can be mixed with others, creating new licenses such as an Attribution-NonCommercial license.

The CC licenses have been wildly successful in helping unleash the power of copying, imitation and sharing. Thousands of open access scientific journals now use CC licenses to make their contents available to anyone for free in perpetuity.[1] Music remix and video mashup communities have flourished. Countless websites and blogs make their content freely accessible, which in turn encourages people to contribute their own talents. According to a report released by Creative Commons in February 2015,[2] the number of CC-licensed works worldwide in 2014 was 882 million – up from an estimated 50 million works in 2006 and 400 million works in 2010. Nine million websites now

---

1 | See essay on open access publishing on pp. 227-228; the essay on the Public Library of Science by Cameron Neylon on pp. 179-181; and the essay on Open Educational Resources by Mary Lou Forward on pp. 186-189.

2 | Creative Commons, "The State of the Commons," February 2015, available at https://stateof.creativecommons.org/report.

use CC licenses, including major sites like YouTube, Wikipedia, Flickr, Public Library of Science, Scribd and Jamendo.

In recent years, there has been mounting frustration with the limits of the GPL and Creative Commons licenses in promoting the creation and protection of commons. Paradoxically, the more shareable the content under these licenses, the more capitalist enterprises are likely to use the "free" content for their profit-making purposes. The classic example of this was the widespread embrace of GNU Linux and other open source software programs by IBM and dozens of other major tech companies. While hackers are pleased that no one can "take private" the code they have worked on, companies are pleased they can use high-quality bodies of software code available at no cost.

This situation is certainly an advance over conventional proprietary software, which does allow any sharing or modification. Yet it still falls short of creating a commons in which the contributors are able capture the value of the work (whether monetary or otherwise) and to protect the integrity of their social commons over time.

To address the limitations of the GPL and CC licenses, Michel Bauwens of the P2P Foundation, working with hacktivist Dmytri Kleiner, developed the idea of commons-based reciprocity licenses, generically known as CCRLs or "CopyFair." These licenses are specifically designed to strike a middle ground between the full-sharing copyleft licenses (such as the GPL and the Creative Commons Non-Commercial license) and conventional copyright law, which make creative works and knowledge strictly private.

The idea is to replace licenses that do not demand direct reciprocity from users, with licenses requiring a basic reciprocity among users in a commercial context. Bauwens and his colleagues are in the process of developing a Peer Production License that would explicitly allow commercialization of a creative work or body of information, but only if the creators, as copyright holders, are able to share in the gains. Bauwens envisions the PPL as a reciprocity license that would serve worker-owned co-operatives and online communities of creators. An early version of the PPL is currently being used experimentally by Guerrilla Translation, a Madrid-based activist/translation project, and the PPL is being discussed in various places, especially among French open agricultural machining and design communities.

As Bauwens explains, "The PPL is designed to enable and empower a counter-hegemonic reciprocal economy that combines commons that are open to all who contribute, while charging a license fee to the for-profit companies who want to use without contributing to the commons. Not that much changes for the multinationals. In practice, they can still use the code as IBM does with

Linux, if they contribute. And for those who don't contribute, they would pay a license fee, a practice they are used to."

The practical effect of the PPL, says Bauwens would be "to direct a stream of income from capital to the commons, but its main effect would be ideological, or, if you like, value-driven."

The PPL should not be confused with the Creative Commons NonCommercial license, which is used by creators who do not want their work used for commercial purposes. That license halts economic development based on open, shareable knowledge and keeps it in nonprofit spheres. But the PPL is intended to allow the commercialization of works developed on open platforms of shared knowledge so long as creators are compensated. The PPL would encourage communities to contribute to a common pool of knowledge, code or creativity, knowing that any resulting profit would help sustain their own cooperative entities; profit would be subsumed to the social goal of sustaining the commons and the commoners.

By using the PPL, Bauwens argues, "peer production would be able to move from a proto-mode of production, unable to perpetuate itself on its own outside capitalism, to an autonomous and real mode of production. It would create a counter-economy that can be the basis for reconstituting a 'counter-hegemony' with a for-benefit circulation of value allied to pro-commons social movements. This could be the basis of the political and social transformation of the political economy." Instead of our being locked into a "communism of capital" in which large companies can amass more capital by appropriating the fruits of sharing on open platforms, peer production mode could self-reproduce itself, socially and financially.

New Ventures in Commons-Based Publishing

Even as commercial publishers struggle to survive in a world of high distribution costs, an aggressive Amazon.com and thin profit margins – many upstarts are discovering the appeal of commons-based publishing. Community building turns out to be a great way to bypass the formidable costs of conventional markets and to bring authors and readers together in highly efficient ways. Below, we profile some noteworthy pioneers of commons-based publishing – for academic journals, books and magazines. These examples show that it is entirely possible to publish important works more cheaply and rapidly than conventional publishers, and without the severe restrictions of copyright law and concentrated markets.

Open Access Scholarly Publishing

For generations, scientists and scholars have used scholarly journals to share their latest research discoveries and theories. These journals – usually run by commercial publishers selling subscriptions to university libraries and research institutes – provide the easiest, most efficient way for academic disciplines to advance their collective knowledge.

But the arrival of the Internet and digital technologies has called into question the expense and information restrictions of this commercially driven system. Thanks to digital publishing, it has become far cheaper and easier for a field of researchers to share their specialized research with anyone on the planet. To be sure, there are still costs associated with editing a journal and the peer review of articles, but Web-based publishing has radically reduced (and sometimes eliminated) the expenses of print production, distribution and marketing.

Most commercial journal publishers, not surprisingly, have seen these developments as a troubling threat to their business models. They have continued to assert strict copyright control over articles, putting them behind Web paywalls and charging high subscription fees. In short, they have limited access to research that could otherwise be made freely available – research that taxpayer money has often financed.

In the early 2000s, a variety of academic researchers in the US and Europe began to address this significant problem by starting the open access, or OA, movement in scholarly publishing. Its goal has been to make academic research freely and openly available to anyone in perpetuity. Open access advocates have had to pioneer new revenue models for academic journal publishing, overcome the limitations of copyright law by using Creative Commons licenses,[1] and fight fierce opposition from commercial publishers, uninformed politicians and slow-moving university administrators.

Happily, these strong, sustained efforts to reclaim research from profit-driven publishers and reclaim it for the academic commons have had many great successes. The open access journals started by the Public Library of Science in 2003[2] have been followed by thousands of other publications that honor open access in one fashion or another. One example is the *International Journal of the Commons*,[3] an open access journal published by the International Association for the Study of the Commons. Major funders of scientific research, including governments, have started to require that research be published under OA principles, and commercial journals have allowed academics to self-archive their work in open access repositories. Some of the largest journal publishers have themselves started OA journals, joining a small group of niche publishers that have pioneered OA publishing as a profitable enterprise.

As of July 2015, the Directory of Open Access Journals had indexed 10,354 open access, peer-reviewed journals that had published more than 1.8 million articles. A flood of major research universities, including Harvard University, now require their faculty to publish works under open access principles. While there remain many challenges in making scientific and scholarly research more accessible, open access journals have become one of the most significant success stories in reclaiming and reinventing knowledge commons.

– *David Bollier*

Book Publishing as a Commons for Regional Culture

Dissatisfied with the costs and slowness of conventional book publishing, some newcomers are trying to re-introduce the craft, care and social relationships that once prevailed in the field. One of the most innovative examples is Levellers Press, a worker-owned and -managed co-operative in Amherst, Massachusetts (USA), the offshoot of a regional photocopying business, Collective Copies.

1 See essay on Creative Commons licenses on pp. 223-226.

2 See essay on PLOS by Cameron Neylon, on pp. 179-181

3 http://www.thecommonsjournal.org/index.php/ijc

Levellers Press – inspired by the seventeenth-century commoners who denounced the privatization of common lands and called for greater equality – wants to give authors new opportunities to reach readers, and first-time authors new opportunities to publish. This means changing the relationships among publishers, authors and readers. As one local observer put it, "It's something of a throwback to a different era, when publishers were also printers and worked more closely with writers on their books – and when books were produced not just for the sales potential but for their literary and informative value."[4]

The authors who publish their books through Levellers Press usually live in the Pioneer Valley of western Massachusetts. Many Levellers books cover regional topics that might not otherwise find a book publisher. Levellers' first book, for example, was *Slavery in the Connecticut Valley of Massachusetts*, by a retired Amherst College professor, Robert Romer. Since its inception in 2009, Levellers has published more than fifty books on a wide range of topics – fiction, poetry memoirs, social issues, health. Books are sold in local markets as well as via the Levellers and Amazon websites.

Two factors have been critical to Levellers' success – its skillful use of new technologies to develop a new publishing model, and its founder, Steve Strimer, a worker-owner of Collective Copies since 1997. Strimer realized that the publishing marketplace was changing radically, and that a niche printer such as Collective Copies could prosper by pioneering a new form of regional publishing. New types of software, printers, scanners and bindery machines now make it possible for a small enterprise like Levellers to do print runs of 100 to 200 books for less than $10 a copy.

Such small-batch "print on demand" publishing helps avoid costly, unsold inventory while also giving unproven authors an opportunity to find their voice and reach readers. This publishing model also allows great flexibility in meeting unpredictable consumer demand. If a spurt of interest arises for *Vital Aging*, a guide for older people, or *Girls Got Kicks*, a popular photo-documentary book about "badass females," Levellers can quickly print a few dozen copies within a few days for a very low cost. Most Levellers' authors sell between 200 and 300 copies. After *The Wealth of the Commons* was rejected by a dozen conventional publishers, Levellers agreed to publish the book in 2012 and welcomed the editors' use of a Creative Commons license. The book went on to sell well and earn a profit for the worker cooperative.

Authors like the Levellers publishing model because it is simple and fair: Levellers absorbs the startup costs of layout, design and printing for any book it chooses to publish, and the author gets no advance payment and must do

---

4 | Steve Pfarrer, "Leveling the Playing Field," *Daily Hampshire Gazette* [Northampton, Massachusetts], January 26, 2012.

most of the marketing. But once production costs have been recouped – usually after sales of 100 to 150 books – the author and publisher split all revenues 50-50. This is a far better deal for authors than the usual royalty rates of 7 to 12 percent. Levellers also has a self-publishing arm called Off the Common Books, which assists authors in printing and marketing books themselves. This was a perfect arrangement for *Patterns of Commoning* because of the greater author autonomy, low pricing, open licensing and production control that Off the Common Books makes possible.

Levellers has enriched the western Massachusetts area by carving out a viable new market for books of local interest – memoirs by community person-alities, biographies, histories, recipe books, and many other books of quirky authenticity. Strimer concedes that he does not need to be as market-focused as conventional publishers to be profitable, and that is mostly the point: the Levellers publishing model blends financial practicality with localism, and makes book publishing a feasible creative outlet for a diverse roster of people who might not otherwise become authors.

– David Bollier

A Community of Commoners in the Guise of a Magazine

The first time the printing presses were fired up for *Oya*, the word "crisis" followed "print media" like a mantra. Since March 2010, thirty issues of this young magazine from Germany have been published every two months. *Oya* emboldens readers to forge new paths in living a "good life." Yet the editors do not themselves decide what a "good life" is supposed to be, but instead set out on an expedition with their readers. The journey winds a varied trail from open workshops and urban gardens to art in public spaces and communal residential projects. The magazine has gone to ecovillages, farms practicing eco-responsible agriculture, and schools in the wild.

Commons principles lie at the core of the projects. They all depend upon voluntary contributions, communal action, self-organization, self-determina-tion and a diversity of participants. As the motto of *Oya's* online edition (www. oya-online.de) puts it, "Much more interesting than a bunch of like-minded people is a community of differently minded people." While *Oya* tends to focus on practical applications, it is also a thoughtful and reflective magazine. Its essays question the foundations of contemporary thinking and squarely face up to failures and disillusionment.

The magazine has been published every two months since March 2010 with a lively layout and strong photos, and of course, on eco-friendly paper. Roughly 90 percent of the print edition is available online under a copyleft license, the Creative Commons Attribution-NonCommercial-ShareAlike license

(BY-NC-SA). The project is run by Oya Medien eG, a cooperative whose preamble states that its goal is not to enrich its members, but to publish a meaningful magazine. *Oya* has a large and loyal following that warrants print runs of 10,000 copies – a cost financed mostly by subscriptions, advertising and sales at select railway news stands. One tenth of the magazine's 4,000 subscribers are members of the cooperative and support it with shares of 200 Euros each: an impressive show of support, but not quite enough to make the magazine financially stable. That will require 5,000 subscriptions. In the meantime, the editorial staff, administrators, and authors made substantial gifts to the magazine in the early years in the form of their work.

Oya is not a glossy lifestyle magazine designed to promote a bit of sustainable consumption. It is a magazine by and for activist-minded people who are deeply concerned with the state of the world and want to make a real difference. In this sense, *Oya* is far more than a magazine. It is a community of commoners trying to develop and share commons-based ways of living and forms of economic activity that can thrive in a world framed by climate change and Peak Oil.

– Lara Mallien

A Growing Network of Commons-Oriented Magazines

A number of magazines are starting to provide regular coverage of the commons and companion-movements. In the United Kingdom, **STIR magazine**, for "stir to action," has introduced a fresh, vigorous voice to the coverage of politics, culture and social transformation. In addition to its coverage of cooperatives, open source projects and alternative economics, *STIR* has focused a great deal on the commons movement and its initiatives. Like *Oya*, *STIR* has re-imagined the idea of a magazine as a focal point for bringing together an active community of reader/activists/thinkers. Many small, local projects with great potential are woven together to suggest hopeful new visions for the future.

Another notable British publication on the commons is **The Commoner**, edited by Massimo De Angelis.[5] The website is a rich body of Web commentary and analyses from an autonomous Marxist political lens. Since May 2001, *The Commoner* has published fifteen substantive collections of essays exploring how the commons is relevant to care work, domestic labor, free software, energy, money, the body and value, among other topics. *The Commoner* explains that it is "about living in a world in which the doing is separated from the deed, in which this separation is extended in an increasing numbers of spheres of life, in which the revolt about this separation is ubiquitous."

---

5 | http://www.commoner.org.uk

In the US, several web and print magazines are providing valuable coverage of the commons. **Shareable**, based in the Bay Area, is a Web magazine with plentiful, cutting-edge coverage of developments in the "sharing and collaborative economy."[6] *Shareable* has pioneered the idea of "shareable cities" with a set of detailed policies, and organized dozens of projects to promote alternative local projects and activism. **Yes! Magazine** – the magazine for alternative futures – features an ongoing series of articles on "commonomics," the development of local alternatives, from local co-ops to public banks to community-owned solar projects.[7] **On the Commons** magazine, published from Minneapolis, generally focuses on the great variety of North American commons, giving special attention to placemaking initiatives, water commons and organizing efforts.

Kosmos, a beautifully designed quarterly magazine with an international readership, has frequently focused on the commons as part of a larger agenda of building a "planetary civilization and world community."[8] Published out of the Berkshires in Massachusetts, Kosmos also explores transformational leadership and spiritual dimensions of making change.

The Case for the Commons is a bimonthly e-publication that explores the implications of dozens of judgments and orders about the commons passed by the Indian Supreme Court, High Court and state governments. Produced by the Foundation for Ecological Security in India, the e-publication interprets and popularizes the legal rulings, with an eye toward improving commons governance.[9]

In Latin America, **Pillku** – "lovers of freedom" – is an online magazine about free technology and culture, commons, good living, collaboration and community property.[10] It is published quarterly by Código Sur, a nonprofit organization whose purpose, among others, is to assist the development and socialization of these concerns by providing basic funding and technical infrastructure. The *Pillku* website provides a collaborative space for debate on free culture and commons in Latin America and seeks to build a society based on the freedom to share. Although it meets the standards of scientific and scholarly journals, *Pillku* as an organization and magazine is dedicated to collective creation, even in its editing processes. Most of the work needed to produce *Pillku* is voluntary. Contributions to the website come from throughout Latin America and the Caribbean, generating a vast commons of information and building relationships among various projects. The extended *Pillku* community and

6 | http://shareable.net

7 | http://yesmagazine.org

8 | http://www.kosmosjournal.org

9 | http://www.fes.org.in/includeAll.php?pld=MiøøNyøy

10 | http://www.pillku.com

editorial board are comprised of committed social organizations in Argentina, Uruguay, Brazil, Ecuador, Costa Rica and Mexico.

In India, **Pratham Books** is a not-for-profit publisher that has the avowed mission of "putting a book in every child's hand."[11] It is an outgrowth of the "Read India Movement," which seeks to cultivate a joy of reading among children and encourage education. Identifying a lack of affordable, quality books for children in India, Pratham Books has set out to publish inexpensive books in English and ten other Indian languages. It works with a range of partners – a foundation, a conservation group, social media enterprises and other publishers – to reach children. To date, it has published over 280 titles and over 12 million books.

Of course, there are also a wide number of blogs and websites devoted to the commons. The leading academic website on the commons include those run by the **International Association for the Study of the Commons**, founded by the late Professor Elinor Ostrom, and the **Digital Library on the Commons**, which hosts an extensive collection of documents.[12] Another much-used resource is the **P2P Foundation's blog and wiki**, a vast archive of materials about digital peer production, the commons and related fields.[13]

– David Bollier and Santiago Hoerth Moura

---

11 | http://prathambooks.org
12 | http://dlc.dlib.indiana.edu
13 | http://p2pfoundation.net

SPACES FOR CO-LEARNING

"Whoever you are, whatever you are, start with that, whether salt of the earth or only white sugar."

Alice Walker

Otelo – Open Technology Labs in Austria

By Hannelore Hollinetz and Martin Hollinetz

The development of the Otelos – the international network of open technology labs – is the story of a group bringing together creative people in rural areas and forging a new culture of innovation with them. The idea for Otelos began in 2009 as Martin Hollinetz, then Director of Regional Management in the Upper Austrian districts of Vöcklabruck and Gmunden, contemplated with dismay the regional development strategies of the EU, the Austrian federal government, and the Austrian states.

He saw the existing strategies as rigidly centralized processes dominated by establishment "experts" and hostile to the idea of public participation. There were neither infrastructures nor organizational models to support a culture of creativity and innovation. Martin wanted to develop a culture in which openness, sharing and cooperation could drive new forms of participatory regional development.

When the two of us set out to find solutions to this challenge, we found answers in the community workshops, Fab Labs and hackerspaces in urban areas. These are the spaces where tech-savvy people, hackers, and people interested in science or digital art come together to exchange ideas and produce new things. Unfortunately, these spaces seemed entirely unsuited to rural areas because they are usually tailored to very narrow groups of specialists. Also, a feasibility study for introducing such spaces in rural regions stressed the importance of collaborating with people from various business, education, media, and political communities. We also realized that is would be crucial to create a structure that would allow any projects to be financially independent.

We imagined Otelos as places where ordinary people could find pleasure in sharing knowledge and building things together. The projects could be about constructing autonomous spider robots or building raised beds for gardening. They could be about making soap and crafting jewelry from recycled materials. The people who might wish to participate in the Otelos could be children, people interested in agriculture, cultural networkers, "mechatronics" technicians, do-it-yourselfers, game developers, and many others.

Capturing People's Imaginations and Making Things Possible

The first Otelos began in 2010 in cooperation with the municipalities of Vöcklabruck and Gmunden. The municipal councils decided that the municipalities would provide the physical spaces and budgets for the Otelos for at least three years (a commitment that many municipalities have since extended to an unlimited period of time).

Those municipal council decisions fulfilled an initial requirement for the independence we desired. In each community, we tried to identify people who were interested in forming a group that would organize and design the individual Otelo venues. In each place, at least five members came together who enjoyed hosting and networking with other people – a model of volunteer organizing that has proved quite successful. This group keeps an eye on new trends and initiates experimental projects of the sort mentioned above.

Soon, the first Otelo jam sessions and "DenkBars" were held – DenkBar being a play on words: "denkbar" means "imaginable" in German, so a Denk-Bar would be a bar or pub for open meetings not dominated by experts imparting knowledge, but by interested amateurs who share a passion for a topic of common interest. We also developed what we call the "node model," which enables groups to use space in the Otelos long-term, free of charge, and without any pressure to achieve results. The only requirement is that the groups share their knowledge and experiences and provide opportunities for others to participate. The nodes let a creative economy project evolve and do in-depth experiments with public funding support.

The resulting projects have been quite diverse. There are electronics do-it-yourselfers who build Tesla coils for making music, light painters and people developing municipal energy-saving projects. There are people exchanging ideas about innovative educational models and others organizing new forms of consumer-producer partnerships for sourcing food. An important aspect of all of the nodes is that participants come from very different contexts. Most of them would never meet each other in "normal" life.

Belonging and Being Able to Grow

What began as an experiment in 2010 became the first major challenge for the Otelo Association in 2012 when two new venues were opened. How should they be managed and relate to each other? It quickly became clear that decentralization would be necessary in order to maintain Otelo's vitality as well as our ability to make decisions.

It was decided to invite individual local projects to start local Otelo associations if they wished. Today, these associations are the governing bodies for local Otelos – with the Otelo Charter serving as a networking element. The Charter outlines our cultural ethic of innovation and formulates the fundamental perspective of all Otelo venues. Today, the associations meet twice a year as a network and participate in activities involving various Otelo venues, such as festivals.

By the end of 2014, there were twenty-six Otelo nodes in eleven locations in Austria and Germany. Otelos are places where people can delve into all sorts of arts and crafts, electronics, 3D printing projects and alternative educational approaches. They are places where people play and dance together, produce free media, design new forms of work, and pursue countless other passions. All of the ideas and projects developed in the Otelos are made available under a Creative Commons license[1] or through workshops or various forms of documentation. This is in keeping with the motto, Knowledge is a commons!

In a few years, the term "Otelo" could be defined like this in the dictionary:

ō tel ō, adjective: Welcoming; being part of a diverse, open community; invited to join in actively; keen to experiment; free, touched, inspired and alive; having found one's place.

Martin Hollinetz *(Germany) is a social pedagogue, vocational educator and regional developer. An Ashoka Fellow since 2013, he is a lecturer at the University of Art and Design Linz and was elected Austrian of the Year in the field of creative industries in 2013.*

Hannelore Hollinetz *(Germany) is a musician and educator. She works as an actress, project developer and facilitator for projects for children and youths, and is a cofounder, with Martin Hollinetz, of the Otelo network and Otelo eGen.*

---

1 | See pp. 223-226.

Medialab-Prado:
A Citizen Lab for Incubating Innovative Commons

By Marcos García

Medialab-Prado is a citizen laboratory in Madrid that hosts a great diversity of commons-based innovation. Through its workshops, collaborative teams, classes and public events, Medialab has enabled the development of open design hives for urban beekeeping,[1] sponsored collaborative translations of books,[2] and assisted development of experimental video games.[3] It has invited anyone who is interested to help develop a new data visualization for air quality in Madrid[4] and a new citizen network of sensors to collect the data.[5] It has hosted research teams that have produced a new typography font[6] and designs for a massive LED screen as a vehicle for urban art and commentary.[7]

It may seem odd to think that passionate amateurs, open source hackers, various professionals and ordinary citizens could actually collaborate and produce interesting new ideas. But that is precisely what Medialab-Prado has succeeded in doing in the last eight years. It has invented a new type of public institution for the production, research and dissemination of cultural projects. It is committed to exploring collaborative forms of experimentation and learning that are emerging from digital networks, especially those practices that enact the commons such as free software, hacker ethics, the Internet as an open infrastructure and peer production dynamics. Medialab-Prado serves as a municipal cultural center that promotes commons-based research, experimentation and peer production, especially through its "Commons Lab."

The model is quite simple: Medialab-Prado acts as a platform where anyone who has an idea can meet other people and form a work team to develop and

---

1 | http://medialab-prado.es/article/colmenasurbanas
2 | http://medialab-prado.es/article/floren_cabello_laboratorio_del_procomun
3 | http://medialab-prado.es/article/playlab_experimentacion_con_videojuegos
4 | http://www.intheair.es
5 | http://medialab-prado.es/article/air_quality_egg
6 | http://medialab-prado.es/article/from_stone_to_spaceship
7 | http://programalaplaza.medialab-prado.es

prototype the idea. Projects developed at the lab vary immensely, as the list above suggests.

The beauty of the Medialab-Prado process is the inclusive invitations to anyone with the knowledge, talent or enthusiasm to develop a new idea. Through different kinds of open calls for proposals and collaborators, teams are often formed to develop projects in production workshops. Each group is an experiment itself in team- and community-building as it blends people with different backgrounds (artistic, scientific, technical), levels of specialization (experts and beginners) and degrees of engagement. Each group, overseen by the promoter of the project, needs to self-organize and arrange the rules and protocols by which the contributions of participants will be incorporated or rejected, and with what types of acknowledgments. This is why Medialab-Prado has been sometimes defined as an incubator of communities – and commons.

At the heart of Medialab-Prado's "innovation hosting" of projects is its commitment to free software tools and free licensing. This facilitates the local participation of those that want to contribute to the common good. It facilitates online participation as well, and also in the proper documentation of projects, which is crucial in replicating them elsewhere and in tracking the reasons for the success, failure and procedures of commoning experiments.

Since its creation in 2007, the Commons Lab has evolved from a seminar in which members' unpublished working documents on the commons were discussed, to an open laboratory that invites the participation of any collaborator, including amateurs, academics and professionals, who wish to join a project.

The Commons Lab has been remarkably productive. Its projects include *Memory as a Commons*,[8] which explore the collective creation of shared memory during conflicts; *guifi.net Madrid*,[9] which imagined and produced a local tele-comunications wifi infrastructure that works as a commons; *Commons Based Enterprises*, which examines recent models of business management that have made contributions to the commons;[10] and *Kune*, a web tool to encourage collaboration, content sharing and free culture.[11]

Besides such projects, the Commons Lab has hosted many public debates on commons-related themes involving cities, rural areas, digital realms and the body. It has also made public presentations about projects such as Guerrilla Translation, a transnational curator and translator of timely cultural memes,[12] and Mapping the Commons, a "research open lab on urban commons."[13]

---

8 | http://medialab-prado.es/article/memoria_procomun
9 | http://madrid.guifi.net
10 | http://www.colaborabora.org/proyectos/empresas-del-procomun
11 | http://kune.ourproject.org
12 | http://guerrillatranslation.com/en
13 | http://mappingthecommons.net/en/world

Guerrilla Translation is a P2P-Commons translation collective and cooperative founded in Spain. It consists of a small but international set of avid readers, content curators and social/environmental issue-focused people who love to translate and love to share. The group seeks to model a cooperative form of global idea-sharing, by enabling a platform and method for opening dialogues. Guerrilla Translation does not rely on volunteers, but on building an innovative cooperative business model which "walks the talk" of much contemporary writing on the new economy and its power to change.[14]

Since moving to a new venue in 2013, the Commons Lab has been less active, even as commoning practices and the commons paradigm have played an increasingly important role in other lines of work and projects at Medialab-Prado. In the near future, the Commons Lab is going to reinvent itself as a project and pull together a history of its achievements to date and comprehensive and introductory material for the general public on the commons theory and practice.

Through public policies and institutions that incubate new commons projects, and enable civil society to create value directly, the commons paradigm may allow us to reinvent public institutions. It can engage people more directly, developing their capacities and participation, and providing accessible open infrastructures that require what anthropologist and free software scholar Christopher Kelty calls "recursive publics" – "a public that is constituted by a shared concern for maintaining the means of association through which they come together as a public."[15]

Medialab-Prado, as a public institution that is part of the Arts Area of Madrid City Hall, tries to advance this point of view. It tries to learn from commons-based practices and apply them in the public realm – sometimes succeeding, and sometimes not. But as an organization committed to commons as a model of governance, Medialab-Prado regards its workshops, convenings and events as an indispensable way to continue this important exploration.

Marcos García *(Spain) is Director of Medialab-Prado, an initiative of Madrid City Hall devised as a citizen laboratory for the production, research and dissemination of cultural projects.*

---

14 | http://www.guerrillatranslation.com

15 | Kelty, Christopher, Two Bits, *The Cultural Significance of Free Software.* Durham, NC: Duke University Press. 2008, at http://twobits.net/read.

Voyaging in the Sea of Ikarian Commons and Beyond

By Maria Bareli-Gaglia

Our story begins in 2006, during my fieldwork at the Greek island of Ikaria in the Aegean sea, when I picked up a hitchhiker, a woman named Frosini. As we began to talk, we realized that we were both anthropologists riding in the same car. This encounter was the start of a discussion on the commons, which still continues. It also marked the beginning of a collaborative endeavor to understand how commons are tied to land and local culture. What do the commons mean to people? What happens when people lose access to their commons? What happens to local cultures when natural and civic commons are enclosed?

Two years after our first encounter, as the 2008 financial crisis was starting to unravel, the daily agenda of Greek politics was marked by enclosures of natural and civic commons, through privatizations and commodification of public goods and services. In the name of "green development," the government has been working closely with private companies to develop industrial wind parks along the mountain ridges of most of the Aegean islands. A new Land Plan was also legislated for the island, which re-designates uses of land in ways that seem incompatible with traditional uses of land. Perhaps the most characteristic example has been the designation of some areas below the mountain range, traditionally pasturelands, as "industrial zones."

In 2012, the government announced its decision to downgrade the Hospital of Ikaria into a branch of the hospital of the nearby island of Samos, thus downgrading the quality and quantity of health services provided at Ikaria. That measure, along with other measures which promoted the commodification of health, threatened to sweep aside the very reason Ikarians, locals and immigrants had built the Panikarian hospital in 1958 – to give all Ikarians equal access to health services. For Ikaria, an island of 8,000 inhabitants, legislation promoting the privatization or commodification of natural resources, public goods and services was seen as a serious threat to their way of life.[1]

---

1 | For an account of the islanders' discourses and the ways they perceive and respond to crisis, see Bareli M., 2014, "Facets of Crisis in a Greek Island Community: The Ikarian Case." in

Frosini Koutsouti and I soon realized that Ikaria was a real-life labora-tory for some key themes of our times: the various enclosures of the island's commons, the people's resistance in defending and/or reclaiming them, and their invention of innovative new commons. But how could we explore and document these phenomena? We concluded that such an endeavor could not be neutral, as if we could stand apart from local struggles. We could not ignore global neoliberal forces that are violently transforming citizens into consumers of goods whose production depends on relentless enclosures.

In 2012, Frosini and I formed a nonprofit group, the Documentation Research and Action Centre of Ikaria (DRACOI), as a "shelter" for our collab-orative work on the commons. One major source of inspiration has been Ivan Illich's Intercultural Documentation Center in Mexico, which he established in 1961 to document the role of "modern development" in the dismemberment of local cultures, the loss of traditional ways of life and the creation of poverty. Like Illich, we entered into collaboration with various locally based village as-sociations, action committees, cooperatives and other collectivities. Our shared goals lay in protecting basic human rights like equal access to health, education and water. We also wanted to use the commons as a lens for understanding the larger processes of political and sociocultural transformation.

We began to realize that local responses to enclosures of commons could be "read" not merely as isolated moments of resistance against a neoliberal wave, but part of a much larger historical process of enclosure that began in England and elsewhere during the late Middle Ages. Local struggles can be seen as part of the *double movement* described by economic anthropologist Karl Polanyi, who explained that enclosures driven by the international market economy inevitably provoke countermovements of people seeking to reclaim their commons and create new ones. Seen in this light, the ideals of "green development"[2] promoted by corporatists as a "solution" to the crisis resembles the "improvements" of nineteenth century Britain that require ongoing enclosure of natural and civic commons (Esteva 1992:6-25).

In the course of our journey in the immense sea of literature, activism and dialogue on issues of the *commons*, we came across thinkers posing issues relevant to our own questions and aims. Each added to our navigational hori-zons. Some became passengers, joining us in common endeavors, for varying periods of time. We also joined larger "ships" of shared inquiry. Such was the "Mataroa" seminar, named after the historical ship that in December 1945 left Greece, loaded with young scientists, students and artists, who, over the course of their lives, contributed to the formation of the thought and visions that was

---

Practicing Anthropology, 36:1 (Winter 2014), pp. 21-27.

2 | See essay by Arturo Escobar on pp. 348-360 of this volume.

culminated with May 1968. Our ambitious idea for Mataroa was that now an imaginary ship would return to Greece, loaded, this time, with concepts and ideas proper for a critical and radical understanding of contemporary reality. Those were the concepts of crisis, critique, and commons and their enclosures, as well as the idea of a Mediterranean imaginary – a vision of what the region could be.[3]

In 2013, the Mataroa seminar "arrived" at the port of Ikaria, bringing together twenty-seven researchers and commoners from the Mediterranean Sea and beyond, to share their stories. One participant brought the other, some found out about the meeting through its blog (mataroanetwork.org), and each found the main concepts of the seminar to be fruitful organizing concepts for telling many different stories. All participants agreed on the need to deconstruct the idea of "crisis," which was not to be taken as an objective condition of contemporary reality but as a powerful discourse for "Othering" as a powerful means of legitimizing conspicuous violations of the social contract and fundamental human rights.[4]

The question posed by the "Mataroans" was whether the main components of a new imaginary challenging the capitalist one could be identified. Instead of conceiving of more and more aspects of life in terms of market norms and "development," could we imagine one that protects and regenerates the very sources of life? Could we discover whether a "Mediterranean Imaginary" existed in contrast to the imaginary of a Hobbesian "war of all against all" – a vision defined by such core values as *offering* and *conviviality* within communal institutions,[5] and within familial and friendly ties?

The seminar was convened without a budget and depended entirely on the local gift economy of Ikarians, who provided hospitality to researchers and commoners. The logic of the gift also penetrated the organization of the seminar, which would "open up" to local society through a series of public talks on current political and social developments in the Mediterranean and beyond, and on issues relevant to Ikarian experiences. With that in mind, the organizing committee invited some of the "Mataroans" to publicly share their experiences

---

3 | The idea for a "Mataroa Summer Seminar" belongs to Nikolas Kosmatopoulos, and the title of the meeting at Ikaria was "Against Crisis For the Commons: Towards a Mediterranean Imaginary." Besides Nikolas Kosmatopoulos, Frosini Koutsouti and me, the organizing committee consisted of Takis Geros (Panteion Universtiy of Athens), Penny Koutrolykou (University of Thessaly), Helena Nassif (Westminster University) and Stavros Stayrides (National Technical University of Athens).

4 | See, for example, the report of the International Federation for Human Rights and its Greek member organization, the Hellenic League for Human Rights, on the downgrading of human rights as a cost of austerity in Greece, Dec. 2014, available at https://www.fidh.org/International-Federation-for-Human-Rights/europe/greece/16675-greece-report-unveils-human-rights-violations-stemming-from-austerity.

5 | See essay by Marianne Gronemeyer in this volume on pp. 50-52.

and ideas. Some discussed the popular uprisings in Egypt (Samah Selim), Turkey (Merve Cagsirli) and Kentucky (Betsy Taylor). Others addressed the international experience of privatizing systems of water management (Dimitris Zikos), the experience of neoliberal environmental management of commons in Tanzania and Senegal (Melis Ece), and the idea of degrowth (Giorgos Kallis). Another presentation, inspired by American and European press accounts of Ikarian longevity, examined "slacker politics" (Kristin Lawler). ("Slackers" are people who always seek to avoid work.)

The Mataroa seminar-ship left the port of Ikaria for unknown destinations of new initiative, leaving behind a wealth of material available to anyone through a Creative Commons Attribution-ShareAlike license. As a kind of countergift to our hosts in Ikaria, the Ikarian stakeholders of the Mataroa initiative prepared a publication that documented this dialogue about the commons.[6] Instead of just publishing the proceedings of the seminar, we created a collection of essays that extended the dialogue sparked by the public talks during the seminar. We invited citizens and groups who are fighting privatizations and commodifications of natural resources, public goods and services, to share their thoughts and experiences. These included the vice chair of the local Association of Health Workers at the Hospital of Ikaria, for example, and SOS Chalkidiki, a coalition of collectives struggling against a huge gold mining plan that will have great environmental, economic and social consequences.[7]

This experience convinced us that, if we are to place the notion of the commons in our analytical epicenter, or use this notion as a compass, we cannot *but* do it in collaboration with people of praxis, within their own moral and social economies. Politically engaged research must facilitate the co-construction and exchange of knowledge in ways that empower people and give them new tools to serve their ongoing struggles. The journey in this immense sea of the commons continues and new initiatives are already planned with new partners and enduring friends.[8] The endeavor of creating a methodology of the commons has just started, many collaborations are to be made, and many more lessons remain to be learned.

---

6 | The fruit of this endeavor was an edited volume, "Dialogues Against Crisis, for the Commons. Towards a Mediterranean Imaginary" (2014), which was made possible by members of the Mataroa initiative as well as of the team behind the electronic local magazine ikariamag.gr, to whom we remain grateful.

7 | The editing of the book was also a collaborative endeavor, which I took up with a woman of praxis, Argyro Fakari, a high school teacher, who is active in the struggles of the educational community to guard the public character of the Greek educational system.

8 | The "Dialogues" project is continued in the journal *Esto*, the quarterly publication of an initiative based at the island of Kefallonia, which aims at the creation of a "Free University."

References

Esteva, Gustavo. 1992. "Development." *In* Wolfgang Sachs, ed., *The Development Dictionary: A Guide to Knowledge as Power*. London, UK: Zed Books, Ltd.

Stiglitz, Joseph E. 2001. "Foreword." *In* Karl Polanyi, *The Great Transformation: The Political and Economic Origins of Our Time*. Boston, Mass.: Beacon Press.

Maria Bareli-Gaglia *(Greece) is an economist, currently pursuing her PhD in Sociology/Social Anthropology (University of Crete). Her thesis involves the study of the annual festivals (paniyiries) at Ikaria. She is chair of DRACOI, a nonprofit, which aims, among others things, at creating the conditions for an equal exchange of knowledge between locals and researchers.*

Learning as an Open Road, Learning as a Commons

By Claudia Gómez-Portugal M.

A number of families in the small Mexican town of Tepoztlán have taken the initiative to create a space for free and independent learning that provides meaning. Some of the 14,000 people who live in the town's seven neighborhoods are indigenous or immigrants, and in keeping with a longstanding Mexican tradition, some land is communal property. In addition, there are numerous initiatives for alternative economic activity – for example, the barter currency "Ollines," the organic market, and TepozTequio, where people come together to work with and for each other.[1]

The TepozHub is an office jointly used by several people and initiatives, where the infrastructure is available to all who contribute. There is also the secondhand and barter online initiative and the community radio station Tepoztlán. Our family decided that all this offered a unique potential to create a special learning context for our children as well as for neighborhood youths and adults...and so we decided to contribute to the transformation from the bottom up and to focus on building an alternative to education with many others who shared our views.

It all began when we as a family had to choose a school for our children to attend. Making a wise choice became more and more intense as we realized that other parents were grappling with the same question. But to us, it became a decision of life beyond the school and even education. We felt it was more important to ask how we wanted our children grow up and learn. We thought about how we would spend the time that we devote to our children, and how we would have to change ourselves so that they could grow up free, being exactly who they are, and make decisions about their own lives.

All these questions made us want to reinvent learning as something deeply connected with the joy of life and something that requires care. They

---

1 | In Tepoztlán, this procedure is used especially for building houses. A group comes together that first builds one family's house, then the next person's, etc. The name takes up the indigenous tradition of *tequio*, which signifies the coordination and performance of work for the community.

strengthened our desire to ensure that we could connect life and learning in our children's lives, and also in other people's lives, and especially in our own. We wanted to open up a path that everyone could take, a path through which we would reinvent ourselves and define what to do, a path on which we would expand our means, opportunities, and skills to learn and take action, and together with other people experience and bring about the vitality that lies in learning itself.

That is how we came to establish Camino Abierto, the Open Road, a space for pursuing alternative forms of learning and living on this planet. The name refers to the poem "Song of the Open Road," written by Walt Whitman in 1856. Camino Abierto sees itself as a community for self-directed learning. This is where we try to integrate learning and living, and in the process, build community ties. Our group includes families whose children go to schools and others whose children do not. We meet on a regular basis to exchange views, and we organize common activities, tours and outings as well as workshops that everyone can participate in.

Our starting point is our own interests, creativity and skills. Every month we compile a calendar with all activities that we want to do. For example, we learn about the balance of life in the orchard and in the biology of the region, about the natural world with expert talks and hiking. We are developing a new global consciousness through our film club. We get to know ourselves through contact with nature, exploring our comfort zones and our boundaries. We learn to reinvent ourselves in the meeting with others, and we learn about the power of the word in reading groups where we grapple our feelings towards others. We work on social integration, occupying the public space where we use bicycles, tricycles and roller skates[2] – which requires redesigning the public space – and we create communal spaces, designing projects for community parks and orchards. In short: We shape and live learning as commons!

Building and revitalizing our community are the most meaningful, essential and useful learning of our time. It takes place from a local initiative in a small and human scale. People assume that learning happens naturally; they integrate it into their family lives and in a natural way, and it leads to actions. Thus the very process of creating networks for mutual support results in more resources and relationships becoming available – and over time, this brings about a learning-friendly context and spaces of communality.

People in many parts of the world are starting to recover and claim learning as a commons, and are creating new structures to make it real. The initiatives vary widely, but they all share the feature that the people are directing their

---

2 | Editors' note: This is not a matter of course in Mexico. The cobbled streets of Tepotzlán, the narrow sidewalks, if they exist at all, are not suitable for bikes, trikes, or skates.

learning themselves. Learning as a commons is embedded in meaningful contexts. It is founded on people developing their own interests and addressing problems and questions in their lives. Doing all this in a self-directed and free way – "unschooling" themselves[3] – lets people find their own ways of learning that exist beyond the logic of the state and the market, both of which are increasingly shaping school curricula and undermining academic freedom.

"Learning as a commons" is a challenge because it always has to be re-thought and re-enacted with others. Also, in contrast to homeschooling, it must take place within the community itself. The challenge lies in developing unique living environments in which children and youth can take courses, work on projects, solve problems, or simply play. Learning as commoning must create an ambiance that is embedded in active life, and in which there is no room for coercion, pressure, manipulation, threats and anxiety. Such "learning communities" do not seek to imitate school, but rather to create environments in which the people involved do things, and in which they do better and better at what they are doing, not least because they themselves benefit from it. Learning in this way is encouraged. Girls, boys, youths, men and women all have the capacity to learn for themselves, provided they are interested, are offered a suitable context, and have the resources and the liberty to do so.

Real learning empowers us to decide how we spend our time and how we give the world meaning – from our identities and relationships with others. That is how learning sticks; people understand and remember it, and it is useful for taking care of ourselves, others and nature. Curiosity and creativity are at the center of attention – and they can unfold in horizontal networks among similarly minded people, supporting solidarity and exchange. At the same time, such a process opens up substantial individual potential for development. All this creates the conditions for people to shape their lives themselves and to live life to the fullest. In other words: learning is living. Learning as commoning has an impact beyond the learning itself. It affects family life in different convivial forms, gender relations, and the organization of work, time and good living. It is a process for building another basis of understanding.

---

3 | Editors' note: Educational reformer John Holt coined this term in the 1970s; he wrote books such as *How Children Learn* (1967) and *The Underachieving School* (1970), always seeking to take the students' perspectives, which led him to the insight: "What goes on in class is not what teachers think." (Quoted in Ian Lister (1974). "The Challenge of Deschooling." in Ian Lister, editor, *Deschooling. A Reader.* London 1974. p. 2.) When he had come to view approaches to school reform as having failed, Holt decided to work directly with the families on "unschooling" children. There is a difference between "unschooling" (following Holt) and "deschooling" (following Illich). Unschooling is to be understood more as a concrete way of learning that is not regimented – apart from the presence of any physical school or educational process – while deschooling is a concept about changing society. Unschooling is a form of deschooling, but the reverse is not necessarily true.

Instead of education what we really need, in the words of Gustavo Esteva, the founder of the Universidad de la Tierra in Oaxaca, is "to find ways to regenerate community in the city, to create a social fabric in which we all, at any age, would be able to learn and in which every kind of apprenticeship might flourish....When we all request education and institutions where our children and young people can stay and learn, we close our eyes to the tragic social desert in which we live" (Esteva 2007).

It is hard for us at Camino Abierto to imagine approaching learning from a culture of individualism, yet at the same time, most of us are not deeply embedded in communities. The reality of our lives does not correspond to the commons. That is why this way of shaping life is also an opportunity for us to establish and enliven our own experience of community in everyday life. Ivan Illich described the magnitude of this task like this: "We have almost lost the ability to dream of a world in which the word is embraced and shared, in which nobody limits the creativity of anybody else, in which every person can change life" (Illich 1978:15).

Yet it is not all that difficult to create alternatives, and the implications are considerable. There are many opportunities for developing a real inter-cultural dialogue that comes from learning by doing. Autonomous learning communities can connect as equals with other worlds beyond "education," and with other learning communities, especially with those that rely on "new commons" created by information and communication technologies. Learning as commoning brings the possibility of building relationships and networks in a horizontal exchange, between those who were born into a culture of indi-vidualism and those who were born into a rich community. Together, they can develop the knowledge and wisdom to build their autonomy: the beginnings of a rich interculturality. All new structures of learning could be conceived of as commons – popular education, community-based and supported schools, educational institutions, vocational training centers, learning communities, even universities.

The **Zapatista communities in Mexico** are an impressive example of taking demands for educational autonomy seriously. As J.I. Zaldívar writes, Zapatista education offers an incredibly strong anchor for "establishing learning from the bottom up and seeking those elements within the communities themselves that combine the local reality with the universal; developing them beginning with their local foundation, and relying on the knowledge present in the indigenous farming communities in the process...." He continues:

> It has succeeded in developing an educational system with various levels that were developed by the Zapatista communities themselves, referring to their history and their geographical surroundings; [...] it

sets its gaze on the Zapatista communities, even when seeking to better organize what these communities have been doing for centuries, namely training those people who will attend to life in the communities, in the final analysis so that they will not die, but will on the contrary be reborn time and again"(Zaldívar 2007:48).

In the Mexican state of Oaxaca, the **Universidad de la Tierra** (in English, the University of the Earth, or "Unitierra" for short) takes a similar approach. It was established in 2001[4] to provide free learning opportunities, especially for youths who have not completed school or vocational training. It employs learning methods that people have always used in their own ways. Unitierra is an example of creating places of conviviality[5] where everyone plays a part, where people learn communally, and every individual can still do what he or she is interested in.

The founder of Uniterra, Gustavo Esteva, puts it like this: "Knowledge is a relationship with others and with the world; it does not mean consuming a good that is packaged in bite-sized insights. In the best case, consuming such a tidbit means receiving information *about* the world. Yet knowledge means learning *from* the world, by entering into relationships with it, with others, and with nature, and by experiencing them. [...] At the university, the youths learn things they are interested in from people who do or produce something in particular; in this way, they not only acquire specific skills and capabilities, but also observe the lives of people who pursue certain activities and can figure out whether that is what they really want to do in life. What they learn is useful for the communities they come from, and the young people derive dignity, esteem, and income from it" (Esteva 2001:10).

Unitierra is also a place where people think about the economization of learning, in other words, the fact that "education is learning under conditions of scarcity and is therefore, seen from a historical perspective, a relatively young practice that [emerged with] the economic society. Everywhere, people and entire peoples are taking up initiatives that are no longer limited to reforming the educational system or making it their own. Instead, they are leaving it behind." Here, Esteva agrees with Holt (Holt 1976) when he adds, "our competence in life emerges from our learning by doing, [...] to be precise, being alive and living means nothing other than learning" (Esteva 2001:9).

Learning as a commons is in fact functioning in a number of countries. In Udaipur, Rajasthan, a de-educational movement called **Shikshantar** is focused on regenerating diverse informal knowledge systems and nurturing radical

---

4 | The Universidad de la Tierra was formally established in May 2001, but since 1996 has operated within the Centre for Intercultural Encounters and Dialogues.

5 | See Marianne Gronemeyer's essay on conviviality on pp. 50-52.

learning communities within the larger spirit of gift culture.[6] Inspired by commons freedom-fighters such as Mahatma Gandhi and Rabindranath Tagore, Shikshantar has created an intergenerational community "unlearning" center with a library, Slow Food café, urban organic farm, upcycling maker space and community media studio. At an annual Learning Societies Unconference, learners can enter into deeper dialogue, friendship and collaboration among learning communities across India that are seeking a radical, systemic rethinking of monoculture education and development.

Another project in India, **Swaraj University**, hosts a two-year self-designed learning program for people between sixteen and thirty years old.[7] The learners, called *khojis* (seekers), are encouraged to reconnect with the wild and explore their deeper passion, purposes, needs and gifts within a larger context of community living. Their co-learners ("faculty") in reclaiming the abundance of the commons include other *khojis*, artisans, healers, tribal fishermen, small farmers, street children, grandmothers and activists, among others. There are no "degrees" required to join and no degrees issued because certification is regarded as another tool of enclosure. To support the program, *khojis* are invited to contribute whatever they can to operating costs and to pay it forward to help others participate in the future. A notable part of Swaraj University is the cycle yatra, in which a group of young people travel in rural areas on bicycles for one week, without any money, digital technologies, medicines or planning.

In Ciudad Bolivar, a neighborhood in the southwest of Colombia's capital Bogotá, **Libertatia** is a social center for children and youths of the most disadvantaged social classes of the city's population.[8] Libertatia is designed as a space for learning and dialogue, for exchanging knowledge, and is managed by the young people themselves. There are neither teachers nor students, but workshops where the people involved learn critical thinking in order to change their living conditions.

The **Purple Thistle Centre**[9] of Vancouver, Canada, was established in 2001 as an alternative to schools that is managed by youths themselves. The focus is on art and activism that help young people gain experience the challenges of community needs and self-organization.

The **Otherwise Club** in London[10] has been a place of self-determined learning for more than twenty years. It was established by mothers for children and youths. The Otherwise Club has been cooperating with the London

---

6　|　http://www.shikshantar.in
7　|　http://www.swarajuniversity.org
8　|　http://www.centrosociallibertatia.org
9　|　http://www.purplethistle.ca
10　|　http://www.theotherwiseclub.org.uk/index.php

Community Neighbourhood Co-operative (LCNC), an ambitious project supporting environmentally sensitive practices in housing, working life, and in the communities and neighborhoods themselves, since 2011.

The **Learning Exchange** started in Evanston, Illinois, in the US in 1971 and rapidly spread to more than forty communities. It is closely tied to the ideas that social critic Ivan Illich set forth in his book *Deschooling Society* (Illich 1971). People documented on file cards what they wanted to learn as well as what they could teach and what they wanted to share. After just two and a half years, 15,000 people had registered to teach or learn 2,000 topics. Today, there are similar "Learning Exchanges" in many states of the US.

The **Synergia Project** at Athabasca University in British Columbia, Canada,[11] uses online tools to share extensive research about cooperation – whether through formal knowledge or tacit knowledge – to teach how to build new types of institutions for a sustainable and socially just future.

Since 2013, the **Cusanus University** in Gründung, Germany, has been an ambitious educational institution that offers a critical, transdisciplinary masters degree program in economics, with a special emphasis on the formation and creation of society and the economy.[12] The state-accredited university is committed to the notion of community. One example of how this is expressed is the campaign *Denken Schenken* ("Thinking Giving") in which the community of students itself raises support for its members and also decides how to distribute funds, including scholarship grants. In their vision statement, the founders of Cusanus speak of "empowering people to educate themselves." By this, they mean that "within the social community, every person should be permitted to educate himself or herself in moral and intellectual freedom." That includes learning how to "creatively develop and reflect on [one's own subject area] beyond pure imparting of knowledge." The school also encourages students to take part in "interdisciplinary dialogue as well as to participate creatively in society rather than focus on narrow specialization." "In the process, we explicitly include the level of values and meaning," the website reads.

That is surely what unites the experience of those who participate at Camino Abierto and so many other commons: learning must have meaning for our lives and for the lives of the people with whom we are in relationships.

---

11 | http://auspace.athabascau.ca/handle/2149/3437

12 | http://www.cusanus-hochschule.de

References

Esteva, Gustavo. 2001. "Más allá de la Educación", Beitrag zum Seminar "Jugend und Bildung." Monterrey. N.L., September 2001.

———. 2007. "Reclaiming Our Freedom to Learn" *YES!* Magazine [USA] November 2007, available at http://www.yesmagazine.org/issues/ liberate-your-space/reclaiming-our-freedom-to-learn.

Illich, Ivan. 1978/2001. *Tools for Conviviality*. Marion Boyars.

———. 1971/2003. *Deschooling Society*. Marion Boyars.

Holt, John. 1976. *Instead of Education*. Dutton.

Zaldívar, J.I. 2007. "La otra educación en territorio Zapatista." No. 371, January 2007. *Cuadernos de Pedagogía* (Pädagogische Hefte); Spanien.

Claudia Gómez-Portugal M. *(Mexico) is a Mexican activist promoter of the transition agenda and founder of the organization SAKBE Commons for Change (Spanish: Comunicación para el Cambio Social) and the Free Learning Communities for Life initiative. She is a strategist in communication for social change, effective participation, knowledge sharing and community revitalization.*

OMNI-COMMONS

"Humans putting their heads together in shared cooperative activities are thus the originators of human culture."

Michael Tomasello

"We Are One Big Conversation": Commoning in Venezuela

An Interview with members of Cecosesola

Cecosesola has been making history for almost half a century. It all began in 1967 when a *cooperativista* in Barquisimeto, a city in Venezuela with a population of more than a million, died, leaving behind a family not only in mourning, but also unable to meet the funeral expenses. Soon thereafter, ten cooperatives, not wishing to leave death to market forces, came together and formed a single cooperative – a funeral home, Cecosesola.

Today, the Central Cooperativa de Servicios Sociales des Estado Lara (www.cecosesola.org) is a network of about sixty cooperatives and grassroots organizations in the Venezuelan state of Lara, with about 20,000 members. The cooperatives sell at weekly markets in Barquisimeto and provide community-backed loans, among many other services.

One of its proudest achievements is its health center, the Centro Integral Cooperativo de Salud, which serves 200,000 patients every year. To start the health center in March 2009, Cecosesola raised US$1.8 million by selling fruit salads at the markets; by soliciting short-term, fixed interest deposits from cooperatives and individuals; and through consensus-based contributions made by all full-time staff.

What follows is an edited interview that Silke Helfrich conducted with several members of Cecosesola in Mexico City in 2012 and in Berlin in 2013.[1] The interviewees were **Jorge Rath**, born and raised in Germany, who has worked with Cecosesola since 1999, chiefly as an acupuncturist; **Gustavo Salas**, a Cecosesola member for forty years who is active in the Escuela Cooperativa and the markets; **Noel Vale Valera**, a member of the Cooperativa El Triunfo since he was 15, who works mostly at the markets and in the computer team;

---

1 | Interviews in Spanish on *Pillku*, at http://www.pillku.com/article/de-la-confianza-emerge-una-fuerza-colectiva-que-es and Remix the Commons, at http://www.remixthecommons.org/?fiche=cecosesola-vivir-lo-comun-dia-a-dia.

and **Lizeth Vargas**, whose grandparents cofounded the federation and is active at the weekly markets and the health center.

Helfrich: Growing food, taking care of the sick, doing business, and burying the dead. How does all that fit together?

Salas: That's just one way of describing what this is really about. We are in a communal process in which we are constantly educating ourselves and arranging our lives. In the process, we are affected by the usual forces: patriarchal structures, property, and so on.

Rath: But we turn those forces toward our own ends, as it were. In philosophical terms, one could say: "We suspend property without abolishing it."[2]

Salas: That's right. Nobody can say: Cecosesola is mine.

Rath: ....and the same thing is – gradually – happening with hierarchies, too. We don't have a manager or a chair or a vice-chair.[3] The only formal thing is our assemblies. And there are loads of them! We are basically one big conversation.

Vale: You have to know something about our history in order to understand that. In the 1970s, many of our members took part in demonstrations against doubling the local bus companies' ticket prices. In 1974, they finally established their own transportation company as a cooperative, a business run by the workers themselves. It failed later on, mostly because of entanglements with political power struggles. Cecosesola learned from this bitter experience. In 1982, the general manager of the funeral home quit. Cecosesola didn't hire a new one. The warehouse manager left. The position remained vacant. The same thing happened when the building manager left. In the end, the secretaries learned how to drive trucks, and the drivers took on administrative tasks.

Helfrich: How are members assigned to their tasks nowadays?

Rath: They rotate. From one task to the next. Everybody is supposed to be able to learn as much as possible. That also helps people to keep their focus on the whole operation rather than claiming their own little fiefdoms.

---

2 | Editors' note: This phrase is a reference to Hegel's concept of "sublation" which has three senses: a lifting to a higher level; a retention of the sustainable parts; and an ending and overcoming.

3 | Editors' note: That was not always the case. In the beginning, the federation and its cooperatives were completely conventional, with an executive director and employees. The executive director earned almost twice as much as his assistant and four times as much as the secretaries. Over time, people became dissatisfied with the lack of transparency and participation in decisions. When the bosses left, they were not replaced – and the current structure organically emerged to replace the organizational hierarchies.

Vale: But there is no rotation plan. It's like agendas at our assemblies. We don't have them, either. We always start out with the principle that everything is voluntary; it depends on what each individual wants to do or learn just then.

Rath: But may I gently remind you that you haven't rotated voluntarily for quite a while now. (laughs)

Vale: Let's use a concrete example. I work in our health center and do massages and hydrotherapy. I take care of bookkeeping and staff scheduling. Sometimes I update the website or work at one of the markets on weekends. It's free-flow rotation, not fixed in advance. I might be working in the office one day, mopping the hallways the next, and cooking the third. Who does what and for how long depends on people's preferences, skills, and the needs at any particular time.

Salas: When we rotate, we encounter new people again and again, and that's in line with our culture of personal contact. These contacts come to life wherever we happen to be working, not only in the assemblies. That's anything but abstract. It's very concrete. We touch the other person – literally.

Helfrich: Sounds exciting, but it also takes a lot of time and effort.

Rath: Well, it isn't easy, but that's how we want it to be. After all, Cecosesola isn't our work. It's the project of our lives.

Vale: In any case, I never have the feeling that I'm working.

Rath: Well, we are less interested in producing "something that's ours" than creating "us." We want to understand and change ourselves. That generates a kind of collective energy. Of course, there are situations in which we don't feel it, but we generate this energy again and again, collectively.

Vale: It's also a question of perspective. We try to conceive of Cecosesola as a personal process of development, not as work. Work! Just thinking about it makes you tired! It isn't always successful, and it isn't for everybody. But we're taking this path, for example, in our assemblies without a fixed agenda. We talk about what needs to be done. Sometimes the same issue is discussed two or three times before we find a consensus.

Helfrich: That brings us to an important question: How do you make decisions?

Rath: Our goal is to reach decisions by consensus. So we never vote, because we don't want to split into a majority and a minority. Instead, we take the time to talk, to deliberate together, and to develop "our common criteria."

Helfrich: Could you describe that in more detail?

Rath: They're criteria that we can use for orientation in all kinds of everyday situations when individual groups or people make decisions. One of the criteria is that whoever makes a decision in the end is also responsible for the decision and for communicating it.

Vale: We never expect to make decisions together in our assemblies. We just talk a lot about how a decision can come about and according to which criteria. In the end, the decision itself can be made by one, two or three people.

Helfrich: And that really works?

Vargas: Yes, and it has been working for decades. Of course, it isn't easy. After all, we're a group of 1,300 people. But we don't have to discuss everything together. We're often confident that the other members will represent us well and tell us about decisions.[4]

Helfrich: What about pay?

Vale: We don't pay ourselves wages. Instead, we pay an advance on what Cecosesola will presumably make.

Rath: ....but we don't work in order to make a profit or to accumulate goods. That isn't what drives us, and that's why our surpluses are relatively modest. A large part of any surplus we make is spent on things for everyone, for the cooperative. In other businesses, you would call that reinvestment. In addition, we have to set aside reserves as required by law. If any money is left over after that – and that usually isn't the case – we adjust the advance. In recent years, we used the inflation rate as our criterion so that the advance wouldn't be eaten up by inflation.

Helfrich: Who gets paid how much?

Vale: In principle, everybody gets the same amount. The cook earns the same as the bookkeeper, but we also take different needs into account, for example, if someone has just had a baby. The only exception is the physicians. They get about twice as much, and their pay also depends on the number of patients they treat. Only a few doctors are prepared to work full-time in Cecosesola for the advance we pay.[5]

---

4 | A German book, *Cecosesola, Auf dem Weg. Gelebte Utopie einer Kooperative in Venezuela* (Berlin: Die Buchmacherei, 2012), describes the cooperative as having a "collective brain."

5 | Three physicians work full-time at the health center, and another sixty operate or treat outpatients there. However, they are not members of Cecosesola, rarely participate in assemblies and consider the work part of their professional lives. This topic is frequently discussed within the network.

Helfrich: So – the more patients, the more they earn?

Vale: Exactly. We would like to change this system, but we haven't been able to agree on a solution. It's easier with the vegetables. We decouple the price of the vegetables from the time and effort we put into them. We use an average price per kilogram.

Helfrich: Does that mean that peppers cost as much as potatoes?

Vale: Yes, it does. We produce a lot of vegetables in the cooperatives. So we explore exactly what is necessary to produce them. We add up the number of kilograms produced – across the entire product range – on the one hand and the costs on the other. Then we divide one by the other to figure out our average price per kilogram. Our yardstick is simply the production costs including what the producers need to live.

Salas: This is how we produce a considerable part of the food eaten by up to 300,000 people. It's pretty tricky to manage such growth and still be as creative as in the early days when five to eight of us brought vegetables to market.

Helfrich: And does your system work?

Vale: Yes, it does. Compared with others, we're doing very well. Of course, there are losses, just like everywhere else. Food goes bad, things are stolen, and so on. We have to "juggle" with that. That is why we are very careful to keep losses as small as possible; we make sure the lettuce doesn't go bad and that we don't damage the manioc.

Rath: By the way, this system saves people quite a lot of money. Many kinds of vegetables cost disproportionately more "outside." Our price per kilogram reduces red tape, we don't work with middlemen, and seasonal fluctuations don't make a difference, either.

Vale: The decisive factor is that we don't follow the market or the market price. If prices for tomatoes and potatoes go up someplace, that doesn't mean that we'll raise prices, too. What matters for us is that we earn what we need.

Helfrich: What is actually the most important thing for your process?

Salas: Respect! Respectful relationships in the comprehensive sense of the term. I don't just mean tolerance, but respect for the other person we are living with. We cannot treat our counterparts like things that we want to profit from. We must perceive the entire person. In order to do that, we need transparency, honesty and responsibility. They are the basis for trust, and that is fundamental. Because trust is the foundation for what we call "collective energy."

Vargas: And that can move mountains.

Salas: By the way, trust can be developed infinitely. That is why we say that our process is limitless. We show that is it possible to relate to other people in a different way. Anyone can take this with them into their own context if they want. We don't have a toolbox for it, though, because we don't assemble things; what we do is shape relationships.

Helfrich: What is your relationship to the state?

Salas: Independence is very important to us. That is why we don't apply to the government for financing. We try to work within our own means, and that is why we always start small. But we work together respectfully where necessary. By the way, working within your own means creates something mystical. Great enthusiasm for what we are doing.

Helfrich: What do commons mean to you?

Rath: There are many theories about the commons. That isn't really our issue. We show what an example of the practice of the commons looks like, or what it can look like. We need more experience, but not in the sense of "models." Cecosesola is not a model and doesn't seek to be one. The theory of the commons can develop only from a collaborative practice, from concrete processes. Cecosesola is our commons.

Salas: We don't assume a dream about what the world or society should be like. Notions about "this is what the world should be like" often end up with the ideas being forced down people's throats. We start out with ourselves and our culture, and we're very much aware that cultural transformation takes time. All this individualism! It isn't the same thing as individuality, which we strongly support. How are you supposed to build up trust if everybody is "chasing after their own opportunities"? That is why we often analyze how our culture affects our relationships, and what constructive things might come out of it.

Helfrich: Could you give an example?

Salas: At some point, the idea came up to start using cash registers at the markets. Cash registers are the norm everywhere, but we don't use them. The *cooperativistas* at the markets take the money to the office in envelopes. That's it. So at some point, this idea to use cash registers came up to make it easier to monitor the transactions. We discussed it in countless assemblies for almost three years. And then we finally realized that these cash registers serve one function above all: to monitor the *cooperativistas* at the markets. That would amount to withdrawing trust. And we didn't want to do that. So we continue as before, without cash registers, and using envelopes. We saved the money for the investment. And we gained trust.

And then, the Venezuelan tax office made cash registers a legal requirement ..."

Helfrich: Thank you very much for this informative conversation!

In December 2014, after this interview was conducted, the Venezuelan government decided to tax the country's cooperatives at a rate approximately 35 percent higher than the rate applied to for-profit businesses, starting immediately. Until then cooperatives had enjoyed special protections under Article 118 of the constitution passed in 1999. The government justified the new tax rate by saying the income of cooperativistas *should be considered taxable surpluses – a claim that Cecosesola says cannot be reconciled with other official statements. On the basis of its revenues in January and February 2015, Cecosesola calculated that its additional taxes total roughly 50 million bolivares (US\$7.25 million) – a sum that would put many co-operatives out of business.*

Cecosesola is resisting the new tax rate. It has launched a number of large and small responses, including a petition drive that had collected more than 200,000 signatures by July 2015, and urgent alerts to its international networks. Cecosesola is also seeking a dialogue with the state, especially the Regulatory Authority for Cooperatives or the Ministerio de las Comunas. On May 4, 2015, Cecosesola led a march of more than 1,000 of its members from five federal states to the headquarters of Corpolara, a development organization representing the state in the federal state of Lara. The three-kilometer protest walk took place in a "thoroughly playful/peaceful atmosphere," as Jorge Rath wrote. Cecosesola members now realize that they must consider the fundamental question of what kind of cooperativism they desire as well as whether and how the government can differentiate between authentic cooperatives on the one hand and capitalist businesses and pseudo-cooperatives on the other. The conflict, which has not yet been resolved, can be followed on Cecosesola's website, http://www.cecosesolaorg.bugs3.com.

Cecosesola By the Numbers

1 integrated health center with operating room, radiology department, lab, alternative therapies, and 12 doctors' offices.

500 tons of vegetables are produced and marketed every week.

1,300 members, including approximately 700 in the productive co-operatives and weekly markets.

3,000 assemblies per year, more or less, including all local, regional and departmental assemblies. That amounts to almost ten per day.

60,000 people buy from Cecosesola every week at the markets.

150,000 people are covered through Cecosesola for funeral costs in the event of their death.

Cooperativa Integral Catalana (CIC): On the Way to a Society of the Communal

By Ariadna Serra and Ale Fernandez

Catalonia has been the cradle of various movements – the cooperative movement, the movement for independence as well as anarchism and nudism,[1] each of which has had important effects on society in the area. Not surprisingly, these movements were influential in the founding of the *Cooperativa Integral Catalana* (CIC) even though it is not dedicated to any particular school of thought. The CIC is dedicated to discussing its own principles, coming to a consensus about them and acting accordingly.

An integral cooperative is a tool to create a grassroots counterpower based on self-management, self-organization and direct democracy, so that it might help overcome the generic state of human dependence on systemic structures. Its aim is to move toward a scenario of freedom and full awareness in which everyone can flourish under equal conditions and opportunities. It is a constructive proposal for disobedience and widespread self-management to rebuild our society from the bottom-up – holistically, across all areas and fields of work and thought – and to recover the affective human relationships based on proximity and trust. The name reflects these values:

- Cooperative, because it is a project practicing economic and political self-management with equal participation of all its members. Also, because it uses the official legal structure of a co-op.
- Integral, because it seeks to unite all the basic elements of an economy such as production, consumption, funding and trade. And at the same time, it seeks to integrate all the activities and sectors needed for the basics of life: food, housing, health, education, energy, transport.
- Catalan, because it is organized and works mainly in the territorial scope of Catalonia.

---

1 | Editors' note: In the early twentieth century, libertarian nudism was seen as a way to criticize the ideas about industrial development as immoral, socially alienating and harmful to the Earth. The central element of nudism is the belief in a natural order and the necessity of living in harmony with nature. Important practical elements include vegetarianism and going nude.

The establishment of the CIC was influenced by many events such as the Degrowth tour in spring 2009, a bicycle tour through all of the Catalan counties whose purpose was to spread information about the principles of economic activity without growth. The CIC's founding was also influenced by several pamphlets – *Crisis*,[2] *Podemos*[3] and *Queremos*[4] – which have had a strong impact on the public discussion about self-government and self-empowerment. Finally, the CIC was influenced by the creation of numerous barter networks (*ecoredes*[5]) that organize bartering using "social currencies"[6] that were created spontaneously and at the same time in various places across the Catalan territory.

The CIC was founded on this fertile soil in May 2010, when it adopted some fundamental principles, including consensual decisionmaking during its first "Assembly Day" (*Jornada Asamblearia*). The assembly days are open and nomadic, which means that they always take place in different towns in Catalonia on a weekend at the end of the month. In this way, the co-operative can get to know associated projects and decentralize itself. The assemblies are the place where we discuss fundamental issues and examine them from a communal point of view. They provide a space to share, to be together, to think, to plan, and also to find playful avenues to approaching things. They often end with an improvised concert.

The topics discussed at assemblies vary widely. In the forty-seven *Jornadas Asamblearias* held in our first four years, CIC members have discussed health, living in community and the principles of the Integral Revolution.[7] The assemblies are also a place for us to establish networks with other cooperatives or interested individuals who support the CIC and are already working on a certain set of problems.

---

2 | *Crisis* was published once on September 17, 2008, with a print run of 200,000. It featured the "Catalan Robin Hood" Enric Duran, who took out loans totaling 492,000 euros from thirty-nine Spanish banks without intending to repay them. Instead, he used the money to pay the printing costs for *Crisis* and to invest in various social projects. http://enricduran.cat/en/statements172013. A lengthy profile of Duran can be found here: Nathan Schneider, "On the Lam with Bank Robber Enric Duran," *Vice*, April 7, 2015, at https://www.vice.com/read/be-the-bank-you-want-to-see-in-the-world-0000626-v22n4.

3 | *Podemos* means: "We can." The paper was subtitled, "Living without capitalism," and was published on March 17, 2009, with a print run of 350,000. The term "integral cooperatives" was used here for the first time.

4 | *Queremos* means: "We want." It was published on September 17, 2009, and presented various projects.

5 | http: //ecoxarxes. cat

6 | Editors' note: Social currencies do not aim to replace state currencies. They circulate in an area of their own and are managed communally. Brazilian-Argentinian Professor Heloisa Primavera coined the term to highlight that official currencies have "antisocial" effects and that the people using them cannot control them. The concept is used today by various actors and with diverse meanings. (Correspondence with H. Primavera on August 20, 2014).

7 | http://integrarevolucio.net

The CIC started as an initiative of just a handful of activists, but in recent years, more and more people have joined. It is a varied bunch of people of all age groups, nationalities and genders. Whether they are men, women, the so-called disabled, girls or boys, CIC members all try to create a space for team spirit and community. This diversity enriches our debates even if the process can sometimes be difficult. For example, there are (unconscious) power and gender expectations that sometime encourage women to fall back into culturally determined, submissive roles while men seek power and recognition as men. The men usually discuss technical questions while the women focus on social issues: a complex of problems for the *Jornada Asamblearia*.

Many things developed very rapidly in these early years, 2010-2011 – the numbers of people and communities with close relationships to us, the number of members, the annual budget, the real estate we use. In August 2014, the CIC had 2,600 members – although that figure is not particularly significant because membership is not a prerequisite for participation. In the four years since our founding, our budget grew from zero to 458,000 euros.

Calafou is the most important of the properties we have collectivized. We are transforming this old industrial settlement that we jointly bought in 2011, and have been renovating it into a post-capitalist eco-industrial neighborhood.[8] Today, thirty people live in Calafou. Several projects are already emerging there – Circe, an experimental lab for producing soaps, essences, and natural remedies; and a hackerspace/FabLab for people to work on free software,[9] network administration, dissemination of open source principles, and security and encryption on the Internet.

The organizational structure that CIC uses to secure the provision of basic essentials, outside of state and market structures, is the *Sistema Público Cooperativista* (SPC). The SPC is not a legal structure, but rather consists of working groups that organize around various topics such as therapy, education and food production. Each of these areas has what we call an "office" – not always a physical space but rather an intentional work group, with an assembly that is used as a space to meet and talk. These projects are autonomous and, like the *Jornadas Asamblearias*, open to anyone.

One such project, "Living Education Albada,"[10] is a space in which families with children can work together to pass on techniques and skills to aid in their personal growth and to follow whatever path they please, in a respectful and loving environment.[11] Another example is the health group, which explores

---

8 | https://calafou.org

9 | See essay on the General Public License on pp. 223-226 and essay on Libre Office on pp. 182-185.

10 | http://albadaviva.blogspot.com.es

11 | http://www.albadaviva.blogspot.fr

the idea of health as a living process, supported by a communal financing model based on mutuality. The transport office attempts to reduce the need to transport people and materials while reducing our own use of fuel through renewable alternatives such as recycled vegetable oil.

A project devoted to food has brought producers and consumers together to create their own system for certifying that foods are produced organically, going beyond the requirements of government labels. Another office is concerned with helping people create common living spaces through, for example, contracts of assignment,[12] subsidized housing or donations. There is even a science and technology working group that helps develop tools that we need for production. Apart from these open workshops, the CIC has a number of internally organized work commissions that are concerned with finances, for example, and support networks for the cooperative. These commissions are open to anyone as well. Although any commission depends on the other commissions and they often reach common agreements, each is autonomous in their decisionmaking.

This entire organizational structure is subject to constant transformation; in each case the structure and process depends on what the people involved need and what motivates them. Besides its internal systems, CIC is connected with many groups in the bioregion that are self-governed or that work on similar topics. We use or contribute to those tools that we produce as commons. One example is IntegralCES, an open source Community Exchange System that is used for the accounting of all CIC goods and services that are distributed internally and bought and sold externally. The system also oversees accounting for numerous barter exchanges that belong to the system as well as the virtual market, an online sales platform for CIC members. One of its special features is that people can pay with social currencies as well as with euros or cryptocurrencies like Bitcoin or Faircoin.

Taken together, these self-organized systems have a fractal structure. That means that one group can represent the whole in one context, but at the same time only part of the whole in another context. That is not possible in hierarchical structures. The groups make all decisions by consensus, which neither gives an advantage to majorities nor discriminates against minorities. The point of the fractal structure is to allow decisionmaking that is optimal for a particular group at a particular time, based on the principles of direct democracy, ecological integrity, equality in diversity, human development, team spirit, integral revolution and voluntary simplicity.

---

12 | A means for assigning another person the right to use your property, usually in return for care or maintenance of the space.

Voluntary simplicity in this context means that the more a person is integrated into the CIC and benefits from it, the less money that person receives, for the logical reason that he/she needs less. After all, the way in which the CIC uses its common resources differs from the wage system in which people are paid money and their pay correlates with people's time, efforts and specific achievements. At the CIC, people are invited to join working groups where they can follow their expectations and interests, switch groups when they wish, and even participate in several ones at the same time.

The CIC work environment is about building trust, which is essential to enable everyone involved to become aware of their own vital needs (food, housing, transportation, etc.). These needs are met by the common project, independently of the number of hours that an individual may contribute to the cooperative and the responsibility he or she bears. The main assembly makes decisions about the distribution of common income to individual members. These decisions are publicly accessible and transparent – just like all the other decisions made by the main assembly and also the social currency balance sheets. Successful social relationships are based on transparency, but also on each person participating to the best of his or her ability, refraining from making value judgments, and showing responsibility for his or her own decisions.[13]

Everyone belonging to the CIC can receive tax-free products and services within the cooperative, from bread to English language courses to plumbing work. The transactions outside the cooperative are subject to taxation. CIC has taken strong stands against the legitimacy of the state following the Spanish government's behavior in the aftermath of the 2008 financial crisis. The government bailed out banks with billions of euros of taxpayer money and, in CIC's words, it committed a "financial coup" in 2011 by changing the Spanish constitution to benefit financial institutions. Meanwhile, banks also foreclosed on millions of people's homes and the government cut budgets for healthcare, social services and unemployment aid. CIC believes that the state has in effect abandoned any legitimate social contract with citizens, and so it openly calls for citizen insubordination to the state and "disobedience to all laws and all policies that we consider unjust." It urges Spanish citizens to deposit their taxes in a "tax treasury" escrow account that withholds funds from the government until it meets CIC demands for institutional transparency. It is redirecting taxes towards self-management in the local assemblies that arose from the M-15 movement.

Our financing ranges from supporting production to microfinancing platforms. Coopfunding is a free website that enables joint financing of self-

---

13 | Editors' note: See the interview with Cecosesola members on pp. 258-264.

organized projects, and uses other currencies in addition to the euro.[14] We have been able to raise 80,000 euros through the finance cooperative CASX.[15] In 2014, we succeeded for the first time in working entirely independently of the banking system, which is regulated by the state. That was unthinkable when we founded the CIC.

We have achieved a lot, but the greatest challenges still lie ahead, not as the Catalan Integral Cooperative, but as people. We speak of what we call Integral Revolution: joining together in networks and supporting and recognizing one another. We are committed to taking this path that leads to a society of the communal.

Ariadna Serra *(Spain) works at l'art du soleil (http://www.lartdusoleil.net), a travelling eco-show in a converted truck, which proposes itself as an alternative approach to the current socioeconomic situation. She co-wrote this essay in Spanish with input from many people at the Cooperativa Integral Catalana interested in sharing our work.*

Ale Fernandez *(Spain) works in the CIC's housing commission (http://habitat-gesocial.cat) and with Guerrilla Translation (http://guerrillatranslation.com). He helped with the English language translation of this essay and with various edits and corrections.*

---

14 | http: //www. coopfunding. net

15 | http: //www. casx. cat/es. Translator's note: CASX (Cooperativa de Autofinanciación Social en Red) means Cooperative for Social Self-Financing in a Network.

INTERMEZZO II

The Internal Dimensions of the External World: On Commons and Commoning

In Part II, we introduced a broad diversity of remarkable commons. The goal was to explain their origins, context and other salient features, and in so doing make this invisible realm of social experience more visible – and thus more easily spoken about and discussed. Unlike many academic monographs, the essays of Part II do not adopt the pose of "neutral" observers, as if a more precise rendering of the motifs and details of diverse commons would be enough to (somehow) reveal their essence. Nor were we attempting to marshal multiple examples as a way to move toward a single, universal definition of "the commons." Instead the profiles of Part II represent an invitation to enter into the distinctive lifeworlds that every commons embodies, to put them into relationship with each other and to invite further reflection and study of them.

In Part III, we would like to delve more deeply. We believe that the diversity of the commons, which may appear confusing at first, can be seen as embodiments of other ways of being and a deeper set of ontological principles. This is precisely what the authors of Part III try to show us in different contexts. In the opening chapters, Étienne LeRoy realizes, after studying land use and property rights systems in Africa for thirty years, that he was in fact studying the commons; the tensions between formal legality and social functionality and legitimacy are illuminating.

Andrea Nightingale then provides a fascinating ethnographic account of how people on the coast of Scotland become and live as fishers through commons. What are the subjective experiences and cultural dimensions of this identity? Anne Salmond in her essay describes the relationships between some indigenous Maori communities, their fishery practices, and the ocean – and how their commoning has come into conflict with the politics and law of the New Zealand state. The other authors of Part III also draw on an anthropological perspective. They focus on commoning as a process of subjectification, outlining the factors, conditions, and ways of thinking that affect our actions as commoners – that is, the kinds of people that we are constantly becoming.

Bringing into focus this constant *process of becoming* is important. It helps emphasize our innate propensity to cooperate with each other and to seek stable social arrangements. As human beings, we are embedded in many and diverse relationships, and we depend on them. They forge our subjectivities. If the processes we are involved in are primarily mediated by money and can be easily measured and calculated, then we become traders or transactionists. We experience ourselves as customers or producers and come to build an identity and culture around those practices. We constantly deliver things, or things are delivered to us, and we become suppliers or recipients of services – often switching roles several times a day. Pressed into using market-oriented infra-structures and social habits, we practice the role of *homo economicus* daily, like actors rehearsing their roles or musicians practicing their parts, often driven by institutional priorities, political considerations, media spectacles, and the artistically contrived illusions of advertising.

If the stories of Part II have any lessons, it is that we must *practice* commoning; after all, it is only commoning itself that makes us commoners. And this "practice" cannot be achieved once and for all; it must be re-enacted time and again, and become a living, pulsating element of social life and culture.

In describing the attitudes, customs and actions of the people who manage common resources, solve problems, and defend their collective rights together – as Nigel Gibson does for the shack dwellers in South Africa – the authors of Part III help us more fully understand a point made in Intermezzo I – that (mature) commons point toward some very different ways of knowing, seeing, being and acting. All this requires a certain amount of perseverance because commoning is a process of constantly trying things out and putting them into practice. It requires the opportunity to make mistakes, to scrap ideas, to consult with others, and to start over, time and again. Commoning needs time and support – not least, and especially, from the realm of politics. It requires protected spaces for experimenting, for developing a sense of independence and confidence, and for acknowledging skepticism and resistance.

Furthermore, people must have psychic room and time for processing (both intellectually and emotionally) what is happening in a particular circumstance so that *something different* can emerge from the interpersonal relationships and the specific relationships between human beings and nature (or other resources). People must have space to make sense of their problems and circumstances, and be able to experiment in finding solutions, without the coercive threat of enclosure. This is an important political challenge: to retain open spaces for commoning. Simply having such spaces free from the threat of market enclosure – whether an open Internet, legally recognized forest commons or protection for lifeforms as shared wealth, not patented commodities – is an important political challenge. Some things must be kept as "nobody's (private) property" – but many people's responsibility. Eventually, this struggle, if it succeeds in creating a new and stable commons, produces its own treasured world of feelings that are experienced by its creators as entirely natural and self-evident.

This perspective on the commons requires that we adopt a different intellectual approach and methodology than one that focuses on inventing or changing laws in existing institutional structures to achieve healthier forests, cleaner bodies of water, more stable fish stocks, and so on. This very idea presumes that experts armed with sufficient authority and resources can generate, through a complex calculus, the results they wish. The struggle for a free, fair and sustainable future must always begin with the question of how we wish to live together, and how this communal life is to be designed so that nobody feels taken advantage of. This implies always asking: Who is affected? Who is responsible? Who can shape things, and for what reasons? Who can say no? Who can support or obstruct things, and why? Such questions inevitably lead to larger questions about the whole economic and social system.

Thinking like this and taking this approach moves us away from linear concepts of development. It cultivates a more helpful set of "pluriversal perspectives," in the words of Arturo Escobar – the theme of his essay. This idea helps reveal that many struggles to defend territories and resources managed as commons are, in fact, ontological debates. Political and policy debates often dismiss the other's worldview as "irrational" when the actual conflicts are fundamentally directed against the worldviews engendered by commoning.

Because each commons is forged by unique forces and circumstances, it is perilous to overgeneralize about commons by claiming a faux taxonomy of institutions, products or results. There are too many floating variables. Evolutionary scientist David Sloan Wilson, who vividly describes his collaboration with Elinor Ostrom in the final years of her life, refers to the many contingencies at play in the functioning of commons, something that receives support from institutional economics, complexity theory and evolutionary biology. Biologist and philosopher Andreas Weber takes this idea one step further at the end of this volume when he writes about reality itself as a commons that is a dynamic matrix of relationships that are alive. "Creative aliveness" is a fundamental dimension of commons, he writes: "Therein slumbers the opportunity to arrive at a new, relational understanding of the world, which encompasses not only structures, algorithms, and causalities, but also the actions and feelings of the actors, and that is thus no longer a dualism."

Seen in this light, the commons opens up new opportunities for pursuing genuine freedom to shape one's own sense of being, identity and purpose in the present moment. Unlike the asocial, individualist fantasies celebrated by market culture, a serious commitment to freedom requires enduring human relationships, a commitment to nature and place, and concrete social actions developed together. Any real emancipation in the future will depend upon the creative energies and innovations that flow from such freedom.

– David Bollier and Silke Helfrich

PART III

THE INNER DYNAMICS OF COMMONING

"Basically, there is no such thing as matter. At least not in the common sense. There is only a fabric of relationships, constant change, vitality. We have trouble imagining this. What is primary is only the interrelationships that exist – that which connects. We could also call it spirit. Something we can only experience spontaneously and cannot grasp."

German physicist Hans Peter Dürr,
Interview in P.M. magazine, May 2007

How I Have Been Conducting Research on the Commons for Thirty Years Without Knowing It

By *Étienne Le Roy*

What Blocked My View of the Commons

Writing about commons as a member of a scientific community, which itself has developed only recently, has raised a number of problems for me.

First, there is the time lag with which the complex problem of the commons gained our attention in the first place. Why didn't that happen fifty years ago? Why did it take so long to overcome the obstacles that made us unable to recognize social phenomena as commons phenomena and to think about them as such? Even though I had answers to many questions and was already writing within the paradigm of sharing, I was still unable to ask the questions using commons terminology.

The second problem lies in the fact that opening up the topic of the commons triggers a kind of domino effect. As soon as the first domino falls over – by invoking the commons – many of the concepts on which the idea of modern Western civilization rests lose their apparent balance, and the whole edifice, previously believed to be well-founded, collapses onto itself: the state, the law, the market, the nation, work, contracts, debts, giving, the juristic person, private property, as well as institutions such as kinship, marital law, and the law of succession, are suddenly called into question. We often consider these concepts to be universally valid, but intercultural comparison reveals that they are only a custom, a folkway that deeply influenced our modern Western legal tradition (which itself proves to be a folk law of its own).

Finally, the third problem has to do with the highly political, even polemic character of the contemporary commons debate, as currently expressed in France by Pierre Laval and Christian Dardot in their book *Commun*. Even the subtitle does not mince words: "Essay on the revolution in the 21st century." Laval and Dardot bring important questions back into the academic debate, questions that Karl Marx raised as early as the mid-nineteenth century when reflecting upon the meaning and the role of capital.

The attention currently granted the commons suggests approaching these problems one by one, first in order to make the "question of the commons" comprehensible, and then to examine how they relate to contemporary law. One thing should be clear from the outset, however: theoretically, commons could be an alternative to the market and the state, but practically, we are a long way from achieving that. And if we follow Professor Elinor Ostrom, then the unresolved social question of the twenty-first century[1] should in any case focus on how commons and private property might coexist and complement each other.

I graduated from university with degrees in anthropology and public law in 1964. While I was conducting research for my thesis (corresponding to a master's degree today), I discovered Michel Alliot, a young professor coming from Africa, as well as the scientific discipline of legal anthropology and the land question in Africa, particularly in Senegal. These three discoveries were to change my life.

I selected Michel Alliot as my academic advisor and wrote my doctoral dissertation, one of the first in legal anthropology in France (Le Roy 1970), about the Senegalese land reform and Law 64-46, which was one of the first dissertations on legal anthropology in France. My ambition was to comment not only on the origins and roots of this reform, but also to explain what it actually sought to cover and regulate: namely consuetudinary law, or customary, unofficial types of law.[2] I dug into the history of possession of land in a sub-Saharan African society, all the way back to the sixteenth century, and discovered the field of the commons, but could not find a concept, a term for it.

I later discovered that this was because of the ethnocentric ideology of colonialism[3] and the foundations on which the thinking of the modern age and the notion of development of that time rested.[4] So-called consuetudinary law was an Unidentified Scientific Object (USO). Only a few scholars had attempted to actually comprehend its more profound features. The scientific community

---

1 | For some authors who speak of revolutionary questions rather than social ones, including Dardot and Laval (2014), the contribution of commons to a new societal model is not marginal or complementary, but quite central.

2 | In France, this type of postcolonial studies began at the end of the colonial period; some anthropologists such as Georges Balandier were already conducting them in the 1950s.

3 | It is common knowledge that nineteenth century colonialization was based on the notion that development was constantly progressing and that the Western societies were at the forefront of that progress. Lewis H. Morgan, an American and one of the founders of ethnology, is a typical example of this, with his study *Ancient Society, Or: Researches in the lines of human progress from savagery through barbarism to civilization* (1877).

4 | Editors' note: On thoughts beyond development, see the contribution by Arturo Escobar on pp. 348-360.

usually dealt with legal phenomena in Africa as if they were the opposite of Western legal concepts developed over the past three centuries. Primitivism[5] and scientific arrogance are never far apart.

This USO status of consuetudinary law also has to do with the fact that its rules are not formulated according to generally recognized standards or the impersonal criteria of modern laws; instead they manifest themselves as enduring patterns of behavior and the willingness of people to engage in certain forms of action that is stable over time. Now, these can be grasped and researched only by employing specific models, so I decided to use a matrix to represent consuetudes as legal acts. Legal acts not in the sense of written law, but in the sense of patterns that are expressed in behavioral rules that can be found in the various communities.

That is how I succeeded in responding to a phenomenon that I had just discovered and that challenged received bodies of research: legal pluralism. It was surprising that even by organizing my research according to the principles of a matrix analysis, I had already discovered the basic elements of the description of the commons – without being aware of it: a community in which everyone has status, an activity recognized and appreciated by the others, and a resource that – symbolically – permits the intentions and dispositions of everyone involved to be interconnected. In sum, a sanctionable system that amounts to "law."

In my early works and in those of the 1970s in which I developed the anthropological models of the relationship of human beings to land (Le Roy 2011), I focused on the problem of communities. I could discern fundamental community-based conceptions that influence actions, and my discussions also included the civil-law concept of common goods. But however surprising from today's perspective, the term "commons" never appeared in my work, even though the *mbock* thinking of the West African *Wolof* had already left its mark on my analyses.

Mbock – in the *Wolof* language – means kinship, and at its core, it also means sharing. At times, it refers to common ancestors, at others, to a particular field (with its specific area and boundaries), a herd, forest areas, and many other things. The discovery that sharing is preferred to exchange suddenly challenges all those insights that anthropology felt to be certain: namely, limited exchange within kinship relations, according to the theory of Claude Lévi-Strauss,[6] the

---

5 | Editors' note: This is about the idea that the life of primitive peoples is "better," similar to life in childhood, and that civilization can basically only destroy it.

6 | Editors' note: Lévi-Strauss (1908-2009) was the founder of ethnological structuralism and probably the most renowned French ethnologist. One of his best-known works is *Tristes Tropiques* (1955, English translation: *Tristes Tropiques*, 1961), to which his first wife Dina made a great but unacknowledged contribution. Even in this fascinating description of cultures without writing, Lévi-Strauss sketches them as *alternatives to Western civilization*, an idea he developed

concept of the gift according to Marcel Mauss,[7] that of property according to Maurice Godelier[8], and others. Sharing is the predominant principle of organization in the commons. But I came to understand that only between 1980 and 1990 while I elaborated a new model for managing land and areas for fruit cultivation (Le Roy 1996). In that model, I attempted to explain how Africans (and other humans, too) combine various legal forms of property and resource uses in their complex practices – transcending cultural boundaries that we imagine as defining. Modern science considers the incompatibility or even incoherence of many such combinations practically a truism.

A Reform of Unforeseen Consequence

I told the stories of all these intellectual adventures in my synthesis on land policy on Senegal, from a theoretical perspective (Le Roy 2011). In it, I combined the legal relationships of individualistic modernity (public and private) with those of communitarianism (external, internal and coalitions). In other words, I correlated the categories *public* and *private*, or a combination of the two, with external and internal, respectively. The concept of the common proved useful in ordering these relationships according to the following logic:

- public = belonging to all
- external = belonging to "n" groups
- alliance = belonging to two or more groups
- internal = belonging to one group
- private = belonging to a juridical or physical individual, or legal entity

---

further in the early 1960s with his programmatic work *Pensée Sauvage* (English translation: *Savage Mind*, 1966). He decided that traditional, holistic and mythically explained ways of thinking are certainly coequal to the Western way: not more or less reasonable, but simply different. Here, LeRoy refers to Lévi-Strauss's analysis of kinship systems, which was published as early as 1949. In this work, Lévi-Strauss formulated the basic idea that a barter system guided by marriage rules (imperatives and prohibitions) replaces natural kinship by socially binding alliances from which mutual obligations emerge.

7 | Editors' note: Marcel Mauss (1872-1950) was a French sociologist and ethnologist. He considered exchange in archaic societies, which he analyzed in *Essai sur le don* (first published in 1923/24; English translation: *Gift; forms and functions of archaic societies*, 1954) as a "total social phenomenon" that points beyond the image of the human as a rational *homo economicus* and the construct of the economy erected on that basis. In Mauss's work, the gift – in principle – retains its nature as an obligation. It produces debt and *requires* a gift in return. This enables Mauss to analyze the principles of service, welfare or the welfare state on the basis of this concept.

8 | Editors' note: Maurice Godelier (born in 1934) is considered the founder of neo-Marxist economic ethnology. He is a specialist in the societies of Oceania and research director at the École des Hautes Études en Sciences Sociales (EHESS) in Paris. His most important work *La production des Grands Hommes* (English translation: *The Making of Great Men*, 1986) was published in 1982.

Doubtless, all these possibilities of collective organization did not already lead to what contemporary commons theory (Bollier 2014; Dardot & Laval 2014) considers to be "commons," but since 1996, *avant la lettre*, at least this concept of the common has been at the center of my analyses of land policy. With a thirty-year time lag!

One of the reasons for this false start lies in the anthropological paradigm itself. It concerns itself with "the law" – in my case, regarding land use in Senegal. Accordingly, the conceptual and methodological tools that are required for understanding what has not and literally cannot be thought in the realm of consuetudinary law, can only be expressed in the intellectual categories of lawyers – in other words, norms and legal provisions. Whereas from the anthropologists' perspective, "law [is] not so much what the texts say, but rather what the actors do with it" (Le Roy 1999). The texts are important, but how they are interpreted and applied is even more important. Or as a French saying goes, "It's a long way from the cup to the mouth." In the endogenous, oral African contexts, there are no texts that could be interpreted and no explicit norms which could be the subject of legal commentary. One can only observe the practices! By granting the requisite attention to the positions and roles of actors, their status, their actions and their interrelationships, anthropologists are able to escape the abstractions that fundamentally structure Western legal systems, but which are not to be found in the *Wolof* and other societies that anthropologists study.

The concept of the commons is an abstraction circulated first and foremost by the field of economics. And it is precisely in economics that Garrett Hardin's all-too-famous "tragedy of the commons" parable has gained currency since its publication in 1968.[9] For at least a generation this make-believe idea that shepherds are unable to use their pastures jointly has undermined and marginalized research on collective resource management. Incidentally, I admit that I did not take this laughable story seriously until the mid-1980s when I began to recognize the collateral damage of this pseudo-theory and its sloppy generalizations.[10]

The second reason for the false start of the commons in the intellectual debate concerns the theories on "development" applied to countries that were called "underdeveloped" at the time. By passing the Law Concerning the Territory of the Country,[11] Senegal finally emancipated itself from a development model that is fundamentally connected to the market and private property.

9 | Editors' note: This was year in which Garrett Hardin's article, "The Tragedy of the Commons," was published in the journal *Science*.

10 | Editors' note: See the contribution by David Sloan Wilson in this volume on pp. 361-368.

11 | Translator's note: In French: *loi sur le domaine national.*

This took place in the name of an African socialism that was at least as open to poet-president Léopold Senghor's[12] *Négritude* – a poetic discovery of African roots – as it was to breaking with capitalism. Yet in this case, it was not about breaking with capitalism, but about placing limits on the outright dominance of private property norms – a legacy of the colonial era. Accordingly, Law 64-46 did not seek to abolish private property; it even permitted completion of all pending proceedings concerning private rights still awaiting resolution in land registry processes. Applications above and beyond this (for example, for recording further private real estate in the land registry) would thereafter be subject to the control of the administration. This provision was intended to prevent private property, which President Senghor called "egoistic" in a 1964 speech, from having direct effects on social relationships.

According to this reform, the only justification for transforming local, endogenous property rights into state property is to enable market transactions for the public good (Article 13), which then authorizes the state to transfer the rights to private individuals. This approach is based on the assumption that public institutions in Senegal, like any institutions of a liberal, democratic state, are neutral and fair-minded – a presumption that was unfortunately disproven by later facts. We shall see how this "nationalization" flirts with socialism. To this end, we shall first examine the wording of the law and then its practical application.

From the Wording of the Law...

Formally speaking, 96 percent of Senegal's territory belongs to the nation-state; the remainder is publicly administered plots of land or private landholdings that have already been recorded in the land registry. This "territory belonging to the nation" has no legal personality and is not a legal entity, and so by default it belongs to the Senegalese state. Accordingly, what truly matters in a legal and political sense is the interpretation of the term "belong." Article 2 interprets it in the sense of trust in a common-law context.

In other words, Law 64-46 changes the arrangements concerning possession of land in a way that is to prove forward-looking for Senegal, for colonial law usually treated these tracts of land as the private property of the state; they were considered unused, "ownerless" areas available to the administration for whatever it chose. Today, by contrast, they are entrusted to specific local administrators and divided into four areas subject to different regulations: 1) urban land; 2) development land (*zones classées*); 3) land in rural areas (*zones de terroirs*); and 4) pioneer areas.

---

12 | Editors' note: Léopold Sédar Senghor (1906-2001) was a Senegalese poet and intellectual, and the first president of the country, from 1960 to 1980.

A substantial part of this very brief law – just seventeen articles – is concerned with these *zones de terroirs* that are managed by rural collectivities (*communautés rurales*). This is where the most references to commons are to be found. The law states that "the land in rural areas (*zones de terroirs*) are used by members of the local municipalities who guarantee its management and conduct it under state control (...)" (Article 8) and that the decisionmaking power for specific uses (Article 9) or setting aside land (Article 15) lies with the relevant councils of the municipality rural community in question. That is one provision that would actually have authorized self-organization among people to create and formalize a culture of the commons – had party politics not interfered. And this is where real life comes into play.

...to Real Life

Building on my first fieldwork in 1969, and making use of my contacts with the Minister of Rural Development, Ben Mady Cissé, I wanted to get to the bottom of the land-policy questions raised by the experimental implementation of Law 64-46. Following the defense of my doctoral dissertation in 1970, I actually sent my research findings to President Senghor, who unfortunately entrusted them to his Minister of the Interior Jean Colin. Colin, a former colonial civil servant, had become Senegalese by marriage. He saw my findings as a threat to his own plans to place the rural communities under government supervision (in typical French-Jacobin manner) and manage them as regional grassroots collectives (*collectivités territoriales de base*). The transition from the principle of self-organization to integration in a central administrative network fundamentally changed the role of the rural municipalities' communities despite the decentralization of government power in 1972.

Commons theory usually underlines the independence of commons from both the market and the state. While markets in Senegal were at a distance from commons, the state got quite involved in land use at the local level by reducing the autonomy of rural communities. The idea of the commons was not only nonexistent as a legal concept, but any disagreements about the commons were settled – at least officially.

Yet the Senegalese people on the ground continued to take up the original reform ideas. Despite a lack of sufficient administrative procedures and overly detailed interventions by the relevant divisions, people took on responsibility for managing their own resources and rallied behind an ethic to curb the spread of private property rights. Even the powerful religious Muslim brotherhoods cooperated, which cannot be said of domestic and foreign investors. They have called for repeal of Law 64-46 since 1980. But despite all the many controversies and conflicts, the law marked its fiftieth anniversary in 2014. Amazingly, despite political, economic, and procedural ambiguities and at times radical opposition in the highest echelons of the Senegalese state, in the end a logic of the commons prevailed in practice. Was this a unique case?

Functional Rather than Institutional Logic

In 2012, I decided to attend a conference for lawyers and legal historians at the University Paris VIII-Saint-Denis on the topic, "The Resurgence of the Commons: Between Illusions and Necessities," whose debates were later documented in a publication (Parance and Saint Victor 2014). The conference painted a much more positive picture of the commons than was discernible at first from the invitation. I developed three arguments in my presentation:

1. Our modern society has lost the experience of commons and commoning.

2. The rediscovery of the commons suggests that the paradigm of sharing is more attractive than that of exchange.

3. The rise of commons necessarily raises the question about legal pluralism.

To provide evidence for this, I referred to two different experiences: land reforms in Africa and the island states of the Indian Ocean, as well as observations about French society in both urban and rural areas.

Land Reforms and the Limits of Private Property

Putting land reform into practice is always a delicate undertaking. In the African context, it also poses conundrums, because one often must create ownership of land in the first place where previously no such ownership existed – and at times the communities involved refuse to accept its existence at all. And for good reason: they feel safer if they are protected by kinship or other relationships where they live, and not by remote civil institutions directed by people unknown to them. The world has surely changed, but not for everyone, and not in a linear fashion.

The Senegalese land reform illustrated a combination of political concerns, lobbying by international donors, and uncertainty about the dynamics of rapidly changing societies. In the end, experts seeking to set policies face a dilemma. On the one hand, there is an officially proclaimed commitment to so-called modernization at the global level, which must in no case be abandoned; and on the other hand, the resilience[13] of communities and societies in the face of countless changes must be supported or there may be outbreaks of unprec-

---

13 | On the concept of resilience, see Rob Hopkins, "Resilience Thinking," in David Bollier and Silke Helfrich editors, *The Wealth of the Commons: A World Beyond Market and State* (Amherst,

edented violence (Appadurai 2013). If it is impossible to reject "progress" in the modern capitalist sense, then at least changes must correspond to the needs of the entire population, and not only to those of the Westernized elite. And they must recognize the limits of reproducible and sustainable "development" driven by globalization.

Even if we researchers have not understood everything over the course of these roughly thirty years, at least we have all learned a lot, in particular through activities of the Association for the Advancement of Research and Studies on the Possession of Land in Africa (APREFA)[14], which I chaired from 1986 until 1996. At the time, we established a technical committee – i.e., without political decisionmaking power – on possession of land and development, within the French Ministry of Foreign Affairs. We sought to bring together the researchers' expertise with diplomats and development cooperation staff who need informed analysis. The committee pursued a notion of applied research and development cooperation practice, and at the same time sought to promote interdisciplinary basic research. Here, too, the central research question was about the extent and form in which private ownership of land was to be recognized.

Our work showed that private property[15] and property (as its equivalent in common law) are necessary only in contexts in which the market, organized along capitalist principles, is ubiquitous. Various intermediate forms between a lack of titles of ownership on the one hand and "absolute" property on the other, can both accommodate the needs of local producers and reduce the risk of land-grabbing. The models for dominance and control of soil and natural resources described above are based on this assumption. So are the solutions used by various communities of practice who also implement a commons logic and ethic, but whose practices have rarely been described theoretically.

This, too, is a lesson arising from our work: the illusions of development, according to which everyone was to somehow become a private property owner and entrepreneur. Such narrative ideals conceal the necessary displacement of populations, the consolidation of land rents into few hands, and the decline of smaller, more locally oriented producers.

Let us remember: good governance in twenty-first century land policy should include variable configurations of private and common property, always aligned to the needs of respective groups of people on the ground. The Senegalese experience began by desiring to control the expansion of private

---

Mass.: Levellers Press, 2012), pp. 19-23, available at http://wealthofthecommons.org/essay/resilience-thinking.

14 | Association pour la Promotion des Recherches et Etudes Foncières en Afrique

15 | In accordance with Article 544 of the French *Code Civil*, property can be understood to be "the right to enjoy and dispose of things in the most absolute way...." – *"Le droit de jouir et de disposer des choses de la manière la plus absolue (...)"*

property rights. For this purpose, the state was accorded a role that it exceeded so tremendously that it in effect eclipsed the commons as a functional and legal entity in Senegalese villages. At the same time, we must recognize the importance of different types of property, just as various kinds of commons exist. This is precisely what my experience on the Comoros has taught me since 1986.

At the time, the FAO (the Food and Agriculture Organization of the United Nations) asked me to head a group of experts tasked with stabilizing land policy on the Comoros. A former French colony, the country experienced a revolutionary crisis between 1975, when it gained independence, and 1978. Among other things, this brought about the occupation of the former colonial properties, where vanilla and flowers for perfume were grown. It also resulted in all land registers being burned; entire archives were annihilated – and with them, the titles of ownership. In 1986, in an economically unstable situation and under pressure from international donors, the government was forced to clarify land policy in order to attract investors, and to do so without provoking new rounds of violence.

Since I was an expert on land rights, my job was to propose various scenarios. I outlined six options and described their potentials and limits. They ranged from "everything" (proactive and rapid expansion of private property to the entire population) to "nothing" (the government would settle for resolving the most sensitive conflicts, thus permitting local power relationships and local forms of negotiation to prevail). If, after almost thirty years, it looks like we are close to "nothing," because no reform was ever formally put into practice, then we would be closing our eyes to the intellectual and technical revolution that permitted the functionaries of rural development to tackle the problem of land use according to the principle of inalienability that the government approved in 1987. The parliament of the Comoros was unable to fully implement the wording of the law because Hamed Abdallah, the president of the republic, was murdered in November 1989.

The future of major transnational corporations was in danger. And our challenge was now to stabilize smallholder agriculture, so that it could feed the country and guarantee the export of certain colonial goods. To do so, some innovations were necessary, for example, the enclosure[16] of plant material on those lands that had previously been freely accessible and had been managed as village commons, but were used by individual families.[17]

---

16 | In contrast to the experience in sixteenth to eighteenth century England, enclosure in this case does not only serve the richest and the powerful dignitaries; it also enhances communal land use in the villages.

17 | Saïd (2009) reminds readers of the diversity of legal forms for land that can be used communally but for different purposes, such as high-altitude pastureland; old, colonial reserves

In addition, technical consultants and rural technicians helped hold regular village administrative council meetings: reliable, but hardly formalized meetings of farmers and elders every Friday evening as they left the mosque. The meetings were intended to prevent problems and resolve local tensions before they developed into conflicts. The options I had presented in my legal texts were implemented in social practices because a culture of negotiation prevailed at all levels of political-administrative life, and because the notion of inalienability was favored over that of absolute property. The development consultants had two beneficial effects: they saved the government the political costs and uncertainties of land reform, and they guaranteed the citizenry a lifestyle that, although modest and often close to poverty, was more dignified than that of many of the country's neighbors (such as Madagascar, which in 1991 had fallen back to its 1896 poverty level again).

Later on, I was to work in Madagascar, too, but only after two more assignments: the first one took me to Niger to contribute to drafting the country's agricultural legislation (*Code rural*), the second to Mali, where I observed numerous legal inconsistencies concerning the possession of land. I had been tasked with helping to rescue the country's cotton industry. All three countries – Niger, Mali and Madagascar – already had their own histories of land tenure law, so simply "copying and pasting" systems that seemed to work in other countries was unthinkable. That would have produced problems similar to those arising in the aftermath of colonialism: private ownership of land that could be used or sold for any purpose; undue state interference in property ownership; and no legal recognition of people's traditional practices in managing land.

In Madagascar, I plunged into the so-called real economy and observed the wood energy sector. The communally managed eucalyptus plantings on the so-called tanety[18] provided a livelihood for the local population. Then I expanded my research to the contractual relationships as I was interested in the substance and extent of leasehold clauses[19] as well as sharecropping[20] and the true nature of the relevant property rights. I collaborated very closely with Alain Karsenty – a social economist working for CIRAD[21], the French research center for international agricultural and development questions – and in 1996,

---

(*réserves indigènes*) which could be used again for growing fruit; old colonial possessions reserved for perfume production; *manyaouli*; matrilineal assets (in Muslim countries); fisheries in lagoons, etc.

18 | Translator's note: A flat hill, previously without trees.

19 | Translator's note: "*clauses de fermage;*" here, a fixed amount is paid in advance to the owner.

20 | Translator's note: In the original: "*clauses de métayage;*" here, it is determined in advance which percentage of the harvest – half to two-thirds – goes to the owner, who usually is responsible for the production infrastructure.

21 | http://www.cirad.fr

I witnessed the adoption of the so-called GELOSE legislation by Madagascar's government.

The law does not refer to "absolute property rights." Instead, it authorizes the parties involved to negotiate resource management contracts, provided the relative security of property rights to land is guaranteed. In 2005 this step resulted in a more far-reaching land reform that permitted a trading office to be established in every municipality where so-called land certificates can be discussed and negotiated. The certificates are legally binding. They are legal documents that ensure the security of the transaction in the relevant administrative region, whereby the desire for more security naturally continues to be linked to the idea of (registered) land registry titles. The certificates provide an interesting middle course between communal management by like-minded people and land titles freely exchangeable on the market, but they are also called into question precisely for this reason. The experience in Madagascar has attracted a great deal of attention internationally, but has not been reproduced elsewhere.

Commons Re-emerge in France, Too

My other world of experience stems from the fact that since the mid-1970s, I have been thinking about how a scientific approach that up to then was exclusively Africanistic could be applied to French (or European) society. The basic idea was to establish legal anthropology, which was still an exotic field, "at home," too, to get beyond ethnocentric perspectives. And while I was asking myself time and again what law actually was, I developed the idea to expand the fieldwork I had done in Senegal in 1969 and then in the Congo in 1972/73. I was looking for ways in which collective aspirations and communitarian practices were expressed in France – in the relationship between humans and land, and then in negotiations for managing conflicts in France's juvenile justice system of the 1980s.

In exploring this question, I selected my own ethnic group as the object of investigation, since my cultural belonging made it easy for me to access certain pieces of information and behavior patterns; also, the people of Picardy in northern France are renowned for their consuetudinary law and I had privileged access to detailed information about a specific area within Picardy, the medieval county of Vermandois: it was genealogical material, "commonplace books," a kind of calendar in which all economic activities, all sales and purchases, all work activities, special weather or political events, even laborers' jokes, were recorded. The commonplace books as well as the business managers' records provided the key to understanding how communal practices were retained in a world of farming that was increasingly subject to the capitalist market.

This world fell victim to the trenches on the Somme in 1916, which destroyed the historical legacy as well as the architecture and the landscape of the area.[22] Since the eighteenth century, private property had become increasingly powerful in this region of the world. And in the nineteenth century, it continued to spread, but various social and legal practices still bore witness to common points of reference, to the obligation to "keep something jointly," just as one "keeps company." For example, commoning means sharing the art of hunting, the social protocols of weddings and funerals, the patronage of one's own clients and workers, and all the traditions that express social belonging and solidarity in the face of life and death. In France as in Africa, the local agricultural milieu is rich in family relationships and professional ones. And just as in Africa, the limitations on one's behavior that this entails are experienced and perceived intensely, but not mentioned – and certainly not to a stranger.

Pluralism is a condition for a community to function harmoniously, but this is usually not made a topic of discussion as such. My interviewees agreed in that regard, yet they had never thought about the problem of land from a pluralist perspective before! Examining the structure of ownership revealed that in the villages where I worked, everything belonged to someone. Not a single place was unowned. The land is expensive and among the best in France. Giving away even the smallest portion of land is unthinkable. And indeed there were only a few communal organizational structures in the swamp landscapes along the rivers running through the area.

Yet the physical areas devoted to specific *common activities* bear witness to longstanding common practices even on "private property," e.g., playing fistball or gathering forest fruits. That was my first lesson. It was to be confirmed in the Amiénois, my own area of Picardy: *a "common" function which is thus inherent and not made explicit can be superimposed on a right of ownership that is exclusive and absolute in principle.* That function would then limit the exercise of this right, to the benefit of all members of a certain community insofar and as long as this function requires it. In the absence of players, for example, the fistball fields were transformed into community squares, flowerbeds, places for storing materials, and the like.[23] Functional logic triumphs over institutional logic!

---

22 | During post-World War I reconstruction in the early 1920s, those real estate companies relying on foreign capital benefited from the psychological state of shock and their financial independence to gain control of considerable tracts of land and to bring their management into a capitalist logic of rationalization.

23 | Professor Carol Rose notes that British legal doctrine once recognized the right of localities to uphold "customs of the manor" overriding common law: "To be held good, the custom in question must have existed without dispute for a time that supposedly ran beyond memory, and it had to be well defined and 'reasonable.'....Custom thus suggests a route by which a 'commons' may be managed – a means different from ownership either by individuals or by organized governments. The intriguing aspect of customary property rights is that they vest property rights in groups that are indefinite and informal yet nevertheless capable of

These practices illustrate that notions about common space that usually remain in the dark emerge when one starts to look at common uses and the sharing of places. These notions about space are familiar in African societies, but have been forgotten here in Europe where geometrical notions about space dominate. Geometrical notions lead to the surveying and measuring of space, thus enabling people to assign an exchange value to the measure and finally to marketize what has been surveyed and measured (Le Roy 2011); social uses disappear from view. In a topocentric concept, by contrast, all spaces are identifiable by a place (location, point) that retain their own functional identities. These spaces can overlap if they fulfill different functions, and they can create borders and even territories if the functions are similar. The functions may be political, economic, religious, or otherwise. All of this characterizes how a territory is formed.

In other words, one can observe how commons with different functions overlap in a single area. At the same time, a physical space is generally assigned to concrete ownership rights according to the rules of positive law. Of course, such "layerings" of the law with various forms of control complicate the understanding of the people's culture and their networks. After all, fundamentally speaking, as soon as we enter into the logic of the commons, some of our accustomed mechanisms for interpreting the functioning of a society and its formal regulatory authorities fail. At times, all they can do is represent information in a distorted way – or more likely, as caricatures.

I returned to Michel Alliot's analyses (2003), in which he asserted that a community shares in three ways: areas of life, a particular type of behavior, and a decision area. This threefold sharing makes communities potentially totalitarian if the practices of sharing are not corrected by plural belongings and identities. By default, as a fact of life, we live in many worlds simultaneously, after all: family, school, political circles, professional life, sports, etc. In each of these worlds, we have a status of our own and an identity of our own. Even if societies transformed by market-oriented norms and state control no longer recognize traditional, communal, threefold sharing as a general rule, practices of sharing continues to flourish among communities comprised of people with multiple part-time identities. I call these groups "neo-communities."

A supplement to Le Monde of April 4, 2014, on sustainable development, with the suggestive title "Betting on sharing," took up the commons from the

self-management. Custom can be the medium through which such an informal group acts; indeed the community claiming customary rights was in some senses not an 'unorganized' public at all, even if it was not a formal government either." "The Comedy of the Commons: Custom, Commerce and Inherently Public Property," [Chapter 5] in Carol M. Rose, *Property and Persuasion: Essays on the History, Theory and Rhetoric of Ownership* (Boulder, Colorado: Westview Press, 1994) pp. 123-124.

perspective of "alternative consumption." Above all, it sketched the effects of carpooling and forms of living in cooperatives as promoted in France by the ALUR Act (Law on access to housing and urban redevelopment) following the German model. Journalist Marie-Béatrice Baudet commented that "customs are changing, especially among young people. That is certain, but not yet a revolution." She quoted Remy Oughiry of the opinion research institute IPSOS: "The followers of collaborative consumption do not reject the consumer society at all. They simply want to regain control over it." And Oughiry added, "The desire to own property remains very strong."

Just as Monsieur Jourdain in Molière's *The Bourgeois Gentleman (Le Bourgeois Gentilhomme)* discovered that he had been speaking prose all his life without knowing it, we have been practicing commoning through and in our common experiences that we no longer call common. After all, under the influence of neoliberalism, the concept of community has been transformed in French political debate into something negative, an antithesis to the idea of the good life and a negative buzzword in the political debate, with all the side effects that entails (Hatzfeld 2011).

As a result, we are confronted with a difficulty that I linked to an enigma in the land question at the beginning of this chapter. We participate in sharing behaviors that are often long-lasting, but are not identified as commoning. And if people try to name these behaviors, then tend to use terms like "common good," which have a convenient semantic and political ambiguity but may in fact be undermined by the legal realities. In civil law, a good is a thing in private possession and which can be disposed of at will in any way desired, while a commons must remain intact as a collective resource and cannot be sold at will. For this reason, I will devote the final section of this essay to the legal status of the commons. In principle, this would require that new categories and legal concepts be introduced, but I will refrain from doing so due to a lack of space.

The Legality of the Commons

The commons, singular or plural[24], confront us with two problems: the fact that the law is silent, and yet a torrent of legal words purports to regulate what existing law cannot regulate effectively at all. This obvious contradiction requires a kind of anthropological demystification of the state of the law in order to clarify the difficulties of conventional law in managing commons.

The fact that lawyers abuse the law is explained by the very practices of their profession. Still, a majority of citizens continue to trust formal law to

---

24 | I usually use the plural to avoid an abstraction that would affirm the philosophical idealism of the positivists, who treat the "common" as a good, an object of ownership, a person, or something similarly fictitious.

deal with problems that it can hardly grasp, or not at all. That is not acceptable. My anthropological experience as a researcher makes me concede that formal law, which we claim is universal in human thinking, is nothing but a construct that credibly corresponds to a particular temporal and local situation and has endured for several generations (for example, in Rome). In Europe, it is only since the seventeenth century that people have come to believe that law can take on a life of its own, largely independent of human agency and more and more specialized, finally brokering an alliance between the state and the market. Bound to political and economic power in this way, and in the course of the colonial adventures of the nineteenth century, this originally Western form of law has now spread to the entire world. Yet the rule of weapons and capital cannot make us forget that what is called "law," and what goes hand in hand with the modern state, does not correspond to the experiences of three or four billion of our contemporaries around the world. For them, law instead triggers their mistrust and resistance.

In terms of the history of mankind, the law is only a folk law, a local interpretation of a process that is much more general. I call this process legality, or *juricidité*. If this legality is barely studied, it is because powerful political, economic and ideological interests prevent it. They are the same interests that do not permit the commons to be apprehended and named.

In addition, there is a problem in how to characterize law. If only the law itself is considered as autonomous (Le Roy 2009) – and if its interpreters derive normative categories from it and can treat them semantically as categories of law – then other experiences, whether they are Confucian, indigenous, Muslim, animist, or other traditions, are in principle heteronomous.[25] They may resemble law, but they are instead based on social traditions. Legality, by contrast, is identifiable in and through those practices that can be held legally responsible by an authority that is nominally empowered by the group itself to exercise appropriate sanctions. Legality in this sense is tautological because its grounding in social practice may or may not even exist!

This apparent lack of formal recognition of what is and is not law is deeply unsettling to European minds, especially for the Cartesian ones. For they tend to practice a kind of juridification (*juridisme*), to use Pierre Bourdieu's (1986) term. Bourdieu considers this a bad habit of anthropologists and others – to formulate legal rules and thus orient rules along the particular conventions of the law in cases where there is actually only habitus, i.e., material for representing structural conditions of existence, preferences that are stable over time. For this reason, it is imperative that two things be respected: on the one

---

25 | Editors' note: "Heteronomous" is the opposite of autonomous, and thus subject to foreign laws, economics, and political, religious and ethical regulations. It refers to someone deprived of self-determination, and dependent on outside influences or the will of others.

hand, not to consider anything to be law which is actually only a standard enacted and recognized by the state (in other words, what is called positive law); and on the other hand, to treat everything else that emerges organically from communities as an authentic product of legality as relevant phenomena: the *li*[26] and *fa*[27] of Confucianism, the Hindu Dharma,[28] the Muslim Fiqh[29] and Sharia, customs and traditions, etc. Laws belong to the legal order and are its dominant expression, but other forms of social expression and regulation have always existed as well, and will continue to unfold – in particular, forms that regulate the relationships among people in managing their shared wealth. It is precisely these practices that we need to use if we are to enable people to "be commoners" and to take paths that are secured in a *different* way – not purely through the legality of laws and property rights. If we think that legality offers inappropriate answers, then we must rely on innovative forms of the legal order. And it is up to us to invent them.[30]

From the Law to Control:
About Masteries for Exploring a New Legal Order

Two innovations have already been put up for discussion. I now come back here to legal dominance and control over soil and resources. The idea has taken hold that one could exercise a right to land (*ius in re*) or could have a claim to be allotted a plot of land or to be a creditor. It has taken hold so firmly that it is difficult to admit that this, too, is only a specific product of our way of thinking. In this way of thinking, law becomes autonomous; it is considered something independent. It is also a condition for constituting the autonomy of the individual in society. The great adventures of democracy in England, America and France are all based on important declarations of rights. Other cultural traditions tend to try and conceive of human beings as parts of complex

---

26 | Editors' note: The word *li* denotes the abstract idea of the totality of all manners and forms of behavior that characterize a good person and an intact societal order. In Western editions of Confucian writings, *li* is usually crudely translated as "rite." Yet Confucian rites are more than spiritual or ceremonial in nature; they also encompass small, everyday patterns of personal behavior. Other translations include ritual propriety, etiquette, or simply rules of proper behavior. Adapted from Wikipedia.

27 | *Fa* is the law, enacted by central power, which is primarily applicable to nonbelievers and strangers, according to the Confucian way.

28 | Editors' note: Dharma characterizes the ethics that determine the personal and social life of a Hindu. Karma depends on the extent to which dharma is fulfilled.

29 | Editors' note: Literally means awareness, understanding, or insight and denotes "Islamic jurisprudence," i.e., the science that concerns itself with Sharia, which regulates all relationships of public and private life in accordance with canonic law. These religious laws are laid out and discussed in the books of the Fiqh.

30 | Editors' note: The editors are planning a volume devoted to this topic in 2017.

networks in their interactions with and their obligations toward others, as well as in their ability to mobilize these networks.

In order to do justice to both approaches, I have decided to use an intercultural concept, that of *maîtrise*,[31] of dominance and control, which I first define as follows:

> The concept of control mastery suggests a power and a force that grants particular responsibility to those who reserve the rights to a territory more or less exclusively because they are actually affected by what happens there. The concept permits sovereignty and property to be combined – the two concepts provide a "frame" for the debate about land use (...) – by emphasizing that rights and responsibilities can arise from a concrete relationship to space [*Translator's note: Here: "land"*] and that this responsibility must be retained or ensured at its core. (Le Roy 1995:489)

By taking up anthropological and intercultural aspects, this concept of control, following Catherine and Olivier Barrière, enables the establishment of "a system for managing the assets of socioecological relationships at the heart of the internal and external relationships of communities." (Barrière & Barrière 2002:315)

This concept – as well as further clarity about the forms in which resources and their communal management are appropriated and used – enables us to evaluate what does and does not stem from a commons logic in accordance with the conventions of each group, community, or society at a particular moment in its history. As a scientific approach, this concept does not require an a priori definition of what commons are "in their essence." Instead, it focuses our view on what people share, and it moves strategies of communal management to the center of attention.

Conclusion

Making commons come alive again in everyday life and in the economic and legal systems seems like a revolution that can be interpreted through two lenses. Is it a rediscovery of precapitalist and prestate organizational principles or is it a break with the current political order? Perhaps even this framing does not do justice to the issue. In the epilogue to their book quoted above, Pierre Dardot and Christian Laval write: "Commons are the new political rationality that must replace the neoliberal rationality" (2014: 572). They regard revolution as the self-institution of society, an idea of Promethean dimensions of greatness.

---

31 | Editors' note: "Maîtrise" can also be translated as "mastery" in the sense of "mastering something/performing something well," but what is meant is dominance and control over one's own living conditions.

I believe their most important hypothesis is summed up in the following quotation: "As a principle, commons define a norm of inappropriability. This indeed requires establishing all social relationships anew, with this idea as a starting point: Inappropriability does not mean... that it would be impossible to appropriate something, but that it is socially unacceptable to appropriate it. In other words, that appropriating something as one's private property is not permitted because that thing is reserved for common use." (Dardot and Laval 2014: 583) "There are no common goods; what matters is creating commons."[32]

References

Alliot, Michel. 2003 [1980]. "Modèles sociétaux : les communautés," *Le droit et le service public au miroir de l'anthropologie*, Paris. Karthala. S. 73-78.

Appadurai, Arjun. 2013. *Condition de l'homme global*. Paris: Payot.

Barrière Catherine aund Olivier. 2002. *Un droit à inventer. Foncier et environnement dans le delta intérieur du Niger*. (Mali), Paris. IRD.

Bollier, David, 2014. *La renaissance des communs, pour une société de coopération et de partage*. Paris. Éditions Charles Léopold Mayer.

Bourdieu, Pierre. 1986. "Habitus, code et codification, *Actes de la recherche en sciences sociales*. Vol. 64, septembre, S. 40-44.

Dardot, Pierre aund Christian Laval. 2014. *Commun, essai sur la révolution au XXI° siècle*. Paris, Le Découverte.

Hatzfeld, Marc. 2011. *Les lascars, une jeunesse en colère*. Paris. Autrement, 2011.

Le Roy, Étienne. 1970. *Système foncier et développement rural, essai d'anthropologie juridique sur la répartition des terres chez les Wolof ruraux de la zone arachidière nord*, Sénégal. DiplomarbeitPH Dissertation. FDSE Paris. Ronéo.

———. 1995. "Le pastoralisme africain face aux problèmes fonciers," Daget Philippe, Godron Michel, editors, *Pastoralisme; Troupeaux, espaces, societies*. Paris. Hatier AUPELF-UREF, S. 487-510.

———. (with A. Karsenty und A. Bertrand). 1996. *La sécurisation foncière en Afrique, pour une gestion viable des ressources renouvelables*. Paris. Karthala.

———. 1999. "Au delà de la relation public-privé, l'apparition de la notion de 'communs' dans les expériences actuelles de décentralisation administrative en Afrique francophone," in Rösel Jacob und von Trotha, Trutz (Hg..), *Dezentralisierung, Demokratisierung und die lokale Repräsentation des Staates*. Köln, Rüdiger Köppe Verlag, S. 69-78.

———. 2009. "Autonomie du droit, hétéronomie de la juridicité." In Sacco Rodolfo, editor, *Le nuove ambizioni del sapere del giurista: anthropologica giuridica e traducttologia giuridica*. Rome. Academia Nazionale dei Lincei, Atti dei convegni Lincei 253, S. 99-133.

———. 2011. La terre de l'autre, une anthropologie des régimes d'appropriation foncière. Paris, LGDJ, col. Droit et société, série anthropologie.

———. 2014 [2012]. "Sous les pavés du monologisme juridique, prolégomènes anthropologiques." In Parance et al. 2014. S. 81-101.

---

32 | *"Il n'y a pas de biens communs, il n'y a que des communs à instituer."*

Parance Béatrice. Saint Victor Jacques de, editors. 2014. Repenser les biens communs. Paris, CNRS éditions. Saïd Mahamouadou, 2009. *Foncier et société aux Comores*. Paris. Karthala.

Étienne Le Roy *(France) is emeritus Professor of Legal Anthropology at the University Panthéon-Sorbonne, Paris 1 where he has directed the research Laboratory for Legal Anthropology of Paris from 1988 to 2007 and Curricula of African Studies, from 1993 to 2003. Since the mid-Sixties he has devoted his fieldwork to the study of land tenure systems and policies governing the appropriation of territories in Africa. Among many publications, Le jeu des lois, (Paris, LGDJ, 1999) offers his theoretical contribution to a legal "dynamic" anthropology and La terre de l'autre, une anthropologie des régimes d'appropriation foncière is the synthesis of forty years of research on land issues.*

Commons and Alternative Rationalities: Subjectivity, Emotion and the (Non)rational Commons

By Andrea J. Nightingale

When I tell people that I work on inshore fisheries management the response is inevitably disparaging. Most people continue to assume that the commons is an ecological disaster waiting to happen and that all fishermen are greedy individuals. Yet my experience on the west coast of Scotland suggests that the fishing ground is governed by a variety of rationalities and subjectivities that often override the desire to maximize individual benefit.

When I first began thinking about ideas of subjectivity and emotion in relation to fisheries most people thought I was crazy. Talk to fishermen about their feelings? But it quickly became clear that I was on the right track. As one fishermen's advocate said to me, laughing, "People are definitely not rational, especially fishermen. They make decisions based on other factors."[1] I became fascinated by what some of these "other" factors might be.

My project begins with the excellent work done by Ostrom (1992) and others on design principles for the commons. Design principles focus on the institutional rules and norms required for effective management of collective resources. This work has been done within a rational choice framework, however, which leaves little space for understanding alternative rationalities or "nonrational" behaviors. If we simply add in perspectives on gender, kinship relations, emotional attachments to resources and land- and seascapes to our understanding of design principles, it prevents us from exploring how design principles emerge in the first place. Rather, I suggest we need to explore how institutions, resources and societies are co-emergent. This starting point shows how the "design" of a commons is a product of personal interactions, histories and relationships that need to be continually renewed.[2]

---

1 | A paraphrase of an unrecorded phone interview.
2 | See essay by Silke Helfrich, "Patterns of Commoning," on pp. 26-46.

Taking co-emergence as a starting point has major implications for how we understand the dynamics of the commons. It is not a question of explaining how resource use *affects* the commons, but rather a question of exploring how the commons, as an institution, a place and an ecosystem, is embedded *within* and *productive of* the communities that rely on commons. The two cannot be neatly separated, spatially, temporally or analytically.

My research has been on the Scottish inshore *Nephrops norvegicus* fishery, which is the largest fishery in Scotland in terms of landings and number of boats. *Nephrops* are also known as Norwegian lobster or prawns and are the main species marketed as scampi or langoustines. They are fished both by creel and by trawl net, although the creel fishery produces a higher value, live product. Skipper-owned boats, operated out of small ports on a daily basis, dominate the fishery.

The west coast is a mixed fishery with creelers (pots on the sea bed) and trawlers (nets towed across the sea bed) sharing the same fishing grounds. One community on the west coast has banned all trawl gear from its fishing grounds and operates a formal (although not legally binding) scheme to limit the number of creels fished per day per boat. They are an unusual case because the UK government sets and distributes prawn quotas, leaving limited opportunities for fishers to make their own rules for managing fish catches. The situation is rapidly changing as the government implemented inshore fisheries groups in 2009 to decentralize management. How much authority they have, however, is still quite restricted. It is in this context that I want to explore the "(non)rational commons."

Design Principles and the (Non)rational

Much of the work done on the commons has centered on the institutions that make collective management of shared resources viable. Institutions (rules and norms) are vital to limiting and monitoring resource extraction. Yet I want to focus on the dynamics of institutions, the everyday practices through which institutions come into being and are reproduced over time and space. In particular, I want to add in a consideration of subjectivities, including gender, race, class and even identities such as "fishermen," which I suggest are equally important to how a common-pool resource is managed. When we take into consideration alternative rationalities, then the reasons that some well-designed institutions fail becomes clearer. It is the ongoing *enactment* of institutions as well as their underlying rules and norms that are crucial to outcomes.

Subjectivities are important to the operation of institutions as they are integrally bound up with how people understand their relationship to others. In a fisheries context, I focus on the practices and interactions that are required for one to be considered a "fisherman" and the contradictory ways in which these interactions both promote and frustrate attempts at collaboration.

For example, when I tell inshore fishermen I am interested in how they cooperate, they laugh and say they do not. And yet, when I have been on boats with them, there is an almost constant stream of communication as skippers radio others about the sea conditions, alert them to a strange boat in their waters, or warn trawlers they are too close to someone's creel line. When I point this out, they readily agree that they cooperate in these ways. In fact, I think most would agree that *they must* cooperate in order to ensure their safety and that of their gear and catch. The question then becomes whether or not these forms of cooperation help to build a foundation for more formal collaboration.[3]

The types of relationships driving cooperation can be considered "rational" in certain respects. Taking account of community obligations, the need to preserve kinship relationships and an emotive attachment to the sea can be seen as "rational," particularly over long time scales. Kinship relationships, for example, can be vital to supporting people during times of crisis and therefore are logically considered important to maintain. This kind of rationality, however, is not the kind of "rational fisherman" that rational choice theorists have in mind. I am therefore interested in challenging the dominant idea of the greedy fisherman by highlighting the alternative or "(non)rational" relations and commitments that underpin cooperation.

Subjectivity and Cooperation

I suggest that subjectivity is an important component of the "(non)rational" relations that underpin informal and formal modes of cooperation. Subjectivity is often conflated with identity, but the two concepts are different in important ways. Subjectivity refers to the ways in which people are brought into relations of power, or subjected, as well as how they resist them. Power is at the heart of social interactions; it is impossible to conceptualize relationships that are not bound by power in some way. Power can operate in the commons in many different forms, from gender, caste, and ethnicity inequalities within commons user-groups, to the relations between fisheries policy or policy makers and fishermen, to more subtle dimensions of power such as those that arise from differences in experience and knowledge of commons resources – all of which produce different subjectivities. These serve to position people engaged in the commons differently in relation to each other and in relation to the commons itself.

---

3 | Editors' note: The essay by Étienne Le Roy in this volume, on pp. 277-296, addresses this point, that the processes of commoning are not necessarily perceived or reflected upon.

In fisheries, to be "a fisherman" requires that one goes to sea and catches fish. This relationship between the resource and subjectivity is crucial for how fishers see themselves and integrate certain attitudes and behaviors into other aspects of their lives, including formal institutions to manage the fishery.

Subjectivities are not necessarily negative; they are a consequence of the multidimensional aspects of power, making it difficult to think of power as simply unidirectional or even bidirectional. Power is what gives the subject the ability to act, and any resistance to a dominating power will always have some contradictory outcomes. In order to resist power, one has to first accept that they are subject to that power.

In Scottish fisheries, the subject "fisherman" is dependent upon a large web of economic, political and social relationships wherein fishing as an historical, cultural, technological and legal activity is defined and policed. If we consider the operation of power in this context, fishers cannot contest fishing regulations without first accepting that they are subject to those regulations. This power over them also provides the power to act in a variety of ways. Similarly, fishermen cannot make claims about protecting their fishing grounds without simultaneously reinforcing the idea that fishermen exploit their fishery and that the fishing grounds belong to *someone*.

In most thinking on the commons, power is either something which might derail an otherwise well functioning community, or as something contained in individuals that they can use to maximize their profits by overexploiting the shared resources in defiance of the rest of the users.

For example, even though overfishing or violating quotas is a familiar phenomenon, recently some Scottish fishers have been at the forefront of voluntary schemes to create sustainable fisheries. One is a scheme for white fish boats to report and actively avoid areas where large concentrations of young cod are found. Another is the case, mentioned above, where mobile gear was banned from a creel fishery. (This is rather unusual in that part of the fishing ground is "protected" by a military zone on one side, and that combined with the topography of the coast lines serves to demarcate a relatively clear "local fishing ground" that is clearly identifiable on a map.) About fifteen years ago fishers in this area became concerned over the decline in their fishery. They engaged in a variety of legal and somewhat more dubious tactics in what is known as the "trawl wars" to exclude mobile gear from their area. One of the most notorious incidents was the sinking of a caravan to interfere with the trawl gear. This was successful in deterring the trawlers but the culprit was identified because, as one informant told me, "they forgot to take off the licence plate, so that wasn't so smart."

The group succeeded in getting a partial ban in the fishing ground that excludes mobile gear and limits the number of creels fished per day, per boat. They also use escape hatches to allow the smaller prawns to leave the creel before it is lifted. These agreements are voluntary, but the exclusion of mobile gear has been legally confirmed, although not permanently. The exclusion has to be renewed regularly (roughly every ten years, but it changes with changes in Scottish fisheries policy). Because this has helped produce excellent fishing ground, "there are more boats, especially in the south end of the area that aren't signed up [to our agreement] and aren't complying. Especially Max [pseudonym]... is not a fisherman, he's just a businessman." My respondent explains why some fishers are committed to limiting the fishery and others are not by invoking the difference between "fishermen" who respect the local customs and seek to limit their fishing, and a "businessman" who simply wants to catch as much profit as possible. In another area, a creeler contrasted the "businessmen" who trawl, with creeling which he described as, "days you're out there and you're barely making a living but you're at sea...It's a way of being." He went on to complain that the large trawlers do not spend money in the village and have no commitment to the community. Not only is the trawl catch more indiscriminate, but he suggests that their emotional attachments to the sea and the community are dissimilar, and as a result, they do not have the same commitments to try to manage the fishery sustainably. Both of these schemes are constructive, pro-active attempts to protect their fishery.

Neither scheme provides short-term financial returns for the fishers although most people involved believe and hope that longer term it will ensure the viability of the fishery. Under a rational choice framework, however, these schemes are considered highly irrational. They are not seen as advancing the best interests of individual fishers because they often result in fishers earning less money from their days at sea. But my point here is that these schemes only appear as "unusual" or "innovative" because of the dominant view (fostered by rational-choice theory itself!) that fishers are only interested in self-improvement or profits. Schemes to limit the fishery are all based on the assumption that fishers will try to catch as many fish as they can when they are out on the sea. Yet the everyday practices of fishers generally do not reflect these assumptions. This is largely because the identity of being a "fisherman" emerges from the act of going to sea and living in a web of kinship, community and peer relationships that are crucial to supporting fishing as an activity and as an industry. Significantly, this identity persists *regardless of the institutional rules and to a certain extent regardless of dominant theoretical paradigms.* Thus attention to alternative rationalities and identities is crucial to understanding how cooperation or noncooperation emerges – and therefore how a commons can function so effectively.

Fishing produces particular kinds of bodies and emotions that are not insignificant when it comes to trying to draw up management agreements. Men who are used to coping with dangerous and physically demanding environments, find it literally uncomfortable, physically and subjectively, to situate their bodies in a meeting room. In other words, this experience changes what it *means* to be a fisherman. This change is as much an embodied experience as it is a political and emotional one. A fisherman working on his boat, providing food and income for his family, is often in a relatively powerful position. I have met few fishers in Scotland who are not proud of their occupation. And yet, that changes to a very different kind of subjectivity when they find themselves the target of decommissioning schemes, blamed personally for degradation of their fishing grounds, or forced to interact with policymakers. The exercise of power changes in profound ways and they end up in a more defensive position relative to their occupational identity.

Conceptualizing power and subjectivity in this way brings into focus the kinds of relationships and practices that shape how cooperation occurs within the commons, many of which are not "rational" as narrowly defined by rational choice theory.[4] Every relationship linked to the commons – from that between policymakers and resource users, to internal user-group dynamics, to those between resource users and the larger community – contain the possibility for power to produce either a resistant, uncooperative subject or a variety of subjectivities that are more conducive to working collectively.

The spaces within which these interactions occur are also important in shaping power and relationships. Therefore, we need to shift the focus in commons work from institutional design (rules and norms) to the everyday spaces, experiences and practices wherein commons management occurs. It is those elements that shape whether management rules are accepted, who accepts them, who polices them and the kinds of social *and* environmental transformations they produce.

Working the Sea: Everyday Practices and the Operation of Power

This discussion, however, still seems remote from the pitching fishing boats and smelly piers wherein fishers spend most of their time. I think that attention needs to be paid to the *embodied experiences of fishermen* in the spaces wherein they interact: the pier, on boats, in meeting halls, and in the community.

4　|　Editors' note: Rational choice theory is used by many conventional economists, political scientists and sociologists as a framework for analyzing individual decisionmaking and behavior. It assumes that individuals use instrumental rationality to acquire more of a given good or service in the most cost-effective way possible.

In Scotland, the inshore fishery is often the lifeblood of small, coastal villages. Many places have few other job possibilities outside of tourism, which itself is dependent on selling the idealized "fishing village" image to guests. In response to a question about what had caused the biggest changes in her west coast community, an older woman said,

> Well, mainly the fishing, the prawn fishing. Years ago now, I suppose ten or fifteen years ago, there weren't that many boats out of here and most of the young ones were really going away from the place. But now a lot of the young ones are back... They are buying houses and they are building houses...

Fishing, then, is far more than an occupation. It is one of the activities that keeps the community viable and lively. As a result, fishers are embedded in a set of relationships that support fishing in symbolic and emotional ways, even if local people buy very little fish directly off the boats. Fishers do not financially gain from the community, but the relationships bind them together – which itself enacts an alternative rationality to profit maximization. The benefits of fishing flow from these relationships and *from that particular place*; they provide subconscious emotional support to fishers when they may not catch any fish. This kind of support is crucial to keeping fishers rooted in place and dissuades them from moving to more productive fishing grounds, as "rational" theory suggests they should.

As more "local" boats have appeared, many fishers are concerned that there are now too many fishers. Yet none of them suggests that people should be actively excluded. Rather they highlight the ways they cooperate, as one fisherman said,

> Everyone is free to go where they want but I mean basically your [fishing ground] is marked and it's...well, it's more of a kind of gentleman's agreement that you don't go and shoot over the top of someone else's creels...I mean it does happen...basically because people think maybe somebody else is getting something better but its generally put down to a mistake with tides...but if someone was blatantly doing it, moved in here and just plastered on top of everyone there would have to be something done that maybe you wouldn't put down on paper. [laughter]

Here, the fisher suggests that the ability to exclude someone from your fishing ground is tied up in being a legitimate member of the community. He assumes that a blatant violator of the "gentlemen's agreement" would be an outsider. Thus being a "fisherman" in a locally understood sense is also to be part of the community.

Another fisherman spoke about how it was unpleasant to have confrontations with people, indicating that relationships are often more important than the catch. In localities where two communities' fishing grounds overlapped, they actively tried to avoid fishing in areas that might cause conflict. People aren't willing to risk causing an altercation just to catch a few more prawns.

These "fishermen" are very different from the "fishermen" of fisheries policy. In many respects, they act "irrationally" in the face of competition in the fishery. One would expect fishers to try to exclude new boats or to capture as much catch as they can individually, even if it meant conflict with people they do not know. While certainly the local men involved in the fishery compete with each other in a variety of ways, they are also highly valued because of the jobs and prosperity they bring into the village. They need to live up to their reputations and feel bound by certain local etiquettes that supersede some of the more blatant forms of self-interested behavior. When I speculated on some of these ideas to a fisherman's wife she immediately broke in, "They don't have a choice. I don't even think it's conscious; they have to be a part of things here. It's part of who they are. It's how we do things here."[5]

Similarly, in two other west coast fisheries, the creelers know that they would have bigger and more prolific prawns if trawlers were banned from their fishing grounds. But they are acutely aware that the fishing ground has to be shared and are against trying to ban the trawlers altogether. In one place, the brother of a successful creeler is physically disabled and while he can run a trawl boat, he would be physically unable to creel. Everyone agrees that he needs to have an opportunity to fish, too. It is also common for fishers to trade in their creels for a trawler when they get older and find the physical demands of creeling to be too difficult. It is these kinds of community obligations and alternative rationalities that make all fishers in those particular areas committed to a mixed gear (creel and trawl) fishery.

Interestingly, this commitment is rapidly changing as fuel prices increase and more trawlers are converting to creeling which uses significantly less fuel. The creel fishermen also federated in late 2012 and their organization is trying to provide an alternative lobbying voice to that of the trawlers. It is also promoting creeling as a clear commitment to conservation of the fishery for the short and long term. For example, the federation issued a public statement embracing the new marine-protected areas along the Scottish coast as a welcome development in marine spatial planning. Some of these areas will allow limited fishing while others will exclude fishers entirely. The trawl-dominated federations have been adamantly against marine protected areas.

Clearly, such relations of power can also lead to noncompliance and defiance of peer pressures to be a "good community (or federation) member." Many fishing communities have at least one such person, and indeed, at one of my field sites I was told to stay away from one man because he is considered

---

5　|　A paraphrase from an unrecorded phone interview.

dangerous. Yet for the vast majority of the fishers I have worked with, they are consciously and unconsciously bound within relations that make them unwilling to resist the subject "good community member."

Fishing in Scotland is very much a masculine activity, with the work and time demands deemed inappropriate for women raising children. With a few exceptions, women (wives) do most of the paperwork and onshore fisheries-related activities but rarely go on the boats themselves. This is important because the kinds of conflicts that emerge are linked to ideas of how men should behave in a west coast fishing village. One woman vividly described for me the priorities of the men in her village: "Oh, you know these West Highland men, it's work, pub, wife." She held her hands up in front of her and placed "work" right in front, "pub" right next to it, and then stretched her arms all the way to the side and placed "wife" there. She continued, "I'm sure in their heads they think it's the opposite but it isn't." [laughter] The notion that "good men" work hard is emphasized along with the idea that men's and women's places are very different. Very few women hang out in the pubs. Maintaining your reputation, providing for your family, working hard and drinking in the pub are key ways in which males become "men," and through their activities on the sea, become "fishermen."[6]

What makes it so difficult to understand the relationships I've described is that attempting to identify patterns or to associate identities with particular motivations is inappropriate. Community obligations can just as easily lead to a ban on mobile gear as it can to a mixed gear fishery – as is the case in different places on the Scottish west coast. It is important to recognize that relationships are complex, contingent and changeable. If the commons is not successful, it is more likely due to problems with these relationships than it is with the institutional design. Therefore I propose the (non)rational commons, one which takes account of how power operates in the fishery, including the kinds of relationships I've described here.

Meetings, Emotion and Subjectivity

In order to understand more fully the relationships relevant for cooperation in the fishery, it is also necessary to consider the meeting room. A variety of meetings occur in relation to fisheries, ranging from informal chats on the pier between skippers and other users of the sea such as tourist boat operators or port authorities, to policy meetings in Edinburgh and Brussels attended by fishers' representatives, policymakers and scientists. The shift from their boats

---

6 | Many of the skippers I know do not spend much time drinking in pubs. They are more likely to drink at parties or at home whereas crew members, who tend to be younger and unmarried, do spend a lot of time in the pub.

to the meeting room subjects fishermen in radically different ways. Here I focus on the consultation meetings that usually involve policymakers and fisheries regulators with fishermen, fishermen's advocates, and occasionally other stakeholders such as environmental groups or local development authorities. Most often, these meetings are held in larger west coast towns or areas central to the dispersed fishing villages.

In the interviews many fishers expressed a much stronger emotion and pragmatic connection with their resources than with policy meetings. One fisherman put it poignantly, "People sitting in their office, they are not even affected by the rain." Another said, "They are so divorced from what it's about. We have a lot of conversations about what it's about to live here. We are surrounded by greens and blues [i.e., nature], [policy makers] coming from the city, they don't have that, they do not understand what that means."[7] These men insist that managers do not understand the realities of the act of fishing and living in a remote coastal village, and this is seen by them as a major problem for collective solutions. In other words, the fishermen and the policymakers inhabit very different relationships with the resource and this is crucial for how relations of power are exercised.

The meeting room itself produces a very different subjectivity among fishermen than time on the boat. They are clear that the meeting room is not their place. One man said, "It's the difference between standing on the landing and jumping in the sea." Another said, "One's real and the other is not. Well yeah, I'm happier for one [on the boat]." Equally importantly, many fishermen pointed out that policy makers are paid to attend meetings whereas they are not. Instead, they take time away from their boats or other activities in order to have their voices heard. The space of the meeting room itself produces particular kinds of subjects for both the fishermen and policymakers that sets them literally, on opposite sides of the room.

The fishermen are well aware of these relations and how the assumptions of fisheries regulators shape meeting dynamics. One man said about a recent meeting, "The guys come with their preconceptions, it's almost like here we go again. We threw them a surprise [when we started talking about limiting the creel fishery in addition to banning trawling]. Someone talking about their own sector, they didn't expect that."[8] Another man said, "You explain your point of view but they don't want to hear it. They've made up their mind before they go in the meeting."

These preconceptions emerge from the normative practices of fishing. Policymakers base their policies and their meeting agendas on ideas of "rational

---

7 | A paraphrase from an unrecorded phone interview.

8 | A paraphrase from an unrecorded phone interview.

fishermen," who by definition need to be policed and regulated. By this reckoning, the creel fishermen I have described here shift from being family providers, bound by "gentlemen's agreements" and subjected by the "community,"to being an overexploiter of the sea who needs to be told about proper fisheries management. This shift in subjectivity is central to why there is so much antagonism between fishermen and policymakers.

Alternative rationalities or the "nonrational" are therefore key components of commons management. The relationships and places within which fishers interact are important components of their subjectivities, which in turn is integral to how power is exercised. My work suggests that these kinds of relations of power are central to whether fishers bond together to cooperate (sometimes to manage the fishery, sometimes to protest against rules) or fiercely resist any kind of collective action.

In terms of management of common-pool resources, then, it is crucial to examine how people's personal relationships within a commons change with the spatial and political context, and especially the configurations of power. These embodied interactions create openings and close down others for particular kinds of cooperation. What emerges is an important difference between "managing a common-pool resource" as fisheries policy schemes try to do, and the "gentlemen's agreements" that emerge out of community commitments and obligations I have described here. While the Scottish case shows that such gentlemen's agreements are vulnerable to noncompliance and even to lack of support from state regulatory structures, they also point to the tremendous possibilities that arise when people bring their commitments to "commoning" into their everyday lives. Or as Silke Helfrich puts it, "If you consider yourself a commoner and if you realize and reflect upon what you're doing in terms of commoning, then it's likely to be a successful commons." Emotional attachments to land and seascape and community subjectivities can help to foster such consciousness.

Reference

Ostrom, Elinor. 1992. "The Rudiments of a Theory of the Origins, Survival, and Performance of Common-Property Institutions." In David Bromley, editor, *Making the Commons Work: Theory, Practice, and Policy*. San Francisco, ICS Press. 293-318.

Andrea J. Nightingale *(Sweden) is a Geographer by training and presently Chair of Rural Development in the Global South at the Swedish University of Agricultural Sciences (SLU) in Uppsala, Sweden. Her current research interests include climate change adaptation and transformation debates; public authority, collective action and state formation; and feminist work on emotion and subjectivity in relation to theories of development, collective action and cooperation. She previously worked at the School of Global Studies, University of Gothenburg, Sweden and the University of Edinburgh, Geography, School of GeoSciences, Scotland.*

I would like to give a special thanks to the people on the west coast who contributed their time, thoughts and patience to my project. They have shown a generosity in working with me that helped me to better understand the importance of the "community obligations" I discuss. I would also like to thank David Donan, Jim Atkinson, Jim Watson and Hamish Mair for discussions on the policy context and pressures facing the fishery and being open to thinking about the social science aspects of the science they do.

The Fountain of Fish: Ontological Collisions at Sea

By Anne Salmond

"If something goes wrong, its not only our beaches that get ruined. It's everyone's."
[Tweedie Waititi, Te Whanau-a-Apanui, *Sunday Star Times*]

In April 2011, a small flotilla of protest vessels headed out to sea from the Eastern Bay of Plenty in New Zealand. Among them was a fishing boat, the *San Pietro*, owned by the local *iwi* (kin group), Te Whanau-a-Apanui, and skippered by Elvis Teddy, an *iwi* member. Rikirangi Gage, a senior tribal leader, was also on board. At that time, a large ship, the Orient Explorer, contracted by the Brazilian oil company Petrobas, was conducting a seismic survey of the Raukumara Basin, about 300 kilometers north of East Cape. In 2010, Petrobas had been granted a permit by the New Zealand government to prospect for oil in these waters, which crossed Te Whanau-a-Apanui's ancestral fishing grounds.

When they learned of this permit from press reports, the *iwi* leaders were incensed. Under the Treaty of Waitangi, signed in 1840, Queen Victoria had guaranteed their ancestors the "full, exclusive, undisturbed possession of their Lands and Estates Forests Fisheries and other properties... so long as it is their wish and desire to retain the same in their possession." (Waitangi Tribunal)

Since 1975 the Waitangi Tribunal, established to inquire into breaches of the Treaty, had held hearings around the country and investigated many complaints by Maori kin groups, including those relating to fishing and the ocean. The Tribunal issued reports and made recommendations, and over this period, successive governments had offered apologies and settlements in cash and kind to many *iwi* around the country.

When Te Whanau-a-Apanui leaders met with the Prime Minister to state their opposition to drilling for oil in their ancestral waters, he expressed sympathy, but refused to revoke the permit. Determined that their point of view should be heard, the tribe put out a call for assistance, and the environmental group Greenpeace responded by sending a flotilla of protest vessels to the Bay of Plenty.

As anger about the oil prospecting increased, placards and signs sprang up on windows and fences along the road between Opotiki and Gisborne. Bonfires were lit in protest, and large-scale *haka* (war-dances) performed on the beaches.

In April 2011 Greenpeace protestors swam into the path of the *Orient Explorer,* watched by members of the Air Force, Navy and police. The police issued notices under the Maritime Act, ordering the protest boats and their crews to stay 200 meters from the ship, or to face a fine of NZ$10,000 or up to a year in jail (Hill 2011).

In a press interview, Tweedie Waititi from Te Whanau-a-Apanui expressed surprise at the depth of feeling among her people: "We are the most placid *iwi* on earth. And I tell you what, the government has awakened some sort of *taniwha* [guardian creature]. It's quite a surprise to see my people react the way they are reacting. We're all virgins at doing this. We never fight." (Waititi 2011).

Like other New Zealanders, tribal members had heard a great deal about the Deep Horizon blowout in the Gulf of Mexico the previous year, and the damage done to the ocean, sea life, coasts and estuaries, and the livelihoods of local people. They were fearful that a similar catastrophe might happen in their ancestral waters.

Tweedie also expressed concern for the *moki*, a sacred fish that migrates every year from Hawaiki, the ancestral homeland, to Te Whanau-a-Apanui waters. "That's the *moki*'s home", she said, "Right where they want to drill. Every June, there is a star that shines in the sky and her name is Autahi, and that's our indication that the *moki* has come home."

The story of the *moki* is told in paintings in the dining hall and carved meeting-house at Kauaetangohia marae, at Whangaparaoa. I had also heard about this sacred fish many years earlier when I worked with Eruera Stirling, a leading elder of the *iwi*, on a book about his ancestors and his life. He told me about a time in his youth when a senior elder, Manihera Waititi, invited him and his elder brother to catch the "first fish" to open the *moki* season.

On that occasion, the two boys went to the Whangaparaoa River before dawn and boarded Manihera's boat. With a land breeze behind them, the elder took them to the *moki* fishing ground about one hundred yards offshore from Ratanui, a beach where ancestral voyaging canoes had come ashore.

After catching several *moki*, they headed out to a deep water fishing ground, where they caught several more of the sacred fish. Back on shore, the old man gave them the *moki* to take home to their mother, Mihi Kotukutuku. As the tribe's senior leader, it was customary for her to be presented with the first fish of the season.

According to Eruera, the waters offshore from Raukokore, his home village, are known as Te Kopua a Hine Mahuru, the deep waters of Hine Mahuru, named after the ancestress of his people. Its fishing grounds and shellfish beds are linked with the carved meeting-house on shore, also named after this high born woman, whose *mana* (ancestral power) extended over the land and sea.

A rock named Whangaipaka stands in these waters, guarded by a *kai-tiaki* or guardian, a large sting-ray. If a stranger went there without permission, a great wave carrying the stingray would sweep over the rock, drowning the intruder. Eruera told me that in his time, shellfish beds and fishing grounds were jealously guarded:

> Each district had its own mussel beds, and they were reserved for the people of that place. If the people saw a stranger picking their mussels, look out! He'd be a dead man if he came ashore. Fishing was very *tapu* [imbued with ancestral presence], and each family had its own fishing grounds, no one else could fish there or there would be a big fight.

> The old people were very particular about the sea, and nobody was allowed to eat or smoke out on the boats. If a man took food with him when he went fishing, he'd sit there all day with his hook and line empty and the fish would stay away.

> Sometimes if the fishing was very bad the people would start asking questions, and if they found out the guilty man, he'd get into big trouble for breaking the sacred law of *tapu*. The people would just about knock him to pieces, and he wouldn't be allowed to go out to sea again for quite a while. If a thing like that happened at home, you were well marked by the people (Stirling 1980:106).

Given the intensity of this bond between people, their land and ancestral waters, it is not surprising that Te Whanau-a-Apanui were outraged when, without prior warning, the government issued a permit for an oil company to explore their ancestral waters. As Tweedie Waititi remarked, it was as though a *taniwha*, a powerful ancestral being, had woken up and was thrashing around in the ocean.

When Rikirangi Gage, an acknowledged senior leader of the *iwi*, joined the protest flotilla, the government ignored this gesture. Several days later, Te Whanau-a-Apanui's fishing boat *San Pietro* motored across the bow of the *Orient Explorer*, trailing tuna fishing lines and a string of buoys tied together with rope. When the captain of the survey ship told them to stay away, Gage replied, "We won't be moving. We'll be doing some fishing."

Soon afterwards police officers boarded the fishing boat and arrested the skipper, Elvis Teddy, charging him with an offense under the Marine Transport Act. Back on shore, Teddy defended his actions, saying that he was simply exercising his right under the Treaty of Waitangi to fish his ancestral waters.

If his boat had come close to the *Orient Explorer*, it was the fault of the drilling ship's commander for not avoiding a fishing vessel.

Teddy was prosecuted, and during his trial in the Auckland District Court, his lawyers argued that since the confrontation had happened outside New Zealand's twelve mile territorial zone, the Maritime Transport Act did not apply. The judge agreed, and the charges were dismissed.

When the police appealed the judgment to the High Court, however, the Court ruled that as a New Zealand vessel, the *San Pietro* came under New Zealand jurisdiction, even on the high seas (Woolford 2013). Although there was no specific provision in the Maritime Transport Act to this effect, the Act must apply beyond the twelve mile limit, or the New Zealand government would be unable to uphold its international obligations under the 1982 UN Convention on the Law of the Sea. (Webster and Monteiro 2013).

After this verdict, Teddy's lawyer issued a statement saying that by granting a drilling permit in their ancestral waters without consulting Te Whanau-a-Apanui, and by sending the Navy, Air Force and police to stop Teddy and Gage from fishing in ancestral waters, the New Zealand Government had breached not only the Treaty of Waitangi but the International Convention of Indigenous Rights, which New Zealand has also signed (Te Whanau-a-Apanui 2012).

Soon afterwards, the New Zealand government took further steps to tighten its control over New Zealand vessels on the high seas, passing a hotly debated act that prohibits protest at sea in the vicinity of oil exploration vessels (Devathasan 2013).

This clash between Te Whanau-a-Apanui on the one hand, and Petrobas and the Crown on the other, was not just a physical confrontation. It was an ontological collision – a clash between different "worlds" or ways of being. Different claims to the sea, different ideas about collective rights, and different kinds of freedoms and constraints were being negotiated.

At the same time, this is not a simple confrontation between different "cultures" or "ethnicities." It is a complex story, with different resonances for different people.

The Sea as a Theater of Protest

For many in New Zealand, the standoff between the *San Pietro* and a large oil drilling ship recalled an episode in 1973 when the New Zealand government tried to stop French nuclear testing in the Pacific. Two naval frigates, one with a cabinet minister on board, were sent to Moruroa atoll, a testing site in the Society Islands. When a Greenpeace yacht was boarded off Moruroa, its skipper was assaulted by French marines.

In 1984 when the New Zealand government declared the nation nuclear-free and refused to allow visits by US nuclear vessels, the country was ejected from the ANZUS alliance. A year later, French agents sank the Greenpeace vessel *Rainbow Warrior*, which was about to lead another protest flotilla to Moruroa, in Auckland harbor (Thakur 1986).

In New Zealand, as one can see, freedom to protest at sea is deeply entangled with national identity, and a concern for environmental issues. For many New Zealanders, by pitting its small boat against the oil drilling ship, Te Whanau-a-Apanui was following in that tradition, fighting to protect the ocean.

For many members of Te Whanau-a-Apanui, on the other hand, this was more a question of protecting the *mana* of their kin group. The *San Pietro* and its crew were asserting the right of their *iwi* to protect their ancestral fisheries against unwanted intrusion, based on the guarantee of "full, exclusive and undisturbed possession" of their fishing grounds under Article 2 of the Treaty of Waitangi.

At the same time, for the Government and many other New Zealanders, it was a matter of upholding the sovereignty of the Crown, and the government's right to manage the 200-mile Exclusive Economic Zone; to issue exploration permits to oil companies; and to protect prospectors from interference by protest vessels, including those owned by *iwi*.

Nevertheless, this was not an ethnic confrontation. Many of the protestors were not Maori, and as Tweedie Waititi remarked, "If something goes wrong, it's not only our beaches that get ruined. It's everyone's. I'm pretty sure that not only Maori have a connection to the sea." Also, some *iwi* were flirting with the idea of supporting oil exploration: "Like our lawyer said," she added, "our *mana*'s not for sale and no amount of money could pay us off. Maybe some *iwi* you could dangle a carrot. But this one's not biting."

In order to explore these ontological collisions, and what they tell us about different relationships between people and the ocean in New Zealand, and different ideas about the commons, I'd like to explore some of the deep, taken-for-granted presuppositions that underpin the positions adopted by different protagonists, along with previous alliances and confrontations.

The Fountain of Fish: The Ocean in Te Ao Maori

As the anthropologist Marshall Sahlins once remarked, "The [Māori] universe is a gigantic kin, a genealogy... a veritable ontology" (Sahlins 1985:195). Te Ao Maori [the Maori world] is ordered by *whakapapa* – vast, intricate networks of relationships in which all forms of life are mutually defined and linked, and animated by *hau* [breath, wind, life force].

In 1907, Elsdon Best, a New Zealand ethnologist who had spent a lifetime studying Maori customs, wrote to an elder called Tamati Ranapiri, asking him to explain the idea of the *hau*. Ranapiri replied:

> As for the *hau*, it isn't the wind that blows, not at all. Let me explain it to you carefully. Now, you have a treasured item (*taonga*) that you give to me, without the two of us putting a price on it, and I give it to someone else. Perhaps after a long while, this person remembers that he has this *taonga*, and that he should give me a return gift, and he does so.

> This is the *hau* of the *taonga* that was previously given to me. I must pass on that treasure to you. It would not be right for me to keep it for myself. Whether it is a very good *taonga* or a bad one, I must give to you, because that treasure is the *hau* of your *taonga*, and if I hold on to it for myself, I will die. This is the *hau*. That's enough (Ranapiri 1907).

The *hau* is at the heart of life itself. As Ranapiri explains, if a person fails to uphold their obligations in such exchanges, their own life force is threatened. As gifts or insults pass back and forth, impelled by the power of the *hau*, patterns of relations are forged and transmuted, for better or for worse.

When Elsdon Best wrote about Ranapiri's account of the *hau*, it captured the imagination of a French sociologist, Marcel Mauss. In 1925, Mauss published *The Gift*, a classic work exploring gift exchange in a range of societies, including his own. Quoting Ranapiri, he contrasted the Maori concept of the *hau* and chiefly generosity with the utilitarian assumption in contemporary capitalism that all transactions are driven by self-interest, arguing that this gives an impoverished, inaccurate view of how relations among people shape social life.

For Mauss, the *hau*, or the "spirit of the thing given" impels a gift in return, creating solidarity. His discussion of the concept is perceptive, but in fact, it only scratches the surface. In Maori philosophy, *hau* drives the whole world, not just human communities. It goes far beyond the exchange of gifts among people.

According to the *tohunga* [experts] in the ancestral *whare wananga* [schools of learning], *hau* emerged at the beginnings of the cosmos. In a chant recorded by Te Kohuora, for example, the world begins with a burst of energy that generates thought, memory and desire (Te Kohuora 1854).

Next comes the Po, long aeons of darkness. Out of the Po comes the Kore, unbound, unpossessed Nothing, the seedbed of the cosmos, described by one of Best's contemporaries as "the Void or negation, yet containing the potentiality of all things afterwards to come" (Tregear 1891:168).

In the Void, *hau ora* and *hau tupu*, the winds of life and growth begin to stir, generating new phenomena. The sky emerges, and then the moon and stars, light, the earth and sky and the ocean.

When the forest ancestor Tane creates the world of light and life by forcing earth and sky apart, his brother Tawhiri, the wind ancestor, attacks him and his children, the trees, smashing their branches, and the ancestors of root crops, forcing their offspring to hide in the ground. In this cosmic battle, only Tu, the ancestor of people, stands tall against the Space Twister. For his bravery, he earns for his descendants the right to harvest the offspring of his brothers – birds, root crops, forest foods and trees, fish, crayfish and shellfish.

Utu, the principle of reciprocity, drives the interactions between individuals and groups and all other life forms in the Maori world, working towards (an always fragile) equilibrium. In the process, *hau* is exchanged among and between people and other life forms, binding their fates together.

Here, individuals are defined by their relationships, and subject and object are not radically divided. From this we can see that any idea of the commons that presupposes this Cartesian division is rooted in a particular modernist cosmo-logic, one that cannot claim universal validity or application.

In Maori life, the mingling of self and other is reflected in many ways. When greeting one another, for instance, Maori people press noses and breathe, mingling their *hau* [wind of life] together. People speak of themselves as *ahau* [myself], and when *rangatira* or chiefs speak of an ancestor in the first person, it is because they are the *kanohi ora* [living face] of that ancestor.

A refusal to enter into reciprocal exchanges, on the other hand, is known as *hau whitia*, or *hau* turned aside. *Hauhauaitu* [or "harm to the *hau*"] is manifested as illness or ill fortune, a breakdown in the balance of reciprocal exchanges. The life force has been affected, showing signs of collapse and failure.

This also applies to people's relations with other life forms. Unless the exchanges between people and the sea are balanced, for instance, the *hau* of both the ocean and the people alike will suffer.

Stories about the sea illustrate this point. According to Timi Waata Rimini, an elder from Te Whanau-a-Apanui, many generations ago the son of the ancestor Pou drowned in the Motu River. Setting off in search of his son, Pou arrived at the home of the sea ancestor Tangaroa, a "fountain of fish" teeming with different species, where he asked the sea ancestor whether he had taken his son. When Tangaroa denied it, knowing that he was lying, Pou asked him to attend his son's *tangi* [funeral].

Returning to the Bay of Plenty, Pou told his people to make a great net. That summer, a huge shoal of *kahawai* (*Arripis trutta*) approached the coast, escorting the sea ancestor to the funeral. On a signal, Pou ordered his people to cast the great net. Thousands of Tangaroa's children were caught and fed to the crowds that had gathered to mourn Pou's son (Rimini 1901).

As Rimini explained, when the *kahawai* arrive at the mouth the Motu River every year, a chiefly youngster was sent out to catch three *kahawai*, which were offered to Pou and the high chief of the region. By acknowledging the *mana* of the sea ancestor, these "first fish" rituals opened the fishing season, protecting the fertility and abundance of the ocean.

Other local customs related to the *kehe* or granite trout, a sacred fish that frequented rocky channels in the reefs, grazing on *kohuwai*, a particular type of seaweed. There were a number of methods used to catch this fish, including shaping channels in the reef with stones, waiting until the *kohuwai* grew back again, and then using a hoop net to scoop up the *kehe* as they grazed on the seaweed, or using a pole to drive them into the net.

When the chief's wife at Omaio became pregnant, he said, the *rahui* or sacred prohibition on a famous *kehe* fishing ground called Te Wharau was lifted, and as people gathered on the beach, men with hoop nets were sent to stand on particular named rocks. When the *tohunga* or expert called out Rukuhia, people dived into the channels, swimming underwater and driving the *kehe* into the hoop nets, in a joyous pandemonium. Afterwards, the fish were cooked and presented to the chieftainness as a delicacy (Te Rangihiroa 1926).

In this onto-logic, the sea itself was alive and breathing. When Te Parata, a powerful being in the heart of the ocean, breathed out, the tide began to flow, and children were born. When he breathed in, a great vortex formed, swallowing canoes at sea. At death, a great *rangatira* might be farewelled with the chant, "The eddy squall is gone, the storm is passed away, the Parata is gone, the big fish has left its dwelling place." (Colenso 1887:422).

Here, ideas about collective rights acknowledge the vitality of other life forms – fish, rivers, mountains and land, for example. Rights in particular localities are distributed between people and other phenomena, nested and linked in exchange relationships at various scales. In relation to the sea, these ideas allow the control of use rights, along lines of kinship and descent or gift exchange.

In contemporary times, these ways of thinking are receiving legal recognition in New Zealand. In 2014, for instance, in a Waitangi settlement with the Whanganui *iwi*, the Crown has recognised their iconic river as a legal being; while in a Waitangi settlement with Tuhoe, an inland people, their ancestral land Te Urewera has been recognized in the same way, with co-management regimes with the Crown and regional authorities being established.

In many ways, these legal innovations echo contemporary biological understandings in which people and other phenomena (such as the ocean) are engaged in complex interactive systems, mutually implicated at every scale, while the idea that people might be linked by kinship with marine life forms is shared with evolutionary biology, for instance.

The virtue of these arrangements is that the well-being of a lake, a river or the ocean can be given legal priority in the allocation of resource rights and management regimes, alongside the interests of human beings.

The Ocean in the Enlightenment

There are both divergences and resonances between Western and Maori ideas about the sea. When Captain Cook's ship *Endeavour* arrived off the east coast of the North Island in October 1769 and brought the first Europeans ashore, for instance, the ship was a travelling sideshow of the Enlightenment in Europe, laden with a cargo of colliding cosmologies.

This was a scientific naval expedition, sponsored by the Royal Society of London to observe the Transit of Venus in Tahiti, and by the Admiralty to find Terra Australis, the Unknown Southern Continent. It is a mistake to think of the meetings that followed as binary clashes between two "cultures," however. As at present, Maori and European ways of thinking alike were diverse.

One strand of Enlightenment thought, for instance, can be traced back at least as far back as the seventeenth century, when the philosopher Descartes had a new vision of reality, at once powerful and intoxicating. In his dream, the Cogito – the "thinking self" or Subject – became the eye of the world, which in turn became an Object for inspection.

The Cartesian division between mind (*res cogitans*) and matter (*res extensa*), Subject and Object is historically and culturally specific. During the Enlightenment in Europe, as culture was separated from nature, the natural sciences and the humanities and social sciences began to diverge (Descola 2013).

As entities were detached from each other, they were objectified and classified, and the different disciplines emerged. This "Order of Things," as Michel Foucault called it, was at the heart of Enlightenment science (Foucault, 1970). It also shaped the law of the sea, and how forms of control were distributed over the ocean.

In this style of thinking, the ancient motif of the grid was used to divide and sort different dimensions and entities into bounded units, bringing them under control for practical purposes. Often, the grid was hierarchical – the old idea of the Great Chain of Being, for example, with God at the apex followed by angels, divine Kings, the aristocracy and successive ranks of people, from "civilized" to "savage," followed by animals, plants and minerals in descending order (Lovejoy 1936, Hodgen 1971).

As the *cogito* or thinking self became the guarantor of being, the all-seeing "Eye of God" was replaced by the "Mind's Eye," and human beings were put in charge of the cosmos. Often, this was understood as a machine, made up of distinct, divisible working parts that performed particular functions.

In the mid-eighteenth century in Europe, the Order of Things went viral. Many aspects of life were transformed – administration (with censuses, surveys, and bureaucratic systems), industry (with manufacturing based on mechanization and standardization, the replication of parts and processes), and science (with the use of instruments and quantification, and the increased specialization of knowledge), for instance (Frängsmyr, Heilbron and Rider 1990). In the case of surveying, this was closely associated with military activities, and the scientific use of force (Edney 1994).

As it happened, Captain James Cook, the first European explorer to land in New Zealand, as a leading hydrographer, was in the vanguard of this way of reimagining the sea. Like his cartographic peers, he adopted an imaginary vantage point high above the earth – an "Eye of God" perspective.

In Cook's charts, the ocean – grey or blue-green, the home of birds, fish and whales, surging with tides and currents, ruffling or roaring in the wind – was transformed into a static, white, two-dimensional expanse, gridded by lines of latitude and longitude and mathematically partitioned and measured.

Near harbors or lagoons, the depth of the coastal seabed was measured with the lead, and these soundings were recorded on his charts. Using a process of instrumental observation, the blurred, shifting liminal zone between land and sea was reduced to a simple line (Salmond 2005).

As Jordan Branch has recently argued, this process of cartographic simplification was intimately entangled with imperial power and the creation of the modernist nation-state. Except for scatters of islands, new stretches of the Pacific were depicted as vacant expanses, waiting to be explored, charted, claimed and ruled by European powers (Branch 2011).

At this time in Europe, the sovereignty of the Crown (or *imperium*) in Europe was held to extend about a league (three nautical miles) from the coastline, or within cannon shot, although property rights [*dominium*] could be granted within that limit (Bess 2011:87). Captain Cook had instructions from the Admiralty to claim any new lands he might "discover" for the British Crown.

At the same time, as Peter Hans Reill has remarked, one should not underestimate the diversity of Enlightenment thinking. In the mid-eighteenth century, for instance, men including Erasmus Darwin and Priestley, many of those involved in the Scottish Enlightenment, Buffon in France, Benjamin Franklin in America, and later the Humboldt brothers, understood reality as living networks of relations among different phenomena, animated by complementary exchanges – an account that has strong resonances with Maori and Polynesian thinking (Reill 2005; see also Israel 2006).

In this Enlightenment tradition – the Order of Relations, one might call it – people are just one life form among many, and the world is constantly changing. Ideas such as justice, truth, equality and honor, and balance and equilibrium suggested how exchanges – particularly among people – should be handled. Here one can find the origins of participatory democracy, and much of contemporary anthropology, earth sciences, cosmology, ecology and evolutionary theory. The World Wide Web and scientific ideas about complex systems and networks also trace back to this strand of modernist thought.

Not surprising, this diversity of views was reflected on board the *Endeavour*. In addition to his orders from the Admiralty, Cook had a set of "Hints" from the Earl of Morton, the President of the Royal Society, which acknowledged the legal rights of Pacific people to control their own lands and coastlines, and suggested how to describe in detail the people, places, plants, animals and minerals that they might encounter during their voyage around the world.

While Cook's charts abstracted the land and sea, the journals, sketches and collections produced by the scientists and the ship's officers restored them to life again, at least in part, with meticulous depictions of local people and landscapes, canoes and fishing gear, different species of fish, as well as currents, tides and the temperature of the ocean (Salmond 2004).

During the *Endeavour's* circumnavigation of New Zealand in 1769-1770, these divergent strands in Enlightenment thought – as reflected in the Admiralty orders and the Earl of Morton's "Hints" in particular – helped to shape what happened. The presence of Tupaia, a brilliant man later described as a "genius" by Georg Forster, also powerfully shifted the dynamics of these encounters. A high priest from one of the homelands of Maori, he was quickly able to master the sound shifts between Maori and Tahitian, and speak with the local people.

The warriors who came out in their canoes to challenge the ship were unsure what this bizarre apparition might be. In Turanga, for instance, the first harbor visited by the *Endeavour* in New Zealand, the people thought this might be Waikawa, a sacred island off the end of the Mahia peninsula, floating into their harbor. Nevertheless, they used their own time-honored rituals for challenging the strangers, performing *wero* [ritual challenges], *karakia* [incantations] and *haka* [war dances].

While Cook followed his Admiralty orders and took possession of New Zealand, marching the marines ashore to set up a British flag, he also followed the "Hints" by negotiating with Maori, using Tupaia, the Ra'iatean star navigator, as his interpreter. When the first encounters on land and sea ended in shootings, Cook was bitterly chagrined.

There were many such clashes around the coastline of New Zealand. When the *Endeavour* arrived at Waikawa, for instance, off the end of the Mahia peninsula, a sacred island and the site of a school of ancestral learning, priests chanted and warriors in canoes threw spears at the hull of the *Endeavour*. As they sailed across Hawke's Bay, flotillas of canoes came out, led by elderly chiefs wearing fine cloaks, chanting, making speeches and brandishing their weapons, preventing the Europeans from making a landing.

When the *Endeavour* headed north and arrived in the Bay of Plenty, a large canoe carrying sixty warriors came out from Whangaparaoa in Te Whanau-a-Apanui waters, and circled the ship, a priest reciting incantations as the crew performed a war dance. They cried out, "Come to land and we will kill you," paddling at high speed to attack the *Endeavour* and stopping only when a volley of grapeshot was fired beside their canoe. When a cannon loaded with round shot was fired overhead, they fled back to the land.

As one can see, there is a strong continuity between Rikirangi Gage's presence on board the *San Pietro* and their confrontation with the oil drilling ship, and these earlier clashes in which Te Whanau-a-Apanui defended their *mana* (ancestral power) over their tribal waters.

On the whole, Captain Cook respected these challenges, retorting with warning shots rather than shooting the warriors. The Earl of Morton had insisted that people in these new lands had the right to defend their own territories, including their coastal waters. Later, this same understanding underpinned the promise in the English text of the Treaty of Waitangi that Maori would enjoy "full, exclusive, undisturbed possession of their Fisheries and other properties... so long as it is their wish and desire to retain the same in their possession."

It was not until quite recently in New Zealand (in 1965) that the Crown's sovereignty was formally extended out to three miles from the coast, to twelve miles in 1977, and in 1982 under the United Nations Convention on the Law of the Sea (or UNCLOS) out to 200 miles, defining an oceanic "Exclusive Economic Zone" that the Government sought to defend against Whanau-a-Apanui and Greenpeace protestors.

Thus in very recent times, the high seas or *mare liberum*[1] – that part of the ocean which falls outside the Exclusive Economic Zones, an expanse free to all nations but belonging to none – has been shrinking, as nation-states expand their terrestrial sovereignty out from their coastlines – a kind of oceanic enclosure. As we have seen, such cartographic visions of the ocean embody particular assumptions about the world. This atomistic, quantifying, abstracting, commodifying logic is still unfolding.

---

1 | *Mare liberum* is a doctrine articulated by Hugo Grotius in defense of the right of the Dutch to sail to the East Indies, as against the Portuguese claim to exclusive control over those waters: "The sea is common to all, because it is so limitless that it cannot become a possession of any one, and because it is adapted for the use of all, whether we consider it from the point of view of navigation or of fisheries." (Grotius, trans. Magoffin 1916:28).

This cosmo-logic fragments the sciences, detaches people from "the environment" and makes the well-being of other life-forms contingent. It therefore is not particularly successful at understanding or safeguarding the vitality of those intricate socio-biophysical systems in which human beings participate, and on which their own well-being and futures rely.

In New Zealand, as in other situations where the government has sought to commodify and privatize resources formerly held in common, Maori have reacted by challenging the Crown's right to make these decisions. As Alex Frame, a law professor in New Zealand, has observed, under the Treaty of Waitangi:

> The commodification of the "common heritage" has provoked novel claims and awakened dormant ones...Claims to water flows, electricity dams, airwaves, forests, flora and fauna, fish quota, geothermal resources, seabed, foreshore, minerals, have followed the tendency to treat these resources, previously viewed as common property, as commodities for sale to private purchases. Not surprisingly, the Maori reaction has been, if it is property, then it is our property (Frame 1999:234).

The Foreshore and Seabed

It would be possible to examine the unfolding of this logic with the quantification of fish stocks in the fisheries quota system in New Zealand, for instance, which provoked one of the first claims to the Waitangi Tribunal. Here, however, I will focus on the confrontations between many Maori and the Crown over the foreshore and seabed, since this forerunner to the clash between Te Whanau-a-Apanui and the Crown also illuminates complexities in contemporary debates about the commons.

The foreshore and seabed saga began in the Marlborough Sounds, at the northern end of the South Island. Although the local tribes had repeatedly applied to the local District Council for licenses to farm mussels in their ancestral *rohe* (territory), none were granted. Finally in frustration, they finally applied to the Maori Land Court to recognize their customary rights over the foreshore and seabed in the Sounds (Bess 2011:90-93; Boast 2005).

In Maori ancestral practice, the foreshore is a fertile place. At the time of the Treaty, clans and families moved from gardens and forests to wetlands, sandy beaches, rocky reefs and out to sea in seasonal migrations, maintaining relations with a complex mosaic of fish, plants and animals, and harvesting at peak times of plenty. Particular groups held nested use rights to particular resources at particular times of the year, creating overlapping, shifting networks of rights that crossed the shoreline, binding people, land and sea together.[2]

---

2 | See Diaw (2008) for an excellent discussion of similar nested mosaics of use rights in the Cameroons, and the implications of these resilient systems for adaptive ideas of the commons.

According to English common law in 1840, on the other hand, land and sea were divided at the high tide mark, and subject to different regimes of control. On land, the Crown held the right of *imperium* or sovereignty, whereas *dominium* or ownership was generally held as private property; whereas at sea, it was assumed that the Crown held both *imperium* and *dominium*, at least as far as three miles offshore, unless it had granted the right of ownership to other parties.

When land began to be surveyed, partitioned into bounded blocks and sold in New Zealand, the government and European purchasers alike generally assumed that if they bought coastal land, they owned it to the high tide mark, but that the foreshore or tidal zone and the seabed belonged to the Crown.

From the beginning, Maori contested this assumption, which clashed with the Article 2 Treaty promise about their control of ancestral fisheries. But in 1963, when the Court of Appeal ruled in a case over the Ninety Mile beach that customary rights to the foreshore had been extinguished when the Native Land Court had issued title to coastal land, the matter was assumed to be legally settled.

The application of the Marlborough *iwi* to the Maori Land Court overturned that legal precedent, however. The judge held that the legislation cited by the Attorney General, including the Ninety Mile Beach case, had not in fact extinguished the customary rights of the Marlborough *iwi*.

The case was appealed, and then referred to the High Court, where the judge reversed the ruling, and then to the Court of Appeal, where the judges ruled unanimously that upon the signing of the Treaty, the Crown had acquired only a radical right or *imperium* over the sea with the acquisition of sovereignty.

Citing the doctrine of aboriginal title, they ruled that unless the rights of *dominium* had been legally extinguished, they remained with Maori kin groups, and that this was also the case with the foreshore and seabed. Furthermore, they argued, the distinction in English common law between land above the high water mark, and land below it, did not apply.[3]

As Judge Elias said, "The common law as received in New Zealand was modified by recognized Maori customary property interests. There is no room for a contrary presumption derived from English common law. The common law of New Zealand is different." The judges referred the case back for the Maori Land Court to determine whether or not the Marlborough *iwi* had customary ownership of the foreshore and seabed in their ancestral territories (Elias, S, in the Court of Appeal of New Zealand, CA 173/01).

By this time, however, most New Zealanders took it for granted that, apart from riparian rights, the foreshore and seabed were owned by the Crown,

3 | This provoked a flurry of legal debates. See, for instance, Brookfield (2004).

and the decision caused a furor. Over the generations, many non-Maori New Zealanders had also formed close ties with particular beaches and stretches of coastline, echoing an ancestral Maori habit of setting up summer fishing camps by heading to beaches and coastal camping grounds, and spending a great deal of time fishing, diving, surfing and sailing.

Although some Maori leaders insisted that they only wished to exercise *kai-tiakitanga* or guardianship over the foreshore and seabed, and not treat them as private property, others were clearly interested in commercial possibilities, and claimed property rights in the ocean. Fearing that their relationship with particular beaches and harbors would be severed, and their recreational as well as commercial interests in these places would be lost to Maori, many non-Maori New Zealanders were incensed by the Court of Appeal's decision.

Again, this was not strictly an ethnic confrontation. None of the Court of Appeal judges, for example, were Maori. Nevertheless, public anger was such that in 2004, the Government hastily passed legislation to ensure that the foreshore and seabed would be owned by the Crown, with open access for all, subject to various regulatory restrictions and acknowledging Maori customary interests (but not allowing this to be translated into freehold title).

When a *hikoi* (march) of thousands of Maori protesters marched on Parliament, they were dismissed by the Prime Minister as "wreckers and haters," a comment that hurt and horrified many of the elders who participated.

In the aftermath, however, as different *iwi* signed Treaty deeds of settlement with the Crown, anger on all sides gradually cooled (Palmer 2006:197-214). When a new Government formed a coalition with the Maori Party, which had been created in protest against the Foreshore and Seabed Act, in 2010 new legislation gave Maori further customary (but not freehold) rights to these areas, while protecting public access and enjoyment by defining the foreshore and seabed as "public domain" (Bess 2011:92-93).

Out at sea, on the other hand, the Crown reserved its right to allocate oil and mineral licences, without public participation. By the time that Te Whanau-a-Apanui's fishing boat confronted the *Orient Explorer*, they had many non-Maori supporters who shared their fears for the future of the ocean. In October 2011 when a container ship the *Rena* ran aground on a reef in the western Bay of Plenty, it seemed that they had been prescient. A cargo including hazardous materials, fuel oil and diesel spilled into the sea, causing widespread environmental and economic damage.

"Tie the Knot of Humankind": Experiments Across Worlds

As one can see, in New Zealand, fundamentally different onto-logics about human relations with the ocean have proved very resilient. At the same time, there have been significant transformations, both to Maori ideas and to modernist thinking.

In the law, for example, at different times, the doctrine of continuity in relation to Maori rights has transformed English common law by the incorporation of Maori customary law. As Sian Elias, now the Chief Justice of New Zealand, put it succinctly, "The common law of New Zealand is different." One can see this in many New Zealand laws that cite *tikanga* (ancestral conventions), whether in general or in particular,[4] including those recent laws giving effect to those Waitangi settlements in which ancestral rivers and stretches of land are recognized as beings with their own legal rights.

At the same time, while particular *tikanga* may be cited in legislation, their content has often fundamentally shifted. One can see this in the case of *kai-tiakitanga*, for example, once exercised by non-human beings such as sharks and stingrays over particular ancestral stretches of the ocean. Today, a more anthropocentric version is common, with people regarding themselves as *kai tiaki* (guardians) of these places.

On the other hand, the assumption that with the signing of the Treaty, sovereignty was transferred to the British Crown, has not been seriously disturbed, despite many challenges, since this provides a fundamental scaffolding for legal processes in New Zealand.

In relation to the sea, this means that mechanisms such as *mataitai* and *taiapure*, where Maori kin groups either exercise or share limited rights over coastal subsistence fishing with other community members, operate within strict limits. For example, Ministers appoint tribal "representatives" to management groups and require that their arrangements not clash with commercial fishing rights.

Simultaneously, however, the idea of the "Crown" itself has also altered, so that any pure opposition between Maori and the Crown is now difficult to sustain. For many years in New Zealand, Maori have been lawyers and judges, officials, members of Parliament and Ministers. In fact, it was a Maori Minister of the Crown, Matiu Rata, who helped to set up the Waitangi Tribunal.

Again, the relation between *iwi* and the Crown is structural rather than strictly ethnic, and this is played out in fisheries management as well, with non-Maori as well as Maori managing fishing quota for *iwi* according to strictly

---

4 | See Henare [Salmond] (2007) for an exploration of the way that the concept of *taonga* (ancestral treasure) has been incorporated in recent New Zealand legislation, for instance.

commercial principles; while in *mataitai* and *taiapure*, the management of customary fishing is usually shared with non-Maori community members (Jacobson and Moller 2009).

At the same time, some non-Maori New Zealanders now speak of themselves as *kai-tiaki* or guardians for rivers, beaches and endangered species. As Maori terms increasingly shift into Kiwi English, both European and Maori ways of thinking are being transformed.

In New Zealand, it seems, a middle ground exists in which experiments across Maori and non-Maori ancestral ways keep creating new ideas and ways of doing things – in the law and governance along with business[5] and many areas of everyday life, from the arts to sport to public ritual.

This holds promise for the future, because in relation to the sea, experiments of this kind are urgently needed. In New Zealand as elsewhere, a radical division between Nature and Culture, born of one strand of modernist thought, and the belief that Nature is there for human beings to exploit without limit and that any damage can be fixed, is fundamentally disruptive to relations between people and the ocean.

While surfers, swimmers, divers and fishers still frequent our beaches and coasts, and sailors still cross the Pacific, their activities are increasingly at risk from water-borne pollution, sedimentation, over-harvesting of reefs, shellfish beds and fisheries, and the intense storms, acidification and current shifts driven by climate change, for example.

Contemporary scientific models, with their fragmented partitions, and the split between Nature and Culture with its deep separation between people and other phenomena (also born of the Order of Things), are flawed. They fail to adequately grasp the cascading dynamics of complex systems in which people are implicated at every scale, putting the future of many marine species *and* coastal human communities at risk.

Ideas of the commons do not always escape these limitations. In New Zealand, these play out in complex ways, sometimes to oppose Maori claims to fisheries or waterways ("No one owns the water!"), whose control may then be privatized – but also to forge alliances with Maori kin groups (in the case of the *San Pietro*, for example) to try and prevent extractive activities that seem too damaging or dangerous.

Until people grasp that their being and that of the sea are bound together, they will not demand that human activities that put our futures at risk are conducted within survivable limits. We need new ways of thinking about the

---

5 | It is interesting that one of the largest companies in New Zealand, the dairy company Fonterra, is in fact a farmer-owned co-operative; and share-milking is common. (See Diaw 2008 for a discussion of share-cropping in Cameroon.)

shifting relations between people and the ocean – and indeed, all the intricate biophysical systems of which human beings are a part.

In New Zealand, deep resonances may be found between relational thinking from the Enlightenment (including the commons); Maori ideas of complex networks that bypass Cartesian divisions between subject and object, mind and matter, society and nature; and the contemporary science of complex systems. These convergences may help to incubate some new ideas about the ocean.[6]

Just as the physicist Niels Bohr drew upon Asian conceptions to grasp quantum theory, or Marcel Mauss reflected on the Maori idea of the *hau* to imagine alternatives to a commodified world, such cross-philosophical experiments (and not just in New Zealand) might help to engender new kinds of environmental science.

They might also foster ideas of the commons based on complex systems – those intricately entangled, cascading, dynamic, interactive networks among people, and between people and other life forms at different scales – and legal arrangements in which rivers and the ocean have their own being and their own rights.

As my mentor, Te Whanau-a-Apanui elder Eruera Stirling, used to chant:

Whakarongo! Whakarongo! Whakarongo!	Listen! Listen! Listen!
Ki te tangi a te manu e karanga nei	To the cry of the bird calling
Tui, tui, tuituiaa!	Bind, join, be one!
Tuia i runga, tuia i raro,	Bind above, bind below
Tuia i roto, tuia i waho,	Bind within, bind without
Tuia i te here tangata	Tie the knot of humankind
Ka rongo te po, ka rongo te po	The night hears, the night hears
Tuia i te kawai tangata i heke mai	Bind the lines of people coming down
I Hawaiki nui, i Hawaiki roa,	From great Hawaiki, from long Hawaiki
I Hawaiki pamamao	From Hawaiki far away
I hono ki te wairua, ki te whai ao	Bind to the spirit, to the day light
Ki te Ao Marama!	To the World of Light!

References

Bess. 2011. "New Zealand's Treaty of Waitangi and the Doctrine of Discovery: Implications for the Foreshore and Seabed." *Marine Policy* 35:85-94.

---

6 | See Schmidt and Mitchell (2013:64-66), who explore some of these possibilities for transfiguring the commons in a Canadian context, with some reference to First Nations; and Cox, Arnold and Tomás (2010) for ways of testing the efficacy of socio-biophysical complex systems in the management of common-pool resources.

Blomley, Nicholas. 2003. "Law, Property and the Geography of Violence: The Frontier, the Survey and the Grid." *Annals of the Association of American Geographers* 93(1):121-141.

Boast, Richard. 2005. *Foreshore and Seabed*. Wellington: LexisNexis.

Branch, Jordan. 2011. "Mapping the Sovereign State: Cartographic Technology, Political Authority, and Systemic Change." PhD thesis in Political Science, Berkeley.

Brookfield, F.M. 2004. "Maori Customary Title in Foreshore and Seabed." *New Zealand Law Journal* 34(1).

Colenso, William. 1887. "Ancient Tide Lore, and Tales of the Sea." *Transactions and Proceedings of the New Zealand Institute* 20:418-22.

Cox, Michael, Arnold, Gwen, and Tomás. 2010. "A Review of Design Principles for Community-based Natural Resource Management." *Ecology and Society* 15(4):38.

Descola, Phillipe. 2013. *Beyond Nature and Culture*. Chicago: University of Chicago Press.

Devathasan, Anna. 2013. "The Crown Minerals Act 2013 and Marine Protest." *Auckland University Law Review* 19:258-263.

Diaw, Mariteuw. 2008. "From Sea to Forest: An Epistemology of Otherness and Institutional Resilience in Non-Conventional Economic Systems." http://dlc.dlib.indiana.edu/dlc/bitstream/handle/10535/312/diaw.pdf?sequence=1

Edney, M.H., 1994. "British Military Education, Mapmaking, and Military 'Map-mindedness' in the Later Enlightenment." *The Cartographic Journal* 31:14-20.

Frame, Alex. 1999. "Property and the Treaty of Waitangi: A Tragedy of the Commodities?" In Janet McLean, editor. *Property and the Constitution*. Oxford: Hart Publishing: 224-234.

Foucault, Michel. 1970. *The Order of Things*. London: Tavistock.

Frängsmyr T., J.L. Heilbron and R. Rider, editors. 1990. *The Quantifying Spirit in the 18th Century*. Berkeley: University of California Press.

Grotius, Hugo, translator. Ralph Magoffin. *The Freedom Of The Seas: Or, The Right Which Belongs To The Dutch To Take Part In The East Indian Trade*. New York: Oxford University Press.

Henare [Salmond] AJM. 2007. "Taonga Maori: Encompassing Rights and Property in New Zealand." In A. Henare, M. Holbraad and S. Wastell, editors. *Thinking through Things: Theorising Artefacts Ethnographically*. London: Routledge. 47-67.

Hill, Marika. 2011. "Police Make Arrest on Protest Ship." *Stuff NZ*, April 23.

Hodgen, Margaret. 1971. *Early Anthropology in the Sixteenth and Seventeenth Centuries*. Philadephia: University of Pennsylvania Press.

Israel, Jonathan. 2006. "Enlightenment. Which Enlightenment?" *Journal of the History of Ideas* 67(3):523-545.

Jacobson C., and H. Moller. 2009. "Two from the same cloth? Comparing the outcomes of *Mātaitai and Taiāpure* for delivering sustainable customary fisheries." He *Kōhinga Rangahau* No. X. Dunedin: University of Otago.

Lovejoy, Arthur. 1936. *The Great Chain of Being: The History of an Idea*. Boston: Harvard University Press.

Mauss, Marcel. 1966. *The Gift: Forms and Functions of Exchange in Archaic Societies*. London: Cohen and West Ltd.

Palmer, M. 2006. "Resolving the Foreshore and Seabed Dispute." In Raymond Miller and Michael Mintrom, editors. *Political Leadership in New Zealand*. Auckland: Auckland University Press, 197-214.

Ranapiri, T, 1907. Letter to Peehi (Elsdon Best), 23 November 1907, p. 2, MS Papers 1187-127, in the Alexander Turnbull Library, Wellington. Anne Salmond, translator.

Reill, P.H. 2005. *Vitalizing Nature in the Enlightenment*. Berkeley, California. University of California Press.

Rimini, Tiimi Waata. 1901. "Te puna kahawai i Motu." *Journal of the Polynesian Society* 10(4):183-190.

Sahlins, Marshall. 1985. "Hierarchy and Humanity in Polynesia." In A. Hooper and J. Huntsman, editors. *Transformations of Polynesian Culture*. Auckland. The Polynesian Society.

Salmond, Anne. 1992. *Maori Understandings of the Treaty of Waitangi*, F19, for the Waitangi Tribunal, Muriwhenua Land Claim.

———. 2004. *The Trial of the Cannibal Dog: Captain Cook in the South Seas*. London: Penguin.

———. 2005. "Their Body is Different, Our Body is Different: European and Tahitian Navigators in the 18th Century." In *History and Anthropology*,16 (2):167 – 186.

———. 2010. Brief of Evidence of Distinguished Professor Dame Anne Salmond, WAI 1040, #A22, for the Waitangi Tribunal.

Stirling, Eruera, as told to Anne Salmond. 1980. Eruera: *The Teachings of a Maori Elder*. Christchurch: Oxford University Press.

Te Kohuora of Rongoroa, dictated to Richard Taylor. 1854. [The Maori text is in Taylor, Richard (1855), *Te Ika a Maui*. London:15-16.]

Te Rangihiroa, Peter Buck. 1926. "The Maori Craft of Netting." *Transactions of the New Zealand Institute* 56: 597-646.

Thakur, Ramesh. 1986. "A Dispute of Many Colours: France, New Zealand, and the Rainbow Warrior Affair." *The World Today* 42(12):209-214

Schmidt, Jeremy and Mitchell, Kyle. "2014 Property and the Right to Water: Towards a Non-Liberal Commons." *Review of Radical Political Economics* 46(1):54-69.

Te Whanau-a-Apanui. 2012. Statement of Te Whanau-a-Apanui, iwimaori. weebly.com/.../te_whanau_a_apanui_statement_16_may_2012

Tregear, Edward. 1891. *The Maori-Polynesian Comparative Dictionary*. Wellington: Lyon and Blair.

Waitangi Tribunal. http://www.justice.govt.nz/tribunals/waitangi-tribunal/treaty-of-waitangi

Waititi, Tweedie. 2011. Quoted in *Sunday Star Times*. April 24.

Woolford, J. 2003. Judgment in NZ Police vs. Elvis Heremia Teddy, CRI-2011-470-00031 [2013, NZHC 432].

Webster, Kerryn and Felicity Monteiro. 2013. "High Court clarifies jurisdiction over New Zealand ships on high seas, International Law Office." http://www.internationallawoffice.com/newsletters/detail.aspx?g=96970d24-7159-4b4c-b41f-71d8c0f58

Anne Salmond *(New Zealand) is a Distinguished Professor of Māori Studies and Anthropology at the University of Auckland. For many years she has worked with indigenous leaders and groups in New Zealand and the Pacific. As a writer, she has won many literary and academic awards. A passionate environmentalist, she has also led major ecological projects in New Zealand. In 2013 she was awarded the Rutherford Medal, New Zealand's top scientific award, and was made the New Zealander of the Year.*

The Ethical Struggle to Be Human:
A Shack Dwellers Movement in South Africa

By Nigel C. Gibson

On March 19, 2005, in a scene reminiscent of the anti-apartheid struggle, 750 Black shack dwellers barricaded a major ring road near the Umgeni Business Park in Durban, fighting the police for four hours.[1] The shack dwellers had been waiting patiently for Nelson Mandela's historic 1994-election promise of housing to be realized. The houses, they believed, were to be built on a nearby piece of land, but under the pressure of real-estate and commercial develop-ment, this promise was broken. Instead of new houses, people found themselves facing bulldozers and threatened with removal to a place miles outside the city, far from work opportunities, schools, hospitals and the communities they had been part of. Not unlike the apartheid practice of treating people as "surplus population," the politics of market forces had thrown into relief the human reality of post-apartheid South Africa and all its broken promises.

The Kennedy Road settlement is squeezed between the Clare Estate and the Bisasar Road garbage dump, the largest in Africa. Trucks continually enter the dump, passing Electron Avenue and other similarly named roads from a bygone age of technological innovation under apartheid "development." Along Kennedy Road, the dump is ringed by a long concrete fence and topped by perfume rods that spray out fumes in an attempt to mask the smell. People walk constantly up and down the hill, to and from their jobs as domestic workers or gardeners in the houses on the Clare Estate, or to pick through the dump. Entry to the noxious and toxic dump is officially prohibited to shack dwellers, but if one walks alongside the fence that abuts the shack settlements one sees that, every few yards, concrete panels have been removed for easy access, and many make a living by sifting through the detritus, collecting cardboard, plastic, or metal to sell to recyclers in the "informal economy."

---

1 | Some of the following was adapted from my introduction to *Challenging Hegemony: Social Movements and the Quest for a New Humanism in Postapartheid South Africa* (Gibson 2006:1-14).

Most of the Kennedy Road "informal settlement" is not "on" Kennedy Road, but is accessible through numerous paths that crisscross the hills.[2] The people there are desperately poor. Forgotten in post-apartheid South Africa, they live without basic services like sanitation, water or electricity, in shacks dug into the side of the hill and built out of advertising boards, corrugated iron, branches and mud; their "temporary" shelter having become more or less permanent. For a long time, there wasn't even refuse collection.

Kennedy Road itself is on the Clare Estate, a mainly Indian, middle- and upper-middle-class residential area that has experienced skyrocketing real-estate prices. In the interstices of the estate – in the valleys and along riverbanks, and against the municipal dump – there are eight different shack settlements, each with different histories and organizations. One of them is the Kennedy Road settlement, which has a radically democratic political culture that took years to develop. Other shack settlements have different forms of government, some based on political patronage which are often overseen by an *induna* (chief), some more respected than others, but often governance is along hierarchical and patronage lines.[3] Because there are material interests at stake, the creation of democracy is often a continually contested and hard-fought struggle. Each settlement is configured by different material realities, often limited by physical space, size and geography, which determine the feasibility of such things as common meeting spaces. But, despite these constraints, looking down from the hilltops, there is something special about this area of Durban. The real-estate developers understand it, and it is not lost on the shack dwellers either.[4]

On March 19, 2005, despite the local councillor's promises, the bulldozers moved in. Seeing their "Promised Land" being levelled, the shack dwellers acted, blockading Umgeni Road with burning tires and mattresses, bringing traffic and businesses to a halt. The police, taken by surprise, called for support. They attacked with dogs, punching protestors. Four hours later, fourteen of the 750 people from the Kennedy Road settlement had been arrested, including two teenage students. Two days later, on March 21 – Human Rights Day in South Africa (the anniversary of the day in 1960, when apartheid police fired on pass-law protesters in Sharpeville, and killed 69 people) – 1,200 people dem-

2 | "Informal settlement" is a term preferred by INGOs and NGOs and gives the impression of temporary accommodation, which is far from the truth. Often families live in these settlements for generations.

3 | Given that so much literature on shack settlements is based on studies by UN-Habitat in Nairobi (where the problem is slumlordism produced by a rental market for shacks), it is necessary to point out that authoritarian modes of governance tend to be based on clientelistic associations, where local leaders try to turn "their people" into vote banks for the ruling party in exchange for favors from above.

4 | A member of the KwaZulu-Natal Cabinet is reported to have stated: "We can't build matchboxes next to three-million-rand houses" (Khan 2006a), while one of the shack dwellers notes simply, "They want it for the rich" (Alfred Ndlovu, quoted in Pithouse 2005b).

onstrated, demanding that the local police release the fourteen people or arrest the whole community. The people themselves had begun to self-consciously mobilize for their own rights; they were finally beginning to press the state to be accountable. For more than a decade, the people's anger had been steadily rising. Many people had given up hope of formal employment, or were being forced to use what the World Bank terms their "entrepreneurial" aspirations and "resourcefulness" in the informal economy. But collecting cardboard, plastic or metal from the stinking dump, or even gardening and cleaning for residents on the Clare Estate, doesn't provide many "opportunities."

The shack dwellers had understood that change promised by the government would be slow and that they needed to take responsibility for their own welfare; but by 2005, it had become crystal clear that their interests weren't being considered at all. As one shack dweller put it, they had finally grown "tired of living and walking in shit" (quoted in Kockott 2005).

So, on that March day, the people from the Kennedy Road settlement organized quickly and staged their protest. They revolted because they felt betrayed. Although they might not have initially seen it in these terms, their action proved to be the beginning of a movement. They saw themselves as being *on their own* against the local government, the police, businesses, the rich, the media and the courts. Characteristically, they did not wait for the media or for professional activists to arrive. What was key to their actions was that they already had a democratic decisionmaking body, the Kennedy Road Development Committee, whose participatory meetings and social demands quickly caught the imagination of adjacent communities.

Indeed, this imagination was captured at the welcome-home party for those who had been arrested, when the chair of the Kennedy Road Development Committee, S'bu Zikode, affirmed the actions of the crowd with a memorable speech: "The first Nelson Mandela was Jesus Christ. The second was Nelson Rolihlahla Mandela. The third Nelson Mandela is the poor people of the world" (quoted in Patel and Pithouse 2005). The resonance was clear. The poor weren't Christ, but Christ was the first Mandela, the first liberator who articulated a new heaven on earth. Mandela is Christ reborn, grounding liberation firmly on South African soil, his long imprisonment during apartheid a metaphor for the nation, just as his release is identified with the birth of a new South Africa.

Yet, the failure of the historical Mandela to really liberate South Africa demanded the birth of a new Mandela: the poor themselves. After many promises, all of them broken, they saw through the empty rhetoric of the local authorities. Enough was enough – *sekwanele, sekwanele!* – truth emanated from their own experiences: they had become the "new reality of the nation," declaring the shack dwellers' movement a university where they "think their own struggles" and "are not poor in mind" (Zikode 2006). Subtly criticising Mandela's historical leadership, the poor were taking matters into their own hands, seeing themselves as the force and reason for their own liberation; they had become their own Mandelas.

This has been the essential aspiration of all commoners, everywhere – to throw off the chains of alien governance that dispossesses them; to assert their own rules for governing themselves and resources that matter to them; and to become protagonists in their own history. In this sense, the shack dwellers' movement has been a pioneering struggle of commoning as a way to secure survival and basic dignity.

Origins of the Shack Dwellers' Movement

Even if they had previously never heard of a "social movement," by March 2005, the shack dwellers had effectively become such a movement by virtue of their self-organization and by developing their own relationships with other shack dwellers. For it was the *universality* of the Kennedy Road shack dwellers' experience and demands that was immediately understood and taken up by neighboring settlements. The development of such horizontal links among shack settlements suggested a new kind of movement in the making. By May 2005, the people from Kennedy Road and five other shack settlements, as well as residents from local municipal flats, had organized a march of over 3,000 people. With banners expressing their collective will ("We want our land") and homegrown political education ("The University of Kennedy Road"), the marchers presented a memorandum of ten demands that they had drawn up through a series of meetings and community discussions. Written by the shack and flat dwellers after careful discussion, this memorandum, which included the need for housing, jobs, sanitation, medical care, education, and safety from police brutality and environmental toxins, became a people's charter [5] – one that sought to represent not only Durban's 800,000 shack dwellers, but the poor across South Africa, where nearly three million households live in "informal" housing.

Their demands were far from revolutionary; they were the demands of loyal citizens making reasonable requests, borne of their citizenship, for inclusion in the "new South Africa."

The march ended at the offices of the local ANC councillor, and there the marchers announced that if the councillor did not resign, they, his constituents, would declare Ward 25 without a councillor. They brought along a coffin to

---

5 | It is important to note that the handful of middle-class activists/intellectuals from the University of KwaZulu-Natal who were involved in the movement adhered to the principle that the people spoke for themselves.

represent the councillor's political death. The point is obvious, but what is also worth noting is the marchers' self-consciousness, both as a class pitted against the interests of property and as a collective pressing the government to deliver not only on its promises, but also to include those promises in its future deliberations. The marchers, in other words, were self-consciously challenging the elite character of the local government and by implication, the class character of the "elite transition" in South Africa.[6]

Some months later, following a meeting of twelve settlements at Kennedy Road, the shack dwellers' movement, Abahlali baseMjondolo, was launched.[7] There was no donor funding, no NGO, no civil-society funding nor political-party backing. Consistently ignored by the local council and often treated as criminals, shack dwellers across Durban began to join the movement. "The only language they understand is when we put thousands of people on the street," proclaimed Zikode (2006:187), and throughout the following year, mass marches and demonstrations brought the plight of the shack dwellers to local, national and even international attention, with stories being featured in *The Economist* and other international and local media, including a full-page story in *The New York Times*.

On a quick learning curve and with few resources, the movement was able not only to represent itself but also to respond to misrepresentation in the media. And soon it became clear that the shack dwellers weren't going away. Daily demonstrations and actions in all of South Africa's major cities continued to occur alongside Abahlali's growing reputation and media presence.[8] Despite President Mbeki's call for these actions to stop, they continued. "These are the things the youth used to do in the struggle against apartheid," he complained, but that was exactly why the actions were legitimate.

In early 2006, Abahlali began to organize a boycott of the local-government elections scheduled for March of that year. This was a logical development following the "burial" of the councillor, and the decision to boycott was marked

---

6 | Legitimation of the shacks could take different forms. One form, which is akin to privatization, is to legalize the shacks by providing title deeds, thus making shack dwellers into individual property owners. The shack dwellers' movement is not advocating this strategy since it would probably undermine the autonomy of the settlement and would prove detrimental to a movement based on community solidarity.

7 | Of the thirty-two elected representatives, fifteen were women and seventeen were men. The roots of the word *mjondolo* (the colloquial word for shacks) are numerous. One line of thought is that *jondolo* originally referred to the John Deere tractor crates that were used for shack construction in the 1970s.

8 | In 2005 alone, there were over 600 community actions across the country (Alexander 2010). These included demonstrations, occupations, and battles with police that resulted in bloodshed. Several new technologies were harnessed to aid communication (particularly mobile phones and SMSes (on SMS activism in Africa, see Erkine 2010). This has enabled the shack dwellers' and other movements to speak for themselves and represent themselves in the media more than was possible in the past.

by a march from the Foreman Road settlement into Durban's city center, under the slogan "No Land, No House, No Vote," which had earlier been employed by the South African Landless People's Movement in a national campaign in 2004. Though the march was legal, it was banned by Durban's city manager, Mike Sutcliffe. Two days later, on February 3, 2006, surrounded by riot police, the 3,000 shack dwellers amassed at the Foreman Road settlement and decided to go ahead with the march. Behind the banners of "University of Abahlali baseMjondolo" and "No Land, No House, No Vote," they marched out of the settlement. As they entered the paved road, the police immediately attacked. A number of people were seriously injured and forty-five were arrested. Sutcliffe issued another ban, this time on a march planned for February 27. The police again cordoned off the exits to three large settlements, and made a number of arrests. But this time the people were prepared. With the support of progressive lawyers, Abahlali was able to take Sutcliffe to the High Court and won an interdict allowing them to march into the city.

Certainly there are continuities between these struggles and the struggles against apartheid. Many in Abahlali see their challenges as unfinished, and even Mandela had acknowledged the shack dwellers' movement in 1993, when it was widely believed that the end of apartheid would see the upgrading of "informal settlements" and that these settlement conditions were a direct consequence of apartheid.[9] In fact, South Africa has always been a country of extremes, of rich and poor, and developments in the South African economy have always been the province of powerful mining and financial interests in the context of global capitalism. The end of apartheid actually strengthened this proprietorship.

While co-opting some of the best brains of the struggle and transforming the formal movements into structures of governance, the ANC promised that the legacies of apartheid would be addressed. Yet, the ANC's actual policies and practices never matched its rhetorical promises. At first this was put down to the politics of transition, especially at the local-government level, where apartheid functionaries lingered. But after the government's embrace of neoliberal economic policies, the shift became clear. Though subject to international pressures, the direct authors of the "homegrown" structural adjustment were the new Black and old White elites. Alan Hirsch (2005) suggests that the neoliberal program was instituted by the government to protect South Africa's sovereignty from the IMF/World Bank's institution of a neoliberal program.

Today it is clear that the main beneficiaries of post-apartheid economic redistribution have been (and continue to be) South Africa's banks and

---

9 | In a 1993 press release, the ANC proclaimed that people living in "squatter areas" should "make their voice heard. 'Your problems are my problems, your solution is my solution,' says President Nelson Mandela." As Dumisani Makhaye put it, 'The crisis in housing in South Africa is...a result of apartheid'" (ANC 1993).

multinationals, now even freer than they were under apartheid. This includes the moneyed White elites, as well as the new much smaller Black elites, and the South African economy is more integrated into the global economy than at any time in its history. Moreover, post-apartheid South Africa's quick move to roll out a neoliberal economic model to encourage global investment shifted priorities and resulted in deep cuts in budgets for social services, below the levels in the first years of the ANC government. Serious discussion of the social and economic consequences of years of colonialism and apartheid in the 1990s has given way to a neoliberal discourse about the poor, who are represented as "undifferentiated, unwilling carriers of social diseases" (Barchiesi 2007:46-7) – in other words, as morally corrupt and behaviorally undisciplined – or, to use the language of apartheid, "surplus population." Needless to say, the post-apartheid housing program is part of this project, ultimately aimed at moving the poor out of the cities. Built far from the urban centers, one-room closet-sized houses are economically nonviable for many. On the contrary, living close to both economic opportunities and to educational opportunities for their children, is vital. Thus, when the Durban municipality described its plan for a "city without slums," it was correctly understood by the shack dwellers as the return of the apartheid policy of "influx control" and the removal of "black spots."[10] Once again, Black people were to be pushed out of the city and dumped in the peripheral ghettoes.

The class character of the situation is plain. This is also evident when it comes to water and electricity supply. Access to "sufficient water" (twenty-five liters per day and person) is guaranteed in the South African Constitution, but this seems to miss the point in the context of the shacks. Reducing general water consumption and controlling it through a metering system are pointless in a situation in which there are few working taps and toilets to serve thousands of people. The same is true for electricity supply.

And it is not simply that those in the shacks can't afford sufficient water and electricity – some can – but insufficient water and no electricity, along with the fact that fire engines are often not dispatched when fires do start, has resulted in frequent fires and avoidable deaths. As S'bu Zikode put it: "We have seen that when the wild forests and plantations of the rich are on fire, there are often large helicopters with hundreds of tons of water to extinguish the fires. But when our shacks are on fire, the helicopters and ambulances are nowhere

---

10 | We should remember that although apartheid minister Piet Koornhof announced in 1981 that forced removals would end, they did not. What changed were the tactics and language, which included "vague promises, ambiguous statements, announcements and retractions, rumors and harassment" (Platzky 1986:395). The same tactics are being used in post-apartheid South Africa. For example, promises to bring electricity to the shacks were retracted because the informal settlements were "temporary" and the shack dwellers would be rehoused by 2010. The 2010 date was later retracted.

to be found...Helicopters only come for us when we march. The state comes for us when we try to say what we think." (Zikode 2008a)

On April 21, 2006, twelve years after the birth of a new South Africa, generated by the first full and free election, 5,000 South African shack dwellers from the fourteen informal settlements that had joined Abahlali the preceding year came out, not to celebrate freedom, but to mourn "Unfreedom day," and they have done so ever since. How can "we celebrate freedom when we only hear tales of freedom or see people's lives changed for the better in other parts of the country, but never in our communities?" asked S'bu Zikode, questioning, in effect, the state of freedom in the whole country.

Zikode, the founding president of the shack dwellers' movement, Abahlali's baseMjondolo, is a forty-year-old former petrol-station worker. (Early in 2007 Zikode lost his job at the petrol station because of his political activity.) A father of four who moved to the Kennedy Road settlement in 1997, he is a former Boy Scout from a small rural town who gained distinction at school but had no money for university. A short, slight man with a welcoming manner and warm smile, Zikode is both engaging and articulate, with a reflective and calm demeanor. A radical humanist, not a firebrand, but a teacher and listener, Zikode has become a significant national public figure, appearing on television, on radio, and in the national and local print media, his words frequently reprinted in pop-culture magazines with a combined circulation of five million (Bryant 2008). (For more of his biography, see Zikode 2009.)

While S'bu Zikode might be viewed as Abahlali's philosopher – indeed he articulates the struggle as "thought on the ground, running" – he has rigorously resisted calls to run for local government or to be the single spokesperson of the movement. He maintains that the problems are systemic, and sees himself only as the people's servant, elected on their behalf and subject to recall. Zikode has remained remarkably consistent and true to the principles of grassroots democracy, shared leadership, and to critically reflecting on these struggles. In 2008, he decided not to run as president of the movement arguing:

> My intention was always to remain strongly committed to the movement but it seemed clear to me that all the positions at all levels of leadership in our movement need to be shared, that the burden of leadership in a movement of volunteers needs to be shared, that I need time for my family and to be able to read and think about what we have achieved with our living politics, a politics that was always based on us thinking carefully about our lives and our struggles. We have to change ourselves before we can change the world and, without time to think, that change becomes difficult (Zikode 2008a).

This is an important articulation of principle. It insists not only on the space for thinking, but also on the centrality of self-reflexive thought to the movement itself. When members called on Zikode to reconsider his decision not to run, he took it seriously, adding that the movement's "calls for a leader who is willing to learn and who is prepared to be led...[is] very important in our Movement's work of defining itself and knowing itself before someone else from somewhere else defines our Movement" (2008a).[11] This, of course, is an expression of a Fanonian principle: the leader does not lead the people, but rather helps in the work of self-clarification; the philosophic idea of "knowing thyself" is and must be a social and collective process.

Zikode has developed a knack of talking over the head of the government to a larger constituency, and his message is a challenge to the nation. "Government officials, politicians and intellectuals who associate the shack dwellers with the Third Force [a term that alludes to the murderous apartheid-sponsored violence of the early 1990s] have no idea what they are talking about. They are too high to really feel what we feel." And quite literally, high up in their offices, they cannot see the people down below – physically, conceptually and experientially – and quite possibly, for this reason, the Third Force may not be something the politicians can understand. Zikode continues: "We are driven by the Third Force, the suffering of the poor. Our betrayers are the Second Force. The First Force was our struggle against apartheid. The Third Force will stop when the Fourth Force comes. The Fourth Force is land, housing, water, electricity, health care, education, and work" (Zikode 2006). The implication is clear: The "Second Force," the ANC in power, had betrayed the struggle and produced not liberation but a "Third Force," namely the suffering of the poor. In this logic, the as-yet unrealized "Fourth Force" is, of course, a vision of an egalitarian future.[12]

A Struggle of Moral Discourse and Democratic Practice

Boycotting the election was not taken lightly, but for Abahlali, democracy means much more than a periodic vote. The decision to boycott represented a real shift in thinking about the core values of post-apartheid society. For Abahlai members, democracy was not about an election every five years, but about day-to-day life that included reciprocity, caring, and the inclusion of those who had been systematically excluded and told that they were too stupid to

---

11 | Zikode is always clear that Abahlalism is about the "movement" not about individuals. Inviting Zikode to speak at one or another workshop, NGOs are often shocked to be told that the movement will first discuss whether or not to attend the workshop and then, if they decide to attend, will send an elected representative or representatives.

12 | The importance of Zikode's analysis should not be underestimated. When Blade Nzimande, general secretary of the South African Communist Party, condemned the protests by the poor in 2009 and dismissed looting and destruction of property as the work of a "third force," newspaper columnists (such as Karumbidza 2009) responded with references to Zikode's "Third Force" argument.

understand. Abahlali was simply speaking a different language that emanated from below, and was grounded in the struggle of the everyday. The organization was concerned not with political negotiations but with principles that flowed from an open and egalitarian moral discourse and democratic practice: "Our struggle is for moral questions, as compared to the political questions as such. It is more about justice," declared Zikode. "Is it good for shack dwellers to live in mud like pigs, as they are living? Why do I live in a cardboard house if there are people who are able to live in a decent house? So it is a moral question" (Zikode quoted in Ngiam 2006).

Just as the struggle against apartheid brought the vote, the shack dwellers' struggle has challenged the meaning of the vote, and given a voice to the poorest of the poor: "Now the tide has turned," argued Zikode in 2006, "you are hearing from the horse's mouth...We have come out to say *this is who we are, this is where we are and this is what we want*" (interview with Zikode in Beresford 2006; original emphasis). Continuously staying open to new creative impulses and questions and to innovation from below remains a core principle. As self-organized shack dwellers, Abahlali was becoming an author of its own history with everyone able to participate – an example, in Fanonian terms, of the "practice of freedom" taking place in the "structure of the people" (1968:143).

Abahlali has consistently refuted the discourse of "service delivery"; they insist instead that their demands are about "being human." "It is not only about physical infrastructure," says Zikode, "we have shifted our thinking"; from the beginning, "the struggle is the human being, the conditions that we live in which translates into demands for housing and land."[13] Through Abahlali, he adds, "people are starting to remember that they are human beings" – even the police. Often harassed and criminalized (with trumped-up murder charges and such), with leaders including Zikode imprisoned and beaten up in Sydenham police station, members of Abahlali have suffered at the hands of the police. But after sustained mobilization in late 2007, a shift in police behavior became apparent, and Abahlali was determined to continue this trend and work with the police around issues of safety.[14]

A deeply rooted humanism guides "the culture of Abahlalism," a set of ethical norms in which everyone shares everyday suffering and pain, as well as laughter. Reflected in the democratic openness and respectfulness with which they conduct their meetings, Abahlalism is a culture of sharing that is rooted in the ideas of community and reciprocity found in the long struggle against

---

13 | Minutes of the Abahlali baseMjondolo meeting to discuss legal and political strategies to oppose the Slums Bill, July 19, 2007, available at http://abahlali.org/node/1718.

14 | This relationship was broken in late September 2009 when the police stood by while Abahlali members were expelled from the Kennedy Road shack settlement and their shacks were destroyed. See http://www.youtube.com/watch?v=-8gQvi9cD4Y.

apartheid. "We fought, died, and voted for this government," Zikode says, "so that we could be free and have decent lives," but "this government does not treat us like people who can speak and think for ourselves" (Butler and Ntseng 2007). Thus life is not only about a struggle for decent living conditions, but also about a mental liberation from years of subservience and the lack of self-confidence that so oppressed the poor during the apartheid period, and sadly also during the post-apartheid period. One of the major goals of Abahlali, therefore, is a kind of moral revolution, the creation of a society where the poor will be treated as human beings with minds of their own.

Yet at every turn, Zikode is reminded that poor people in post-apartheid South Africa are not valued as much as others. While Abahlali has successfully forced itself onto the agendas of government institutions and "civil society," there is a constant struggle not only to keep these spaces open but through their inclusion to transform them. Whatever tactic has been employed, from mass marches to challenges in the courts, from meeting with local government to the No Vote campaign, what remains essential is that no actions take place without ongoing discussion and decisionmaking at the meetings in the shack settlements. Court cases (including appeals to the Constitutional Court), for example, can be long, procedural and expensive affairs that can drain the resources and challenge the integrity of any poor people's movement. And while it appreciates the *pro bono* work of lawyers, Abahlali has always been careful to develop and sustain a mode of organizing from the bottom-up, through constant consultation and principled refusal of "biryani money." Thus, as a movement, it has avoided two pitfalls, namely dependency on donors and professionalization:

> All decisions about money are taken collectively, publicly and democratically in the movement's open weekly meetings and all donations should therefore be channeled through the movement's official structures so that decisions about how to use the money can be taken in these meetings. Abahlali is a 100 percent volunteer organization and no member is paid for any work undertaken for the organization and no money is allocated to individuals – it all goes for collective expenses such as lawyers, bail, transport, sound hire, etc. as determined by the discussion at the weekly meetings (Abahlali 2006a).

Abahlali's critique of the discourse of service delivery thus emerges from the conception of being counted as active participants in decisions and actions, rather than being seen as pariahs to be managed and controlled. They have deliberately chosen to force themselves into those spaces where they have not been invited, and make their presence in these spaces a kind of "insurgent citizenship" (Holston 2007), one that contests the elite form of South Africa's democracy. Their claim to practical and intellectual equity, remarks Cooper-Knock

(2009:57), "does not rest on claims to equal, technical knowledge but...in their capacity to reason through their situation." In other words, the shack dwellers' knowledge derives from their existentially experienced situation of being in the shacks, and their politics from theorizing their situation.

Thinking in Communities

The shack dwellers' movement cannot be explained by issues of resource mobilization, or the aid of outside forces, or even the event's material success. What was expressed through the shack settlement's initial self-mobilization was its insistence on open meetings where all could speak and hash out issues, coupled with the straightforwardness and moral suasion of their demands. The growth of the movement came about through word-of-mouth and personal communication, which, by the end of the first year, 2005, had engendered a new organization, Abahlali baseMjondolo. And if Abahlali's commitment to growth is tempered, it is only because it is invested in the principle of discussing things openly and thoroughly in meetings, and making decisions with the commitment of all.

Each shack settlement that joins, each new branch that forms, has to follow the democratic principles of Abahlali.[15] This means that each demonstration or march requires a number of meetings, then meetings of subcommittees, as well as communication among settlements. Press releases are discussed, written and distributed. And each settlement and branch, through its own autonomous committees, sends delegates to Abahlali. The Abahlali meetings rotate among all the affiliated settlements, are usually attended by about thirty to forty elected representatives from the various committees, and are open to all residents from the local settlements (Beresford 2006). It is worth noting that, though the democratic culture of the organization has spread across the settlements, it doesn't always overcome authoritarianism or conservative ideas. Even where settlements have strong Abahlali activists, it has been difficult, at times, to get beyond the armed authoritarianism of "leaders" who trade votes for private deals with the state.

Governed on such a grassroots democratic basis, with meetings open to all adults (regardless of age, gender,[16] ethnicity, origin, and length of time in residence), each settlement has at least one weekly meeting, and representatives

---

15 | This, of course, becomes more challenging as Abahlali has grown and shack dwellers join Abahlali for an immediate goal, such as to stop an eviction, and become fairly inactive after that goal is achieved and thus do not play an active part in the organization's culture of grassroots democratic participation and "living learning" (see Pithouse 2006). This became apparent for a short while after the attacks at Kennedy Road in 2009, when many of the movement's activists were in hiding.

16 | Pithouse (2006:61) notes that while all are included, it is mostly young women without children or older women with teenage or adult children who are able to go. He says that

from each of the settlements elected each week meet as Abahlali baseMjondolo every Saturday. Every day there are a number of meetings of various subcommittees. The meetings are very formal, with decisions arrived at by consensus and with an emphasis on the inclusive process of "listening to others' ideas" and "being together" (Bryant 2008:48).

Through these process the movement has consistently rejected offers of money, proffered mostly by NGOs and parties attempting to buy political credibility. It has remained very suspicious of outsiders who try to speak for it or take control and, over time, it has come to understand who its real friends and enemies are. At its inception, three "outsiders" – activist academics at the University of KwaZulu-Natal, Fazel Khan, Raj Patel and Richard Pithouse – were directly involved with the movement on a daily basis. Committed to the Fanonian belief that a movement of the poor should speak for itself, these activist academics had put themselves "in the school of the people," to be educated by the movement. They not only helped put the shack dwellers' organization in touch with committed lawyers, typed up press releases and developed a website, but took the thinking being done in the communities seriously.

In *The Wretched of the Earth*, Fanon writes, "It is true that if care is taken to use only a language that is understood by graduates in law and economics, you can easily prove that the masses have to be managed from above. But if you speak the language of the everyday...then you will realize that the masses are quick to seize every shade of meaning...Everything can be explained to the people, on the single condition that you really want them to understand...The more people understand, the more watchful they become and the more they come to realize that everything depends on them." This idea helps explain, as noted by Zkorde (2008a), how the shack dwellers' conception of politics is not about political office; it is a politics of the poor in the language of the people. Participation is based on shared experience, and their political practice is dependent on democratic meetings in the settlements: "Our politics is a traditional home politics which is understood very well by all the old mamas and *gogos* [grannies] because it affects their lives and gives them a home." It is a language which all can speak and understand; it is simple and transparent and thus creates a situation which is consciously collective and inclusive.[17] In Zikode's words, "We look after each other and think about the situation and plan our fight together" (2008:115). Zikode's notion is a challenge to the elite

---

for meetings to be fully democratic, childcare will have to be provided, although, in some settlements there just isn't a physical space large enough for collective childcare arrangements.

17 | And thus reminiscent of Aristide's liberation theology and its three principles of a people's program: dignity, transparent simplicity and participation. For Aristide, "The democracy to be built," he argues in his autobiography, "should be in the image of *Lavalas*: participatory, uncomplicated, and in permanent motion" (1993:126).

politics that has characterized the post-apartheid transition and its corporate and technicist aftermath. It is not a question of empowerment or inclusion in terms of having a seat at the policy table, nor it is not simply a question of being consulted, although that would be an important beginning; it is a challenge to the alienation inherent in the attitudes and proposals of the housing-policy experts, an alienation that arises out of their attitude towards the poor, and the poor's systemic exclusion from the policy decisions made about them.

Thus, at first, the Kennedy Road movement saw itself as a movement unto itself, local and immediate, utterly divorced from liberal NGO or left anti-globalization discourses. A year later, in his 2006 presentation, Zikode directly linked the self-activity of the shack dwellers, not only to housing politics, but also to national politics:

> We believe that the housing policy does not only require housing special-ists, rich consultants and government. We believe that housing policy requires most importantly, the people who need the houses. *But* we also know, as poor communities and as shack dwellers that the broader poor have no choice but to play a role in shaping and reshaping this country into an anti-capitalist system (Zikode 2008: 115; my emphasis).

And this alternative, he added, comes out of "the thinking that we do in communities." The challenge to academics and intellectuals in the university setting is quite clear; their work requires listening to, and taking seriously, the thinking that is done in the communities. In other words, it requires shifting the geography of reason, and challenging preconceived ideas of who does the thinking and where it is done. This is not simply about territoriality, but about restoring agency to the people who know the situation, who can and should do the thinking so that they can demand, in a Fanonian sense, a more reality-based and a more rational[18] and effective mode of operation that will lead to a self-conscious realization that they are "equal to the problems that confront them" (Fanon 1968:193). In practice, this has meant that Abahlali's meetings, its finances and its organizational structures are open to all.

Beyond Liberal Ideas of "Freedom" and "Inclusion"

In the early days of the movement, the struggle's discourse centered on ideas of dignity and self-respect. The declaration that "we are human beings" was echoed in the shack dwellers' outrage at the politicians who ignored their plight. Thus, from its beginnings the struggle was not over a technical issue about

---

18 | Hegel famously said that "truth is concrete" and that "the real is rational." Here the challenge to theory is the reality of the situation, expressed by the thinking (rationality) of the shack dwellers. Rather than a source of theory, the thinking done in the communities is itself a form of theory (see Dunayevskaya 2002). Dunayevskaya's argument (1958) that Marx re-organized *Capital* on the basis of ongoing struggles and the "limits of an intellectual work" is a point lost on many Marxists.

the redistribution of resources (though it includes that) but a most concrete reflection on being human, about the fact that human beings should live in homes fit for human beings. The shack dwellers don't only demand recognition as human beings. Their demand for recognition has been consistent and goes beyond the liberal tradition of "inclusion" in a political or legal system. They take the freedom won in the struggles against apartheid seriously, and thus reject the equation of freedom with neoliberal ideas as "unfreedom" since for them those ideas only amount to absence of freedom. They want freedom to be truly equal.

Thus, while fighting for what is guaranteed by the South African Constitution is important,[19] what is at stake is the need to address deep-rooted structures of economic inequality that are legacies of apartheid and colonialism, reproduced in contemporary neoliberal South Africa. In that sense, the demand for "redistribution" is a real and urgent one, but it also implies a critique of elite-driven politics (or the anti-politics discourse of "service delivery"), be that right-wing, top-down technocracy, NGO paternalism, vanguardism,[20] or left-wing technocratism. The latter describes a situation in which too much attention is paid to technical instruments, and too little to popular participation. In contrast to reforms developed by scholars and NGO staff "while the poor and their grassroots organizations play only a very secondary role in terms of strategy building and intellectual elaboration" (De Souza 2006:337), the shack dwellers seek to be an essential part of decisionmaking and thus agents of refashioning democracy.

When Fanon wrote in *The Wretched* that intellectuals needed to put themselves in the school of the people, he had in mind the grounding of new concepts in what Zikode calls "thinking that is done in the communities." This thinking, which emerges from experience, is at once pragmatic and critical. Ideas and formulas repeated at meetings help generate new ways of knowing in the communities and, in the case of Abahlali, the movement's intellectuals are truly organic to it. They live in the settlements, and this goes a long way

---

19 | South Africa has a liberal Constitution that grants recognition to individuals and to "minorities." Indeed, in contrast to its apartheid past, South Africa is promoted as a rainbow nation celebrating multiculturalism. And in the mid-1990s, Nelson Mandela went to great lengths to stress, "I love each of you – of all races." Additionally material rights, such as housing, are included in the Constitution even if the extent of their guarantee is debatable. The fact that the Constitution includes language about second-generation human rights means that the law courts, however weighted, are still a terrain of struggle in which the shack dwellers' movement can operate. But at the same time, in practice, the law courts are constrained by the state.

20 | Abahlali is far from alone. Writing in the *Mail and Guardian*, Richard Calland (2007) argues that South Africans deserve more from democracy than a government of experts with a plan. Explicitly criticizing Durban city manager and ANC stalwart Mike Sutcliffe, he argues for "a very different vision of a participatory democracy, in which citizens are provided with meaningful opportunities to engage government in a permanent conversation, as opposed to the anachronistic, five-yearly episodic model of representative democracy."

towards overcoming the separation of intellectuals from the masses that so preoccupied Fanon.

Over time, some NGOs and other individuals have given practical support, but Abahlali is not dependent on any external funds. It remains particularly concerned about its ability to maintain political autonomy within the democratic structure of the organization. "It's quite interesting because sometimes we are aware that these organizations have got money but they don't have constituents, you know, people," argued Zikode, "Abahlali is the poor struggle – struggle of the poor – therefore money will not tempt us...we cannot therefore be bought" (Zikode quoted in Pithouse 2006). In other words, Abahlali became aware of the potentially disastrous effects of external funding on a poor people's movement, that it may not only broker a movement but also potentially destroy it.

Again, Zikode (2008:122) reminds us that human beings do not live on bread alone. "We are poor," he says, "we know that, and we might be poor in life, but we are not poor in mind," recognizing, as Marx put it, the real wealth of the individual depends entirely on the wealth of real social and intellectual relationships.

References

Abahlali baseMjondolo. 2006. "Supporting Abahlali." http://www.abahlali.org/node/269.

Alexander, Neville. 1993. *Some Are More Equal Than Others: Essays on the Transition in South Africa*. Cape Town: Buchu Books.

ANC [African National Congress, South Africa]. 1993. "Southern Natal Statement on the Housing Crisis." November 9.

Aristide, Jean-Bertrand and Christophe Wargny. 1993. *Aristide: An Autobiography* Maryknoll, NY: Orbis Books.

Barchiesi, Franco. 2007. "Wage Labor and Social Citizenship in the Making of Post-Apartheid South Africa." *Journal of Asian and African Studies* 42(1):39-72.

Beresford, Alex. 2006. 'Trapped in Corporatism? Trade Union Linkages to the Abahlali baseMjondolo Movement in Durban'. http://www.abahlali.org/files/Beresford.pdf

Bryant, Jacob. 2008. "Toward Delivery and Dignity." *Journal of Asian and African Studies* 43(1):41-62.

Butler, Mark and David Ntseng. 2007. "Minutes of the Abahlali baseMjondolo Meeting to Discuss Legal and Political Strategies to Oppose the Slums Bill." July, 13. Kennedy Road Hall, Durban. http://abahlali.org/node/1718.

Calland, Richard. 2007. "Resist the Prison of Expertocracy." *Mail and Guardian*, January 21.

Cooper-Knock, Sarah. 2009. "The Role of Citizens in Post-Apartheid South Africa: a Case-Study of Citizen Involvement in Informal Settlement Projects," M.A. Thesis, Oxford University.

De Souza, Marcelo Lopes. 2006. "Together with the State, Despite the State, Against the State: Social Movements as 'Critical Urban Planning' Agents." *City* 10(3):327-42.

Dunayevskaya, Raya. 2002. *The Power of Negativity. Selected Writings on the Dialectic in Hegel and Marx.* Peter Hudis and Kevin B. Anderson, editors. Lanham, MD. Lexington Books.

Fanon, Frantz. 1968. *The Wretched of the Earth.* Constance Farrington, translator. New York. Grove Press.

Gibson, Nigel C., editor. 2006. *Challenging Hegemony: Social Movements and the Quest for a New Humanism in Post-Apartheid South Africa.* Trenton: Africa World Press, 1-14.

Hirsch, Alan. 2005. *Season of Hope: Economic Reform Under Mandela And Mbeki Pietermaritzburg:* University of KwaZulu-Natal Press.

Holston, James. 2007. *Insurgent Citizenship: Disjunctions of Democracy and Modernity in Brazil.* Princeton: Princeton University Press.

Khan, Fazel. 2006. "Outside the ICC again." Independent Media Centre, September 12. http://www.southafrica.indymedia.org/news/2006/09/11083.php

Kockott, Fred. 2005. "Shack Dwellers' Fury Erupts." *Tribune.* March 20.

Loftus, Alex. 2006. "Reification and the Dictatorship of the Water Meter." *Antipode* 38(5):1023-45.

Ngiam, Xin Wei. 2006. "Taking Poverty Seriously: What the Poor Are Saying and Why it Matters." http://www.abahlali.org.

Patel, Raj and Richard Pithouse. 2005. "The Third Nelson Mandela." http://www.voiceoftheturtle.org/show_article.php?aid=435.

Pithouse, Richard. 2005. "The Left in the Slum: The Rise of a Shack Dwellers' Movement in Durban, South Africa" (History and African Studies Seminar, November 23, 2005, University of KwaZulu-Natal).

———. 2006. "Our Struggle is Thought on the Ground Running": The University of Abahlali baseMjondolo. Centre for Civil Society Research Report, No. 40, University of KwaZulu-Natal, Durban.

———. 2009. "A Progressive Policy without a Progressive Politics: Lessons from the Failure to Implement Breaking New Ground." *Town Planning Journal* 54: 1-14.

Platzky, Laurine. 1986. "Relocation in South Africa." *South African Review* 3. Johannesburg: Ravan.

Zikode, S'bu. 2006. "We Are the Third Force." *Journal of Asian and African Studies* 41(1/2):185-9. Also, http://www.abahlali.org/node/17.

———. 2008. "Sekwanele Sekwanele" (Enough is Enough). *Journal of Asian and African Studies* 43(1):119-24.

———. 2008a. "Post Annual General Meeting Speech." December 14. http://abahlali.org/node/4666

————. 2009. "To Resist All Degradations and Divisions." Interview by Richard Pithouse. http://antieviction.org.za/2009/04/28/ to-resist-all-degradations-divisions-an-interview-with-sbu-zikode

This essay is derived from a chapter by Nigel Gibson, "Unfinished Struggles for Freedom: The Birth of a New Shack Dwellers' Movement," in *Fanonian Practices: From Steve Biko to Abahlali baseMjondolo*, Pietermaritzburg: University of Kwa-Zulu Natal Press and New York: Palgrave Press: 2011.

Nigel C. Gibson *(USA) is Associate Professor of Interdisciplinary Studies at Emerson College and research associate at the University of Kwa-Zulu Natal. In addition to* Fanonian Practices, *he is the author of* Fanon: The Postcolonial Imagination *and the editor of eight books, including* Rethinking Fanon *and* Biko Lives.

Commons in the Pluriverse

By Arturo Escobar

I. Commons and Worlds

Commons exist within worlds. Long before private property showed its ugly head and started to devour territories, people created what today we call commons as a principal strategy to enact their worlds. These worlds, made up of human and nonhuman, living and nonliving, material and spiritual beings and forms woven together in inextricably entangled ways, have continued to persevere nevertheless.

Colombian sociologist Orlando Fals Borda (1984) describes how the introduction of barbwire for cattle ranching in the Caribbean Coast region of Colombia at the dawn of the twentieth century interrupted flows of people and animals, regularized landscapes and even desiccated wetlands and lagoons in some areas. Despite these challenges, the region's people had a resilient culture and strove time and again to reconstitute their commons. They sought to recreate the sensual wholeness that Raoul Vaneigem describes as a casualty of the economy:

> The economy is everywhere that life is not....Economics is the most durable lie of the approximately ten millennia mistakenly accepted as history....With the intrusion of work the body loses its sensual wholeness...work existed from the moment one part of life was devoted to the service of the economy while the other was denied and repressed (Vaneigem 1994:17, 18, 27, 28).

And so, and against all odds, and like many other people throughout the world, the Caribbean people described by Fals go on enacting a world of their own, creating with every act and every practice worlds in which the commons – indeed, commoning – still find a breathing space and at times even the chance to flourish. Commoners are like that. They refuse to abide by the rules of the One-World World (OWW) that wishes to organize everything in terms of individuals, private property, markets, profits, and a single notion of the Real.

OWW seeks to banish nature and the sacred from the domain of an exclusively human-driven life (Law 2011).

Those who insist on commoning defy this civilization of the One-World (capitalist, secular, liberal, patriarchal, white) that arrogates for itself the right to be "the world" and that reduces all other worlds to nonexistence or noncredible alternatives to what exist (Santos 2002). Vaneigem is again instructive:

> Civilization was identified with obedience to a universal and eternal market relationship....The commodity is the original form of pollution.... Nature cannot be liberated from the economy until the economy has been driven out of human life....(From the moment the market system minimizes the fruits of the earth by seeing them only in terms of the fruits of labor, the market system treats nature as its slave)... As the economy's hold weakens, life is more able to clear a path for itself (Vaneigem 1994).

This reality has always been evident to most of the world's peoples-territory (*pueblos-territorio*).[1] An activist from the Process of Black Communities of Colombia said: "The territory has no price. Our ancestors cared for the territory with a great sense of belonging. This is why we have to create our economies not from the outside coming in but the other way around: from the inside going outwards."[2] The world this activist talks about has persevered, again despite all odds. Let us visit this this world for a brief moment.

II. Yurumanguí: Introducing Relational Worlds

In Colombia's southern Pacific rainforest region, picture a seemingly simple scene from the Yurumanguí River, one of the many rivers that flow from the Western Andean mountain range towards the Pacific Ocean, an area inhabited largely by Afrodescendant communities.[3] A father and his six-year old daughter paddling with their *canaletes* (oars) seemingly upstream in their *potrillos* (local dugout canoes) at the end of the afternoon, taking advantage of the rising tide; perhaps they are returning home after having taken their harvested plantains

---

1 | By *pueblos-territorio* (peoples-territory) I mean those peoples and social groups who have maintained a historical attachment to their places and landscapes. By hyphenating the term, I emphasize that for these groups (usually ethnic minorities and peasants, but not only; they also exist in urban settings) there are profound links between humans and not-humans, and between the natural, human and spiritual worlds.

2 | Statement by an Afro-Colombian activist at the Forum "Other Economies are Possible," Buga, Colombia, July 17-21, 2013.

3 | The Yurumangui River is one of five rivers that flow into the bay of Buenaventura in the Pacific Ocean. A population of about 6,000 people live on its banks. In 1999, thanks to active local organizing, the communities succeeded in securing the collective title to about 52,000 hectares, or 82 percent of the river basin. Locals have not been able to exercise effective control of the territory, however, because of armed conflict, the pressure from illegal crops, and mega-development projects in the Buenaventura area. Nevertheless, the collective title implied a big step in the defense of their commons and the basis for autonomous territories and livelihoods.

and their catch of the day to the town downstream, and bringing back some items they bought at the town store – unrefined cane sugar, cooking fuel, salt, notebooks for the children, or what have you.

On first inspection, we may say that the father is "socializing" his daughter into the correct way to navigate the *potrillo*, an important skill as life in the region greatly depends on the ceaseless going back and forth in the *potrillos* through rivers, mangroves and estuaries. This interpretation is correct in some ways; but something else is also going on. As locals are wont to say, speaking of the river territory, *acá nacimos, acá crecimos, acá hemos conocido qué es el mundo* ("Here we were born, here we grew up, here we have known what the world is"). Through their *nacer~crecer~conocer* they enact the manifold practices through which their territories/worlds have been made since they became *libres* (i.e., free, not enslaved peoples) and became entangled with living beings of all kinds in these forest and mangrove worlds.

Let us travel to this river and immerse ourselves deeply within it and experience it with the eyes of relationality; an entire way of worlding emerges for us. Looking attentively from the perspective of the manifold relations that make this world what it is, we see that the *potrillo* was made out of a mangrove tree with the knowledge the father received from his predecessors; the mangrove forest is intimately known by the inhabitants who traverse with great ease the fractal estuaries it creates with the rivers and the always moving sea; we begin to see the endless connections keeping together and always in motion this intertidal "aquatic space," (Oslender 2008) including connections with the moon and the tides that enact a nonlinear temporality. The mangrove forest involves many relational entities among what we might call minerals, mollusks, nutrients, algae, microorganisms, birds, plant, and insects – an entire assemblage of underwater, surface and areal life. Ethnographers of these worlds describe it in terms of three non-separate worlds – *el mundo de abajo* or infraworld; *este mundo*, or the human world; and *el mundo de arriba*, or spiritual/supraworld. There are comings and goings between these worlds, and particular places and beings connecting them, including "visions" and spiritual beings. This entire world is narrated in oral forms that include storytelling, chants and poetry.

This dense network of interrelations may be called a "relational ontology." The mangrove-world, to give it a short name, is enacted minute by minute, day by day, through an infinite set of practices carried out by all kinds of beings and life forms, involving a complex organic and inorganic materiality of water, minerals, degrees of salinity, forms of energy (sun, tides, moon, relations of force), and so forth. There is a rhizome "logic" to these entanglements, a logic that is impossible to follow in any simple way, and very difficult to map and measure, if at all; it reveals an altogether different way of being and becoming in territory and place. These experiences constitute relational worlds or ontologies. To put it abstractly, a relational ontology of this sort can be defined as one in which *nothing preexists the relations that constitute it.* Said otherwise, things and beings are their relations; they do not exist prior to them.

As the anthropologist from Aberdeen Tim Ingold says, these "worlds without objects" (2011:131) are always in movement, made up of materials in motion, flux and becoming; in these worlds, living beings of all kinds constitute each other's conditions for existence; they "interweave to form an immense and continually evolving tapestry." (2011:10) Going back to the river scene, one may say that "father" and "daughter" get to know their local world not through distancing reflection but by going about it, that is, by being alive to their world. These worlds do not require the divide between nature and culture in order to exist – in fact, they exist as such only because they are enacted by practices that do not rely on such divide. In a relational ontology, "beings do not simply occupy the world, they *inhabit* it, and in so doing – in threading their own paths through the meshwork – they contribute to their ever-evolving weave." (Ingold 2011: 71) Commons exist in these relational worlds, not in worlds that are imagined as inert and waiting to be occupied.

Even if the relations that keep the mangrove-world always in a state of becoming are always changing, to disrupt them significantly often results in the degradation of such worlds. Such is the case with industrial shrimp farming schemes and oil palm plantations for agrofuels, which have proliferated in many tropical regions of the world. These market systems, often built at the expense of mangrove and humid forest lands, aim to transform "worthless swamp" into agroindustrial complexes (Ogden 2012; Escobar 2008).

Here, of course, we find many of the operations of the One-World World at play: the conversion of everything that exists in the mangrove-world into "nature" and "nature" into "resources"; the effacing of the life-enabling materiality of the entire domains of the inorganic and the nonhuman, and its treatment as "objects" to be had, destroyed or extracted; and linking the forest worlds so transformed to "world markets," to generate profit. In these cases, the insatiable appetite of the One-World World spells out the progressive destruction of the mangrove-world, its ontological capture and reconversion by capital and the State (Deleuze and Guattari 1987). The OWW, in short, denies the mangrove-world its possibility of existing as such. Local struggles constitute attempts to (re)establish some degree of symmetry by seeking to influence the partial connections that the mangrove-worlds inevitably maintain with the OWW.

III. Territoriality, Ancestrality and Worlds

Elders and young activists in many territorial communities worldwide (includ-ing increasingly in urban areas) eloquently express why they defend their worlds even at the price of their lives. An activist from the Afrodescendant community of La Toma of Colombia's southwest, which has struggled against gold mining since 2008, said: "It is patently clear to us that we are confronting monsters such as transnational corporations and the State. Yet nobody is willing to leave her/his territory; I might get killed here but I am not leaving."[4]

Such resistance takes place within a long history of domination and re-sistance, and this is essential for understanding commoning as an ontologi-cal political practice. La Toma communities, for instance, have knowledge of their continued presence in the territory since the first half of the seventeenth century. It's an eloquent example of what activists call "ancestrality," referring to the ancestral mandate that inspires today's struggles and that persists in the memory of the elders, amply documented by oral history and scholars. (Lisifrey et al. 2013) This mandate is joyfully celebrated in oral poetry and song: *Del Africa llegamos con un legado ancestral; la memoria del mundo debemos recuperar* ("From Africa we arrived with an ancestral legacy; the memory of our world we need to bring back").[5] Far from an intransigent attachment to the past, ancestrality stems from a living memory that orients itself to a future reality that imagines, and struggles for, conditions that will allow them to persevere as a distinct, living mode of existence.

Within relational worlds, the defense of territory, life and the commons are one and the same. This is the ontological dimension of commoning. To this extent, this chapter's argument can be stated as follows: The perseverance of communities, commons, and movements and the struggles for their defense and reconstitution can be described as ontological. At its best and most radical, this is particularly true for those struggles that incorporate explicitly ethno-territorial dimensions and involve resistance and the defense and affirmation of commons.

Conversely, whereas the occupation of territories implies economic, tech-nological, cultural, ecological, and often armed aspects, its most fundamental dimension is ontological. From this perspective, what occupies territories and commons is a particular ontology, that of the universal world of individuals and markets (the OWW) that attempts to transform all other worlds into one;

---

4 | Statement by Francia Marquez of the Community Council of La Toma, taken from the documentary *La Toma*, by Paula Mendoza, available at http://www.youtube.com/watch?v=BrgVcdnwUoM. Most of this brief section on La Toma comes from meetings in which I have participated with La Toma leaders in 2009, 2012 and 2014, as well as campaigns to stop illegal mining in this ancestral territory.

5 | From the documentary by Mendoza cited above.

this is another way of interpreting the historical enclosure of the commons. By interrupting the neoliberal globalizing project of constructing One World, many indigenous, Afrodescendant, peasant, and poor urban communities are advancing *ontological struggles*. The struggle to maintain multiple worlds – the pluriverse – is best embodied by the Zapatista dictum, *Un mundo donde quepan muchos mundos*, a world where many worlds fit. Many of these worlds can thus be seen as struggles over the pluriverse.

Another clear case of ontological occupation of territories comes from the southernmost area in the Colombian Pacific, around the port city of Tumaco. Here, since the early 1980s, the forest has been destroyed and communities displaced to give way to oil palm plantations. Nonexistent in the 1970s, by the mid-1990s they had expanded to over 30,000 hectares. The monotony of the plantation – row after row of palm as far as you can see, a green desert of sorts – replaced the diverse, heterogeneous and entangled world of forest and communities.

There are two important aspects to remark from this dramatic change: first, the "plantation form" effaces the socioecological relations that maintain the forest-world. The plantation emerges from a dualist ontology of human dominance over so-called "nature" understood as "inert space" or "resources" to be had, and can thus be said to be the most effective means for the ontological occupation and ultimate erasure of the local relational world. Conversely, the same plantation form is unthinkable from the perspective of the forest-world; within this world, forest utilization and cultivation practices take on an entirely different form, closer to agroforestry; even the landscape, of course, is entirely different. Not far from the oil palm plantations, industrial shrimp farming was also busy in the 1980s and 1990s transforming the mangrove-world into disciplined succession of rectangular pools, "scientifically" controlled. A very polluting and destructive industry especially when constructed on mangrove swamps, this type of shrimp farming constitutes another clear example of ontological occupation and politics at play (Escobar 2008).

IV. Commons Beyond Development: Commoning and Pluriversal Studies

The ontological occupation of commons and worlds just described often takes place in the name of development. Development and growth continue to be among the most naturalized concepts in the social and policy domains. The very idea of development, however, has been questioned by cultural critics since the mid-1980s; they questioned the core assumptions of development, including growth, progress, and instrumental rationality. These critiques came of age with the publication in 1992 of a collective volume, *The Development Dictionary*. The book started with the startling claim: "The last forty years can be called the age of development. This epoch is coming to an end. The time is ripe to write its obituary." (Sachs 1992; Rist 1997) If development was dead, what would come after? Some started to talk about a "post-development era" in response to this question (Rahnema 1997). Degrowth theorists, notably Latouche (2009), contributed to disseminate this perspective in the North.

Postdevelopment advocates argued that it is possible for activists and policymakers to think about the end of development, emphasizing the notion of alternatives to development, rather than development alternatives. The idea of alternatives *to* development has become more concrete in South America in recent years with the notions of *Buen Vivir* (good living, or collective well-being according to culturally appropriate ways) and the rights of Nature. Defined as a holistic view of social life that no longer gives overriding centrality to the economy, *Buen Vivir* (BV) "constitutes an alternative to development, and as such it represents a potential response to the substantial critiques of post-development" (Gudynas and Acosta 2011; Acosta and Martínez 2009). Very succinctly, *Buen Vivir* grew out of indigenous struggles for social change waged by peasants, Afrodescendants, environmentalists, students, women and youth. Echoing indigenous ontologies, BV implies a different philosophy of life which subordinates economic objectives to ecological criteria, human dignity and social justice. Debates about the form BV might take in modern urban contexts and other parts of the world, such as Europe, are beginning to take place. Degrowth, commons and BV are "fellow travelers" in this endeavor.

Buen Vivir resonates with broader challenges to the "civilizational model" of globalized development. The crisis of the Western *modelo civilizatorio* is invoked by many movements as the underlying cause of the current crisis of climate, energy, poverty and meaning. This emphasis is strongest among ethnic movements, yet it is also found, for instance, in peasant networks such as Via Campesina for which only a shift toward agroecological food production systems can lead us out of the climate and food crises. Originally proposed by the Centro Latinoamericano de Ecología Social (CLAES) in Montevideo and closely related to the "transitions to post-extractivism" framework, *Buen Vivir* has become an important intellectual-activist debate in many South American countries (Alayza and Gudynas 2011; Gudynas 2011; Massuh 2012). The point of departure is a critique of the intensification of extractivist models based on large-scale mining, hydrocarbon exploitation or extensive agricultural operations, particularly for agrofuels such as soy, sugar cane or oil palm. Whether they take the form of conventional – often brutal – neoliberal extractivist policies in countries like Colombia, Perú or México, or the neoextractivism of the center-left regimes, these models are legitimized as efficient growth strategies.

This implies a transition from One-World concepts such as "globalization" to concepts centered on the pluriverse as made up of a multiplicity of mutually entangled and co-constituting but distinct worlds (Blaser, de la Cadena and Escobar 2013; Blaser 2010). There are many signs that suggest that the One-World doctrine is unraveling. The growing visibility of struggles to defend mountains, landscapes, forests and so forth by appealing to a relational (non-dualist) and pluriversal understanding of life is a manifestation of the OWW's crisis. Santos has powerfully described this conjuncture with the following paradox: *We are facing modern problems for which there are no longer modern solutions* (Santos 2002:13).

This conjuncture defines a rich context for commons studies from the perspective of pluriversal studies: on the one hand, the need to understand the conditions by which the one world of neoliberal globalization continues to maintain its dominance; and on the other hand, the (re)emergence of projects based on different ways of "worlding" (that is, the socioecological processes implied in building collectively a distinctive reality or world), including commoning, and how they might weaken the One-World project while widening their spaces of (re)existence.

The notion of the pluriverse, it should be made clear, has two main sources: theoretical critiques of dualism, and the perseverance of pluriversal and non-dualist worlds (more often known as "cosmovisions") that reflect a deeply relational understanding of life. Notable examples include *Muntu* and *Ubuntu* in parts of Africa, the *Pachamama* or *Mama Kiwe* among South American indigenous peoples, Native US and Canadian cosmologies, and even the entire Buddhist philosophy of mind. Examples also exist within the West as "alternative Wests" or nondominant forms of modernity. Some of the current struggles going on in Europe over the commons, energy transitions, and the relocalization of food, for instance, could be seen as struggles to reconnect with the stream of life. They also constitute forms of resistance against the dominant ontology of capitalist modernity. Worldwide, the multiple struggles for the reconstruction of communal spaces and for reconnecting with nature are giving rise to political mobilizations for the defense of the relational fabric of life – for instance, for the recognition of territorial rights, local knowledges, and local biodiversity. Struggles over the commons are key examples of such activation.

V. The Commons and Transitions Towards the Pluriverse

Economically, culturally, and militarily, we are witnessing a renewed attack on anything collective; land grabbing and the privatization of the commons (including sea, land, even the atmosphere through carbon markets) are signs of this attack. This is the merciless world of the global 10 percent, foisted upon the 90 percent and the natural world with a seemingly ever-increasing degree of virulence and cynicism. In this sense, the world created by the OWW has brought about untold devastation and suffering. The remoteness and separation it effects from the worlds that we inevitably weave with other earth-beings are themselves a cause of the ecological and social crisis (Rose 2008). These are aspects of what Nonini (2007) has insightfully described as "the wearing-down of the commons."

The emergence, over the past decade, of an array of discourses on the cultural and ecological transitions necessary to deal with the interrelated crises of climate, food, energy and poverty, is powerful evidence that the dominant model of social life is exhausted. In the global North and the global South, multiple transition narratives and forms of activism are going beyond One-World strategic solutions (e.g., "sustainable development" and the "green economy") to articulate sweeping cultural and ecological transitions to different societal models. These Transition discourses (TDs) are emerging today with particular richness, diversity and intensity. Those writing on the subject are not limited to the academy; in fact, the most visionary TD thinkers are located outside of it, even if most engage with critical currents in the academy. TDs are emerging from a multiplicity of sites, principally social movements and some NGOs, from emerging scientific paradigms and academic theories, and from intellectuals with significant connections to environmental and cultural struggles. TDs are prominent in several fields, including those of culture, ecology, religion and spirituality, alternative science (e.g., complexity), futures studies, feminist studies, political economy, and digital technologies and the commons.

The range of TDs can only be hinted at here. In the North, the most prominent include degrowth; a variety of transition initiatives (TIs); the Anthropocene; forecasting trends (e.g., Club of Rome, Randers 2012); and the movement towards commons and the care economy as a different way of seeing and being (e.g., Bollier 2014). Some approaches involving interreligious dialogues and UN processes are also crafting TDs. Among the explicit TIs are the Transition Town Initiative (TTI, UK), the Great Transition Initiative (GTI, Tellus Institute, US), the Great Turning, (Macy and Johnstone 2012) the Great Work or transition to an Ecozoic era, (Berry 1999) and the transition from The Enlightenment to an age of Sustainment. (Fry 2012) In the global South, TDs include the crisis of civilizational model, postdevelopment and alternatives to development, *Buen Vivir*, communal logics and autonomía, subsistence and food sovereignty, and transitions to post-extractivism. While the features of the new era in the North include post-growth, post-materialist, post-economic, post-capitalist and post-dualist, those for the south are expressed in terms of post-development, post/non-liberal, post/non-capitalist, and post-extractivist. (Escobar 2011)

VI. Conclusion: Commoning and the Commons as Umbrella and Bridge Discourses

What follows is a provisional exploration, as a way to conclude, on the relation between commoning and the commons and political ontology and pluriversal studies. To begin with TDs, it is clear that there needs to be a concerted effort at bringing together TDs in the global North and the global South. There are tensions and complementarities across these transition visions and strategies – for instance, between degrowth and postdevelopment. The commons could be among the most effective umbrellas for bringing together Northern and Southern discourses, contributing to dissolve this very dichotomy. As Bollier (2014) points out, the commons entails a different way of seeing and being, a different model of socionatural life. Seen in this way, the commons is a powerful shared interest across worlds. Struggles over the commons are found across the global North and the global South, and the interconnections among them are increasingly visible and practicable (see, e.g., Bollier and Helfrich 2012). Commons debates show that diverse peoples and worlds have "an interest in common," which is nevertheless not "the same interest" for all involved, as visions and practices of the commons are world-specific (de la Cadena, 2015). Second, reflection on commons and commoning makes visible commons-destroying dualistic conceptions, particular those between nature and culture, humans and nonhumans, the individual and the communal, mind and body, and so forth (see Introduction to the volume). Commons reflection reminds those of all existing in the densest urban and liberal worlds that we dwell in a world that is alive. Reflection on the commons resituates the human within the ceaseless flow of life in which everything is inevitably immersed; it enables us to see ourselves again as part of the stream of life. Commons have this tremendous life-enhancing potential today.

Third, debates on the commons share with political ontology the goal of deconstructing the worldview and practice of the individual and the economy. No single cultural invention in the West has been more damaging to relational worlds than the disembedded "economy" and its closely associated cognate, "the autonomous individual." These two cornerstones of the dominant forms of Western liberalism and modernity need to be questioned time and again, particularly by making evident their role in destroying the commons-constructing practices of peoples throughout the planet. Working towards a "commons-creating economy" (Helfrich 2013) also means working towards the (re)constitution of relational world, ones in which the economy is re-embedded in society and nature (ecological economics); it means the individual integrated within a community, the human within the nonhuman, and knowledge within the inevitable contiguity of knowing, being and doing.

Fourth, there are a whole series of issues that could be fruitfully explored from the double perspective of commons and political ontology as paired domains. These would include, among others: alternatives to development such as *Buen Vivir*; transitions to post-extractive models of economic and social life; movements for the relocalization of food, energy, transport, building construction, and other social, cultural, and economic activities; and the revisioning and reconstruction of the economy, including proposals such as the diverse economy as suggested by Gibson-Graham et al. (2013), subsistence and community economies, and social and solidarity economies (e.g., Coraggio and Laville 2014). There are many ontological and political questions relating to these issues that cross-cut both commons and political ontology, from how to question hegemonic forms of thinking more effectively to how to imagine truly innovative ways of knowing, being and doing with respect to "the economy," "development," "resources," "sustainability," and so forth. Along the way, new lexicons will emerge – indeed, are emerging – for transitions to a pluriverse within which commoning and relational ways of being might find auspicious conditions for their flourishing.

Today, the multiple ontological struggles in defense of commons and territories, and for reconnection with nature and the stream of life, are catalyzing a veritable political awakening focused on relationality. Struggles over the commons are key examples of such activation. Moving beyond "development" and "the economy" are primary aspects of such struggles. But in the last instance our human ability to common will depend on our determination to rejoin the unending field of relations and build movements that honor the pluriverse of life.

References

Acosta, Alberto, and Esperanza Martínez, editors. 2009. *El buen vivir. Una vía para el desarrollo*. Quito: Abya-Yala.

Alayza, A. and Eduardo Gudynas, eds. 2011. *Transiciones, post-extractivismo y alternativas al extractivismo en el Perú*. Lima: RedGE y CEPES.

Berry, Thomas. 1999. *The Great Work: Our Way into the Future*. New York, NY: Bell Tower

Blaser, Mario. 2010. *Storytelling Globalization from the Chaco and Beyond*. Durham, NC: Duke University Press.

Blaser, Mario, Marisol de la Cadena, and Arturo Escobar. 2013. "Introduction: The Anthropocene and the One-World." Draft in progress for the *Pluriversal Studies Reader*.

Bollier, David. 2014. *Think Like a Commoner. A Short Introduction to the Life of the Commons*. Gabriola Island, BC: New Society Publishers.

Bollier, David, and Silke Helfrich, editors. 2012. *The Wealth of the Commons: A World Beyond Market and the State*. Amherst, MA: Levellers Press.

Coraggio, José Luis, and Jean-Louis Laville, eds. *Reinventar la izquierda en el siglo XXI. Hacia un diálogo norte-sur*. 191-206. Buenos Aires: Universidad de General Sarmiento.

Deleuze, Gilles, and Félix Guattari. 1987. *A Thousand Plateaus*. Minneapolis, MN: University of Minnesota Press.

de la Cadena, Marisol. 2015. *Earth Beings: Provincializing Nature and the Human through Andean Worlds*. Durham, NC: Duke University Press.

Escobar, Arturo. 2008. *Territories of Difference: Place~Movements~Life~Redes*. Durham, NC: Duke University Press.

Escobar, Arturo. 2011. *Encountering Development: The Making and Unmaking of the Third World*. Second Edition. Princeton: Princeton University Press.

Fals Borda, Orlando. 1984. *Resistencia en el San Jorge*. Bogota: Carlos Valencia Editores.

Fry, Tony. 2012. *Becoming Human by Design*. London: Berg.

Gibson-Graham, J.K., Jenny Cameron, and Stephen Healy. 2013. *Take Back the Economy. An Ethical Guide for Transforming Our Communities*. Minneapolis, MN: University of Minnesota Press.

Gudynas, Eduardo. 2011. "Más allá del nuevo extractivismo: transiciones sostenibles y alternativas al desarrollo". En: *El desarrollo en cuestión. Reflexiones desde América Latina*. Ivonne Farah y Fernanda Wanderley, coordinator. CIDES UMSA, La Paz, Bolivia. 379-410. http://www.gudynas.com/publicaciones/GudynasExtractivismoTransicionesCides11.pdf

Gudynas, Eduardo., and Acosta, Alberto. 2011. "La renovación de la crítica al desarrollo y el buen vivir como alternativa". *Utopía y Praxis Latinoamericana* 16(53):71-83. Venezuela. http://www.gudynas.com/publicaciones/GudynasAcostaCriticaDesarrolloBVivirUtopia11.pdf

Helfrich, Silke. 2013. "Economics and Commons?! Towards a Commons-Creating Peer Economy." presentation at "Economics and the Commons Conference," Berlin, Germany, May 22, 2013. See report on the conference, pp. 12-15, at http://www.boell.de/sites/default/files/ecc_report_final.pdf.

Ingold, Tim. 2011. *Being Alive. Essays on Movement, Knowledge, and Description*. New York, NY: Routledge.

Latouche, Serge. 2009. *Farewell to Growth*. London: Polity Press.

Law, John. 2011. "What's Wrong with a One-World World." Presented to the Center for the Humanities, Wesleyan University, September 19. Published by *heterogeneities* on September 25, www.heterogeneities.net/publications/Law 2111WhatsWrongWithAOneWorldWorld.pdf

Lisifrey, Ararat, Luis A. Vargas, Eduar Mina, Axel Rojas, Ana María Solarte, Gildardo Vanegas and Anibal Vega. 2013. *La Toma. Historias de territorio, resistencia y autonomía en la cuenca del Alto Cauca*. Bogotá: Universidad Javeriana y Consejo Comunitario de La Toma.

Massuh, Gabriela, editor. 2012. *Renunciar al bien común. Extractivismo y (pos) desarrollo en America Latina*. Buenos Aires: Mardulce.

Macy, Joanna, and Chris Johnstone. 2012. *Active Hope: How to Face the Mess We're in without Going Crazy.* Novato, California. New World Library.

Nonini, Donald. 2007. *The Global Idea of the Commons.* New York. Berghahn Books.

Ogden, Laura. 2012. *Swamplife. People, Gators, and Mangroves Entangled in the Everglades.* Minneapolis, Minnesota. University of Minnesota Press, 2011.

Oslender, Ulrich. 2008. *Comunidades negras y espacio en el Pacífico colombiano: hacia un giro geográfico en el estudio de los movimientos sociales.* Bogotá: ICANH

Randers, Jorgen. 2012. *2052: A Global Forecast for the Next Forty Years.* White River Junction, VT: Chelsea Green Publishing.

Rahnema, M. and V. Bawtree, editors. 1997. *The Post-Development Reader.* London: Zed Books.

Rist, G. 1997. *The History of Development.* London: Zed Books.

Rose, Deborah B. 2008. "On History, Trees, and Ethical Proximity." *Postcolonial Studies* 11(2):157-167.

Sachs, Wolfgang, editor. 1992. *The Development Dictionary: A Guide to Knowledge as Power.* London. Zed Books.

Santos, Boaventura de Sousa. 2002. *Towards a New Legal Common Sense.* London. Butterworth.

Vaneigem, Raoul. 1994. *The Movement of the Free Spirit.* New York. Zone Books.

Arturo Escobar *(Colombia/USA) is Professor of Anthropology at the University of North Carolina, Chapel Hill and Research Associate, Grupo Nación/Cultura/ Memoria, Universidad del Valle, Cali.*

Generalizing the Commons

By David Sloan Wilson

As an evolutionary biologist who received my PhD in 1975, I grew up with Garrett Hardin's essay "The Tragedy of the Commons," published in *Science* magazine in 1968. His parable of villagers adding too many cows to their common pasture captured the essence of the problem that my thesis research was designed to solve. The farmer who added an extra cow gained an advantage over other farmers in his village but it also led to an overgrazed pasture. The biological world is full of similar examples in which individuals who behave for the good of their groups lose out in the struggle for existence with more self-serving individuals, resulting in overexploited resources and other tragedies of non-cooperation.

Is the so-called tragedy of the commons[1] ever averted in the biological world and might this possibility provide solutions for our own species? One plausible scenario is natural selection at the level of groups. A selfish farmer might have an advantage over other farmers in his village, but a village that somehow solved the tragedy of the commons would have a decisive advantage over other villages. Most species are subdivided into local populations at various scales, just as humans are subdivided into villages, cities and nations. If natural selection between groups (favoring cooperation) can successfully oppose natural selection within groups (favoring non-cooperation), then the tragedy of the commons can be averted for humans and non-human species alike.

At the time that Hardin published his article and I was working on my thesis, this possibility had been considered and largely rejected. A book titled *Adaptation and Natural Selection*, written by evolutionary biologist George C. Williams and published in 1966, was on its way to becoming a modern classic. Williams described between-group selection as theoretically possible but almost invariably weak compared to within-group selection. By his account, attempts to explain evolutionary adaptations as "for the good of the group" reflected

---

1 | Hardin was not in fact describing a commons, but an open-access regime or free-for-all in which there is no community, rules, monitoring of usage or other features typically found in a commons.

sloppy and wishful thinking. Hardin's article reflected the same pessimism about avoiding the tragedy of the commons other than by top-down regulation. My interest in rethinking the plausibility of group selection placed me in a very small group of heretics (see Okasha 2006, Sober and Wilson 1998, Wilson and Wilson 2007, and Wilson 2015 for more on the controversy over group selection, which in my opinion has now been mostly resolved).

Evolutionary theory's individualistic turn coincided with individualistic turns in other areas of thought. Economics in the postwar decades was dominated by rational choice theory, which used individual self-interest as a grand explanatory principle. The social sciences were dominated by a position known as methodological individualism, which treated all social phenomena as reducible to individual-level phenomena, as if groups were not legitimate units of analysis in their own right (Campbell 1990). And UK Prime Minister Margaret Thatcher became notorious for saying during a speech in 1987 that "there is no such thing as society; only individuals and families." It was as if the entire culture had become individualistic and the formal scientific theories were obediently following suit.

Unbeknownst to me, another heretic named Elinor Ostrom was also challenging the received wisdom in her field of political science. Starting with her thesis research on how a group of stakeholders in southern California cobbled together a system for managing their water table, and culminating in her worldwide study of common-pool resource (CPR) groups, the message of her work was that *groups are capable of avoiding the tragedy of the commons without requiring top-down regulation*, at least if certain conditions are met (Ostrom 1990, 2010). She summarized the conditions in the form of eight core design principles: 1) Clearly defined boundaries; 2) Proportional equivalence between benefits and costs; 3) Collective choice arrangements; 4) Monitoring; 5) Graduated sanctions; 6) Fast and fair conflict resolution; 7) Local autonomy; 8) Appropriate relations with other tiers of rule-making authority (polycentric governance). This work was so groundbreaking that Ostrom was awarded the Nobel Prize in economics in 2009.

I first met Lin (as she preferred to be called) just a few months before she was awarded the prize, at a workshop held in Florence, Italy, titled "Do Institutions Evolve?" (recounted in Wilson 2011a). Similar events were taking place all over the world in 2009 to celebrate the 200th anniversary of Darwin's birth and the 150th anniversary of *On the Origin of Species*. Multilevel selection theory, which envisions natural selection operating on a multi-tier hierarchy of units, had become more widely accepted by then, especially with respect to human cultural evolution, making me much in demand as a speaker. I had also cofounded a think tank called the Evolution Institute[2] that formulates public policy from an evolutionary perspective, giving me a strong interest in the workshop topic. I had become somewhat familiar with Lin's work but having the opportunity to talk with her at length had a transformative impact.

I quickly realized that Lin's core design principle approach dovetailed with multilevel selection theory, which my fellow-heretics and I had worked so hard to revive. Her approach is especially pertinent to the concept of major evolutionary transitions, whereby members of groups become so cooperative that the group becomes a higher-level organism in its own right. This idea was first proposed by cell biologist Lynn Margulis (1970) to explain how nucleated cells evolved from symbiotic associations of bacteria. It was then generalized during the 1990s to explain other major transitions, such as the rise of the first bacterial cells, multicellular organisms, eusocial insect colonies and human evolution (Maynard Smith and Szathmary 1995, 1999).

Hunter-gatherer societies are famously egalitarian, not because everyone is nice, but because members of a group can collectively suppress bullying and other self-aggrandizing behaviors within their ranks – the defining criterion of a major evolutionary transition (Boehm 1993, 1999, 2011). With disruptive competition within groups held largely in check, succeeding as a group became the main selective force in human evolution. The entire package of traits regarded as distinctively human – including our ability to cooperate in groups of unrelated individuals, our ability to transmit learned information across generations, and our capacity for language and other forms of symbolic thought – can be regarded as forms of physical and mental teamwork made possible by a major evolutionary transition.

Lin's design principles (DP) had "major evolutionary transition" written all over them. Clearly defined boundaries (DP1) meant that members knew they were part of a group and what the group was about (e.g., fisherman with access to a bay or farmers managing an irrigation system). Proportional equivalence of costs and benefits (DP2) meant that members had to earn their benefits and couldn't just appropriate them. Collective choice arrangements (DP3) meant that group members had to agree upon decisions so nobody could be bossed around. Monitoring (DP4) and graduated sanctions (DP5) meant that disruptive self-serving behaviors could be detected and punished. Fast and fair conflict resolution (DP6) meant that the group would not be torn apart by internal conflicts of interest. Local autonomy (DP7) meant that the group had the elbow room to manage its own affairs. Appropriate relations with other tiers of rule making authority (DP8) meant that everything regulating the conduct

---

2 | http://evolution-institute.org

of individuals within a given group also was needed to regulate conduct among groups in a multi group population.

The concordance between Lin's core design principle approach and multilevel selection theory had three major implications. First, it placed the core design principle approach on a more general theoretical foundation. Lin's "Institutional Analysis and Development (IAD)" framework emanated from political science and she was an early adopter of economic game theory, but her main case for the design principle approach was the empirical database that she compiled for common-pool resource groups around the world, as described in her most influential book *Governing the Commons* (Ostrom 1990). Multilevel selection theory showed how the core design principle approach follows from the evolutionary dynamics of cooperation in all species and from our own evolutionary history as a highly cooperative species.

Second, because of its theoretical generality, the core design principle approach is likely to apply to a much broader range of human groups than those attempting to manage common-pool resources (CPRs). Almost any group whose members must work together to achieve a common goal is vulnerable to self-serving behaviors and should benefit from the same principles. An analysis of business groups, churches, voluntary associations and urban neighborhoods should yield the same results as Lin's analysis of CPR groups.

Third, the core design principle approach can provide a practical framework for improving the efficacy of groups in the real world. It should be possible for almost any kind of group to assess itself with respect to the design principles, address shortcomings, and function better as a result. This prospect was especially appealing to me as president of the Evolution Institute, since I was now actively engaged in formulating and implementing public policy from an evolutionary perspective.

Lin inspired me to begin several projects in parallel with each other. One was to collaborate with her and her postdoctoral associate Michael Cox to write an academic article, "Generalizing the Core Design Principle for the Efficacy of Groups" that established the three major implications listed above for an academic audience (Wilson, Ostrom and Cox 2013). Michael was the lead author of a 2010 article that evaluated the core design principle approach for the literature on CPR groups that had accumulated since Lin's original analysis (Cox et al. 2010). Our article was published in a special issue of the *Journal of Economic Behavior & Organization* titled "Evolution as a General Theoretical Framework for Economics and Public Policy." Both the article and the special issue should be consulted for more on the theoretical framework that underpins the design principle approach.

In addition, I started to use the design principle approach in projects that involved working with real-world groups in Binghamton, New York. One was a collaboration with the City of Binghamton and United Way of Broome County called "Design Your Own Park," which used the opportunity to turn a neglected space into a neighborhood park. Neighborhood groups that formed to create a park would be coached in the core design principles and start to manage the affairs of their neighborhood in other respects. This project led to the creation of four neighborhood parks—and their groups—in our city (Wilson 2011b).

The second project was a collaboration with the Binghamton City School District to create a "school within a school" for at-risk youth called the Regents Academy (Wilson, Kaufmann, and Purdy 2011). This was our most ambitious and best documented project because we were able to employ the gold standard of scientific assessment, the randomized control trial, which randomly assigns participants into an experimental group and a control group to identify significant variables that might affect outcomes. To the best of its ability, the Regents Academy implemented the eight core design principles and two auxiliary design principles deemed to be important in a learning context (a relaxed and playful atmosphere and short-term rewards for long-term learning goals). Not only did the Regents Academy students vastly outperform the comparison group, but they even performed on a par with the average high school student on the state-mandated Regents exam (see Wilson, Kauffman and Purdy 2011 for details). This is a strong indication that the design principle approach can be generalized beyond CPR groups and can be used as a practical framework for improving the efficacy of groups in our everyday lives.

The third project was a collaboration with a number of religious congregations in Binghamton to reflect upon the core design principles in relation to their faith and social organization. These conversations did not lead to a formal effort to change practices but they were invaluable for exploring how the success of religious groups can be understood in terms of the design principles approach.

All of these projects were instructive and broadly confirmed the relevance of the core design principle approach for any group whose members must work together to achieve a common purpose. They also showed how the design principles can be sadly lacking in some groups, such as disadvantaged neighborhoods and public schools. It is important to remember that Ostrom was able to derive the core design principles for CPR groups because they varied in how well the design principles were implemented. Some did well without needing to be taught, while others did poorly and might benefit from some coaching. Based on my own projects, I became convinced that all groups are likely to face similar challenges in implementing the core design principles.

At the same time that I was working with Lin, I was working with three leaders in the applied behavioral sciences: Tony Biglan, past president of the US-based Society for Prevention Research; Steven C. Hayes, cofounder of the Association for Contextual Behavioral Science; and Dennis Embry, a scientific entrepreneur who markets evidence-based practices for positive behavior change. I was excited to work with them because they had much more experience accomplishing positive behavioral change in real-world settings than I did. They were excited to work with me because they saw that evolutionary theory could provide a more general theoretical framework for their disciplines, in the same way as for the core design principles.

This experience underscored what's special about evolutionary theory: Now that its generality within the biological sciences has been established, it can expand its domain into the basic and applied human behavioral sciences. One result of our collaboration was a major review article, "Evolving the Future: Toward a Science of Intentional Change" (followed by peer commentaries and a reply), published in the academic journal *Behavioral and Brain Sciences* (Wilson, Hayes, Biglan and Embry 2014), a piece that expanded the theoretical foundation I was building with Lin and Michael. The first half of the article sketches a basic science of intentional change centered on evolutionary theory. The second half reviews examples of successful positive behavioral and cultural change from the applied disciplines, which illustrate the concept of wisely managing the process of cultural evolution but are little known outside their disciplinary boundaries. As we conclude our article, we are closer to a science of intentional change than one might think.

These collaborations have resulted in an ambitious Evolution Institute project called PROSOCIAL (Wilson 2014), which has three objectives. The first is to create an Internet platform that will enable any group, anywhere in the world, to evaluate itself and increase its efficacy based on a fusion of the core design principle approach and evidence-based methods from the applied behavioral sciences. The second objective is to provide a way for these groups to interact with and learn directly from each other, which is an example of facilitating the process of cultural evolution. The third objective is to use information provided by these groups to create a scientific database, much as Lin had done for common-pool resource groups, which enabled her to identify the core design principles in the first place. This project has been in the development phase for several years and should be operational and accessible through the Evolution Institute website by mid-2015.

Sadly, Lin died of cancer in June 2012. I was with her only a few months before at a workshop, "Rules as Genotypes in Cultural Evolution," which we organized together and hosted at her Workshop in Political Theory and Policy

Analysis, at Indiana University. She was simultaneously trying to care for her aging husband Vincent, satisfy the worldwide demand for speaking appearances, manage her projects and care for herself. I am grateful to be among the many who were touched by her and proud to contribute to her legacy by helping to generalize the core design principle approach and make it available to any group whose members must work together to achieve shared goals.

References

Boehm, Christopher. 1993. "Egalitarian Society and Reverse Dominance Hierarchy." *Current Anthropology*, 34:227 – 254.

———. 1999. *Hierarchy in the Forest: Egalitarianism and the Evolution of Human Altruism*. Cambridge, Mass: Harvard University Press.

———. 2011. *Moral Origins: The Evolution of Virtue, Altruism, and Shame*. New York: Basic Books.

Campbell, Donald T. 1990. "Levels of Organization, Downward Causation, and the Selection-Theory Approach to Evolutionary Epistemology." In G. Greenberg & E. Tobach, editors, *Theories of the Evolution of Knowing*, 1 – 17. Hillsdale, NJ: Lawrence Erlbaum Associates.

Cox, M., G. Arnold & S. Villamayor-Tomas. 2010. "A Review of Design Principles for Community-based Natural Resource Management." *Ecology and Society*. 15.

Hardin, Garrett. 1968. "The Tragedy of the Commons." *Science*. 162:1243-1248.

Margulis, Lynn. 1970. *Origin of Eukaryotic cells*. New Haven: Yale University Press.

Maynard Smith, John, & E. Szathmary. 1995. *The Major Transitions of Life*. New York: W.H. Freeman.

———. 1999. *The Origins of Life: From the Birth of Life to the Origin of Language*. Oxford: Oxford University Press.

Okasha, Samir. 2006. *Evolution and the Levels of Selection*. Oxford, UK: Oxford University Press.

Ostrom, Elinor. 1990. *Governing the Commons: The Evolution of Institutions for Collective Action*. Cambridge, UK: Cambridge University Press.

———. 2010. "Polycentric Systems for Coping with Collective Action and Global Environmental Change." *Global Environmental Change*. 20:550 – 557.

Sober, Elliot, & Wilson, D. S. 1998. *Unto Others: The Evolution and Psychology of Unselfish Behavior*. Cambridge, MA: Harvard University Press.

Williams, George. C. 1966. *Adaptation and Natural Selection: A Critique of Some Current Evolutionary Thought*. Princeton: Princeton University Press.

Wilson, D.S. 2011a. *The Neighborhood Project: Using Evolution to Improve My City, One Block at a Time*. New York: Little, Brown.

———. 2011b. "The Design Your Own Park Competition: Empowering Neighborhoods and Restoring Outdoor Play on a Citywide Scale." *American Journal of Play*. 3:538 – 551.

———. 2014. "Introducing PROSOCIAL: Using the Science of Cooperation to Improve the Efficacy of Your Group." *This View of Life*.

————. 2015. *Does Altruism Exist? Culture, Genes, and the Welfare of Others*. New Haven: Yale University Press.

Wilson, D.S., Kauffman, R. A., & Purdy, M. S. 2011. "A Program for At-risk High School Students Informed by Evolutionary Science." PLoS ONE, 6(11), e27826. doi:10.1371/journal.pone.0027826

Wilson, D.S., & Gowdy, J. M. 2013. "Evolution as a General Theoretical Framework for Economics and Public Policy." *Journal of Economic Behavior & Organization*. 90:S3 – S10. doi:10.1016/j.jebo.2012.12.008

Wilson, D.S., Hayes, S. C., Biglan, A., & Embry, D. 2014. "Evolving the Future: Toward a Science of Intentional Change." *Behavioral and Brain Sciences*. 37:395 – 460.

Wilson, D.S., E. Ostrom & M. Cox. 2013. "Generalizing the Design Principles for Improving the Efficacy of Groups." *Journal of Economic Behavior & Organization*. 90:supplement, S21 – S32.

Wilson, D.S., & E.O. Wilson. 2007. "Rethinking the Theoretical Foundation of Sociobiology." *Quarterly Review of Biology*. 82:327 – 348.

David Sloan Wilson *(USA) is SUNY Distinguished Professor of Biology and Anthropology at Binghamton University in Binghamton New York, President of the Evolution Institute, and Editor in Chief of the online magazine* This View of Life. *His books include* Darwin's Cathedral: Evolution, Religion, and the Nature of Society *(2002),* Evolution for Everyone: How Darwin's Theory Can Change the Way We Think About Our Lives *(2007),* The Neighborhood Project: Using Evolution to Improve My City, One Block at a Time *(2011), and* Does Altruism Exist? *(2015).*

Reality as Commons:
A Poetics of Participation for the Anthropocene

By Andreas Weber

> *"What is, then, a philosophy of relation?*
> *Something impossible, as long as it is not conceived of as poetics."*
> – Edouard Glissant

The World as Consciousness

Near Sant'Andrea, Italy, the sea laps onto the slabs of rock that form the edge of the island of Elba. The waves, smooth as fish bellies, slate gray, white, and aquamarine, shatter into liquid fragments on the rock. In the distance lies Corsica, barely visible in the haze, under a fan of fingers of light. The water that strokes the stones, the boulder rounded and worn away, the wind tousling one's hair, the birds blown by and lost again, come together in a dance. We are commoners of a commons of perception from which our own experiences, our own identities and those of the world emerge.

Our identities arise through that which we are not: through impressions and touch, through sensory exchanges with that which is stone and water, molecule and light quantum, all of which somehow transform themselves into the energy of the body. All life, from the very beginning, derives from solar energy that is given to all. Our existence in an ecosphere suffused with life is part of a vast commons even before individuality can be perceived. Each individual belongs to the world and is at the same time its owner, owner of the rough stone speckled by the waves, ruffled by the wind, stroked by rays. All perception is commons, which is to say, the result of a dance of interdependency with the world. The world belongs to us completely, and at the same time, we are fully entrusted to it. It is only through this exchange that we become conscious of it and of ourselves.

Beyond Humanism

A new self-understanding that aspires to supplant modernity is currently developing. It is still in a state of flux, unformed in many ways. But often, it can be discerned as a struggle by humanism to overcome the limits of Enlightenment rationality. It questions the separation of the world into a sphere of humans and a sphere of things that consists of natural resources, animals, objects and ideas. Humans are no longer to be at the center – but the idea of nature as an independent order is also rejected.

Proponents of this type of thinking have given it various names – "Anthropocene," "Posthumanism" and "Metahumanism," among others. What they all share is an attempt to reconceive the relationship between humanity and nature, thus articulating the human in a different way. The proponents of this project – for example, the Italian philosopher and writer Francesca Ferrando – see "an urgency for the integral redefinition of the notion of the human" (Ferrando 2013:26).

This quest will shift completely our understanding of ourselves and of the world we are part of. As a consequence it will also imply a reordering of the realms of politics and economics. If we do not see the world any longer under a duality of "human actors" and "natural resources," then the boundaries between that which is being distributed and those who are using it become blurred. In such a world, socioeconomics can no longer pursue only the goals of just and fair distribution because "producers" and "consumers" are often the same people. We can already witness this in the many commons now arising, and in those that have always been there and are now being rediscovered.

In other words, in the epoch of the Anthropocene and the posthumanist thinking it entails, a new metaphysics of "householding" is emerging, revealing how exchanges of matter and metabolites – and human meaning – are deeply intertwined. This is an astonishing opportunity to escape the dilemmas of modernity and to reimagine our ontological condition. It might be compared to the great transformation occurring at the beginning of the Enlightenment period.

Seeking a new concept of what is human, numerous thinkers are doing away with the separations between humans and "nature," "nature" and "culture," and body and mind, which have dominated our self-understanding since the Enlightenment. New propositions are challenging these dualisms and, in turn, undermining the worldview that has given rise to the neoliberal "free market" economy and the biological ideology that all organisms strive to be "efficient." The old conceptual barriers that thwarted a more benevolent relationship between humanity and the rest of the living world can now be overcome, or at least the terms of the relationships can be shifted.

Today, we are not only in a time of economic or social upheaval, but also in a crisis of self-awareness; the very metaphors we use to describe our role in the world are inadequate. This crisis of normative perception and thought offers the rare opportunity to achieve a more balanced relationship between humans and the earth than was possible with thinking that presumes a human/nature separation. But our crisis today could also result in the opposite, namely, a more commanding, coercive vision of human dominance. Will a new form of anthropocentrism, a new toxic utopia, emerge from the current competition between perspectives? Will this worldview ultimately dominate natural history by comprehending the biological solely as an object of technical creativity? Will it treat the human as a derivative version of the cyborg – a perspective that some representatives of Anthropocene thought seem to believe? Or can we instead develop a comprehensive ontology of creative aliveness?

It is imperative to go beyond Enlightenment categories of thought to recover those currents of humanism that earlier, rationalizing streams of the Western world banished. It is equally important to evaluate some important new perspectives that contemporary thought are able to add, drawing upon co-creative perspectives in biology, anthropology and poetics. To date, theories of the Anthropocene and Posthumanism do not sufficiently include the perspective of creative aliveness; this is the diagnosis of this essay. These theories still follow mainly the notion that the world can be accurately understood as a body of inert physical matter, or, that it needs human stewardship as a controlling agent or a "gardener" (Marris 2013) to fully reach its creative potential.

This essay challenges this belief by recovering the dimension that has been forgotten since the Enlightenment and has not yet been rediscovered in the Anthropocene – the radical philosophical practice and perspective of the commons, without which the relationship of humans to reality cannot be understood. I argue that reality, from which we are descended and through which we experience and engender ourselves, is itself a commons that must be understood and connected to as such.

The commons of reality is a matrix of relationships through which aliveness is unfolding in ecosystems and history. It conveys the aliveness of biological and human communities from a perspective of metabolic dependency, exchanges of gifts, and the entanglement of actors within their vectors of activity. Living participants bring each other into being by establishing relationships (metabolism, predator/prey relationships, social ties), thus producing not only their environments but their very identities (Weber 2014).

Thus, the commons describes an ontology of relations that is at the same time existential, economic and ecological. It emphasizes a process of transformation and identity formation that arises out of a mutuality that is not only material, but also experienced. For humans, then, this ontology produces meaning and emotional reality. This process also encompasses what has recently been described as "conviviality" – "an art of living together (*con-vivere*) that allows humans to take care of each other and of Nature, without denying the legitimacy of conflict, yet by using it as a dynamizing and creativity-sparking force" (Alphandéry et al 2014).

In the following pages, I will attempt to describe a perspective of reality based on connecting *all* humans and *all* other creatures. I seek to shatter the familiar categories of "culture" and "nature," which are invariably seen by moderns as separate and distinct. The two realms are in fact one, if we can recognize that reality is founded upon aliveness as the critical, connecting element. Aliveness is not limited to "nature" or "culture." It is intrinsic to all social and biological systems. It has an objective, empirical substance and a subjective, tangible dimension, and it is always interweaving dimensions of matter with perception and experience (Weber 2013).

It is therefore essential that we elucidate a self-understanding of the Anthropocene from this perspective – an ontology of the commons. After all, without this perspective to complete the picture, the Anthropocene – the new epoch characterized by the dominance of human beings – would disregard a core attribute of reality. To distinguish the necessary new perspective from the technical rationality of the Enlightenment, I refer to this emerging perspective as Enlivenment – a theme that I explored in a previous essay (Weber 2013). Enlivenment is an ontology of aliveness, of coming to life, that is at once physical and intangible, and scientific and spiritual. It calls people to live in an unfolding natural history of freedom and self-realization.

The Anthropocene Hypothesis as a Commodification of the Creative

How, exactly, do the many, burgeoning posthumanist interpretations of our time fail to grasp the cosmos as a creative reality? Let us begin with the Anthropocene. Today, climate researchers assume that humans have become the defining biogeochemical force on Earth since the year 1800, more or less, and that the Holocene era, the phase that started with the last Ice Age, has ended (Crutzen & Stoermer 2000:17-18). Today, we are living in the "epoch of mankind," the Anthropocene. This hypothesis, of course, is not only a scientific finding about the history of the climate: it is simultaneously a cosmological statement about the status of human beings, one that eliminates the familiar division of reality into a sphere of human activity and a sphere of nature.

It is this variant of the Anthropocene hypothesis that is increasingly affecting our deliberations on how to achieve sustainability. Its focus is frankly solipsistic – how should we humans deal with other animals and plants, and what changes should we make to our economic system? But this view lacks a critical element – an account of the more-than-human world as a living reality. The Anthropocene hypothesis may help us overcome thinking that pits humans against nature, but it fails precisely in that endeavor as long as it celebrates humans as the masters of nature. Anthropocene thinkers often enthusiastically annex the planet into the sphere of culture in what appears like a philosophical equivalent of globalization; reality is re-cast to ratify the triumph of human beings over the natural world.

To be sure, our earlier concepts of "nature" are obsolete, but not in the sense that they would have to find their place in the human world. Rather, the Anthropocene is misguided because it projects human methods for solving problems onto a cosmos that is still not understood. It speaks from within the mindset of human power. Sustainability pioneer Wolfgang Sachs observes, "At first, the term 'Anthropocene' expressed the diagnosis of anxiety. Ten years on, it meant power of authority" – a methodology of domination (personal communication, July 21, 2014).

If we consider "nature" to be formed predominantly by culture and technology, the Anthropocene consummates the colonialization of elemental nonhuman creative forces that Western culture has dreamed of for centuries. In other words, Anthropocene thinking is proving to be a new, more extensive iteration of enclosure. To advance narrow human purposes, it not only seizes control of self-organizing creative forces in nature (e.g., genetic engineering, nanotechnologies); it also seizes the self-organizing wild creativity within us.

Admittedly, it is hard to determine who is to blame for this habit of thinking, which is so deeply anchored in the self-understanding of the West as to be utterly invisible. We are not talking about a particular discourse, but the very foundation of our concept of reality. Forms of thinking and feeling that deviate from this sense of reality are hardly possible. Or they are considered "unscientific" and thus unserious. This subtle cognitive form of enclosure occurs with the best of intentions. Since the early modern period, the "Bacon project" has sought to achieve the separation of humans and resources. This is the quest for total self-empowerment of mankind that began with the British Renaissance scholar Francis Bacon's "*novum organon*" (Schäfer 1993). This project was intended to improve human life and keep death in check. The logic and appeal of this worldview remain very much in force today. In the realm of ecology, for example, humans often regard "nature" as an inert physical Other – or they may consider themselves stewards of natural systems and their functions, which are essential for our survival.

Yet this arrangement paradoxically deepens the gulf between what is human and the rest of the world. In the end, such a stance tempts people to conceive of everything nonhuman as a soulless physical resource. From here, it is only a small step to its actual transformation into a commodity, a saleable good that can be used however we wish. Once we adopt this orientation toward the world, all further enclosures seem as necessary and desirable steps. Every physical enclosure of wild and emotionally unbridled reality can be traced back to this separation of living entities from the living context of which they are a part – a separation that neutralizes the generative power of life itself.

This dynamic can be seen in the enclosures of commons in sixteenth century England, the patenting of the human genome and in the sterile, proprietary seeds produced by gene patenting. Such outcomes are the inevitable physical expressions of a conceptual dualism, as it were, that elevates a narrow human instrumentality over the essential wildness of reality.

Dualism as an Invisible Colonialization of the Soul

This dualism is not a mere abstraction; it has been the driving force separating humans from the experience of creative vitality. It also lies at the heart of the historical Enlightenment idea that the world can become a habitable place only by means of reason, which itself is the basis for the logic of the market that also differentiates between actors and things. All of these phenomena have the same roots and are the consequence of an enclosure that is initially imaginary. The liberal market system, which makes a distinction between resources (which are traded) and subjects (who trade or who want to be supplied with things), is the product of this dualism. Dualism has appeal because it is a method for asserting control by dividing the world in two: an inanimate sphere ("nature") that is to be dominated and a sphere of human subjects ordained to assert control.

From this perspective, there is no difference between enclosure, commodification, and colonialization. All three not only attack living systems that have no single owner, they at the same time trample on the psychological and emotional identities connected to these resources. They are all attacks on "aliveness" itself – a capacity of life that is unavailable and incomprehensible to the dualistic mind. Therefore, they are also attacks on reality. In this vein, political scientist David Johns (2014:42) observes, "Colonialism is nowhere more apparent and thriving than in the relationship between humanity and the rest of the earth."

Actual action thus is always preceded by a tacit enclosure sanctioned by the deep assumptions of the mind. Enclosure usurps the categories of existence and disparages the concept of aliveness as well as the dimensions of experience linked to it. The practices of conceptual enclosure preemptively deny the existence of an unavailable Other, making it impossible to conceptualize and honor real, subjective experience. This Other is not only "nature" or a person from a foreign culture; it is *the experience* of a dimension of reality that can only be lived and not captured by rational conceptualization. This Other is the domain of physically experienced reality that precedes all conceptualization and colonialization: it is the bliss when we watch the sun rise or see a beloved partner or a young dog, or the dimension of meaning in a piece of work that benefits everyone and not just ourselves. It is the domain of what Manfred Max-Neef catalogues as "human needs" – the existential dimensions of healthy relationships to self and others (Smith & Max-Neef 2010).

Enclosure occurs through a type of thinking that ignores creative processes and the meanings of emotions, both of which originate in the body. Enclosure instead subordinates these feelings to "rationality," "stewardship," empiricism, discursivity and control. Such thinking culminates in the idea that "nature" and the body themselves do not exist, but are solely artifacts of culture. In modern culture, it is considered naïve to believe that "nature" can be experienced as a domain of creative unfolding, or that there is a perceptible kinship of being alive that is shared by all living things and which can be experienced. This reality is denied by our cognitive frameworks and language, resulting in what amounts to mental and spiritual enclosure. This colonialization of our innermost essence inescapably results in an "empty self," as biophilosopher David Kidner (2014:10) predicts. This de facto "empty self" is indeed diagnosed by many as a current psychopathological "civilizational narcissism" that marks our times.

In humanity's resurgent obsession with treating Earth as a raw, inert resource (e.g., geoengineering to forestall climate change, synthetic biology to "improve upon" nature, etc.), the Enlightenment is pushing one last time for sovereignty over the cosmos. Here the Anthropocene is completely identical with Anthropocentrism. The old notions of human superiority, control and technical mastery are concealed by *equating* humans and "nature," putting them on an equal footing. Even a sophisticated theorist such as Bruno Latour falls for this category error when he reassures his readers, "The sin is not to wish to have dominion over nature but to believe that this dominion means emancipation and not attachment" (quoted in Shellenberger & Nordhaus 2011). Since people are in fact connected in relationships (with the Earth, with each other), the fallacy lies in attempting to dominate what embraces them in ways they do not understand; they are blind to reality and prone to act destructively.

Italian philosopher Ugo Mattei believes that even the act of dividing the world into subject and object results in commodifying both (quoted in Bollier 2014). The commodification of the spirit inevitably finds a warped expression at the real and political level. "Nature" is banished to the periphery of the human world even though it still nourishes and sustains us, produces everything we eat, and remains the wellspring of creative energy. Every separation into subject and object divides the world into two realms, resources and profiteers. This boundary is not necessarily between things and people (or between matter and creatures), but between that which is used up, and those who benefit from that consumption.

Thus, we are suffering not only because of the commodification of the natural and social world. We are suffering because our conceptualization of the world itself allows commodification as the sole way to relate to it. It is no longer possible to speak about the world in the categories of subjective aliveness. We are suffering because of the enclosure of the spiritual through myriad cultural fictions of separation and domination that falsely parse the world into an outside (resource) and inside (actor). Concepts such as strict cause-and-effect relationships, causal mechanisms, the separation of body and soul – all of them fundamental premises of Enlightenment thinking – result in our taking reality hostage. We colonize it by believing in the concept of a treatable, repairable, controllable world. Any experience that contradicts this enclosure of reality must be discounted or denied.

Yet hardly anyone is aware of the profoundly misleading taxonomic screens of our language and worldview. We can barely imagine the extent to which our view of reality is distorted by spiritual enclosure. We do not realize that the self-organizing nature of our everyday lives has disappeared from view – a dispossession far more radical than the one experienced by commoners locked out of their forests a few hundred years ago. We do not appreciate how conceiving of our own selves as biomachines has impoverished us as humans, and how treating our emotional feelings chiefly as "chemical imbalances" (to be corrected through pharmaceuticals) denies an elemental dimension of our humanity.

Cutting living subjects off from participating in the commons of reality and its mixture of practices and emotions, objects and aspects of meaning, is destructive in another serious respect: It blinds us to the nature of enclosure itself. As psychologists Miguel Benasayag and Gérard Schmit (2007:101f) observe, the overarching ideology of enclosure is an ideology of control and dominance, and a denial of enduring relationships. This systemic worldview is not simply unjust and dangerous, it brazenly defies reality. It is cruel because it violates the web of relational exchange which reality *is*.

Every metaphysics that separates humans from the world furtively transforms itself into an inhumane ideology. The ideology of enclosure is inhumane because it generates a hierarchy in reality, ostensibly for human benefit, by installing humanity as custodian of the rational, the protector of the ordered, the knight battling chaos. Yet reality is not chaotic. On the contrary, it simply embodies an order that we are not always able to discern. Reality is structured as a creative expression of living agents, both human and more-than-human. Its structure, however, is sometimes invisible because its systems cannot be universalized, regimented or monetized without destroying life itself.

Posthumanism as an Extension of Our Machine Dreams

A flurry of new critiques are ostensibly seeking to break away from the dualisms of the Enlightenment by using "post" in their names – for example, postenvironmentalism or posthumanism. Regrettably, they do not really come to terms with creative reality. Instead they put forward hybrid versions of human nature that exist between "object" and "subject." But ultimately they are not rooted in the processes of the creative wild, but in technological artifacts made by humans.

Posthumanism is in fact fixated on machines. It is mostly about cyborgs and hybrid humans, and has little interest in grasshoppers, geckos or the integration of the natural and the social as we see, say, in indigenous communities' systems of thought. With the notable exception of the influential Donna Haraway, a feminist scholar who writes extensively about human-machine and human-animal relations, posthumanism wants little to do with other species. Posthumanism is oriented toward machines because they are our species-specific creations. They are artifacts that bear witness to this special feature of ours, namely being not only biological creatures of the cosmos, but also sovereign creators, controllers and engineers. Technical hybrids – i.e., humans whose cognitive abilities are enhanced by means of electronic tools or combinations of humans and machines – represent a type of the wild that fascinates many posthumanist thinkers. But a genuine posthumanism would recognize that we must imagine the deconstruction of the machines as functional essence of what is human. The "function" of our hands, after all, is not just to pick up things, but to be able to sensitively caress a stone, a loved one's neck, or a black poodle's fur in the warm sun.

Posthumanism as now conceived still erects walls around a colony of abstraction. It strictly guards an enclave of rationality and shies away from the practice of living connectedness. And so except for sporadic lapses when the metaphysical fabric accidentally rips, posthumanism continues to overlook the enclosure of the living body as a place of experience, feeling and self. It fails to see itself as a vehicle for any sort of exchange with the Other. Every self-styled philosophy of emancipation is on shaky ground if it is not clear about the self-concealed enclosures of the wild that it commits against our selves, our thinking and our identities.

Recognizing the Commons of Existence: The Key to the Anthropocene

The hypothesis of the Anthropocene, namely that "man and nature are one today," can be considered in a meaningful way only if it acknowledges a theory of reality as a commons. A concept of the Anthropocene can be fruitful only if we do not grasp it as yet another "epoch of humankind," but as an epoch in which the living co-creative reality of ecosystems becomes the foundation for how humans perceive and experience reality.

To this end, we must recognize reality itself as a commons that is pressing forward to unfold in a natural history of freedom. This history must embrace the role of the bodies and subjective experiences of all living subjects. The point is that commons are not only entities designed by humans. They are an existential, self-created necessity of all living exchange – i.e., of life itself. As theologian Martin Buber (1937) puts it, "all actual life is encounter." All reality, every act of perception which accesses and produces the world, is a negotiation, a creative transformation between two poles, each of which is at the same time object and actor.

Even in our absence, reality is a commons. We can approach it by shaping it according to a pattern of mutual giving and giving in return, and then witness the transformational ripples following from each act of giving. Human culture has the opportunity to shape the world as a commons as it participates in the web of interdependent living things, thus making the world more real. In the Anthropocene, this new perspective on natural history as the unfolding of freedom and depth of experience and expression should be put at center stage. This idea, not a narrow vision of human instrumentality, should explicitly guide our self-understanding and our economic and political agenda. Without such an orientation, we will continue to act destructively toward other living things and our planet.

As a philosophy and practice, commoning considers the coexistence of living things on this planet as a joint, creative process, one that increases the aliveness of the biosphere and the cultural sphere. Thinking in the categories of the commons actualizes an ontology that, while not fundamentally new in Western thinking, has been underestimated and suppressed for a long time. This ontology alone makes it possible for us to grasp the conditions of evolutionary reality in which we exist and then to play a constructive part in shaping the unfolding reality. The existential realities of the world have brought us forth as participants in the natural history of the cosmos and its social, metabolical, and existential dimensions; we in turn are continually extending and recreating this natural history.

A commons is a way of entering into relationships with the world, both materially and conceptually. It does so without the usual dualistic concepts of the Enlightenment (culture/nature, animate/inanimate, etc.) and it fuses theory and practice as one. Principles of acting are embedded in concrete, situational processes of conflict, negotiation and cooperation, which in turn alter reality and generate new situations.

All principles that animate this process are intrinsic to it and cannot come from "outside" of it. The principles do not fall into our laps, and no god, state or moral-philosophical process of any kind can posit them. At the same time, however, the process of commoning – and this is true of the commons of reality, too – is anything but devoid of rules. It follows the principles for how creative relationships arise among various counterparties and thereby create their identities, shape their bodies and determine their interests. Commoning is an ecological and evolutionary reality based on concrete interactions, which always have to mediate between the flourishing of individuals and the pros-perity of the encompassing whole. In this sense, existential success always is a negotiation between autonomy and fusion. Its shape can never be codified because it is a living, dynamic process; existential success can only be lived.

In this reading, all commons are "posthuman." Our undeniable human agency is inscribed within a living system of other animate forces, each of which is both sovereign and interdependent at the same time. In commons, humankind does not hold arbitrary sway as a ruler, but as an attentive subject in a network of relationships. The effects of (inter)actions reflect back on those acting and all other nodes, animated or metaphorical – human subjects, bats, fungi, bacteria, aesthetic obsessions, infections, or guiding concepts – are active as well. Every commons is a rhizome – a material and informal network of living connections which constantly changes as it mutates and evolves.

The innermost core of aliveness cannot be classified and negotiated ratio-nally. It is only possible to be involved in experiences and creative expression. That is why the idea of the commons, which is fundamentally about real subjects seeking nourishment and meaning through physical, pragmatic, material and symbolical means, is the best way to describe a "posthuman" connection to the rest of the biosphere. For a commons is always an embodied, material, perceptible, existential and symbolic negotiation of individual existence through the Other and the whole. It is an attempt to echo the forms of order implied in the self-creating wild through acts of creative transformation, in response to the existential imperatives of the wild.

Each of these acts involves both self-awareness and material interactions. Each is real and metabolic in that the participants of the ecosystem are linked together through the exchange of eating and being devoured, of taking and giving, and of subtly influencing the order of the whole and being influenced by it. This process is imaginative because it is triggered by the experiences of joy, fear and other feelings – which in turn are the basis for consequential actions and material changes.

The concept of the commons helps bridge – and transcend – the dualities that otherwise structure our self-awareness. It bridges the connection between the "natural" – the world of beings and species – and the "social" or "cultural" – the sphere of human-made symbolic systems, discourses and practices – by generating an interdependent, organic whole. For this reason, conceiving of "nature" as a commons of living entities is also a way of understanding ourselves anew. It helps us see and name our biological and our social aliveness as an indivisible whole conjoined to the rest of the world.

An ontology that describes reality through the lens of the commons, in other words, makes it possible to focus on aliveness as both a conceptual idea and experience. Therein slumbers the opportunity to arrive at a new, relational understanding of ourselves and the world. Going beyond "objective" structures, algorithms, and cause-and-effect scenarios that look at observable external behaviors, we can also take account of the internal feelings of the actors (which are motive-forces in their own right), and thereby escape the sterile dualism that has crippled the Western mind for so long.

The Anthropocene can reconcile and integrate humans and "nature" only if we comprehend that we exist as agents who are continuously transformed in a process that is both material and filled with meaning – a process that experiences itself emotionally and reproduces itself creatively, and in so doing generates and expresses ever more complex degrees of freedom (in a larger context of dependency on other living systems).

In this sense, "nature" and "human" are aligned and quite literally identical. Both rely on "imagination" to produce a world and self-reproduce themselves. Our identities are rooted in the uncontrollable wild and in creative self-organization, neither of which can be entirely subject to control or "stewardship." Such control (even when asserted through enclosure) cannot prevail ultimately because the instruments of control that we devise are themselves built on "uncontrollable forms" – wildness – which remain beyond strict control and understanding. So while humans may "dominate" "nature" in ways that posthumanism celebrates, conversely, we humans are grounded by forces of wildness that ultimately cannot be subdued and mastered through cultural control because culture relies on them as the basic principles of creation, self-organization and co-creative relations.

In regarding reality as commons, we do not resolve the contradictions of existence by reducing them to one aspect – only mind, only matter, only discourse, only market. Nor do we seek anything such as a higher synthesis – the classic, devastating response to the paradoxes of existence ever since Hegel and then his student Marx, who promised a contradiction-free, higher state of being that drove utopians mad in violent anticipation.

The mundane reality is that true being is "higher" and "lower" at the same moment. And for a simple reason: What is alive resists any and all synthesis. Inner, immaterial and experiential identity, coiled within a material body, is itself the greatest paradox. This identity, which becomes real only through a body, has no separate physical mass and occupies no space. And yet still it profoundly alters the physical world and space through a continual and self-referential process.

This dimension of living reality should follow a "dialogic" rather than a binary logic, as French philosopher Edgar Morin claims. Morin's dialogic does not try to eliminate contradictions but explicitly seizes them to illuminate the point. Living reality is a logic of dialogue and polyphony, of encounters, conversations, mutual transformations and interpretations, in the logic of negotiation and striking compromises (Morin 2001:272). It is this stance of negotiating, adapting and enduring that has determined the way in which humans have dealt with the commons since time immemorial. It is what is called commoning.

Poetic Materialism

The Anthropocene lacks the understanding that any exchange – of things (in the economy), of meanings (in communication), of identities (in the bond between subjects) – always has two sides: an external, material side and also an internal, existential side in which meaning is expressed and experienced. *Reality is creative and expressive precisely because it never lets itself be reduced to one of these sides.* Since all processes are founded upon relationships that convey meanings (which all subjects experience as emotions), the most appropriate way to formulate such a reality is through the idea of *poetics*.

The poetic dimension is the world of our feelings, our social bonds, and everything that we experience as significant and meaningful. Poetics is at the same time symbolic and material and therefore it is inextricably linked to social communication, exchange and interactions with others and the environment. Poetics describes the world that we experience in the perspective of the first person – the world in which we are at home in an intimate way and the world that we seek to protect through political arrangements. Economic exchange, which is always a meaningful householding among living beings, also takes place in this world described by a poetic reality.

In our time, the great discourses – empirical rationality, human freedom as a rational actor, instrumental reason in economics – are being exposed as deficient, provoking a mad scramble to salvage them as coherent perspectives. The real issue of our time, then, is to activate a new language. After 300 years of Enlightenment thinking, the challenge is to redefine aliveness and humanity within it by complementing *techné* with the concept of *poiesis*. *Techné* means explainability, analysis and successful replication. *Poiesis*, by contrast, means creative self-realization – an element that brings forth reality, that cannot be suppressed, and that can never be sufficiently understood to be successfully controlled.

In the end, everything is *techné* in one sense – but in another, everything is also *poiesis*. *Techné* is cause and effect, control, management, understanding, exchange. *Poiesis* is inner goal-directedness, bringing forth oneself, giving oneself over, self-expression, feeling, and accepting. *Techné* is planning and sustainability. *Poiesis* is the "wasteful" promiscuity of creation. Life needs both. Reality is both. Creative transformation grows out of the tension of this contradiction without ever resolving it.

Perhaps one could call such a perspective *poetic materialism*. Any thinking in relationships can take place only in the form of poetic acts. Living relationships, however, organize themselves only among bodies which constantly transform themselves, which grow and decay. In systems in which change occurs dynamically as participants seek to negotiate and transform each other, experience cannot be expressed as a fixed identity, but only as the transient expression of one through the other – in other words, poetically.

The poetic dimension is simultaneously a modification of the individual and a modification of the whole. It becomes distinct and visible in an individual only through forms of experience and symbolic expression. In this sense, as a poetics of relationships defines the individual reality, and a poetics of relationships can be understood as a commons, reality appears to the individual as a commons. Systematic thinking joined with the lived practice of commons – commoning – are based on a poetics of relations. Their idea of exchange considers both embodied things and the existential (inner) reality of meaning and feeling. All are aspects of a "creative householding" – the ability to express and experience things, which constitute the freedom that is constantly being enacted in natural history.

The idea of understanding reality through the lens of a "poetics of relation" was first formulated by the French-Carribean poet and philosopher Edouard Glissant. Glissant calls his poetics a "creolization of thinking": a mutual transformation and fertilization of self and other without clear hierarchies. Everyone involved has equal standing. They are actors and objects. They belong to themselves. And they can be means – even food – to everyone else (see Glissant 1997).

A creolization of thinking requires "peership" between empirical reality and feeling. All processes take place inside and outside an organism simultaneously; they are always conceptual and spiritual, but they are also always real in space and time. Taking the step across the abyss between the two cultures means understanding and reevaluating creative aliveness as the center of reality. Creative action is the experience of what is alive, as experienced from the inside, subjectively. One might call it "affective objectivity" – a universal and real phenomenon, but one that is also evanescent and resistant to measurement.

Indian geographer Neera Singh has shown the extent to which this emotive power encourages commoners to act and provides subjective rewards for their action. She demonstrates that villagers in rural India not only make resources more productive through their commoning with forests. They also satisfy emotional needs and "transform their individual and collective subjectivities" (Singh 2013). They are engaging in an active poetics of relating, in which the human affect and the "material world" commune with each other and alter one another.

It bears emphasizing that "collective subjectivity" extends beyond the human community to include the subjectivities of the living environment – the trees, the supportive vegetation, the birds, the flows of water, the "real" ecosystem elements that human subjectivities actually alter. Commoners, one could say, follow a *poetic reason* that has emotive substance, but also material manifestations in people's bodies, community life and local ecosystems. The poetic moment of their action manifests itself when the living forest and social community flourish together, in entangled synergy. This is something that can be perceived by the senses and experienced emotionally through the forest's opulent biodiversity (and yes, also measured, but the measurements will invariably fail to grasp the animating power of the human affect).

It is telling that cultures for whom participation in natural processes amounts to emotional engagement in a poetic reality, do not make the distinctions between "animate" and "inanimate" or "nature" and "culture" – dualities that are taken for granted in Western thinking. The basic affective experience of being in a lively exchange with the world, taking from it and contributing to it, is denied by the West's worldview and language: a perniciously subliminal type of enclosure.

Singh calls the psychological-emotional engagement arising from caring for a commons "emotional work." In the absence of this affective dimension, both subject and object lose their paired identities: those working on the land, say, as well as the object of such work, the animate whole. Geographers and philosophers are increasingly beginning to comprehend land and people as a lived reality – a factor of real interactions and an existential, poetic enactment.

If such a commons is colonized – which today would mean to be reduced to a mere resource by industrial agriculture – the emotional needs of the people involved – belonging, meaning, identity – can no longer be fulfilled. This is precisely what has happened to our purportedly modern minds – a colonization of emotions that are denounced as backward, superstitious, unenlightened or unscientific. The emotional work of caring for a commons, however, is both an ecological necessity and a material reality, as well as it is a psychological need. Therefore the collapse of affect (belonging, meaning, identity) has material consequences. As human relationships to an ecosystem erode, so does respect for the ecosystem, and the ecosystem's stability. A kind of ecological death occurs, in turn, one that has both spiritual and biodiversity-related dimensions. The two depend on one another and balance one another.

In other words, *a healthy culture is a co-creative interpretation of nature in all its irrepressible aliveness.* That is why subjectivity, cooperation, negotiation and irreconcilable otherness must not be seen as patterns that only we lay upon the world, as is currently done by most economy and culture approaches. Rather it is the other way round: Subjectivity, meaning-creation, "weak" non-causal interaction, code and interpretation are deep features of living nature. Its most basic principle comes down to the paradoxical self-realization of an individual through the whole, which at the same time is "the other" that needs to be fenced off.

Need, distance and momentary balance in beauty: Aliveness as such is a commoning process. Perception thus becomes a co-creative commons integrating a subject concerned with care for its self and its environment – which both mutually imagine, nourish and bring forth one another. In this perspective our deeper feelings are themselves a distinguishing feature of patterns of creative aliveness. They affect the perceptions of subjects and impel them to participate in a co-creative commons with their environment; subjects and environment actively imagine, nourish and engender each other.

Culture therefore is not structurally different from nature in the sense that it is only human – a feature putting man apart as incommensurate with the remainder of the world. Nature, on the other hand, is not underlying human culture in a reductionist sense. Nor can all cultural structures can be explained (socio-)biologically. The causal-mechanic, efficiency-centered approach as a whole is mistaken. Nature is based on meaning, open to creative change and constantly bringing forth agents with subjective experiences. It is always creative in order to mediate the realization of the individual through the whole. Any exchange-relationship in Nature always involves both metabolism and meaning, and in this way generates feeling. Nature is a process of unfolding freedom, tapping inexhaustible creativity and intensifying experiential and expressive depth (Weber 2015).

In this sense (although not in any superficial, reductionistic pattern), culture has to be like nature. This is an idea somewhat parallel to what philosopher

Theodor W. Adorno (2013) is claiming when he argues that any art worthy of its name does not copy nature's objects but rather follows its deep process of creative unfolding, freedom and "non-identity" – the impossibility of reducing an agent to just one substance, be that a causal mechanism or language-games. Culture is structurally not different from ecological exchange processes, but echoes them in the human species-specific creative forms. It expresses our own poetic interpretation of the ever-recurring theme of coping with the ir- resolvable paradox of autonomy and wholeness. That is why human culture cannot control and engineer nature as a passive, non-living object. Because we humans are implicated in the creative aliveness of nature, our culture must also honor our own aliveness as the best way to foster our own freedom and long-term survival. We must shape our selfhood according to the needs of a larger whole that is necessary to all life. Autonomy is always inscribed within a larger whole and only possible through it. Paradoxically, autonomy is possible only through relation.

Seen from this perspective, it becomes essential to adopt a first-person viewpoint as a counterpoint to the purportedly scientific perspective of "objective reality," which is typically expressed in the third person. In the ontological reality that we are describing here, the first-person perspective is both poetic (rich with meaning, feeling and implications for identity) while genuinely objective (material, scientifically measurable). The first-person viewpoint mediates our perception with our material reality, which is only possible from the perspec- tive of a meaning-making self (see Weber & Varela 2002 for more details). Internal, first-person insights that were ruled out by a worldview that accepts only the empirical/objective point of view – because they are not "real" in the material, physical sense – become valid. Once natural ecosystems are seen as creatively alive, it becomes necessary to complement rational thinking and empirical observation with the "empirical subjectivity" of living things, and its complement, the "poetic objectivity" of meaningful experiences. This new standpoint cannot be dismissed as a soft, vague emotion, but must be heeded as a critical genre of evolutionary intelligence.

As living organisms, we must learn to experience and describe the world "from the inside" (emotionally, subjectively, socially) while at the same time treating it as a physical reality outside of us. Poetic objectivity is a solution to the destructive dualities that since the Enlightenment have separated the human species as above and apart from "nature." Poetic objectivity represents the missing first-person-centered perspective in human culture that must act as a complement to the dominant but partial objectivist approach.

Commoning as Partaking in Reality

This essay has so far focused on the philosophical dimensions of the challenge facing humankind, but of course, the practical test is how to bring this ontological sensibility into the world and make it real. Fortunately, the social practices of creating and maintaining a commons – commoning – offer excellent opportunities for blending the subjective and objective, humanity and "nature," and for overcoming the many other dualisms that deny our creative aliveness.

The process of commoning challenges the dualisms upon which "the economy" as conventionally understood is based. It does this by enacting different roles than those ordained by neoliberal economics and policy (such as "producer" and "consumer," and "investor" and "natural resource") and by building provisioning systems that are oriented toward meeting basic needs in situated contexts, and in ways that generate a sense of life and personal integration. The point of commoning projects and policies is to restore enlivenment to the center of any economy activity, which means it must strive to reflect the shared interests of all, subjective human needs and the integrity of natural ecosystems.

This can be seen in Anne Salmond's essay in this volume (pp. 309-329), which describes how the culture of the Māori people in New Zealand expresses "the fundamental kinship between people and other life forms....They are linked together in an open-ended, dynamic set of complex networks and exchanges." The same idea is expressed by the notion of *Buen Vivir*, the idea of "good living" that people in Ecuador and Bolivia use to speak about living in mindful ways with *Pachamama* ("Mother Earth"), the community and one's ancestors. Needless to say, this poses serious challenges to the "modernist cosmo-logic" of the nation-state and capitalist markets. Traditional and contemporary examples add to an endless number of human ways to relate to the Other, social and natural, and defy the artificial borders of animate and inanimate. In so doing, these forms of commoning represent identity systems "beyond nature and culture," as Collège-de-France anthropologist Philippe Descola (2013) has it.

Such patterns of commoning are not confined to people with premodern cultural roots. Even people raised in that modernist cosmo-logic of globalized industry and commerce are building commons that nourish an ontology of creative aliveness. The permaculture network is deliberately designing and engineering forms of agriculture in alignment with ecological forces. A key principle of permaculture is "integrate rather than separate," so that farming practices build relationships among those things that work together and support each other.[1] For its part, the Burning Man community celebrates the principles of "radical inclusion" and "communal effort" in conjunction with

---

1 | See "Twelve Design Principles of Permaculture," on pp. 113-114.

"radical self-reliance," "participation" and "immediacy."[2] The point is to honor the wildness within every human being while insisting upon a civil social order and sustainable relationship to the land.

The idea of *working with* the forces of nature and the social dynamics of living communities – rather than trying to deny them, bureaucratize them or forcibly overpower them – is a key principle of commons-based governance. It is why social critics like Ivan Illich embraced the commons as a path for the spiritual reintegration of people in the face of a dehumanizing modernity. The commons helps move in this direction because it honors "affective labor" as a critical force binding people to each other, to natural systems and to earlier and future generations. The commons cultivates identity, meaning, ritual and culture among people as they work with resources to meet their everyday needs. In the process "resources" are retransformed into things that are inflected with personal and community meaning. The artful blending of the social, moral and physical into an integrated commons is what gives the commons paradigm such durability and power. It taps into wellsprings of creative aliveness in people and in so doing engenders deep satisfaction, identity, commitment, flexibility and vitality.

It is admittedly a difficult challenge for the nation-state born of ultra-rational Enlightenment principles to engineer new types of law and public policy to recognize and support commoning. The cosmo-logic of a liberal, modernist polity has trouble understanding the efficacy or desirability of governance based on subjective feelings, locally rooted knowledge and singular historical relationships; the bureaucratic state prefers to govern with universalized abstractions and atomized individuals shorn of their histories and contexts. Paradoxically, this is arguably why the nation-state and bureaucratic organizations are increasingly losing the loyalty, respect and commitment of people – their remote, impersonal modes of governance have become indifferent to the creative aliveness that human beings need and invariably seek.

The idea of citizen/consumers interacting with the market/state duopoly to advance their self-interests corresponds to the individual seeking to act smartly and efficiently to be a sovereign agent using all available resources to build up an identity and resilient self. When personal identity is regarded from this standpoint, it naturally follows that other subjects, human or otherwise, to whom the self becomes attached, are legitimately seen as mere resources for advancing one's interests. Relationships in this picture become solely a means to a selfish end, a way of functionalizing the Other, rather than open-ended, imperfect processes of transformative exchange.

---

2 | See Larry Harvey, "The Principles of Burning Man," on pp. 140-141.

This may also be why so many commoners working on open networks – e.g., open source software, open design and production, open source agriculture, and much else – are outflanking markets that prize predictable financial gains over all else. Businesses may recognize the abundance that can be produced through common-based peer production, which necessarily draws upon people's creative aliveness – but they are structurally designed to enclose the commons because of their ontological commitment to the subject/object division which is perfectly executed by money. Money is a means to objectify and separate. Putting a price on something reduces self-contained purpose to mere function. Therefore cash-based relationships generally disdain the value of "affective labor" and long-term commitments. Through its deep alliance with markets, the state generally colludes in denying the ontological reality of living systems despite the existential catastrophes that are now raining down on the entire planet, notably in the form of climate change.

The guardians of the state and "free market" would do well to admit their own structural limitations and legally recognize commons as a salutary form of governance. But as products of modernity and its cosmo-logic, the Market/State is mostly unable to participate as a respectful peer in the natural history of the planet; it is unwilling to acknowledge creative aliveness as an ontological foundation of reality.

It is telling that many proponents of the Anthropocene who interpret it as an epoch of world-gardening and technological stewardship over the biosphere – such as Shellenberger and Nordhaus (2013) and Marris (2013) – celebrate ultra-neoliberal free-market approaches as the best way to organize human interactions with the rest of the biosphere, and to distribute and allocate goods, and make sense of the world. They hail market creativity as the key force for inventing planet-healing technologies. This alone confirms that the postdualism of the Anthropocene is in fact still entirely anthropocentric; we are still enacting Enlightenment principles, but this time it hides behind a different mask.

This is why the tendency of certain sustainablity thinkers to hail "green economy" ecological economics and "green accounting" is questionable. To "factor in" natural services may be a quick, expedient amendment and it may in fact help otherwise-endangered ecosystems. Still, it deeply misunderstands the nature of our relationship with reality. As explained above, it fails to recognize that any exchange process is always and inevitably happening on many entangled, mutually dependent levels that reciprocally co-create one another, from the physiological to the spiritual. In a reality that consists of a dynamic and mutual unfolding of transformative relations, or existential commoning, that inescapably transforms both sides of an exchange, an economics and policy regime based on anthropocentric dualisms, including "posthumanism," can never truly heal.

Epilogue: The Affirmation of Belonging

Modernity has sought human emancipation from nature by dominating it. The thinkers of the Anthropocene and posthumanism strive to put an end to this stance – but they continue (tacitly) to separate humans from the rest of reality. In contrast, the poetic materialism of Enlivenment outlined here, which expresses itself in successful processes of commoning, sees humans and "nature" as inextricably entangled in an exchange of mutual responsibilities, materially and culturally. The sharing of creative principles is both material and symbolic. It accepts that aliveness is a defining principle of nature just as for all species, one of which is *Homo sapiens*. The principles of exchange include physical embodiment, co-creativity with other living creatures, birth through death, mutual transformation through commoning, and the paradox that every connection is also a separation – because to connect, a separation is needed in the first place. It is a oneness achieved through the conjunction of two distinct unities. Identity is not wholeness, but "interpenetration," as the Canadian literary critic Northrop Frye would have put it.

The Anthropocene as a reconciliation of humans and nature will function only if we grasp that we are "nature" because we share aliveness with every being, and that creative aliveness is the underlying character according to which reality unfolds. We are transient transformations in a larger process defined by of material/semiotic referentialities. Viewed in this light, reality is revealed as a commons of those perceiving and those perceived, and their ongoing interactions. Its objectivity is not simply an academic discourse. Nor is it invented or constructed by human culture. Instead, reality is both a way of describing the world as it is and as a set of experiential practices. Like Aristotle's ethical ideal of a mediation between the "wise and the many" (Nussbaum 2001), the ontology of the world is never fixed and unequivocal; it is always process, always birth, always becoming. The goal lies in participating in the enterprise of creative aliveness in order to make the world more real.

After the sun has set in Sant'Andrea off Elba, the thunderstorm, gray and violet, has moved on toward Corsica. The sea simultaneously mirrors the colors of the atmosphere and shakes them off, while its choppy suit of armor takes on every hue: turquoise, sky blue, gray, orange, violet, ultramarine. The ocean has no colors, it has nothing but energy. The ocean is the "wine-dark sea" that Homer celebrated in song, the power that enables the actualization of living things. It is a power that makes things more real and that lends itself to everyone who carries it further and transforms it.

We can overcome the misunderstanding of the Anthropocene that celebrates itself as the "era of humans." To do so, however, we need an attitude of inclusivity, of mutual acceptance between attitudes, bodies, identities and sensations. We need the affirmation of belonging and a willingness to engage in an ongoing negotiation within a reality that we recognize as a commons. We can adapt our behaviors to its ongoing transformations and amalgamation. Since this is the inescapable existential reality of life itself, we must acknowledge that the fertile wild ultimately cannot be denied, suppressed or enclosed without a profound constriction on our own freedom.

References

Adorno, Theodor W. 2013. *Aesthetic Theory*. New York. Bloomsbury.

Alphandéry, Claude et al. 2014. *Abridged version of the Convivialist Manifesto*, http://lesconvivialistes.fr.

Benasayag, Miguel and Gérard Schmit. 2007. *L'epoca delle passioni tristi*. Milano: Feltrinelli.

Bilgrami, Akeel et al. 2013. "The Anthropocene Project: An Introduction." Haus der Kulturen der Welt, Berlin.

Bollier, David. 2014. *Think like a Commoner: A Short Introduction to the Life of the Commons*. Gabriola Island, B.C. New Society Publishers.

Buber, Martin. 1937. *I and Thou*. Eastford, CT: Martino (2010 reprint of the original American edition).

Crutzen, Paul J. and E. Stoermer. 2000. "The 'Anthropocene'." *Global Change Newsletter* 41:S. 17 – 18.

Descola, Philippe. 2013. *Beyond Nature and Culture*. Chicago. Chicago University Press.

Ferrando, Francesca. 2013. "Posthumanism, Transhumanism, Antihumanism, Metahumanism, and New Materialisms: Differences and Relations." *Existenz* 8(2):26-32.

Frye, Nortrop. 1991. *Double Vision. Identity and Meaning in Religion*. Toronto, Ontario. Toronto University Press.

Glissant, Édouard. 1997. *Poetics of Relation*. East Lansing: Michigan State University Press.

Hardt, Michael and Antonio Negri. 2009. *Commonwealth*. Cambridge, Massachusetts. Harvard University Press.

Johns, David. 2014. "With Friends Like These, Wilderness and Biodiversity Do Not Need Enemies." In: George Wuerthner, Eileen Crist and Tom Butler, editors. *Keeping the Wild. Against the Domestication of the Earth*. Washington, D.C. Island Press.

Kidner, David W. 2014. "The Conceptual Assassination of Wilderness." In Wuerthner et al. 2014.

Marris, Emma. 2013. *The Rambunctious Garden: Saving Nature in a Post-Wild World*. New York. Bloomsbury.

Morin, Edgar. 2001. *L'identité humaine. La methode, tome 5, L'humanité de l'humanité*. Paris. Seuil.

Nussbaum, Martha. 2001. *The Fragility of Goodness: Luck and Ethics in Greek Tragedy And Philosophy*. Cambridge, Massachusetts. Harvard University Press.

Schäfer, Lothar. 1993. *Das Bacon-Projekt*. Frankfurt am Main: Suhrkamp.

Shellenberger, Michael and Ted Nordhaus, 2011. "Evolve: The Case for Modernization as the Road to Salvation." In Dies, *Love Your Monsters. Postenvironmentalism and the Anthropocene*. Oakland, California. The Breakthrough Institute.

Singh, Neera M. 2013. "The Affective Labor of Growing Forests and the Becoming of Environmental Subjects: Rethinking Environmentality in Odisha, India." *Geoforum* 47:189-198.

Smith, Philip B. and Manfred Max-Neef, 2010. *Economics Unmasked: From Power and Greed to Compassion and the Common Good*. Green Press.

Weber, Andreas. 2012. "The Economy of Wastefulness. The Biology of the Commons." In David Bollier and Silke Helfrich, editors., *The Wealth of the Commons: A World Beyond Market and State*. Amherst, MA: Levellers Press.

———. 2013. *Enlivenment: Towards a Fundamental Shift in the Concepts of Nature, Culture and Politics*. Berlin: Heinrich Böll Foundation.

———. 2014. *Lebendigkeit. Eine erotische Ökologie*. München: Kösel.

———. 2015. *Healing Ecology. Finding the Human in Nature*. Gabriola Island, B.C.: New Society Publishers.

Weber, Andreas & Varela, Francisco J. 2002. "Life After Kant: Natural Purposes and the Autopoietic Foundations of Biological Individuality." *Phenomenology and the Cognitive Sciences* 1:97 – 125.

Andreas Weber *(Germany) is a biologist, philosopher and book and magazine writer based in Berlin. His longstanding interest is how human feeling, subjectivity and social identity are related to biological worldmaking and cognition. He recently published* Enlivenment: Towards a Fundamental Shift in the Concepts of Nature, Culture and Politics *(Heinrich Böll Foundation 2013), and* Healing Ecology: Finding the Human in Nature *(New Society Publishers, 2015).*

Special thanks to David Bollier for inspiration, corrections and support, particularly for the section on commoning.

FINALE

If there is one recurring theme described in this book, it is the importance of exploring the inner dimensions of commoning as a social form, moving beyond economistic notions of the commons as a mere resource to be managed. Commoning is an attitude, an ethic, an impulse, a need and a satisfaction – a way of being that is deeply inscribed within the human species. But it is up to us to make it thrive. We must *choose* to practice commoning and reflect on its impact on our lives and the Earth, the more consciously, the better.

The great appeal of commoning is simultaneously a reason for its invisibility: it calls on us to see the world from a fundamentally different perspective, acknowledging that the *self* emerges from relationships with others and can exist only through these relationships and as a result of them. Failing to perceive the diverse types of "we's" that exist and their complex dynamics and logics is tantamount to trying to live on Earth without an atmosphere. Our lives are enframed and defined by "we's." These collectives are not merely the sum of individuals, but distinct systems of organization that emerge from our encounters with each other and committed joint action.

More: a commons is dynamic and evolving, and therefore proposes a more realistic idea of human life. It does not propose a static economic perspective that assumes what we supposedly *are*; it recognizes that we are always *becoming*. Commoning draws upon our distinct, situated identities, cultures and roots as essential elements of governance, production, law and culture. This perspective helps us grasp that we not only create the world; the world in turn shapes and creates us. So we must attend to the larger, holistic consequences of our own world-creating capacities, to make sure that the selves that we each cultivate through our relationships and world-making are the selves that we truly wish to be and worlds we wish to live in. Or as Lau Tzu put it with such wisdom, "Be a pattern for the world."

The commons quivers with aliveness precisely because it is a reflexive, open system that resists attempts to make it schematic, regularized and tightly controlled. The commons is alive because it offers space for people to apply their own imaginations and energy to solve problems – and human ingenuity and cooperation tend to produce many surprising results. In their self-created zones of freedom, commoners have the latitude to build their own worlds without the tyranny of the Market/State, bureaucratic procedures or confining social roles (consumer, seller, employee, expert).

Needless to say, an economy and society that truly respects commons requires a re-imagination of politics itself. They require social processes that invite collective participation and express collective sentiments, not "leaders" who may be only crudely accountable to people and captive to capital and its imperatives. Commons require a primary focus on meeting everyone's needs, not on catering to the ever-proliferating wants of the few. Expanding the scope and scale of commons so that they can become a powerful alternative to capital driven markets, and spur mutual coordination and federation, introduces a whole new set of challenges, of course. It requires that we work for new configurations of state authority and clear limits on market power. Yet there are many promising scenarios of policy, law, governance and politics that seek to advance this vision: the focus of our next anthology.

Index

A

Abahlali baseMjondolo, 334-347
Abdallah, Hamed, 286
activism, 128-129, 154, 156-157, 208, 330-347
Adaptation and Natural Selection (book), 361
Adorno, Theodor W., 385
Andalusia, 210
Andes, 103-107349
adivasi (India), 77-82
Africa, 71-74, 110, 112, 192, 199-203-216, 271, 277-296, 330-347, 355
African National Congress (ANC), 333, 335, 338
agriculture, 39-41, 43-45, 61-63, 83-85, 103-107, 108-112, 113-114, 130, 145-150, 154-156, 225, 230, 251-252, 268, 284-294, 361 *See also* food *and* fisheries.
agronomy, 108-112
Aguas de Tunari (Bolivia), 86
Alexander, Christopher, 6, 15-25, 26
aliveness, 3, 273, 275, 349-351, 358, 371-375, 383-385, 389, 394
Alliot, Michel, 278, 290
Amazon.com, 227
Amazonia, 133
Amherst, Massachusetts (US), 229
Amherst College, 229
Amiénois, France, 289-291
Amsterdam, Netherlands, 119
Anarchist Collective, 191
Andes, 103-107
Anna Adamolo, 129
Anonymous, 128
Anthropocene, 356, 369-371, 378, 388. 390
anthropology, 278, 291
Apache (software), 149, 182
Apache Open Office, 184
Apache Software Foundation, 184
apartheid, 335-338

apartment buildings, 37-38, 98-99
Arab Spring, 128
Archidiacono, Stefano, 87
architectural design, 15-16, 19
archives, 117-121, 130
Arduino, 55, 151-153, 169
ArduSat, 151
Argumedo, Alejandro, 103
Article Level Metrics, 181
Aristotle, 389
arts and culture, 122-124, 126-131, 136-139, 162
Ashoka, 25
Asia, 110
AS220 (Rhode Island), 136-139
Association for the Advancement of Research and Studies on the Possession of Land in Africa, 285
Association for the Protection of Torrent-Neuf (Switzerland), 62, 63
Association of German Housing and Real Estate Companies, 94
Association Tefy Saina, 109
Astrachan, Russia, 98-99
Athens, Greece, 218
Atlee, Tom, 37
Atsme Irist (land tenure system), 71-74
Augenstein, Patrick, 190
Austria, 66, 221, 237
avaaz (website), 161

B

Bacon, Francis, 373
Bai, Dhani, 79
Bai, Sharmi, 78, 80
Baines, Paul, 219
Bangladesh, Kenya, 199-203
Bangla-Pesa, 199-203
Banzi, Massimo, 151

Barcelona, Spain, 132, 209, 210, 212

Barra da Tijuca (Brazil), 97

Barrière, Catherine and Olivier, 294

barter, 195-198, 205, 266

basic income, 159-160, 164-165

Basque country, Spain, 210, 212

Baudet, Marie-Béatrice, 291

Bauhaus, 160

Bauwens, Michel, 225

Bechstedt, Germany, 28, 31, 48

Beck, Kent, 18

Behavioral and Brain Sciences (journal), 366

Benasayag, Miguel, 376

Berlin, Germany, 216

Best, Elsdon, 314

Betahaus (Berlin), 161

Biblioteka Narodawa, 117

Bien Vivir, 132, 220, 222, 354, 356, 358, 386

Big Transition Map, 222

Biglan, Tony, 366

Bill and Melinda Gates Foundation, 180

Binghamton, New York, 365

biology, 16, 172-175, 350, 361

Biomed Central, 180

bisse de Savièse (irrigation canals), 61-64

Blissett, Luther, 128

BMI, 138

Bogotá, Colombia, 253

Bohr, Niels, 326

Boliva, 86-91, 386

Böll Foundation, xi

Bollier, David, 191, 357

Bologna, Italy, 92-93, 219

book publishing, 228-230

bookcrossing (website), 161

Boston, Massachusetts, US, 145

Bourdieu, Pierre, 292

Branch, Jordan, 318

Brazil, 96-98, 219

Brewin, Kester, 192

British Columbia Open Textbook Project, 189

Brodbeck, K.H., 11

Brown, Patrick, 179

Brückner, Peter, 50

buen vivir, 132, 354, 356, 358, 386

bureaucracy, 10, 53, 78-81, 92, 318, 387, 394

Burn Station, 210

Burning Man festival, 55, 140-141, 386

C

Cagsirli, Merve, 246

Calafou, Spain, 267

Camino Abierto, 249-251

Canada, 31, 132, 146, 192, 219

care work, 44, 53, 78, 93, 196, 201, 202, 228, 231, 248, 250, 259, 342, 349, 356, 372, 384

Caribbean, 348

Carpathians, Eastern, 1, 65-70

CartONG, 216

Case for the Commons, The (web journal), 232

Castells, Manuel, 206

Catalonia, Spain, 265, 266

Centro Latinoamericano de Ecología Social, 354

Cecosesola, 258-264

Cissé, Ben Mady, 283

cities, 92-99, 122, 127

citizen-science, 110, 157-158

City Repair Project (US), 95-96

Coast, Steve, 214

Cochabamba, Bolivia, 86-91

Código Sur, 232

Colin, Jean, 283

Collective Copies, 229

Collective Impact Framework, 149

Collis, Stephen, 57

Cologne, Germany, 93-94

Colombia, 89, 253, 348, 349, 354

common-pool resources, 28, 47, 221, 307, 362, 364-365

commoning, xii, 1-12, 27, 30, 32, 53-56, 119, 122-125, 128, 131, 134-135, 139, 175, 184, 196, 197, 207, 214, 223, 241-242, 250, 251, 258, 271-274, 348-358, 369-390, 393-4

   affective dimensions of, 37, 65, 68-69, 271-274

   and "common-washing," 10, 134

   and fairness, 37-45, 162

   inner dynamics of, 8, 271-391

   and democracy, 9, 124, 333-345

   and inclusiveness, 49-50, 111, 123-125, 140, 161, 210, 214, 237-239, 241, 259, 386 *See also openness.*

   and intentionality, 11, 27

   vs. minimum wage, 43-45

   patterns of, 26-46, 113

   as performative creation of meanings, 32, 126

and piracy, 192

and rationality, 297-307, 370, 375, 379, 381

as a self-organized process, 1, 8, 93-94, 96, 108-112, 140, 168, 268, 339

and subjectivity, 9, 27, 30, 37, 54-55, 271-273, 297-307, 369-390

and systemic power, 50

commons

See also commoning; and maps.

and anarchism, 191

arts and culture commons, 115-141

biocultural commons, 101-114

and biodiversity, 103-107, 350

and Cartesian logic, 318-321, 326, 374-376, 380

collaborative technology commons, 143-175

and co-learning, 235-255

collective property rights in, 66-68, 124-125

and conflict-resolution, 37-45, 69

and consensus, 38, 39, 40-41, 340-343

currency and, 193-206

and design, 9, 30 *See also* Ostrom, Elinor – design principles of commons.

DIY commons, 154-157, 1159, 168, 170-175, 196, 238

and education, 30, 186-189

exchange and credit commons, 193-206

films about, 190-191

and finances, 181, 200, 261-262, 269-270

Francophone network of commoners, 134

free riders and theft in, 62, 73, 78

and gift economy, 164-165, 205, 245, 253, 280, 314-315

governance in, 38-43, 55, 62, 67, 71-74, 87-89, 92-93, 123-125, 140-141, 147, 155, 161, 184-185, 196-197, 212, 213, 215, 238-239, 259-263, 266-269, 333-343

and housing, 94

and identity, 68-69, 369-370, 375, 385, 389, 393

and inalienability, 67, 163-164, 295, 349, 286-287, 295

indigenous peoples' commons, 71-74

and law, 98, 104-106, 122-125, 141, 201, 223-226, 261, 269, 272-273, 277-296, 311-312, 317, 322, 324-325, 340, 344

and liberal democracy, 338-345

long-lasting commons, 59-74

vs. conventional market logic, 10, 19, 23, 37-45, 54, 81, 85, 96-98, 98-99, 106, 119, 131, 137, 147-149, 157, 162-166, 175, 187, 198, 227-228, 272, 297-301, 348-358, 374, 388

multiple definitions of, 132-133

mutualizing benefits of, 95, 199-203

neighborhood commons, 75-99

omni-commons, 257-274

and ontology, 309-329, 348-358, 370-394

and organizational forms, 10, 137

and participation, 11, 67, 87, 123-124, 127-129, 141, 145-147, 156-157, 200-202, 210, 215, 387

pastureland, 71-74, 243

and patterns of, 6, 26-46130

public/commons partnerships, 93

and public policy, 10

as social systems, 2

and spirituality, 104-106
and the state, 65-69, 88-90, 122-125, 127, 136, 187, 197-198, 201, 212, 238, 263-264, 269, 298, 309-329, 330-347, 348-358

urban commons, 92-99, 241

videos, about, 134, 190-194

and western epistemology, 8-9, 11, 30, 277, 280-296, 297-307, 309-329, 348-358

women in, 62, 72, 74, 77-82, 105-106, 305

as worldview, 8-9, 11, 309-329, 348-358

Commoner, The (web magazine), 231-232

Commons Based Enterprises, 241

Commons Lab, 240-242

CommonsScope, 221

Commons Summer School (Bechstadt, Germany), 28

Communist Party, 65-66, 69

community currencies, 195-198, 199-203, 204-206, 248, 266, 268-270

Community Exchange System, 195, 268

Community Land Trust (CLT), 95, 221, 222

Community Supported Agriculture (CSA), 39-41

Confucius, 292-293

Congo, Republic of, 216, 288

Connexions, 187

consciousness, 349-351, 369

consuetudinary law, 278-294

Converse, 163

conviviality, 50-52

Cook, Captain James, 318-321

cooperation, 32, 33, 141, 147, 153-158, 163, 166,
    168, 186, 195-198, 218-222, 237-239, 258-
    264, 299-307, 341-343, 363-364

Cooperativa Integral Catalan, 54, 265-270

co-operatives, 10, 38, 86-91, 196-197, 220,
    225, 228-230, 231, 253-254, 265-270, 291

Coordination for the Defense of Water and
    Life (Bolivia), 87

Copenhagen, Denmark, 195

CopyFair license, 225-226

copyleft. See General Public License and
    Creative Commons licenses.

copyright, 120, 138, 162, 163, 182, 223-226,
    227, 228

Cornell University, 109-112

Corner House, 55

Council of Canadians, 219

Creative Commons licenses, xii, 120, 138, 151,
    163, 180, 187, 189, 210, 220, 228, 229,
    231, 246

Crenca, Umberto, 136-137

Crespo, Carlos, 88

crowdfunding, 208-213

Cuartielles, David, 151

cultural heritage, 19, 23, 63, 104, 117-121,
    320-321

Commun (book), 277

Cox, Michael, 364

currency, 195-198, 199-203

Cusanus University, 254

Cusco Valley, Peru, 103-107

D

Dakar, 132

Dardot, Christian, 277, 294

Darwin, Charles, 362

Darwin, Erasmus, 318

Declaration of the Rights of Mother Earth, 90

De Angelis, Massimo, 231

degrowth, 246, 266

democracy, 9, 16, 22

Dempster, Martha, 136

design, 9, 15-25, 159-165
    holistic, 22-23
    participatory, 19, 22-24
    and pattern language, 15-25
    and people, 22-23

de Soto, Pablo, 218, 219

Descola, Philippe, 386

"development," 285-296, 348-358

Deutsche Bank, 97

Development Dictionary (book), 353-354

Dibbits, Taco, 119

digital arts, 126-131

Digital Library on the Commons, 233

Directory of Open Access Journals, 228

Document Foundation, 184

Documentation Research and Action Center
    of Ikaria, 244

Doctors Without Borders, 216

Drayton, Bill, 25

Drupal, 149

Durban, South Africa, 330-331, 336

Dürr, Hans Peter, 275

Dvorchak, David, 138

E

Earl of Morton, 319-320

Earp, Jeremy, 191

Ebola, 216

ecological economics, 358, 388

Ecuador, 132, 386

Ece, Melis, 246

economics, 2, 28, 348, 362, 388 See also
    Commons, vs. conventional market logic.

EDGE Funders Alliance, 191

education, 30, 129, 186-189, 208, 365

Egypt, 245

Eisen, Michael, 179

Elias, Sian, 324

Elba, Italy, 389

Embry, Dennis, 366

Emma, Steven, 136

enclosure, xii, 4, 7, 33, 37, 53, 56, 104, 134,
    182-183, 191, 243, 244-246, 253, 273, 286,
    320, 330-333, 353, 373-377, 380, 383

Encyclopedia of Practical Farm Knowledge
    (book), 148

England, 293, 374

Enlightenment, 11, 147, 317-321, 356, 370-375,
    379, 385, 387

Enlivenment, 26, 35, 45, 372, 389

environment, 78-81, 85, 90, 117-118, 157

ethics, 5-6, 22, 32

Equator Prize, 74

Escobar, Arturo, 273

Esteva, Gustavo, 250, 251-252
Ethiopia, 71-74
European Commission, 120
European Cultural Foundation, 124
European Molecular Biology Laboratory, 172
Europeana, 120
Evolution Institute, 363, 366
evolutionary science, 361-366, 379

F

Fab Labs, 8, 136, 167-169, 237-239, 267
Fab Lab St. Pauli, 55, 167-169
Fabrica, 168, 169
Fairey, Shepard, 137
Falling Fruit, 221, 222
Fals Borda, Orlando, 348
Fanon, Franz, 339, 342, 343, 344
Farm Hack, 145-150, 156
Field Papers (software), 216
Fiji/ImageJ (software), 174
Finland, 134, 195-198
Fisher, Irving, 204
fisheries, 271, 298-307, 309-329
Flanders, Laura, 191
Flexible Learning for Open Education, 189
Flickr, 225
Flickr Commons, 120
Florence, Italy, 362
Folderapa, 210
Fondazione Teatro Valle Bene Comune,
    122-125
food, 5, 30, 78, 79, 84-85, 105, 108-112, 146,
    192, 196, 200, 260-263, 268 See also
    agriculture.
Food and Agriculture Organization of the
    United Nations, 286
Forest Rights Act (India), 78-81
forestry, 65-70, 77-82, 353
Foucault, Michel, 317
Foundation for Ecological Security, 190, 192
France, 83-85, 146, 192, 278, 288, 289-291,
    293
Frame, Alex, 321
Frankfurt Zoological Society, 74
Franklin, Benjamin, 147, 318
Free Little Library Map, 222
free software, 33
freedom, 16, 32

Fromm, Erich, 163
Frye, Northop, 389
Fundación Fuentes Abiertas, 212
Fureai Kippu, 206
furniture design, 156-157, 160-161

G

Gage, Rikirangi, 311, 320
Galeano, Eduardo, 53
Gandhi, Mahatma, 253
Garden City Letchworth (UK), 94-95
Gatina-Pesa, 199
General Public License (GPL), 213, 223-225
geographical indicators, 105
German Institute for Human Rights, 192
German Sommerschool on the Commons, 48
German translation of words, 16-17
Germany, 28, 43, 93-94, 146, 161, 167-169,
    172-173, 184, 192, 221, 230-231, 237-239
Gershenfeld, Neil, 167
Gesell, Silvio, 204
Gibson, Nigel, 272
Gibson-Graham, J.K., 358
Github, 213
Glissant, Edouard, 369, 382
Gmunden, Austria, 237-239
Global Village Construction Set, 155
Google, 157, 185
Google Docs, 184-185
Google Maps, 161
Gordon and Betty Moore Foundation, 180
Gorenflo, Neal, 220
Goteo, 208-213
Gourmet magazine, 103, 106
Governing the Commons (book), 47, 364
government procurement, 152, 184
Great Britain, 94-95, 244
Great Lakes Commons Map, 219, 222
Great Transformation, The (book), 205
Great Transition Initiative, 356
Great Turning, 356
Greece, 243-247
Greenhorns, 145
Greenpeace, 310, 311, 320
GreenStart, 145
Group Works Deck, 35
Guassa area, Ethiopia, 71-74
Guerrilla Translation, 225, 241-242

guifi.net Madrid, 241
Guinea, 216
Gulf of Mexico, 310

H

Habermann, Friederike, 31
hackerspaces, 8, 218, 221, 222, 237, 267
hacktivism, 209, 225
Haiti, 214
Hamburg, Germany, 167-169
Hansen, Kevin, 190
Haraway, Donna, 377
Hardin, Garrett, 281, 361-362
Hartz IV Möbel, 159, 161, 162
Harvard University, 179, 228
Harvey, Larry, 140-141
Hawaiki, 310
Hayes, Steven C., 366
healthcare, 258, 333
Heidelberg, Germany, 172
Helfrich, Silke 25, 159-165
Helsinki, 132, 195-198
Helsinki Timebank, 54, 194, 195-198
Henry, Joseph, 119
Hirsch, Alan, 335
Hirst, Damien, 162
Hitler, Adolf, 117
Holmgren, David, 113
homo economicus, 4, 5, 272, 280
Hopkins, Rob, 18
HOT project, 56
housing, 156, 159-165, 268, 330-347
Howard, Ebenezer, 94-95
HowlRound, 131
Huisken, Jan, 172
Human Ecosystems Project, 127
humanism, 339, 370-371
Humanitarian OpenStreetMap Team (HOT), 214
Humboldt brothers, 318

I

Iaione, Christian, 92
IBM, 182, 225
Ierodiaconou, Nicolas, 156
    Igoe, Tom, 151
Ikaria, Greece, 243-247
IKEA, 163

Illich, Ivan, 7, 50-51, 244, 250, 251, 254, 387
India, 1, 77-82, 190, 233, 252-253
Indiana University, 367
Indigenous Biocultural Heritage Area (Peru), 104-106
indigenous people, 71-74, 103-107, 248, 251, 252, 271, 292, 309-329, 348-358, 377
individualism, 2, 11, 95, 140, 251, 263, 274, 280, 362, 369-370
infrastructure, 56, 67, 139, 152, 210, 237
Ingold, Tim, 351
Institute for Advanced Sustainability Studies, 192
Institutional Analysis and Development (IAD) framework, 9, 29, 364
institutional economics, 28
Intel, 152, 180, 182
Intercultural Documentation Center, 244
International Association for the Study of the Commons, 192, 233
International Commons Conference (2010), 133
International Convention of Indigenous Rights, 312
International Institute for Food, Agriculture and Development (CIIFAD), 109
International Journal of the Commons, 228
International Monetary Fund, 86, 335
International Mountain Protection Commission, 74
International Potato Center, 105
International Union for the Conservation of Nature, 106
Internet, 8, 128-129, 130, 134, 163, 182, 210, 227, 273
Internet Archive, 130
Invisible Committee (France), 115
irrigation canals, 61-64
Istanbul, Turkey, 218
Italian Theatre Authority, 122
Italy, 66, 92-93, 122-125, 128-129, 219, 369
Iteration, 35
Iterator, 35

J

Jacarepaguá Lagoon, Brazil, 96
Jakubowski, Marcin, 154-155
Jamendo, 225
Jefferson, Thomas, 147
Jesus Christ, 332

Jhally, Sut, 191
Johns, David, 374
Journal of Economic Behavior & Organization, 364
journals, 179-181

K

Kahle, Brewster, 130
Kallis, Giorgos, 246
Kant, Immanuel, 193
Karma Chakhs, 160, 163
Karsenty, Alain, 287
Keio University (Tokyo), 21
Kelty, Christopher, 242
Kennedy Road (Durban), 330-343
Kentucky, US, 245
Kenya, 199-203
Kenyans Organizing Regional Unity, 202
Khan, Fazel, 342
Kickstarter, 211
Kidner, David, 375
Kikai, 151
King Haile Selassie, 73
Kiva, 211
Kleiner, Dmytri, 225
Knutzen, Matt, 119
Kobeissi, Nadim, 177
Kosmos journal, 232
Koutsouti, Frosini, 244
Kumpula exchange rink, 195-198
Kune, 241

L

LabGov (Laboratory for the Governance of Commons), 92, 219
labor market, 29, 30, 43-45, 163-165, 197, 202-203
Labsus (Laboratory for Subsidiarity), 219
Lakeman, Mark, 96
land, 71-74, 83-85, 94-95, 96-98, 192, 278-296, 322
Latin America, 86-91, 103-107, 110, 220, 232-233
La Toma, Colombia, 352
Latour, Bruno, 375
Lau Tzu, 393
Laulanié, Henri, 108
Laval, Pierre, 277, 294

law, 10, 309-329
Lawler, Kristin, 246
legal pluralism, 279, 289
Le Roy, Étienne, 11, 271, 277-296
learning, 248-255
Learning Exchange, 254
legality, 291
Leitner, Helmut, 26-27, 31
Le-Mentzel, Van Bo, 159-166
Lessig, Lawrence, 224
LETS, 206
Levellers Press, xi-xiii, 228-230
Lévi-Strauss, Claude, 279-280
Liberia, 216
Libertatia, 253
Library of Congress, 130
LibreOffice, 182-185
libraries, 117-121
licenses, 213, 223-226. *See also* Creative Commons licenses.
Lietaer, Bernard, 205
Linebaugh, Peter, 27, 191, 197
Linux, 182-184, 224, 225, 226
Liu, John D., 190
Living Education Albada, 267
living systems, 15, 16-17, 19, 23. *See also* aliveness.
Locke, John, 147
London, UK, 95, 253
London Community Neighbourhood Co-operative, 253-254
London School of Economics, 97
Longstocking, Pippi, 163
Loong, Wong, Bernard Yun, 103
Löschmann, Heike, xi

M

Madagascar, 108-109, 287-288
Madrid, 225, 240-241
Magna Carta, 191
makers, 145, 237-239
Mali, 287
Mandela, Nelson, 330, 332, 335
Mantua, Italy, 219
Maori, 271, 309-329, 386
Maori Land Court, 321-322
MapAction, 214
Mapping The Commons(.net), 218, 222

Mapping The Commons(.org), 219, 222
maps, 119, 134, 157, 214-217, 218-222, 318
Margulis, Lynn, 363
MariaDB (software), 185
Maricopa Community Colleges, 188
market system, 1, 2, 4, 10 *See also* Commons,
    vs. logic of conventional markets.
Marlborough Sounds, 321-322
Martino, Gianluca, 151
Marx, Karl, 278, 345
Mataroa, 244-247
Mattei, Ugo, 375
Mauss, Marcel, 280, 314, 326
Max Planck Institute for Molecular Cell
    Biology and Genetics, 173, 174
Max-Neef, Manfred, 375
Maysville, Missouri, 155
Mbecki, Thabo, 334
Medialab-Prado, 240-242
Mediatek, 152
Médicins Sans Frontières, 216
Mediterranean Sea, 245
Mellis, David, 151, 169
Menz-Guassa Community Conservation Area
    (Ethiopia), 55, 71-74
Merkel, Angela, 164
metaphysics, 369-390
Mexico, 190, 244, 248, 354
microscopy, 170175
Microsoft, 180, 182-185
Microsoft Office, 182-184
Middle Ages, 62, 244
Miethäuser Syndikat (Germany), 37-38
minimum wage, 43-45
Missouri, US, 155
M.I.T., 145, 169, 186-187
Molière, 291
Mombosa, Kenya, 199
money, 195-206, 388
Montevideo, 354
Montreal, 31, 132
Morales, Evo, 90
Morin, Edgar, 381
Moruroa, 312-313
Moscow, 98
Mother Earth, 90, 103-106
Motu River, 315
Munich, Germany, 184

Museo dell'Informatica Funzionante
    (Museum of Working Informatics), 129
museums, 117-121, 129
MySQL (software), 185

N

Nahrada, Franz, 32
Nairobi, Kenya, 199
Nantes, France, 212
nation-state, 11
Nature (journal), 175
Nature Methods (journal), 175
Nature of Order, The (book), 6, 16
Négritude, 282
neighborhoods, 248, 253, 267, 364, 365
neoliberalism, 122, 244, 246, 291, 294, 335-
    336, 344, 353-355, 370, 386, 388
Nepal, 1, 189, 190
New Hampshire, US, 146
New York Public Library, 119
New Zealand, 272, 309-329, 386
Niger, 287
Nightingale, Andrea, 271
Nodo Móvil, 208
Noguero, Susan, 211
Nonini, Donald, 356
Nordhaus, Ted, 388
Nupedia, 23

O

Oaxaca, Mexico, 250
Obama, Barack, 137
obştea forest commons, 65-70
ocean, 271, 284, 309-239
Occupy movement, 128
Ochieng, Fredrick, 201
OER Commons, 187
Off the Commons Books, 230
On the Commons, 219, 232
On the Origin of Species (book), 362
One-Square-Meter-House, 164
One-World World (OWW), 348-349, 351, 355,
    356
open access journals, 179-181, 227-228
open brands, 128
OpenCourseWare, 55, 186-189
open data, 127, 157, 181, 215

Open Data Commons Open Database License, 214

open design, 151-153, 154-158, 159-166, 170-175, 225, 240

Open Design (shoe project), 160

Open Desk, 156, 158

Open Document Format, 183

Open Education Consortium, 187

Open Education Week, 189

Open Educational Resources (OER) movement, 186-189

open hardware, 151-153, 158, 170-175

Open Layers, 149

Open Learning Initiative, 189

OpenOffice.org, 183-184

Open Source Ecology, 154-145, 158

open source gasifier, 209

open source paradigm, 8, 111, 128-129, 145-150, 151-153, 154-158, 159-165, 167-169, 170-175, 182-185, 186-189, 209-213, 218-222, 223-226

Opensource Opencourseware Prototype System, 187

openness, 23, 111, 120, 160-161, 388

OpenSPIM, 170-175

Open Stax College, 187

open textbooks, 189

open standards, 182-185

OpenStreetMap, 214-217, 221

Oracle, 184

Ostrom, Elinor, 9, 28-29, 30, 33, 37, 47, 48-49, 133, 273, 278, 298, 362-367
    design principles of commons, 37, 47, 48-49, 362-364

Ostrom, Vincent, 367

Otelo, 237-239

Otherwise Club, 253

Oughiry, Remy, 291

Oya, 230-231

P

P2P Foundation, 221, 222, 233

P2PValue project, 220, 222

P2P Wikisprint, 222

pachamama, 90, 104, 106, 355, 386

Pacific Ocean, 349, 353

Pakistan, 188

Paris, France, 187

Parker, Barry, 95

Parvin, Alastair, 156

Patel, Raj, 342

patents, 104-106, 374

pattern collections, 18-19

pattern language, 6, 17-18, 24-25, 26, 31, 32, 33

Pattern Language, A (book), 6, 15, 17

patterns, 15-25, 27, 30-31, 130
    and anti-patterns, 43
    and commons movement, 24
    developing patterns, 34
    general and specific (box), 28

patterns of commoning, 26-46

Peer Production Licenses, 225-226

peer-to-peer (P2P), 127, 196, 220

Pennsylvania, US, 146

permaculture, 34, 113-114, 386

Peru, 1, 54, 103-107, 354

PESA Act (Panchayats Extension to Scheduled Areas), India, 79

Peterman, Aaron, 137

Philippines, 215

photography, 120

Physiocrats, 147

Picardy, France, 289-291

Pillku (web magazine), 232-233

Pithouse, Richard, 342

Pixelache conference (2014), 134

Placemaking, 96

Platoniq collective, 210-211, 213

pluriverse, 273, 348-358

poetics, 381-383

Polanyi, Karl, 205, 244

Pór, George, 134

Portland, Oregon, 95-96

Portland Pattern Repository, 15

Posthumanism, 371, 377-390

Potato Park, Peru, 54, 103-107

potatoes, 103-107

poverty, 200, 203, 330-347

Prabé Mountain, 62

Pratham Books, 233

Priestley, Joseph, 318

privatization, 37, 86, 122, 125, 224, 229, 243, 246, 355

profit, 19, 23, 54, 67, 69, 104, 119, 162, 165, 167, 182-185, 210, 226, 227-229, 261, 262, 300, 301, 301, 348, 351, 376 property rights, 66-68, 85, 124-125, 273, 278, 282-296 *See also* licenses; Creative Commons licenses; *and* General Public License.

PROSOCIAL project, 366

Providence, Rhode Island, 136-139

public domain, 118, 120, 130, 138, 323

public goods, 28, 122-124, 243, 246, 282

Public Lab, 157-158

Public Library of Science, 55, 179-181, 225, 228

publishing, 179-181, 227-233

Purple Thistle Center, 2253

PURPLSOC (PURsuit of Pattern Languages for Societal Change), 16

Putin, Vladimir, 98

Q

Qero Indigenous Management System, 72-73

quantum theory, 326

Quebec, 146

Quechua people, 103-107

Queen Victoria, 309

Quesnay, François, 147

Quién Manda, 209

Quito, Ecuador, 218

QWAN (Quality Without a Name), 16-17

R

Rajasthan, India, 77-82, 252-253

Ranapiri, Tamati, 314

Rata, Matiu, 324

Rath, Jorge, 258-263

real estate, 83-85, 96-98

Red Cross, 216

Regents Academy, 365

Reill, Peter Hans, 318

Remix The Commons, 132, 192

renewable resources, 113

Reynard, Denis, 62

Rhode Island, US, 136-139

rice, 108-112

right to the city, 122, 168

Rijksmuseum (Amsterdam), 119

Rimini, Timi Waata, 315-316

Rio de Janeiro, Brazil, 96-98, 134, 218

Rio+20 conference, 134

RIP: A Remix Manifesto (film), 133

Robinson, Sir Ken, 162

robotics, 152

Rodale Institute, 146

RomaEuropa FakeFactory, 128

Romania, 54, 65-70

Rome 122-125, 128, 219

Romer, Robert, 229

Rosling, Hans, 162

Rost, Norbert, 56

Royal Society of London, 317, 319

Ruddick, Will, 199-203

Russia, 98-99

Rwanda, 189

S

Samos, Greece, 243

São Paulo, Brazil, 218

Savièse, Switzerland, 62, 63

Sahlins, Marshall, 313

Saint Dizier, France, 83

Saint Petersburg, Russia, 98

Salas, Gustavo, 258-263

Salmond, Anne, 271, 386

San Francisco, California, 130, 172, 181

San Francisco Declaration on Research Assessment, 181

San Precario, 128

SAP, 152

Sauti ya wakulima (The Voice of the Farmers), 130

Schmit, Gérard, 376

Schulbaum, Olivier, 211

science, 170-175, 179-181

Scotland, 271, 297-307

Scribd, 225

Searle, Lucie, 137

seed banks, 33

seeds, 33, 104-105, 108-112, 221, 222, 374

Senegal, 134, 246, 278-285, 288

Senghor, Léopold, 282, 283

Serpica Naro, 128

shackdwellers, 330-347

Shareable magazine, 220, 232

Sharing Cities Network, 220

"sharing economy," 8

Sharpeville, South Africa, 331

Shellenberger, Michael, 388

Shikshantar, 252-253

Sicily, Italy, 129
Siedentopf, 171
Sierra Leone, 216
Singh, Neera, 383
Sipaswarmi Medicinal Plants Women's Collective, 105
Smart Citizen kit, 209
Smithsonian Institution, 119, 130
Sochi, Russia, 98
Social-Ecological Systems Framework, 29
social ethics, 5-6
Social Market, 210
social sciences, 3, 26
Society for Prevention Research, 366
Society Islands, 312
software programming, 18, 35
solidarity economy, 85, 197, 210, 220
South Africa, 272, 330-347
Spain, 152, 209-213, 220
Spain in Flames, 210
SSM (Sozialistische Selbsthilfe Mühlheim), Germany, 93-94
Stallman, Richard, 223
Stelzer, Ernst, 172
Stephen the Great, 68
STIR magazine, 231
Stirling, Eruera, 310
strikingly (software), 161
Strimer, Steven 229, 230
Sun Microsystems, 183
Sutcliffe, Mike, 335
Swaraj University, 253
Swift, Jonathan, 149
Switzerland, 1, 61-64, 204-206
Synergia project, 254
System of Crop Intensification (SCI), 111
System of Rice Intensification (SRI), 108-112

T

Tagore, Rabindranath, 253
Tahiti, 317
Tanzania, 130, 246
Taranto, Italy, 219
taxes, 197-198
Taylor, Betsy, 246
Te Kohuora, 314
Te Whanau-a-Apanui, 309-311, 315, 320, 326
Teatro Valle (Rome), 122-125

Teddy, Elvis, 309, 311-312
Tepoztlán, Mexico, 248-252
Terre de Liens (France), 83-85
Thatcher, Margaret, 362
theater, 122-125, 130
Time Heals Network, 197
timebanking, 195-198, 206
Timeless Way of Building, The (book), 15, 17
Tisselli, Eugenio, 130
To Have or To Be (book), 163
Tomancak, Pavel, 173, 174
Tomasello, Michael, 257
Tokyo, 21
Toronto, Canada, 219
Tracz, Vitek, 180
TransforMap, 221, 222
transition movement, 18, 34, 36, 356
Treaty of Waitangi, 309, 311, 320
Tumaco, Colombia, 353
Tunis, 134
Turanga, New Zealand, 319
Turkey, 245
Typhon Haiyan, 215-216

U

Ubiquitous Commons, 127
Ubuntu, 5, 355
unMonastery, 219
UNESCO, 187
United Nations, 90, 214
United Nations Convention on the Law of the Sea, 312, 320
United Nations Development Programme, 74
United States, 119, 130, 131, 228-230, 293
Univeridad de la Tierra, 250
University of California at Berkeley, 16
University of KwaZulu-Natal
University Paris VIII-Saint Denis, 284
Unmüssig, Barbara, xi
Unreal Estate House, 159, 164
Unwin, Raymond, 95
Uruguay, 89
US Department of Labor, 187
USDA Sustainable Agriculture Research and Education, 147

V

Valais (Switzerland), 1, 61-64

Vale Valera, Noel, 258-263
Vancouver, BC, 253
Vaneigem, Raoul, 348, 349
Vargus, Lizeth, 259-263
Varmus, Harold, 179
Vautier, Auguste, 61
Venezuela, 258, 264
Vest, Charles, 186
Cia Campesina, 354
Vienna, Austria, 220
Vila Autódromo (Brazil), 96-98
Virtual University of Pakistan, 188
Vitra, 163
Viumasters, 192
Vivir Bien (website), 220, 222
Vöcklabruck, Austria, 237-239
Volkswagen, 164
Vrancea Mountains, 65-70

W

Waitangi Tribunal, 309, 321, 324
Waititi, Manihera, 310
Walker, Alice, 235
Warren, Jeff, 158
Warsaw, Poland, 117
water, 61-64, 86-91, 219, 246, 336
Wealth of Commons, The (book), 4, 7, 27, 229
Weber, Andreas, 273
Welwyn Garden City (UK), 95
Whanau-a-Apanui, 320
Whangaipaka, 311
Whangaparaoa River, 310
Whitman, Walt, 249
Wikihouse, 156-157
Wikimedia Commons, 120
Wikipedia, 15, 20, 23, 121, 149, 161, 214, 225
wikis, 15
Williams, George C., 361
Wilson, David Sloan, 273
WIR, 204-206
Workshop in Political Theory and Policy
    Analysis, 366-367
World Bank, 86, 112, 214, 332, 335
World of Commons map, 219, 222
World Social Forum, 132, 133
"worlding," 355
Wretched of the Earth (book), 342, 344
Wu-Ming, 128

Y

Yes! magazine, 232
YouTube, 225
Yurumanguí River, Colombia, 349

Z

Zaldíyar, J.I., 251-252
Zapatistas, 251-252, 353
Zeballos, Gastón, 89
ZEISS, 172
Zero Zero Architecture, 156
Zikode, S'bu, 332, 334, 336-340, 344, 345
Zikos, Dimitris, 246
Zsigmondy, Richard, 171